Knowledge Governance and Learning for Organizational Creativity and Transformation

Series on Innovation and Knowledge Management

Series Editor: Suliman Hawamdeh   **ISSN: 1793-1533**
                (University of North Texas)

Published*

*The complete list of the published volumes in the series can be found at
http://www.worldscientific.com/series/sikm

Series on Innovation and Knowledge Management – Vol. 15

Knowledge Governance and Learning for Organizational Creativity and Transformation

Edited by

Patricia de Sá Freire
Universidade Federal de Santa Catarina, Brazil

Suliman Hawamdeh
University of North Texas, USA

Gertrudes Aparecida Dandolini
Universidade Federal de Santa Catarina, Brazil

World Scientific

NEW JERSEY · LONDON · SINGAPORE · BEIJING · SHANGHAI · HONG KONG · TAIPEI · CHENNAI · TOKYO

Published by

World Scientific Publishing Co. Pte. Ltd.

5 Toh Tuck Link, Singapore 596224

USA office: 27 Warren Street, Suite 401-402, Hackensack, NJ 07601

UK office: 57 Shelton Street, Covent Garden, London WC2H 9HE

Library of Congress Cataloging-in-Publication Data
Names: Sá Freire, Patricia de, editor. | Hawamdeh, Suliman, 1955– editor. |
    Dandolini, Gertrudes Aparecida, editor.
Title: Knowledge governance and learning for organizational creativity and transformation /
    edited by Patricia de Sá Freire, Universidade Federal de Santa Catarina, Brazil,
    Suliman Hawamdeh, University of North Texas, USA,
    Gertrudes Aparecida Dandolini, Universidade Federal de Santa Catarina, Brazil.
Description: Hackensack, NJ : World Scientific, 2022. | Series: Series on innovation and
    knowledge management, 1793-1533 ; Vol. 15 | Includes bibliographical references and index.
Identifiers: LCCN 2021035793 | ISBN 9789811224102 (hardcover) |
    ISBN 9789811224119 (ebook) | ISBN 9789811224126 (ebook other)
Subjects: LCSH: Intellectual capital--Management. | Knowledge management. |
    Organizational learning. | Organizational change. | Strategic planning.
Classification: LCC HD53 .K5937 2022 | DDC 658.4/063--dc23
LC record available at https://lccn.loc.gov/2021035793

British Library Cataloguing-in-Publication Data
A catalogue record for this book is available from the British Library.

For any available supplementary material, please visit
https://www.worldscientific.com/worldscibooks/10.1142/11933#t=suppl

Desk Editors: Aanand Jayaraman/Yulin Jiang

Typeset by Stallion Press
Email: enquiries@stallionpress.com

Printed in Singapore

Preface

Most organizations today understand the importance of knowledge and learning for the development of human capital and the talent needed to compete and stay relevant. Knowledge Management and Learning are essential for the creation of products and services and maintaining a competitive advantage. Knowledge Management is responsible for monitoring, facilitating, and managing the processes of creating and internalizing knowledge at the individual and organizational level. To effectively create, share, and leverage knowledge, organizations need to develop a better understanding of the issues that might hinder their progress. It is necessary to understand how key issues such as culture, leadership, policies, and situational strategies play a role in the enhancement of knowledge management and learning at individual and the organizational level. Organizational learning, on the other hand, is the process by which the organization learns over time. It is similar to individual learning in the sense that organizations do gain experience over time through the development of organizational culture, organizational leadership, and the evolution of processes and practices. The ability of the organization to develop knowledge management practices, such as communities of practice, best practices, and lessons learned, reflects the ability of the organization to learn, adapt, and gain experience over time.

Knowledge governance is at the intersection of knowledge management practices and learning. Currently, there is a gap in the literature regarding studies investigating knowledge management and learning constructs at the intersection of knowledge governance. This book is an effort to understand the interrelationship, interdependence, and interorganizational issues that affect knowledge governance and learning governance. We want to express gratitude to participating authors for their valuable contributions to this book.

In the first chapter of the book, Patricia de Sá Freire, Suliman Hawamdeh, Gertrudes Aparecida Dandolini, and Graziela Grando Bresolin discuss the need for a new governance approach that takes into account knowledge governance and learning governance. They highlighted the importance of the alignment between knowledge governance and learning governance.

Following this chapter, the book is divided into four different parts. Part I contains five chapters under the theme of Knowledge Governance and include chapter on "Knowledge Governance: Addressing Complexity Throughout the Knowledge Processing Cycle" by Kimiz Dalkir; "Multilevel Governance and Organizational Knowledge: Contextual and Theoretical Elements for its Configuration" by Fernanda Kempner-Moreira and Patricia de Sá Freire; "Beyond Organizational Knowledge: Governance Mechanisms Applied to Knowledge-Intensive Organizations" by Ricardo Pereira, Sicilia Vechi, Rosane Malvestiti, and Neri dos Santos; "Framework for Knowledge Governance and Organizational Learning: The Interrelationship of Constructs" by Giselly Rizzatti and Patricia de Sá Freire; and "Discovery, Entropy, Organization, and Trust" by Bart Nooteboom.

Part II contains four chapters with the theme interrelated to the theory of Organizational Learning and include "The Learning Process of Project Teams: An Experience-Based Approach" by Ana María Ortegón and Andrea Valéria Steil; "Knowledge Governance to Create Socially Understanding Communities" by Muhammad Asim Qayyum and Arif Khan; "Knowledge Governance as a Key Factor in Interorganizational Learning" by Julieta K. Watanabe-Wilbert, Carla S. Zandavalli, and Gertrudes Aparecida Dandolini; "Interorganizational Learning: The Central Role of Social Spaces and Learning Episodes" by Anelise Rebelato Mozzato and Claudia Cristina Bitencourt.

Next, we have Part III, in which the theme of Innovation will be addressed, based on the collaboration of 15 authors distributed into five chapters. The first chapter is "Ideas Management: From a Management Perspective" by Elina Mikelsone, Aivars Spilbergs,Tatjana Volkova, and Elita Lielā, followed by "Maturity Model for Ideas Management" by Aline de Brittos Valdati, João Artur de Souza, Maria Isabel Sanchez Segura, and Cynthya Garcia de Jesus; "Networked Innovation Laboratory Model for Public Sector" by Willian Rochadel, Aline de Brittos Valdati, João Artur de Souza, and Gertrudes Aparecida Dandolini; "Cross-Sector Partnerships in Social Innovation Initiatives: A Multiple Case Study in Portugal" by Michele Andréia Borges, Márcia Aparecida Prim, and João Artur de Souza; and "Highlighting the Paths of Social Innovation" by Daniela de Oliveira Massad, Rosane Malvestiti, Ricardo Pereira, and Gertrudes Aparecida Dandolini.

And finally, in Part IV, where 10 authors present in four chapters their studies on the application of this knowledge in academic and corporate universities, the book brings the chapters "University Governance for Innovation: How to Nurture Creativity Through a Successful Academic Entrepreneurship Process" by Valério Vincenzo De Luca and Alessandro Margherita; "Knowledge Ecosystems, Universities, and Innovation in Small and Medium-Sized Enterprises: Establishing a Knowledge Governance Infrastructure Theoretical Framework and the Conditions for Success" by Joyline Makani, Angelo Dossou-Yovo, and Michelle McPherson; "The Corporate Education System and the Governance of Knowledge and Organizational Learning: A Method for Assessing the Maturity of the System" by Marta Silva Neves, Patrícia de Sá Freire, and Talita Caetano Silva and, closing the book, the chapter entitled "Maturity Criteria of the Networked Corporate University Model to Support Knowledge and Organizational Learning Governance" by Graziela Grando Bresolin, Patricia de Sá Freire and Solange Maria da Silva.

We invite the readers to immerse into these new themes.

Patricia de Sá Freire
Suliman Hawamdeh
Gertrudes Aparecida Dandolini

About the Editors

Patricia de Sá Freire graduated in pedagogy, specializes in psychopedagogy and marketing, and holds Masters and Ph.D. degrees in Engineering and Knowledge Management. Dr. Freire is the vice coordinator of the Post-Graduate Program in Engineering and Knowledge Management at the Federal University of Santa Catarina. Dr. Freire is also a professor and the teaching coordinator of the Department of Knowledge Engineering and Post-Graduate Programs in Engineering and Knowledge Management (EGC). She has authored more than 200 scientific publications in national and international conferences, periodicals, and book chapters. For two consecutive years, 2011 and 2012, she was one of the five executives of excellence in knowledge management in Brazil chosen by the MAKE Award. Dr. Freire has more than 30 years of experience as an organizational restructuring consultant to diversify industrial and service companies, including technology-based organizations. She is currently the leader of the ENGIN (Engineering of Integration and Knowledge Governance) Laboratory, and member of IGTI (Laboratory of Intelligence, Management and Technology for Innovation), and KLOM (Knowledge, Learning and Organizational Memory). Patricia de Sá Freire is one of the editors of the *International Journal of Knowledge Engineering Management* (IJKEM). Her research interests include Knowledge Management practices, Networked Corporate University Model; Transformational and Change Management Model, which included topics such as strategic management of people; organizational intelligence; multilevel governance; organizational knowledge and learning; open innovation; absorptive capacity; collaborative management; leadership and organizational culture; intellectual capital, relational capital and intangible assets; shared strategic planning, archives, documentation centers, and study and research centers.

 **Suliman Hawamdeh** is a Professor in the College of Information, University of North Texas (UNT). Prior to joining UNT in August 2010, he taught and coordinated the Master of Science in Knowledge Management in the School of Library and Information Studies at University of Oklahoma. He also founded and directed the first Master of Science in Knowledge Management in Asia in the College of Communication and Information at Nanyang Technological University in Singapore. Dr. Hawamdeh has extensive industrial experience — he was the Managing Director of ITC Information Technology Consultant Ltd, a company developed and marketed a line of products in imaging, document, and record management, engineering drawing management, and library automation software. He worked as a consultant to several organizations. Dr. Hawamdeh also worked as a researcher and a project leader at the Institute of System Science in Singapore. Dr. Hawamdeh has authored and edited several books on knowledge management, including *Information and Knowledge Society*, published by McGraw Hill and *Knowledge Management: Cultivating the Knowledge Professionals*, published by Chandos Publishing. He is the editor of a book series on *Innovation and Knowledge Management* published by World Scientific. He is also the founder and editor-in-chief of the *Journal of Information Knowledge Management*,

one of the first refereed journals in knowledge management. He is a member of the editorial board and a reviewer for several journals. He is the founding president of the Knowledge and Information Professional Association (KIPA). He was also the founding president of the Information and Knowledge Management Society from 1999–2003.

 **Gertrudes Aparecida Dandolini** is a Full Professor at the Federal University of Santa Catarina (UFSC) at the Postgraduate Program in Engineering and Knowledge Management (PPGEGC) and coordinates the Research Center in Intelligence, Management and Technologies for Innovation (IGTI/UFSC). She holds a Master's degree and a Ph.D. in Production Engineering from the UFSC and an undergraduate degree in Mathematics from the UFSC. Dr. Dandolini worked as a lecturer at the Federal University of Pelotas and has coordinated the Mathematics course and the distance learning Mathematics course (2001–2007), worked as a researcher at the Open University of Brazil (UAB), and was the Coordinator of the PPGEGC (2016–2019). Her research focuses on Front End of Innovation, Innovation Management, Innovation in the Public Sector, Social Innovation, Systemic View, and Corporate University.

About the Contributors

Aivars Spilbergs is the Head of Economics and Finance Department in BA. His previous experience includes working in economics and finance research (from 1976–1996, he was engaged in research work at the departments of cybernetics in economics and mathematical economics at University of Latvia) and professional work in banking sector (from 1995–2016, he was the head of multiple departments at SEB banka, in credit management, risk management, and risk center). His recent activities include working as a project manager of a Basel II project "Development and implementation of a credit risk assessment model" at SEB banka (2005–2014); development and implementation of assessment methods and stress tests for internal capital adequacy assessment in banks (2009–2017); development and implementation of a model for assessing expected credit losses in accordance to IFRS9 (2015–2017); council member of *Global Lending Conference* (2015–2018); and Chair of the Risk Management Committee of Association of Latvian Commercial Banks (2014–2016).

Alessandro Margherita Ph.D. is a Senior Researcher at the Department of Engineering for Innovation of the University of Salento (Italy), where he teaches business and project management courses. He holds the qualification for the role of Associate Professor. His research is cross-disciplinary and focuses on topics such as digital and organizational transformation, collective intelligence systems, and technology entrepreneurship. He has published in journals like *Technological Forecasting & Social Change*, *Expert Systems with Applications*, *Human Resource Management Review*, *Technology Analysis and Strategic Management*, *Journal of Intellectual Capital*, and *Business Horizons*. He was a visiting researcher at the Peking University (China) and a Research Affiliate at the Center for Collective Intelligence (CCI) of MIT Sloan (USA).

Aline de Brittos Valdati is a Ph.D. student and holds a Master's degree in Engineering and Knowledge Management (UFSC), integrating the Center for Studies in Intelligence, Management and Technologies for Innovation (IGTI), and the Engineering Nucleus of Integration and Knowledge Governance (ENGIN). She graduated in Information and Communication Technologies (UFSC) and worked with Project Management in systems development and as a teacher in the area of Informatics at the Federal Institute Catarinense. Currently, she is researching on innovation management and management ideas and their practices, techniques, and tools.

Ana María Ortegón is a psychologist and Ph.D. in Knowledge Management Engineering, Master in Psychology, Specialist in Human Resources Management, and has been a consultant and project manager on projects relating to human development, entrepreneurship, organizational change, and innovation. Her work has been financed by public and private organizations, as well as international agencies. She is an active researcher in organizational team learning, knowledge management, team leadership, business and social innovation, and entrepreneurship and is the founding partner of Empreser Tejido Empresarial.

Andrea Valéria Steil is a Full Professor in the Graduate Program in Engineering and Knowledge Management and in the Graduate Program in Psychology at the Federal University of Santa Catarina, Brazil. Prior to joining academia, she spent 10 years in for-profit and not-for-profit organizations in HRM and executive roles. Dr. Steil is an active researcher in organizational learning and memory, work and organizational psychology, behavioral intentions, and employee retention.

Anelise Rebelato Mozzato is a psychologist and a specialist in Business Management. She holds a Master's degree in Education and Ph.D. in Administration from Unisinos. She is a Full Professor and researcher at University of Passo Fundo (UPF) — Rio Grande do Sul, Brazil. She is a collaborating professor in MBA specialization in several educational institutions and leader of the research group "Studies in People Management," registered at CNPq. She has professional and academic experience in Human Resources focusing on behavioral emphasis. She is a researcher with dozens of published articles. Her topics of research interest include strategic people management, organizational behavior, organizational and interorganizational learning, education and professional development, cooperation and interorganizational relations, critical organizational studies, diversities, and qualitative research methods.

Angelo Dossou-Yovo is an Associate Professor in the Department of International Studies at York University (Toronto, Canada), where he teaches Management and Entrepreneurship in the dual degree program in International Studies and Business Administration, a program jointly offered with Emlyon Business School (France). His research interests focus on the processes of opportunity recognition, growth, and innovation in small and medium-sized businesses in the information technology industry, as well as innovation and entrepreneurial ecosystems.

Arif Khan is currently pursuing his Ph.D. in Information Studies at Charles Sturt University, Australia. Mr. Khan has been publishing on different themes related to the library and information science (LIS) profession. His areas of research interest include Knowledge Management, Web Impact Factor, Experiential Learning, Web Accessibility and Usability, Social Information Seeking, and Information Literacy. Besides research, Mr. Khan has extensive experience in designing and conducting professional training programs for the LIS professionals. His areas of training and teaching expertise involve information management and community participation, data analytics, computer-assisted research applications, gender mainstreaming, and collaborative learning. He has a background in computer science and work experience in information management, participatory web, policy development, and project management with respect to the LIS profession.

Muhammad Asim Qayyum is a senior lecturer at the School of Information Studies (Australia) and is currently the deputy Presiding Officer of the university's Human Research Ethics Committee. He has extensive teaching experience in face-to-face and distance learning environments, and currently coordinates the Knowledge Management specialization in the school. Along with his teaching duties, Asim continues to work on individual and collaborative research projects in a variety of contexts where his research is currently focused on two topics: (1) the role of wisdom in knowledge creation works and (2) community engagement practices of public libraries. Asim's research has been published broadly, and he has several research awards to his credit and has conducted research projects funded by national and institutional grants.

Bart Nooteboom studied mathematics and economics. He wrote 18 books and 350 articles and received three international prizes for his work on learning and innovation, trust, and a cognitive theory of the firm. He is member of the Dutch Academy of Sciences. Next to his scientific career, he read philosophy all his life and started writing on it after retirement in 2008. Since 2012, he writes a blog: https://philosophyonthemove. For more information, see his website www.bartnooteboom.nl

Carla S. Zandavalli is a Ph.D. student in Engineering and Knowledge Management at the Federal University of Santa Catarina (Brazil) since 2019. As a researcher, she has experience in research in the field of social innovation and interorganizational learning. She earned her Master's degree at the Federal University of Rio Grande do Sul, and her research was on the area of storage logistics. She earned a degree in Business Administration in

2015, and a degree in Technology in Data Processing in 1997. She was a Professor of Business Administration and Logistics courses. From 1995 to 2005, she worked in a multinational company in National and International Logistics area, with Mercosul and Europe markets. At present, she is a public employee at the Federal Catarinense Institute with experience as International Relations Advisor and Coordination of the Technological Innovation Center.

Claudia Cristina Bitencourt holds a Ph.D. in Administration from PPGA/UFRGS. She is a Full Professor and Researcher at the Graduate Program of Business at Unisinos and the Dean of the Unisinos Business School. She was a Fulbright Scholar at the Thunderbird School of Global Management. She was a visiting professor at the following institutions: TU Dortmund, University of Stavanger, University of Texas Pan American, Technical University of Lisbon, and The University of Queensland. Her research interests are in the areas of strategy and organizational behavior. She serves as an Ambassador of the Human Resources Division at the Academy of Management. She is a member of the International Councils: Association to Advance Collegiate Schools of Business Latin America and Caribbean (AACSB/LATAM) and International Association of Jesuit Business Schools (IAJBS). She is also a Research Productivity Fellow at CNPq (PQ 2).

Cynthya Garcia de Jesus obtained her Master's degree from the Technological Institute of Orizaba, Veracruz, México, and a Ph.D. in Computer Science and Technology at the University Carlos III of Madrid in Leganés, Madrid, Spain. The lines of research to which she is dedicated are software engineering, knowledge Management in software engineering processes, and guidelines and best practices for improving knowledge management processes of R&D. She has developed and worked on projects with the following languages and tools: Language C, HTML, Java, Access, Educational Platforms, PHP, Postgres, Networks and Telecommunications, Software Engineering, Web Development, ASP, JSP, Visual Basic, Web Services, and Data Mining.

Daniela de Oliveira Massad is a doctoral student and holds a Master's degree in Knowledge Management from the Graduate Program in Engineering and Knowledge Management at the Federal University of Santa Catarina (UFSC). She holds a Bachelor of Production Engineering with an emphasis on Chemical Quality from the State University of Rio de Janeiro. She has experience in economic feasibility analysis of nationalization projects, and modifications of automotive parts, having worked for five years in a multinational automobile company. She served as a Technical-Administrative Server in Education at UFSC and is a member of the Research Group on Innovation in Science and Technology — CoMovI (UFSC/CNPq). She has authored book chapters and has articles published in specialized journals and in the annals of national and international events. She is active in the Entrepreneurship, Innovation, and Sustainability research line, conducting research mainly in the areas of social innovation, social entrepreneurship, and absorptive capacity of knowledge.

Elina Mikelsone professionally and academically has experience in management of technology. In last six years, she has participated in more than 20 scientific conferences and has published more than 20 articles. Mikelsone has more than 10 years experience as an international- and national-level project manager and assistant. Elina is also a reviewer of scientific journals in Latvia and internationally. To promote innovation and introduction of new technology in organizations, she has established an NGO: Idea and Innovation Institute. In 2021, she started her post-doctoral project about idea management.

Elita Lielā is an Assistant Professor and Program Director at BA School of Business and Finance in Riga. She graduated from the University of Latvia, Faculty Finance and Trade and holds a doctoral degree in Economics from University of Latvia. She has more than 20 years of professional experience in a public sector (ministries and government institutions of Latvia) as well as in a private sector, e.g. pharmacy, consultations, etc. Her research focuses on Innovation Policy and Innovation Management.

Fernanda Kempner-Moreira is a Ph.D. student of the Graduate Program in Engineering and Knowledge Management (EGC/UFSC) and holds a Master's degree in Administration (2011). She studied specialist courses in Marketing and People Management (2002) and Financial and Accounting Management (2008). She graduated in Administration (2001) and is a member of the LabENGIN Research Group (Integration Engineering and Knowledge Governance). She is an education analyst at SENAI and a lecturer in subjects of the Administration, Production Engineering, and Management Processes. She is the author of several articles published in national and international congresses, magazines, and book chapters. Currently, her research is focused on Governance, Learning Networks, Interorganizational Networks, Multilevel Governance, and Public Security.

Giselly Rizzatti has a Ph.D. from the Graduate Program in Engineering and Knowledge Management at the Federal University of Santa Catarina (EGC/UFSC) (2020) and a Master's degree in Administration (2014). She is a specialist in Consumer Law (2012) and graduate in Law (2007) and undergraduate in Administration. She is a member of the LabENGIN Research Group (Integration Engineering and Knowledge Governance) and the author of several articles published in national and international congresses, magazines, and book chapters. Currently, her research is focused on Learning Governance, Knowledge Governance, Organizational Learning, and Knowledge Management.

Graziela Grando Bresolin is a Ph.D. student and holds a Master's degree in Engineering and Knowledge Management from the Federal University of Santa Catarina (2020). She has a Bachelor's degree in Business Administration (2017) and Tourism (2015) and is a Researcher at the Engineering of Integration and Knowledge Governance Laboratory (ENGIN). She is the technical editor of *International Journal of Knowledge Engineering and Management*. Her research interests focus on innovation in higher education, andragogy, experiential and expansive learning, and the Corporate Education System, specifically planning and assessment multilevel learning applied to the Networked Corporate University Model.

João Artur de Souza holds a Ph.D. in Production Engineering and a Master's degree and an undergraduate degree in Mathematics, all from the Federal University of Santa Catarina (UFSC), Brazil. He also holds a law undergraduate degree from UNISUL. He worked as a lecturer at the Federal University of Pelotas (UFPel), Brazil, where he coordinated its classroom and distance learning Mathematics undergraduate courses, and worked as a researcher at the Open University of Brazil (UAB), and was a university council member. He is currently a full professor at the Federal University of Santa Catarina at the Postgraduate Program in Engineering and Knowledge Management (PPGEGC) of the Department of Knowledge Engineering, and coordinates the Research Center in Intelligence, Management and Technologies for Innovation (IGTI/UFSC) and the Integration Engineering and Knowledge Governance Research Group (ENGIN/UFSC). Dr. Souza is an active researcher on Innovation,

Artificial Intelligence, Governance, Integrity, Internal Control and Risk Management, and Corporate University.

Joyline Makani is an Assistant Professor and Management Librarian at Dalhousie University. She has taught courses in information resources management, knowledge management, virtual teams, collaboration, and leadership at the Faculty of Management's undergraduate, graduate, and executive programs. Her current research activities sit at the intersection of information science, data management, and knowledge management, as well as collaboration, entrepreneurship, and innovation. She focuses on exploring how organizations, in a bid to align and sustain innovation, growth, and success, continuously learn and build or deploy systems to effectively and efficiently create new knowledge.

Julieta K. Watanabe-Wilbert has doctoral and Master's degrees in Engineering and Knowledge Management from the Federal University of Santa Catarina (Brazil), where she currently contributes as a researcher. She has over 25 years of working experience at Correios — the Brazilian Postal Service. There, her main activities were related to Training and Development, Strategic Planning, and Quality Management. In all these areas, she worked as an internal consultant, instructor, and manager of small groups. She also holds a Civil Engineering Degree from the Federal University of Paraná (Brazil), a DESS in Adult Education from the University of Strasbourg (France), and a Master's Degree from the German University of Administrative Sciences, Speyer (Germany). She has authored and co-authored conference papers, journal articles, and book chapters in fields related to her work and studies.

Kimiz Dalkir is the Director of the School of Information Studies at McGill University. She published the third edition of *Knowledge Management in Theory and Practice* in 2019 (MIT Press), which has had an international impact on Knowledge Management education and practice. She has also co-edited *Utilizing Evidence-Based Lessons Learned for Enhanced Organizational Innovation* (with S. McIntyre) and *Change* as well as the more recent *Navigating Fake News, Alternative Facts and Misinformation in a Post-Truth World* (with R. Katz). Dr. Dalkir's research focuses on tacit knowledge sharing and organizational learning to promote reuse and innovation. Her research projects span diverse sectors in both the private and public sectors with outcomes that have influenced organizational and national knowledge management policies.

Márcia Aparecida Prim is a Ph.D. student and holds a Master's degree in Knowledge Management from the Graduate Program in Engineering and Knowledge Management at the Federal University of Santa Catarina (UFSC). She is a Professor at the Faculty of Technology AeroTD. She holds a Bachelor of Business Administration with Marketing Qualification (2010) from the Educational Society of Santa Catarina Única/SOCIESC and won the Productivity Student Merit Award in 2015 and 2017, and the Academic Merit of Única/SOCIESC in 2010. She has experience in the areas of project management, company management, private sector, and third sector and works as a member of the Center for Studies in Intelligence, Management and Technologies for Innovation (IGTI) (UFSC/CAPES), in the line of research in Entrepreneurship, Innovation and Sustainability. She also conducts research in the areas of social innovation and governance.

Maria-Isabel Sanchez-Segura has been a faculty member in the Computer Science Department at Carlos III University of Madrid since 1998. She is a Full Professor at this Department. Her research interests include usability of interactive systems and software engineering in general, focusing on processes, methodologies, reuse, management and software configuration management, and recently Intelligent Organizations. Maria-Isabel holds a B.S. in Computer Science (1997), an M.S. in Software Engineering (1999), and a Ph.D. in Computer Science (2001) from the Universidad Politecnica of Madrid. She is the author of several papers published in journals such as *IEEE Transactions on Education, IEEE Transactions on Software Engineering, Software Practice and Experience, Interacting with Computers, Journal of Systems and Software*, etc.

Marta Silva Neves is a pedagogue with training in Group Dynamics at the Brazilian Society of Group Dynamics (SBDG). She holds a Specialization in Third Sector Management from the Federal University of Rio Grande do Sul (UFRGS), Brazil; Master's degree in Health Teaching from the Federal University of Health Sciences of Porto Alegre (UFCSPA), Brazil; and is a doctorate student in Engineering and Knowledge Management at UFSC. She is a researcher at the Engineering of Integration and Knowledge Governance Laboratory (ENGIN) and works at the Corporate University in a financial institution. She is currently dedicated to the studies of the corporate education system and its maturity stages according to the guidelines of the Networked Corporate University Model.

Michele Andréia Borges holds a Ph.D. in Engineering and Knowledge Management from the Federal University of Santa Catarina (UFSC) with a focus on social innovations and has a degree in Mathematics. She worked as a technical agent and trainer of school teams in the networks of Santa Catarina and São Paulo by Instituto Ayrton Senna. She is a Postgraduate Professor in Education in the specializations of Teacher Training and Management of Educational Centers and Information and Communication Technologies in the Classroom at the Universidad Internacional Iberoamericana and Universidad del Atlántico. She is a content teacher in the production of didactic material with a focus on the articulation of socio-emotional competences with essential cognitive skills in mathematical learning.

Michelle McPherson completed both an undergraduate degree in Biology as well as a Master's degree in Earth Science at St. Francis Xavier University. Her Masters work focused on the impacts of climate change on Lyme disease in Canada. Michelle is the Program and Membership Officer at a non-profit organization called Science Atlantic, which seeks to provide opportunities for STEM faculty and students in the Atlantic region. To continue her work in the research field, Michelle also works part-time as a Research Coordinator at Dalhousie University. Within this role, she provides assistance with data collection and extraction, data analysis, knowledge mobilization, event planning, literature review, and drafting of reports and papers.

Neri dos Santos is a Senior Professor of the Graduate Program in Engineering and Knowledge Management at the Federal University of Santa Catarina (EGC/UFSC) and CEO of the STELA Institute. He holds a B.Sc degree in Mechanical Engineering from the Federal University of Santa Catarina (1976); specialization in Occupational Safety Engineering from the Federal University of Santa Catarina (1977); an M.Sc Degree in Ergonomics from the Paris XIII University, France (1982); a Ph.D. in Ergonomics from Engineering in the "Conservatoire National des Arts et Metiers," France (1985); and Postdoctoral in Cognitive Engineering from Polytechnic School of Montreal, Canada. Former President of ABEPRO — 92/93 and 94/95. Former Dean of the Polytechnic School of the Pontifical Catholic University of Paraná — PUCPR 2015/2018. He serves on the Editorial Board of the following magazines: *American Journal of Industrial Engineering*, *International Journal of Knowledge Engineering and Management*, *Ergonomic Action and Production*, and *Journal of Science & Technology*. His fields of research and teaching specialize in Engineering & Knowledge Management.

Ricardo Pereira is a Doctoral student in the post-graduate program in Engineering and knowledge management (EGC/UFSC). He has a Master's degree in Production Engineering from the Federal University of Santa Catarina (UFSC) and Business Administration (2002) and Law (2013) from the Federal University of Santa Catarina (UFSC). Researcher at the Leadership and Responsible Management Laboratory EGC/UFSC. He is currently conducting research on leadership, knowledge management, innovation, social innovation, applied intelligence, strategic management, public management and law. LATTES: http://lattes.cnpq.br/6740685077297299. SCOPUS ID: 57218597763. ORCID: https://orcid.org/0000-0003-4744-4891. WoS ID P-8095-2018 LinkedIn: https://www.linkedin.com/in/ricardo-pereira-4941979/

Rosane Malvestiti is a doctoral degree student at the Postgraduate Program in Engineering and Knowledge Management at the Federal University of Santa Catarina, Brazil. She holds a Master's degree in Human Movement Sciences from the Cruzeiro do Sul University, graduating in 2014, and is a nurse and physical educator. She graduated in 1986 from the Centro Universitário Hermínio Ometto de Araras, UNIARARAS, and in 1990 at Pontifical Catholic University of Campinas. Her research has been supported by the Center for Studies in Intelligence, Management and Technologies for Innovation (IGTI-EGC-UFSC). She also holds a CAPES-PROEX studentship, with full dedication. Lattes: http://lattes.cnpq.br/0763887115764377. Orcid: https://orcid.org/0000–0002–4927–5721

Sicilia Vechi is a Doctoral student in the Postgraduate Program in Engineering and Knowledge Management from the Federal University of Santa Catarina, Brazil (PPGEGC/UFSC). She holds a Master's degree in Engineering and Knowledge Management, with research on knowledge flows in digital curation, and is a Specialist in Editorial Management from Tuiuti University and graduated in Social Communication (Journalism) from the University of Vale do Itajaí (Univali). She was a member of the Research Group VIA (/EGC/UFSC) on Innovation Habitats and a support advisor to the Project Management of the Santa Catarina Innovation Network (RECEPETI). She acts as communication advisor for the State Government of Santa Catarina. Lattes: http://lattes.cnpq.br/8607286811172683. Orcid: https://orcid.org/0000–0002–8983–1032.

Solange Maria da Silva has a degree in Administration from ESAG/UDESC (1995), a Master's degree (1999), and a Ph.D. (2007) in Production Engineering at the Federal University of Santa Catarina (UFSC). She is a Professor at the Federal University of Santa Catarina — UFSC/Campus Araranguá. She is a member of the research groups LGR (Leadership and Responsible Management Laboratory), ENGIN (Engineering of Integration and Knowledge Governance Laboratory), and KLOM (Interdisciplinary in Knowledge, Learning and Organizational Memory). She is a teacher of Business Management at the Graduate Program in Information and Communication Technologies and at the Graduate Course in Information and Communication Technology, both from UFSC. She has experience in strategic research and extension projects in the following areas: Strategic and Process Management, Leadership, Digital Business Management, Networked Corporate University Model, Innovation Management, Entrepreneurship, and Quality in Services.

Talita Caetano Silva is a psychologist and holds a Master's degree in Organizational and Work Psychology and Specialist in Strategic People Management. She holds a doctorate in Engineering and Knowledge Management from the Post-Graduate Program in Engineering and Knowledge Management of Federal University of Santa Catarina. She is a Senior Researcher at the Engineering of Integration and Knowledge Governance Laboratory (ENGIN) and an executive at one of the largest technology companies in Brazil. She is currently dedicated to the studies of the corporate education system and its interrelationships with the learning curve and transference to work practice, with the objective of substantiating the application of the Networked Corporate University Model.

Tatjana Volkova is a Professor of Strategic Management and Innovation Management and a leading researcher at BA School of Business and Finance in Riga, Latvia. She has extensive practical experience in management and consultancy, including working as Manager of Rotterdam Consult, Ltd, HR recruiting professional at Amrop International office, and Training Officer at WOCCU office in Riga. Her research findings have been published in a number of peer-reviewed books and journals nationally and internationally and presented at numerous international conferences. Tatjana is also a member of editorial committee of scientific journals (e.g. editor and reviewer of *Journal of Business Management, SBS Journal of Applied Business Research and Banks*, and *Banks System Journal*) and has participated in international research projects. Her research interests are related to Innovation Management, Strategic Management, Design Management, etc. As a professor, Tatjana Volkova has delivered lectures in India, Kazakhstan, Greece, Georgia, Norway, Switzerland, and Luxembourg, among countries.

Valério Vincenzo De Luca, Ph.D., is a Researcher at the Faculty of Economic, Social and Political Sciences of the Catholic University "Our Lady of Good Counsel" (Albania), where he teaches business, production, and waste management courses and is in charge of the university incubator. His research interests include different topics such as sustainable entrepreneurship, business modelling, innovative financing, and circular economy. He was a visiting researcher at the Jinan University (China).

Willian Rochadel is a Ph.D. student at the Postgraduate Program in Knowledge Engineering and Management (PPGEGC) of the Federal University of Santa Catarina (UFSC) and holds a Master's degree in Knowledge Engineering (PPGEGC/UFSC) and graduated in Information & Communication Technologies (UFSC). He is an Administrative Staff and IT Technician at the Federal University of Rio Grande do Sul (UFRGS) and Researcher at IGTI (Intelligence, Management, and Technologies for Innovation). His current work focuses on analyzing Collective Knowledge, combining open participation and idea management with Social Semantic Web.

Contents

1

Why Knowledge Governance and Learning

Patricia de Sá Freire[*,‡], *Suliman Hawamdeh*[†,§],
Gertrudes Aparecida Dandolini[*,¶] *and Graziela Grando Bresolin*[*,**]

[*]*Federal University of Santa Catarina, Graduate Program in
Knowledge Management and Engineering, R. Delfino Conti, s/n,
Trindade, Florianópolis — SC, 88040-900, Brazil*

[†]*University of North Texas, Department of Information Sciences,
College of Information, Denton, TX, USA*

[‡]*patriciadesafreire@gmail.com*

[§]*Suliman.Hawamdeh@unt.edu*

[¶]*gertrudes.dandolini@ufsc.br*

[**]*grazielabresolin@gmail.com*

This introductory chapter discusses the various concepts of knowledge governance and their relationships to learning at the individual and organizational level. The governance of learning and governance of knowledge are complimentary concepts increasingly used in relation to the traditional concept of corporate governance. The chapter also discusses knowledge management and organizational learning and their relevance to the various concepts used in this book such as NGov, LGov and KGov.

1.1. Introduction

Knowledge has long been recognized as the most important factor for human development and survival. It has played a key role in gaining a better understanding of nature and the world around us. Humans, through the advances in science and technology, were able to learn how to work the fields, grow crops, raise animals, build infrastructure, and fight diseases. More importantly, humans were able to utilize cumulative knowledge to build governing systems, enact rules and regulations, and create civic societies. Today, societal transformation and development is characterized not only by the advances in science and technology but also by the degree to which these societies are able to learn and adapt. Our society today faces some of the most difficult challenges and complex issues that could have been easily created by the advances in science and technology. Some of these complex issues include the environment, the stockpile of nuclear weapons, and the increased threat to our privacy and security caused by Internet hacking and cybersecurity attacks. Our ability to address these issues depends largely on our ability to learn, adapt, and recognize the interconnectedness of the various governing systems.

1.2. Knowledge Management

Organizations today, small and big, have realized the importance of knowledge as an indispensable element for their survival. Knowledge management and learning are essential elements in creating a distinctive value for the organization and maintaining organizational competitive advantage in both private and public sectors.

Knowledge management comprises a set of processes and practices designed to help organizations improve performance and achieve a competitive advantage. Knowledge management is responsible for monitoring, facilitating, and managing the processes of creating and internalizing knowledge at the levels of individual and organization. Thus, due to its relevance throughout the organizational value chain, it has been recognized by organizations as a strategic tool.[1-8]

However, to create knowledge and manage it in such a way as to overcome existing and new organizational challenges of innovation and transformation, there is a need to engage in theoretical and empirical research. Research is needed to understand how key drivers such as culture, leadership, policies, and situational strategies play a role in the enhancement of knowledge management and learning processes and practices at the individual and organizational level.[9-11] Organizational learning is not much different from that of individual learning in the sense that organizations do gain experience over time through the development of organizational culture, organizational leadership, and norms and practices. The ability of the organization to develop knowledge management practices such as communities of practice, best practices, and lessons learned reflects the ability of the organization to learn overtime and gain experience.

Knowledge is normally created as a result of a learning process that takes into account historical data and social interaction. The drivers of organizational transformation, knowledge creation, and innovation are largely dependent on governance structures that could facilitate or undermine the knowledge management processes and practices needed achieve the intended results.[11,12]

There is a lack of studies investigating knowledge management and learning constructs concomitantly with Knowledge Governance (KGov). There is a need for better understanding the interrelationship, interdependence, and interconnection of governance mechanisms and components with intra- and inter-organizational networks. The most recent studies on these relationships show that the mechanisms and components addressed by the traditional Corporate Governance have not deepened the issues of knowledge management and organizational learning.[13-16] As a result, this ends up hampering the transformation and innovation planned by the organization's strategy.

1.3. Corporate Governance

The traditional Corporate Governance model, currently in force in organizations, began to be questioned for having a narrow focus on monitoring and control of results and offering few mechanisms that support the cycles of knowledge and organizational learning that promote innovation.

It is worth remembering that the Corporate Governance model emerged with the idea of cooperation and interaction among stakeholders as a way to ensure the achievement of common goals, optimize company performance, and facilitate access to capital.[17] However, what is noticeable is that the term has become synonymous with monitoring and control of the actions of managers.[18]

According to Marques,[19] Corporate Governance is:

> ... mechanisms or principles that govern the decision-making process within a company, whose central objective would be to balance the competitiveness and productivity of a company with a responsible and transparent management (p. 13).

While not excluding the need for monitoring and control, it is necessary to move forward to face the challenges generated by the collaborative economy and the new intelligent technologies (which are changing and improving ever more rapidly). A Corporate Governance model must be based on mechanisms and organizational components that recognize the value of sharing, exchanging and transferring knowledge for the creation of value, such as the multi-level governance model.[20–23] In addition, governance is a tool that allows the creation of policies and a dynamic corporate structure through the collaboration of internal and external stakeholders.[24]

Multilevel Governance (MultiGov) is a term derived from the dynamics of decision-making at multiple levels in the European Union. It presents a different perspective and provide a more complete answer to problems related to integration and trust between institutions.[22] In a MultiGov environment, decisions are made as a result of a complex cooperative and adjustment processes that work from the bottom up and from the top down, at all levels.[20] It focuses more on individual and collective goals to be achieved than on a roadmap on how to achieve them. This process allows more freedom in the creation and innovation within legal and strategic principles of the common good.

MultiGov involves stakeholders from different organizational structures that interact with each other and enables horizontal, vertical, and diagonal relationships between different organizations, promoting collaboration for the development of strategies, policies, and controls and feedback channels and the regulation of multiple participants. It helps in maintaining collective coherence between stakeholders, monitoring the results of multilevel evaluation for continuous improvement of the organizational system and creating co-production environments for system innovation.[24–26]

MultiGov is normally proposed for contemporary organizations to better deal with the complexity of the challenges facing society. This can be better achieved through the integration of different organizational competencies for the elaboration of policies and corporate structures aimed at governing with a special focus on economic, social, and environmental sustainability (see Ref. 11, p. 32).[11] Piattoni (Ref. 21, p. 71) points out that the novelty of MultiGov lies in coordinating participants at different territorial levels so that they are not aligned with traditional hierarchical relationships. In other words, the basis for MultiGov is in their relationships, where the formation of intra- and inter-organizational networks allows the sharing of responsibilities and power of influence, both horizontally (between organizations) and vertically (between levels), with respect to the development of strategies and policies of action, as well as the implementation and realization of actions for the common good (Table 1.1).[27]

Table 1.1. Multilevel governance mechanisms.

MultiGov Mechanisms	Authors
Collaborative intra- and inter-organizational networks	Couto,[22] Freire et al.[11]
Decentralization of authority	Freire et al.,[11] Brandão,[28] Ivan and Cuglesan,[29] Dallabrida and Becker[30]
System self-organization	Touati et al.,[31] Maillet et al.,[24] Stoker[25]
Distribution of power and responsibilities	Knopp,[26] Brandão,[28] Dallabrida and Becker[30]
Respect for autonomy	Divay and Paquin,[32] Brandão,[28] Dallabrida and Becker[30]
Integration	Touati et al.,[31] Freire et al.,[11] Divay and Paquin,[32] Knopp[26]
Multi-level learning	Freire,[15] Rizzatti,[16] Touati et al.,[31] Freire et al.[11]

Source: Freire et al.[23]

These mechanisms shown in Table 1.1 and listed by Freire *et al.*[23] interrelate knowledge, learning, and inter-organizational networks. This corroborates the work by Foss and Klein,[33] where they point out that mechanisms should be created for the integration and sharing of knowledge, making changes happen which in return adds value to the organization and the profession. It is also important to note that, in order to implement MultiGov mechanisms, the components of KGov, organizational learning (LGov), and inter-organizational network (NGov) must be taken into account.

1.4. Organizational Learning

As discussed earlier, organizational learning is a process by which organizations create, develop, and institutionalize knowledge. The knowledge resulting from the learning process, in turn, directs the future activities of individuals and groups within the organization. It influences how groups interpret their work environment, develop new insights, make decisions, and solve problems.[34,35] Learning is the result of social relationships, and it depends on intra- and inter-organizational networks. According to Pereira,[36] networks enhance efficiency gains by:

> ... (i) identifying problems and opportunities, producing flexible solutions that allow for their adjustment according to the complexity and variety of problems, i.e., they favor proactive governance; (ii) sharing and aggregating information and knowledge among stakeholders, which become an added value in policy formulation; (iii) establishing a framework for building consensus or for minimizing conflicts among stakeholders; (iv) reducing the risk of stakeholder resistance to the implementation of agreed policies (p. 9).

In this context, a contemporary organization is one that is capable of creating, acquiring, and sharing knowledge, and at the same time, it modifies its behavior to generate new knowledge and create value.[37] KGov in this case becomes essential, as it involves the governance of networks for the collection and sharing of data and information for the creation of new knowledge.[1] KGov implied learning as a key to the process of knowledge creation and sharing. Ikujiro Nonaka and Hirotaka Takeuchi's Spiral Knowledge model distinguishes four stages that include socialization, externalization, combination, and internalization. The model explains how knowledge is continuously converted and created through collaboration, interaction, and learning. The concepts of NGov, KGov, and LGov have been studied by the scientific literature separately since the late 1990s (NGov) and early 2000s (KGov and LGov). However, no publication has been found in international databases that seek to describe or understand their inter-relationships.

1.5. KGov

The term KGov was first coined by Grandori.[38] It is currently in the theoretical and empirical consolidation phase.[39–42] After a thorough study of the definitions of the term, Freire *et al.*[11] defined the concept of KGov as:

> … as a set of formal and relational mechanisms generated by corporate governance and the knowledge management processes to optimize the organization's economic results (p. 32).

The term Learning Governance was first introduced by Rizzatti[16] and defined as:

> … a system through which organizations direct cognitive and behavioral processes involving a set of mechanisms, components and learning environments that allow internal and external stakeholders to develop a collective organization with capacity for change (p. 204).

LGov is aimed at creating clarity and continuity by aligning learning strategy within the organization with the business strategy Vitry and Chia.[43] It is a process by which organization can enhance training with the organization and enhance talent development.

The inter-organizational Network Governance (NGov) has been recognized by academics and professionals as a relevant element for network effectiveness.[44] According to Jones *et al.*,[45] NGov involves:

> … a select, persistent, and structured set of autonomous firms (as well as nonprofit agencies) engaged in creating products or services based on implicit and open-ended contracts to adapt to environmental contingencies and to coordinate and safeguard exchanges (p. 914).

In the current context, internal and external collaborations with partners generate a flow of knowledge between those involved. Good governance of inter- and intra-organizational networks (NGov), of generated knowledge (KGov), and of its learning (LGov) increases the capacity of organizations to successfully integrate internal and external sources of knowledge and subsequently enhanced their capacity for innovation.[46] The relevance of these terms and elements (NGov, KGov, and LGov) for the effective development of knowledge management practices, organizational learning, and innovations in both private and public sector organizations is very important.[47–49]

1.6. Conclusion

The implementation of MultiGov models to promote the capacity of organizations to innovate requires a better understanding of the interrelationships between LGov, KGov, and NGov models. The governance of learning and the governance of knowledge are considered complementary approaches that transcend the boundaries of the traditional model of Corporate Governance. They both recognize the importance of knowledge creation and knowledge sharing, at the individual and organizational level, as well as via inter-organizational networks. KGov and LGov are both in alignment with the concepts of organizational learning and the goal of achieving the learning organizations status.[50] As a learning organization, there is a need for a learning and KGov structure that allows the continuous creation, sharing, and leveraging of knowledge resources within the organizations.

Acknowledgments

This study was financed in part by the Coordination for the Improvement of Higher Education Personnel - Brazil (CAPES) - Finance Code 001.

References

1. I. Nonaka and H. Takeuchi. *Criação de conhecimento na empresa: como as empresas japonesas geram a dinâmica da inovação*. 18th ed. Rio de Janeiro: Campus (2004).

2. I. Nonaka and H. Takeuchi. Teoria da criação do conhecimento organizacional. In: *Gestão do conhecimento*, H. Takeuchi and I. Nonaka (eds.), Porto Alegre: Bookman (2008), pp. 54–90.

3. K. Dalkir. *Knowledge Management in Theory and Practice*. Boston, Elsevier (2005).

4. T.H. Davenport and L. Prusak, *Conhecimento empresarial: como as organizações gerenciam o seu capital intelectual*. 8th ed. Rio de Janeiro: Campus (2004).

5. I Nonaka and R. Toyama. The knowledge-creating theory revisited: Knowledge creation as a synthesizing process. *Knowledge Management Research e Practice*, **1**(1), 2–10 (2003).

6. K.E. Sveiby. *A nova riqueza das organizações*: gerenciando e avaliando patrimônios de conhecimento. 7th ed. Rio de Janeiro: Campus (2003).

7. I. Nonaka and N. Konno. The concept of "BA": Building a foundation for knowledge creation. *California Management Review*, **40**(3), 40–54 (1998).

8. I. Nonaka, R. Toyama and N. Konno. SECI, BA and leadership: A unified model of dynamic knowledge creation. In: *Managing Knowledge: An Essential Reader*, S.E. Little and T. Ray (eds.), London: Sage Publications, 23–50 (2002).

9. N.J. Foss. The emerging knowledge governance approach: Challenges and characteristics. *Organization*, **14**(1), 29–52 (2007).

10. T.C. Silva, R.M. Couto and P.S. Freire. Governança do conhecimento: uma revisão em direção à conceituação e diferenciação da gestão do conhecimento. *Produção em Foco*, **7**(1), 33–49 (2017).

11. P.S. Freire, G.A. Dandolini, J.A. Souza, T.C. Silva and R.M. Couto. Knowledge governance (GovC): The state of the art about the term. *Biblios*, (69), 21–40 (2017), doi:10.5195/biblios.2017.469.

12. M.T.L. Fleury and M.M. Oliveira Junior. *Gestão Estratégica do Conhecimento*: integrando aprendizagem, conhecimento e competências. São Paulo: Atlas (2001).

13. N.J. Foss and J.T. Mahoney. Exploring knowledge governance. *International Journal Strategic Change Management*, **2**(2/3), 93–101 (2010).

14. S. Pemsel and R. Müller. The governance of knowledge in project-based organizations. *International Journal of Project Management*, **30**(8), 865–876 (2012).

15. G. Rizzatti, and P.S. Freire. Governança da Aprendizagem Organizacional (GovA): o estado da arte sobre o termo, *Revista Espacios*, **41**(3) (2020).

16. G. Rizzatti. *Framework de Governança da Aprendizagem Organizacional*. 283 f. Tese (Doutorado em Engenharia e Gestão do Conhecimento). Universidade Federal de Santa Catarina, Florianópolis (2020).

17. Instituto Brasileiro de Governança Corporativa [IBGC]. *Código das melhores práticas de governança corporativa*. São Paulo: IBGC (2015).
18. F.K. Moreira, P.S. Freire and S.M. Silva. Governança corporativa como propulsora da inovação: uma análise a partir da revisão sistemática da literatura. *Annals of VIII International Congress on Knowledge and Innovation-Ciki*. Guadalajara: Universidad de Guadalajara, 1(1), 1–14 (2018).
19. M.C.C. Marques. Aplicação dos princípios da governança corporativa aplicação dos princípios da governança corporativa ao sector público. *Revista de Administração Contemporânea*, 11(2), 11–26, (2007).
20. L. Bobbio. Governance multilivello e democrazia. *Rivista delle Politiche sociali*, 2, 51–62 (2005).
21. S. Piattoni. Subnational governments and non-governmental organizations: a difficult coexistence within multi-level governance? In: *Committee of the Regions, the Contributions to the 2008 Ateliers*, S. Piattoni (ed.). Brussels: Forward Studies/Cellule de prospective, 71 (2008).
22. R.M. Couto. *Governança nas Instituições de Ensino Superior*: análise dos mecanismos de governança na Universidade Federal de Santa Catarina à luz do modelo *multilevel governance*. Dissertação (Mestrado) — Universidade Federal de Santa Catarina, Centro Tecnológico. Programa de Pós-Graduação em Engenharia e Gestão do Conhecimento, 137 f., Florianópolis (2018).
23. P.S. Freire, F. Kempner-Moreira and J.L. Hott Jr. Governança Multinível Em Rede: reflexões sobre um novo modelo de governança para a segurança pública. *VII Encontro Brasileiro de Administração Pública*, (2020).
24. L. Maillet, P. Lamarche, B. Roy and M. Lemire. At the heart of adapting healthcare organizations. *Emergence: Complexity & Organization*, 17(2), (2015).
25. G. Stoker. Urban political science and the challenge of urban governance. In: *Debating Governance: Authority, Steering and Democracy*, J. Pierre (ed.). New York: Oxford University Press (2000), pp. 91–109.
26. G. Knopp. Governança social, território e desenvolvimento. *Perspectivas em Políticas Públicas*, 4(8), 53–74 (2011).
27. I. Bache and M. Flinders. Themes and issues in multi-level governance. In: *Multi-level Governance*, I. Bache and M. Flinders (Orgs.). Oxford: University Press (2004).
28. C.A. Brandão. Descentralização enquanto modo de ordenamento espacial do poder e do reescalonamento territorial do Estado: trajetórias e desafios para o Brasil. In: *Governança territorial e desenvolvimento: descentralização político-administrativa, estruturas subnacionais de gestão do desenvolvimento e capacidades estatais*, V.R. Dallabrida (org.). Rio de Janeiro: Garamond, 115–135 (2011).

29. A. Ivan and N. Cuglesan. Multi-level governance and decentralization in the unitary states of the European Union. Case study: France and Romania. *New England Journal*, **14**(1), 47–59 (2009).

30. V.R. Dallabrida and D.F. Becker. Governança territorial: um primeiro passo na construção de uma proposta teórico-metodológica. *Revista Desenvolvimento em Questão*, Ijuí, **1**(2), 73–97, jul/dez (2003).

31. N. Touati, L. Maillet, P. Marie-Andrée, D. Jean-Louis and C. Rodríguez. Understanding multilevel governance processes through complexity theory: An empirical case study of the Quebec health-care system. *International Journal of Public Administration*, **42**(3), 205–217 (2019).

32. G. Divay and S. Paquin. L'administration publique dans la gouvernance mul- tiniveau infranationale: état de la question et perspectives. *Télescope: revue d'analyse comparée en administration publique*, **19**(1), 1–24 (2013).

33. N.J. Foss and P.G. Klein. The theory of the firm and its critics: A stocktaking and assessment. In *New Institutional Economics: A Guidebook*, E. Brousseau and J.M. Gachant (eds.), Cambridge, UK: Cambridge University Press (2008), pp. 425–442.

34. M.M. Crossan, H.W. Lane and R.E. White. An organizational learning *Framework*: From intuition to institution. *Academy of Management Review*, **24**(3), 522–537 (1999).

35. D.Vera and M. Crossan. Organizational learning and knowledge manage- ment: Toward an integrative *Framework*. In: *Handbook of Organizational Learning and Knowledge Management*, M. Easterbysmith and M. Lyles (eds.), Malden: Blackwell, (2005), pp. 122–141.

36. M. Pereira. Governança territorial multinível: Fratura (s) entre teoria e prática (s). *Desenvolvimento Regional em debate: DRd*, **4**(2), 4–20 (2014).

37. M.J. Kiernan. *Os 11 mandamentos da administração do século XXI*. São Paulo: Makron Books (1998).

38. A. Grandori. Neither hierarchy nor identity: Knowledge governance mecha- nisms ad the theory of the firm. *Journal of Management and Governance*, **5**, 381–399 (2001).

39. Y. Cao and Y. Xiang. The impact of knowledge governance on knowledge sharing: The mediating role of the guanxi effect. *Chinese Management Studies*, **7**(1), 36–52 (2013).

40. L. Van Kerkhoff and V. Pilbeam. Understanding socio-cultural dimensions of environmental decision-making: A knowledge governance approach. *Environmental Science & Policy*, **73**, 29–37 (2017).

41. C. Múnera and L. van Kerkhoff. Diversifying knowledge governance for climate adaptation in protected areas in Colombia. *Environmental Science and Policy*, **94**, 39–48 (2019).

42. R. Bernsteiner, T. Dilger and C. Ploder. A knowledge governance framework for open innovation projects. *International Journal of Web Engineering and Technology*, **15**(2), 189–212 (2020).
43. C. Vitry and E. Chia. Governance learning: Building a network around managerial innovations. *Studies in Public and Non-Profit Governance*, **4**, 275–302 (2015).
44. K.G. Provan and P.K. Tilburg. Modes of network governance: Structure, management, and effectiveness. *Journal of Public Administration Research and Theory*, **18**, 229–252 (2007).
45. C. Jones, W.S. Hesterly and S.P. Borgatti. A general theory of network governance: Exchange conditions and social mechanisms. *Academy of Management Review*, **22**(4), 911–945 (1997).
46. A. Howell. Agglomeration, absorptive capacity and knowledge governance: implications for public-private firm innovation in China. *Regional Studies*, **54**(8), 1069–1083 (2020).
47. E.H. Klijn and J.F.M. Koppenjan. Governance network theory: Past, present and future. *Policy and Politics*, **40**(4), 187–206 (2012).
48. K.A. Borges, G.A. Dandolini and A.L. Soares. O processo de formação de parcerias intersetoriais em iniciativas de inovação social em Portugal. *Análise Social*, **234**, 118–143 (2020).
49. J. Bruneel, B. Clarisse, S. Weemaes and M. Staessens. Breaking with the past: The need for innovation in the governance of nonprofit social enterprises, *Academy of Management Perspectives*. **34**(2), 209–225 (2020).
50. P.M. Senge. *The Fifth Discipline: The Art and Practice of the Learning Organization*. London: Random House Business (1990).

Part I

Knowledge Governance

Knowledge Governance: Addressing Complexity Throughout the Knowledge Processing Cycle

Kimiz Dalkir

McGill University, School of Information Studies, Canada
kimiz.dalkir@mcgill.ca

Effective knowledge governance requires organizations to develop core competencies as well as organizational structures and policies. Knowledge governance mechanisms must be put into place for the creation, sharing, storage, and transfer of knowledge, which in turn foster synergy and create value. However, knowledge governance needs to go beyond the "simple" knowledge management (KM) process cycle to also encompass organizational learning and improvement processes for both explicit and tacit knowledge.[1] An integrated knowledge governance (IKG) model is needed for the processes of knowledge creation, sharing/dissemination, organizing/storing, using/reusing, and learning for organizational improvement. An IKG can also better address the complexity in governing knowledge at three levels (individual, group, and organizational) using both formal and informal approaches. This chapter uses the Evans *et al.*[2] holistic knowledge process cycle to map specific governance activities to each knowledge process as it provides a holistic view of the knowledge life cycle by building on previous life cycles models and by extending previous models to integrate the notion of second order or double loop learning. Best practices from research and an illustrative organizational implementation will be used to highlight recommendations. The chapter will conclude with some research gaps that still remain to be addressed.

2.1. Introduction

What are some of the salient features of knowledge governance and why is it important in all organizations regardless of sector? All organizations have at a minimum an organizational structure and decision-making rules that govern or order how things need to be done in order to attain organizational goals. The complexity of knowledge governance quickly builds up, however, as governance is needed at three interrelated levels in an organization: the level of an individual employee; the group, team, or network level; and the organization-wide level. In addition, knowledge governance requires an integration of both formal and informal governance mechanisms in order to be effective. The final layer of complexity is added as knowledge governance is also needed for each step of the knowledge management (KM) process lifecycle in an organization, namely: for knowledge creation, sharing, storage, use, and reuse. These steps must be applied to both explicit (tangible, e.g. document) and tacit (intangible, e.g. human expertise) forms of knowledge, with the latter usually providing additional challenges. Effective organizational improvement and learning can only be achieved if all of these facets of governance are integrated in a strategic yet implementable approach to knowledge governance. The chapter identifies best practices in knowledge governance throughout the KM process cycle, at all three levels, for the two knowledge forms using both formal and informal approaches in order to propose a comprehensive and integrated knowledge governance approach (IKG). An example from an organization that was successful in implementing this approach is described. The research gaps that remain to be addressed are then discussed together with recommendations to conclude the chapter.

2.2. The Importance of Knowledge Governance

Governance is typically defined in terms of three major components: authority, decision-making, and accountability. This implies that there are organizational roles and responsibilities to identify who has what type of authority; that there are policies, rules, and guidelines that determine how decisions are made; and that there are expectations if not consequences that result when governance is not successful (i.e. accountability).

Governance can be defined as: "the act or process of governing or overseeing the control and direction of something, such as a country or an organization" (Merriam Webster[a]). It refers to the ability "to control, direct, or strongly influence the actions and conduct of" of an organization.[b] Governance can be distinguished from management as being at a higher level. Governance is the strategic task of setting the organization's goals, direction, limitations, and accountability frameworks. Management, on the other hand, is closer to the operational level and refers to the allocation of resources and overseeing the day-to-day operations of the organization. Governance is an overarching framework, such as the organizational structure (the "why"), whereas the "what" of management is more at the level of individual organizational units.[3]

Another distinction lies in the "who" in that governance is the job of the governing body, such as a committee or board, to provide direction, leadership, and control. Management is typically the job of a management or executive team, led by a president or Chief Executive Officer (CEO). The board of directors is responsible for making decisions about the direction of the company. Duties such as oversight, strategic planning, decision-making, and financial planning fall under their governance activities. The board will typically create the company's bylaws, which are a set of core policies that outline the company's mission, values, vision, and structure. On an as-needed basis, the board will also create and approve major policies[3] as well as provide general oversight for the organization.

Another way to distinguish between governance and management responsibilities is to determine whether a duty or responsibility focuses on the big picture. In a paper called "Distinguishing Governance from

---

[a]https://www.merriam-webster.com/dictionary/governance.
[b]https://www.merriam-webster.com/dictionary/govern.

Management" (2008), author Barry S. Bader proposes seven guiding questions to determine whether something falls under governance and is thus the board's responsibility. These questions include whether or not the issue or problem is about the future, whether it is core or mission critical, whether it is a big-picture scope, and if it is a high-level policy to solve a problem. Other parameters include whether it represents the raising of a red flag (e.g. an ethical issue), whether it requires a watchdog intervention, and also whether the CEO simply would like or would need to have the board's support.

Managers make routine operational decisions and handle all of the administrative work that makes the operation tick. While the board of directors creates company policies, managers are responsible for enforcing company policy and holding employees accountable for their actions.

All of the general aspects of governance can and should be found in an organization's knowledge governance. Some definitions of knowledge governance include:

Knowledge governance is defined as the formal and informal rules and conventions that shape the ways we conduct or engage in knowledge processes, such as creating new knowledge, sharing or protecting knowledge, accessing it and applying or using it.[4]

Knowledge governance refers to the suite of formal and informal rules that coordinate, guide, and regulate knowledge processes, including production; whether it is shared and with whom (including who decides, and on what normative basis?); access (e.g. paywalls and professional reward systems); and use (what are the expectations around how decisions or actions should be justified?).[5]

> Knowledge governance refers to how the deployment of governance mechanisms influences knowledge processes, such as sharing, retaining and creating knowledge. It insists on clear micro (behavioural) foundations, adopts an economizing perspective, and examines the links between knowledge-based units of analysis with diverse characteristics and governance mechanisms with diverse capabilities of handling these transactions (Ref. 1, p. 1).

Although governance is more high level than management, the boundaries become easily blurred when it comes to knowledge. This is partly because managing knowledge is new compared to other more firmly established roles in organizations. For example, not all organizations have a Chief Knowledge Office (CKO) who is involved in strategic planning and leadership. The other reason is that KM does not fit neatly within a single business unit nor function. KM is not just about HR (the people) or just about IT (the tools). As a result, the highest "ranking" KM person will need to take on a knowledge governance role and this will sometimes be in addition to their more operational role. For this reason, it is important, at least for the short term, for knowledge governance to be very closely tied to the more operational aspects of KM. The knowledge processing cycle outlined in Evans *et al.*[2] will be used to align the knowledge governance needed for each process (see Figure 2.1). One of the major advantages of this model is that the organizational learning process (single and double loop learning) is aligned and integrated with the knowledge processing stages.[6] This addresses one of the major limitations of most existing models as they are too specific: either for knowledge processing or for lessons learned cycle or an organizational learning model.[7]

The key parameters of knowledge governance include formal and informal rules that are applied to specific knowledge processes. How does this framework apply to knowledge? More specifically, can this

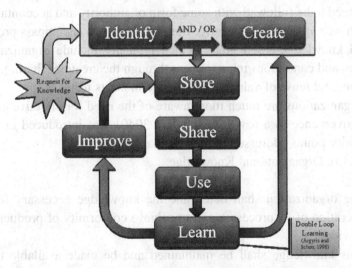

Figure 2.1. The knowledge management cycle (KMC) model.

framework of governance apply to tacit knowledge? Some of the major challenges in knowledge governance are related to tacit knowledge, i.e. knowledge which is difficult to "capture" in tangible form and thus remains in the minds of the knowledgeable people. Organizations often do not know what valuable knowledge exists unless they have undertaken a knowledge asset audit and mapped out where their valuable knowledge is located such as in experts, documents, archives, etc.[7] Organizations are at a significant risk of "forgetting" what they knew which necessitates reengineering their own innovations. Arnold Kransdorff[8] coined the term "organizational amnesia" to refer to this phenomenon which occurs when experts leave (e.g. retire).

Valuable knowledge can also be impossible to locate. While not lost, the employees who knew where this knowledge was are no longer at the organization. An example is NASA's tape of the original 1969 moon landing.[9] Finally, organizations do not "own" their valuable knowledge in the same sense that they own inventory or patents. "Valuable knowledge walks out the door every day" when employees leave for the day, when they go on leave, when they retire.[10]

Governance is therefore an important overarching framework that needs to be in place to ensure the organization is continuously monitored and assessed as it learns and improves. Progress toward organizational goals need to be followed with some form of authority and accountability. Governance applied to knowledge therefore needs to encompass progress toward knowledge-based goals, which typically include organizational learning and continuous improvement through the creation, sharing, preservation, and reuse of valuable knowledge in all its forms.

Organizations are much more aware of the need for effective knowledge governance as a new ISO standard 30401 was introduced in 2018. The major points addressed by this standard are:
"7.1.6, Organizational Knowledge

- The organization shall determine the knowledge necessary for the operation of its processes and to achieve conformity of products and services.
- This knowledge shall be maintained and be made available to the extent necessary.

- When addressing changing needs and trends, the organization shall consider its current knowledge and determine how to acquire or access any necessary additional knowledge and required updates."[11]

This standard has led to knowledge governance becoming much more mandated and prescriptive, especially as the standard is still fairly recent (e.g. Lindsay[12]).

2.2.1. *The Complexity of Knowledge Governance*

Coleman[13] distinguishes between macro- and micro-level governance, where the former is concerned with the organization and the latter with individuals. There is, of course, a third level to take into consideration — that of the group or community level. This leads to yet another dichotomy, that between formal and informal knowledge governance. Formal knowledge governance consists of official policies and organizational structures (e.g. organizational charts) whereas informal knowledge governance looks at emergent mechanisms such as those governing knowledge sharing in networks built on trust.

The focus in KM to date has largely been on informal governance in informal groups, such as communities of practice at the expense of formal knowledge governance. The fear has been that introducing too much formality may "kill" effective knowledge sharing and innovation benefits of these informal groups. However, Foss[1] notes that the focus in KM has been on informal organizational collections (e.g. communities of practice or knowledge networks) rather than formal governance models. As these networks are not part of the official organization (i.e. they do not appear on the organizational chart), their costs as well as their benefits are often much less visible. Michailova and Foss (Ref. 14, p. 8) argued that the knowledge governance approach is an "emerging attempt to think systematically about the intersection of knowledge and organizations." Gooderham et al.[15] contended knowledge governance has an indirect influence on knowledge sharing through the medium of social capital which is created by informal knowledge networks.

As a result, organizations must balance institutionalizing and integrating mechanisms in order to achieve their knowledge-based goals.

Institutionalizing mechanisms help organizations routinize behavior and decision-making[16] typically through the use of formal governance mechanisms such as policies and standards. Integrating mechanisms support knowledge sharing and integration by encouraging interactions and experimental learning. They represent informal methods of governance that rely more on the building of trust through reciprocity between different people in the organization. An organization that relies too heavily on institutionalizing mechanisms may become overconfident, which could result in outdated knowledge and incorrect causal inferences.[17]

In general, knowledge governance has emphasized formal mechanisms over informal ones, leading to an imbalance in the organizational governance. Too much formality can impede the organic and emergent nature of knowledge-sharing networks built on "voluntary" rather than mandated participation. Knowledge governance has been more visible at the level of organizational and individual rules and guidelines whereas the group level has been less well addressed. Knowledge exists, and therefore needs to be governed, at three interlinked levels: the individual level (human capital), the group level (social capital), and the organizational level (structural capital).

Knowledge governance is also needed throughout the KM process, including knowledge creation, knowledge sharing, knowledge dissemination, knowledge preservation, and reuse. Formal and informal knowledge governance mechanisms are needed for each KM process at the individual, group and organizational levels for both explicit and tacit knowledge. Table 2.1 outlines the recommended comprehensive approach

Table 2.1. Comprehensive knowledge governance for knowledge processes.

	Level of Intervention		
KM Process	**Individual**	**Group**	**Organizational**
Creation/capture			
Organize/store		Formal/informal	
Share/disseminate		Explicit/tacit	
Use/reuse			
Learn/improve			

to knowledge governance that is discussed in this chapter. Two illustrative examples are used to show how this comprehensive framework can be applied in an organization.

The framework in Table 2.1 can thus be used as a type of checklist to ensure that knowledge governance encompasses the complexity of the organization. Within each cell in the table, the knowledge governance needs to be identified in terms of who has the authority for what decision-making and what type of accountability exists (i.e. for each knowledge processing step and for both formal and informal mechanisms at all three levels). At the risk of introducing even more complexity, the tacitness of the knowledge should also be taken into account. For example, is the knowledge fairly well documented or fairly widely shared within the organization? If not, then the tacit nature of the knowledge included in the knowledge governance framework needs particular attention. One example could be more in-depth "exit" interviews in anticipation of a planned or unplanned departure of the employee (e.g. Kransdorff[8]). This also needs to be done for both explicit and tacit organizational knowledge that is of value (e.g. critical to attain the organizational goals).

Mintzberg[18] also pointed out the dangers of only considering informal governance in that there will necessarily be less standardization, which is a prerequisite to improving efficiency through reuse and learning processes. Combining formal and informal governance is the only way to create efficient and effective knowledge processes. The knowledge governance toolkit should therefore include a series of policies, incentives, systems, and decision authority that apply to individuals. These individuals in turn are then expected to influence the functioning of groups and ultimately the organization. Knowledge processes can be influenced and directed through a number of governance mechanisms such as hierarchies, community-based, identity-based, and market- or incentive-based.[19] Mechanisms to gain more value from knowledge assets through knowledge sharing (an organizational outcome) may be implemented by:

(1) setting up reward systems for knowledge sharing (and knowledge creating) and
(2) installing monitoring mechanisms that make sure that knowledge that is shared is actually knowledge that has value for the organization.[1]

A first example of a knowledge governance best practice can be found in Cao and Xiang's[20] research that looked at the impact of both formal and informal governance on knowledge sharing in Chinese firms. They looked at formal governance mechanisms such as the organizational structure, incentives, job and task descriptions, and leadership authority. They also looked at informal governance mechanisms such as knowledge networks, organizational culture, management style, and support. In one of the few empirical studies on the topic, the authors found that both formal and informal knowledge governance had a positive impact on individual knowledge sharing. Their findings reveal that formal knowledge governance can influence informal knowledge governance, such as mechanisms used to foster knowledge sharing.

A second example comes from the research of Gooderham *et al.*,[15] who looked at the creation of social capital through knowledge transfer. Their work focused on a large sample of data collected from employees working at two multinational companies in the same industry. Multinationals have to deal with cultural, institutional, and physical distance factors, which all make it more difficult to create and share social capital. The authors studied how social mechanisms such as goodwill can be used by individuals to share knowledge across their organization. They looked at market-based, hierarchy-based, and social mechanisms for individuals. Market relations are characterized by external rewards (also called "extrinsic" rewards or motivation) for sharing knowledge. Hierarchical mechanisms include direct reporting structures, rules, and regulations and social mechanisms involve trust, peer-to-peer mentoring, and professional development. Each one of these mechanisms can help or hinder social capital creation, and they are most likely highly interdependent on one another. The authors found that social mechanisms did lead to greater social capital and hierarchical mechanisms inhibited the creation of social capital (market-based mechanisms had no effect). Social mechanisms are much more informal and are sometimes referred to as "intrinsic" rewards or motivation.

Management is also involved in allocating rewards, exercising authority, and promoting collegial ways of working, and they can impact all three governance mechanisms. The degree to which social capital is generated in a multinational company was found to depend on how individuals perceive the governance mechanisms implemented by management. The more individuals perceive that goodwill exists, the more they will share knowledge with others and the more value will be created for the organization. Gooderham *et al.*[15] propose that hierarchical governance mechanisms such as authority, rules, and regulation be applied carefully so as to not prevent the creation of social capital. They note that more research is needed in order to be able to "determine at precisely which point hierarchical governance mechanisms begin to undermine the development of social capital." (Ref. 15, p. 146). Further discussion of some of the existing research gaps include the need for more empirical research as well as further work on how to integrate governance mechanisms at all three levels, i.e. organizational, group, and individual, is presenting in the concluding section.

2.3. Some Recommendations

Knowledge governance will require balanced governance: a balance between formal and informal governance approaches, a balance extending over all the key stages of KM and over the three levels, as well as across the two forms of knowledge. In general, organizations operate more effectively and better attain their organizational goals when they have a balanced governance across all these facets. In many organizations, however, knowledge reuse is less well monitored and the group level is harder to govern. However, the greatest imbalance exists between the formal and informal mechanisms of governance and this is discussed in greater detail here.

2.3.1. *Formal and Informal Governance Approaches*

Formal governance is typically linked to organizational governance, which is in turn explicitly shown in the organizational structure. The organizational chart will show the direct reporting of each employee and hence encapsulates the authority structure. Highly formal mechanisms of governance will most often be found in very hierarchical organizational structures. The type of leadership will likely also be very formal (e.g. formal meetings with documented minutes of the meeting, formal modes of communication, etc.). Governance will consist primarily of policies, rules, and regulations that are shared in a top-down fashion, following the organizational chart pathways of authority and reporting. Organizational roles and responsibilities will be similarly very well documented and widely disseminated. In other words, everyone should be able to easily find out who is responsible for making what type of decision and who is accountable for what. Formal incentives will also be favored, such as monetary rewards in promotions in order to motivate the performance of employees.[21]

Informal governance mechanisms, on the other hand, are typically linked to organizational culture. For example, how is collaboration viewed (e.g. positive or loss of status?) Are there opportunities for knowledge networking (time during the day; physical/virtual space)? Are there barriers to knowledge sharing (e.g. linguistic, geographical proximity, time zones)? What is the level of trust? Does peer-to-peer mentoring occur? Are leaders good role models of positive behaviors such as knowledge sharing? Informal governance is often overlooked and this leads to it being the missing critical success factor for KM. It is easier to overlook due to its less visible and less authority-dependent nature. There is a need to shift the balance toward more informal governance. Informal governance relies on the development of an organizational culture that encourages the knowledge processing stages but without mandating this in any formal way — e.g. influencing without having direct authority over knowledgeable people in the organization.[21] Knowledge governance, in particular, needs greater emphasis on informal mechanisms.

Some best practices for formal governance include having a Chief Knowledge Office (CKO) and a formal KM team; having knowledge addressed in organizational policy; having clear policies on intellectual property, non-disclosure, non-compete clauses in employee contracts and extrinsic rewards for desired knowledge behavior in the form of monetary compensation. Some best practices for informal governance include having leaders who are good role models, consensus on the "charter" for each knowledge sharing network (clear goal, eligibility criteria for membership), clearly identified KM roles (e.g. discussion moderators), mentoring to help engage rules of conduct (the do's and don'ts of the organizational culture and/or group micro-culture), as well as intrinsic rewards such as recognition for desired knowledge behaviors.

An illustrative example will be used to describe a successful implementation of both formal and informal knowledge governance. A multi-national company with over 30,000 employees in the transportation sector operates in a highly competitive environment where, despite multiple rounds of downsizing, the KM unit has remained intact. One of the major reasons for this was that the KM "home" was within the strategic management unit of the organization. This is an excellent best practice as it will ensure that KM is always directly aligned with organizational goals and, similarly, knowledge governance fits in seamlessly with overall governance.

They accomplished several key KM goals over the course of five years by addressing problems such as a significant amount of rework that was being done, weak incentives to create new knowledge, and little sharing of valuable knowledge and loss of this knowledge due not only to retirements but high turnover rates. They were able to reduce the time spent looking for information and the number of mistakes made by creating knowledge communities with clear goals and eligibility criteria for membership. New employees were immediately connected to their knowledge networks based not only on their job description but their areas of expertise. Each network had a document that outlined their purpose and member expectations. Extensive peer-to-peer mentoring (at events and one-on-one) helped each member understand how they could contribute to the network and how their network could help them on their job.

The knowledge networks documented their collective knowledge and made this content reusable through their internal collaboration system. They also implemented a detailed company expertise directory in the same central system so that it became easier to find out who knows what and ask them for help or find experts for specific projects. Leaders were excellent role models as they were all members of the networks and participated in the peer-to-peer mentoring. Everyone in the company is a member of one or more knowledge networks, including all C-level executives (CEO, Chief Financial Officer, VP Human Resources, and so on). As a result, professional networking between experts was greatly improved.

Valuable knowledge was not only easy to find but easy to reuse, thus reducing the need for costly rework.

The KM Leader was part of the organizational governance model as KM was "housed" in the strategic management unit. This resulted in better communication with change management (CM team member at regular KM meetings) and organizational learning (Learning Academy in regular communication with KM team). It is important to note that the KM leader (and their KM team) ensured an accurate tracking of KM improvements (e.g. time reduced to find content, number of reworked tasks reduced, etc.) and thus show tangible value even from intangible knowledge. They were able to demonstrate that knowledge worker productivity was increased by 38% after these metrics were implemented and monitored.

Over 25 knowledge networks were established in such areas of expertise as project management, quality assurance, and safety. Each network is governed by a "knowledge owner" who is a strategic, inspirational, and technical leader. The knowledge owner oversees subject matter experts in the network, ensures their onboarding (they join their networks when they are hired), and connects people, ensuring knowledge is shared. Knowledge networks are informal units that are embedded in a fairly traditional hierarchical formal organizational structure, which is an example of good balance between formal and informal governance. Knowledge owners are able to connect experts fostering ongoing innovation. Connecting people in turn led to sharing best practices across existing silos, solving problems, and helping each other out.

Another critical success factor in this organization is that all knowledge governance roles are clearly defined. A good model is that provided by the APQC:

Knowledge governance role and responsibilities:

(1) Ensures that KM activities align with enterprise vision, mission, and goals.
    (a) Leads the development of a knowledge strategy aligned with the business strategy.
    (b) Works with the KM team to identify the knowledge assets critical to enterprise KM.

(2) Collaborates with HR and Chief Learning Officer (CLO).

(3) Collaborates with IT and/or the Chief Information Officer (CIO)'s office.

(4) Facilitates and drives the KM projects selected by the KM steering committee.

(5) Promotes KM and the use of common approaches across business units.

   (a) Works with other KM team business-unit representatives and business-unit leadership to establish a common understanding and focus for KM.

(6) Facilitates the development of the enterprise KM toolkit.

   (a) Monitors the effectiveness and use of IT tools and systems as they apply to KM, and suggests improvements.

KM governance in this organization was successful due to a very strong alignment with HR (e.g. in-depth knowledge interviews with departing employees) and the use of key performance indicators (KPIs) and success stories to show progress toward organizational goals. Change management strategy was implemented hand-in-hand with KM strategy and there were dedicated KM roles and responsibilities.

Another best practice that can be derived from this example is that it is very important to integrate or closely align knowledge-based units with learning-based organizational units. For example, many organizations have a "Learning Academy," such as the one described here that help KM work in conjunction with change management, or CM (as KM cannot occur without catalyzing organizational change); similarly, KM should also work in conjunction with organizational learning or OL (as KM cannot occur without catalyzing learning at all three levels: individual, group, and organizational).

A review of the scholarly and practitioner literature shows that there are very few successful case studies in knowledge governance. The reasons for this could be that most organizations do not include knowledge assets as part of the governance framework. This means there is no systematic way of aligning knowledge with organization's strategic priorities. The new ISO 301401 KM standard may help to change this over the short to medium term. Another reason is that most organizations have a governance structure but knowledge governance tends to be apart (e.g. KM team does not fit in anywhere). This could be because it is harder to govern knowledge, particularly tacit knowledge, when it is not something like inventory that is "owned" by the organization. It is even more difficult to assess and ensure compliance with knowledge governance.

The recommended approach is to build on existing governance, both formal and informal, at all three levels of the organization, for both explicit and tacit knowledge. Knowledge governance should be integrated into this existing framework. The guaranteed way to fail is to develop an entirely separate knowledge governance as it needs to be carried out throughout the organization and not just by the KM unit. Knowledge governance authority, decision-making, and accountability are woven into the organizational governance, otherwise KM becomes and remains a silo. This recommended comprehensive and integrated approach to knowledge governance was presented in Table 2.1 and is further updated in Table 2.2.

Last but not the least, organizational maturity models can help with the implementation of knowledge governance, as well as with the monitoring of progression toward organizational goals. Maturity models are a tool used to assess the organizational readiness of an organization for a given intervention.[7] For example, if the organization is undergoing a merger and acquisition or is in the process of downsizing, it may not be advisable to introduce KM or CM initiatives. This approach can be used to assess the organizational readiness for the integrated knowledge

Table 2.2.   Recommended integrated knowledge governance approach.

Knowledge Governance Process	Level of Intervention		
	Individual	Group	Organizational
KM: Create, share, preserve and reuse valuable knowledge			
CM: Change and improve		Formal/informal	
OL: Learn and improve		Explicit/tacit	
IKG: Integrated knowledge governance			

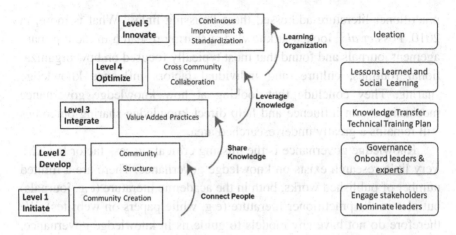

Figure 2.2. Organizational readiness assessment for knowledge governance.

approach. The maturity model for the organization we have been using as an illustrative example is shown in Figure 2.2.

2.4. Conclusions and Future Work

A key challenge remains to integrate the three governance levels: individual, group, and organizational. The organizational capability depends mostly on individual employees' beliefs, information, and motivation to create, share, and learn from valuable knowledge.[7] How to link individuals and groups to organizational goals through governance mechanisms that promote efficiency and innovation remains to be addressed. In 2007, Foss[1] signaled the need for:

> … empirical work that can assist in identifying knowledge-based hazards, ascertain how organizations deal with such hazards by deploying governance mechanisms, find out how these mechanisms are characteristically combined, and examine the performance implications of knowledge (p. 46).

Individual knowledge processing mechanisms need to be linked to governance mechanisms however much of the existing research and practitioner literature addressed these "missing links." What is more, in 2010, Foss *et al.*[22] looked at knowledge sharing research in the top management journals and found that most typically focused on how organizational routines, culture, and individual factors influence knowledge sharing. They conclude that looking at how knowledge governance mechanisms can influence and help direct knowledge-sharing outcomes still remains a greatly underresearched area.

Knowledge governance is the missing critical success factor for KM. Very little research exists on knowledge governance. There are a limited number of published works, both in the academic literature (e.g. journals) but also in the practitioner literature (e.g. white papers on websites). We therefore do not have any models to guide us in knowledge governance. A framework is suggested as a way of seeding more theoretical work in this topic area. The proposed IKG could also be used to guide further work as it can serve as a checklist to ensure that all governance aspects are taken into consideration. This mirrors the current widespread use of the Evans *et al.*[2] knowledge processing model.

Further research is also needed to better understand knowledge governance can be effectively implemented. Further work could include benchmarking knowledge governance in different organizations to identify best practices and good case studies from successful knowledge governance experiences. This will become particularly important as we can now track compliance with the new ISO KM standard. In general, more needs to be done to understand how to effectively manage organizational knowledge and we need contributions from both researchers and practitioners.

References

1. N. Foss. The emerging knowledge governance approach: Challenges and characteristics. *Organization*, **14**(1), 29–52 (2007).
2. M. Evans, K. Dalkir and C. Bidian, A holistic view of the knowledge life cycle: The Knowledge Management Cycle (KMC) model. *Electronic Journal of Knowledge Management (EJKM)*, **12**(2), 85–97 (2014).
3. B. Bader. Distinguishing governance from management. *Great Boards*, **8**(3), 2–5 (2008).

4. L. Van Kerkhoff. Knowledge governance for sustainable development: A review. *Challenges in Sustainability*, **1**(2), 82–93 (2014).

5. W.C. Clark, L. Van Kerkhoff, L. Lebel, and G. C. Gallopin. Crafting usable knowledge for sustainable development. *Proceedings of the National Academy of Sciences*, **113**(17), 4570–4578 (2016).

6. S. McIntyre, K. Dalkir, P. Perry and I. Kitimbo (Eds.). *Utilizing Evidence-Based Lessons Learned for Enhanced Organizational Innovation and Change*. Hershey, PA: IGI Global (2015).

7. K. Dalkir. *Knowledge Management in Theory and Practice*. Third Edition. Cambridge, MA: MIT Press (2017).

8. A. Kransdorff. *Corporate Amnesia*. Oxford, UK: Butterworth Heinemann (1998).

9. D. DeLong. *Lost Knowledge: Confronting the Threat of an Aging Workforce*. Oxford, UK: Oxford University Press (2004).

10. H. Beazley, J. Boenisch and D. Harden. *Continuity Management: Preserving Corporate Knowledge and Productivity When Employees Leave*. Hoboken, NJ: John Wiley & Sons (2002).

11. J. McNenly. The ISO 30401 standard on knowledge management systems-requirements. *TALL Q*, **38**(6) (2019).

12. D. Lindsay. What progress on knowledge management systems–requirements (BS ISO 30401). *Refer*, **34**(1), 18–21 (2018).

13. J.S. Coleman. *Foundations of Social Theory*. Cambridge, MA: The Belknap Press of Harvard University Press (1990).

14. N. Foss and S. Michailova. *Knowledge Governance Approach*. Oxford, UK: Oxford University Press (2009).

15. P. Gooderham, D.B. Minbaeva and T. Pedersen. Governance mechanisms for the promotion of social capital for knowledge transfer in multinational corporations. *Journal of Management Studies*, **48**(1), 123–150 (2011).

16. K.H. Heimeriks and M. Schreiner. Relational quality, alliance capability, and alliance performance: An integrated framework. In: *Enhancing Competences for Competitive Advantage*, A. Heene, R. Sanchez (eds.), Bingley, UK: Emerald Group Publishing Limited, pp. 145–171 (2010).

17. S. Pemsel, R. Müller and J. Söderlund. Knowledge governance strategies in project-based organizations. *Long Range Planning*, **49**(6), 648–660 (2016).

18. H. Mintzberg. *The Structuring of Organizations*. Englewood Cliffs, NJ: Prentice-Hall (1979).

19. A. Grandori. Neither hierarchy nor identity: Knowledge governance mechanisms and the theory of the firm. *Journal of Management and Governance*, **5**, 381–99 (2001).

20. Y. Cao and Y. Xiang. The impact of knowledge governance on knowledge sharing. *Management Decision*, **50**(4), 591–610 (2012).
21. N. Boesen. Governance and accountability: How do the formal and informal interplay and change? In *Informal Institutions, How Social Norms Help or Hinder Development*, pp. 83–98. Paris, France: OECD Development Centre (2007).
22. N. Foss, K. Husted and S. Michailova. Governing knowledge sharing in organizations: Levels of analysis, governance mechanisms and research directions. *Journal of Management Studies*, **47**(3), 455–482 (2010).

Multilevel Governance and Organizational Knowledge: Contextual and Theoretical Elements for its Configuration

Fernanda Kempner-Moreira and *Patricia de Sá Freire*

Federal University of Santa Catarina,
Graduate Program in Knowledge Management and Engineering,
R. Delfino Conti, s/n, Trindade, Florianópolis — SC,
88040–900, Brazil

*fernanda.kempner.moreira@gmail.com

This chapter aims to describe the contextual and theoretical elements about the Multilevel Governance (MultiGov) construct, in order to analyze the state of the art of the term. To accomplish it, a research study with a theoretical approach and descriptive purposes was carried out using the systematic literature review technique, followed by an integrative analysis of the studies found. As a contribution, this chapter describes the objectives, benefits, and challenges of MultiGov today and lists the theoretical elements proposed by the scientific literature: the approaches, assumptions, definitions, and guidelines for its configuration. In the end, it is possible to interrelate the contextual and theoretical elements and to highlight that the MultiGov model is interconnected to organizational knowledge, because, with the MultiGov configuration, where the sharing of authority and knowledge is required, the knowledge produced in one organizational level can influence processes at other levels, promoting the co-production of knowledge in the organization's horizontal, vertical, and transversal networks.

3.1. Introduction

The emergence of a new contemporary world is observed and characterized by the flows that recreate it, giving it dynamicity[1] and increasing its complexity, in which the effective solution of problems requires collective efforts and performance in internal and external organizational networks. This requires new patterns of authority, as the conventional hierarchy and the search for isolated solutions can no longer generate satisfactory results.[2,3] Therefore, governance systems that do not consider the diversity of players at multiple levels become unable to deal with the complexity and diversity of actions necessary to generate effective results.[4]

Among the governance models found in the literature, one in particular is based on learning networks[1] and the common good theories[5-7]: it is the Multilevel Governance model (MultiGov), studied since the beginning of the 2000s as an option for the governance of inter-territorial and inter-organizational networks[2-4,8-10] by involving the integration and cooperation of multiple players at different levels of performance.[11]

It is a vertically differentiated structure that does not meet the limiting principles of command and control, but observes the changes in relationships between players located at all different levels, and the hierarchy is replaced by asymmetric but coordinated interaction between these players.[12] To act effectively at multiple levels, it is necessary to decentralize authority, distribute power and responsibilities, and form internal and external networks to enable collaboration among the different players.[3,5] Connections and interactions become fundamental in this new intra-organizational and inter-organizational context, in which many players are involved in achieving results, in search of collaborative solutions, which is why we understand that the MultiGov model can be the way forward.

Authors like Monios[7] present MultiGov as the governance for innovation, learning, adaptation, reliability, and levels of cooperation of the participants and obtaining more effective, equitable, and sustainable results on multiple scales — benefits desired by public governance in facing complex situations. The author points out other strengths of the model that strengthen its indication for public governance, such as promoting institutional adaptation and empowerment to develop collective solutions to local problems. Thus, it proves to be suitable for a new emerging challenge, overcoming the path dependence of traditional hierarchical models, as it can make socio-ecological systems less prone to collapse (redundancy mitigates risk).

However, even considering MultiGov as a model to be appreciated by public governance, the understanding of the term is still a complex study, discussed by different approaches and, therefore, it has been used much more as a metaphor than specifically as a form of action.[3,9,10] Alcantara *et al.*[3] also understand that MultiGov is not a theory. According to these authors, it is closer to a descriptive concept anchored at the level of institutionalized players, not at the level of whole systems, since systems theory makes it difficult to apply the model, but in instances, i.e. processes of interaction among different players, in which formal large-scale rules do not specifically prevail.

On the other hand, according to Stephenson,[8] taking MultiGov as a mere concept is unfair, since the fact that it explains how the new organizational and governance arrangements are structured already constitutes a great theoretical contribution that points to the decision-making configurations, the dispersion, and the redistribution of powers and competencies for different levels of activities and different functions, incorporating and interconnecting public and private players. Following the logic of a descriptive concept, Dobbs[13] explains that a normative role must be added to this vision for MultiGov to direct the division and assignment of powers, suggesting the concept of subsidiarity to determine the appropriate level of authority and responsibility in terms of efficiency and legitimacy.

Either way, be it a metaphor, a theory, or a descriptive concept, there are some elements that must be respected. As Yang *et al.*[14] describe, even though there is a diversity of interpretations of MultiGov, from the original definition to other uses of the theory, the concept addresses the coordination, development, and implementation of policies, including the delegation of power to lower levels of authority, in a process of decentralization, as well as the description and development of strategies that include broader players, encompassing governmental, non-governmental, and informal institutions. These elements announce that the transformation from a hierarchical model to a MultiGov model will not be easy.

Due to these ambiguities and lack of consensus among theorists, clarifying the MultiGov concept is important due to the growing demand for its application in different contexts, in addition to the territorial one originally applied, mainly and urgently in the context of governance of complex, multidimensional problems. This requires a collective academic effort.[10] With this perspective in mind, this chapter aims to describe the contextual and theoretical elements of the MultiGov construct in order to analyze the state of the art of the term.

3.2. Methodological Procedures

This research can be classified as a theoretical approach, of descriptive purposes, using the technique of systematic literature review, followed by an integrative analysis of the knowledge found about the term *Multilevel Governance*, mainly the determinations of the authors regarding the objectives, benefits, challenges, and theoretical and governance elements for the configuration of this new model. In the *Scopus* database, international and interdisciplinary, the search with the descriptor *Multilevel Governance* in the keyword, title, and summary of journal articles returned 247 documents. Another search using the descriptor *Multilevel Governance* returned 468 documents, of which articles with more than 100 citations were considered more relevant; then 10 more documents were selected. From the *Scopus* database search, the 257 abstracts of the articles were read, and those that did not have adherence to the objective of this research and those that did not allow free access were excluded. Added to these were the results of a search directed to the subject and other publications that already composed the authors' studies on the subject and that were not indexed to the Scopus database, but were confirmed as adherent to the study as a doctoral thesis, adding 17 more documents to the search. At the end of this process, 91 documents were read in their entirety, and 66 documents directly contributed to the objective of the integrative review that followed.

The integrative revision allowed identifying, understanding, and describing the contextual and theoretical elements of the MultiGov construct, as well as the analysis of the contents, categorizing them between **objectives, benefits, challenges, approaches, assumptions, definitions, and guidelines of MultiGov**. They are presented in the following sections.

3.3. Contextual Elements of MultiGov: Objectives, Benefits, and Challenges

From the studies by Stokerr,[15] Knopp,[16] Maillet *et al.*,[17] and, more recently, Freire *et al.*,[18] it is understood that MultiGov has the main objective of establishing the dynamic capacity of the organizational system for the prompt response to transformation and contextual challenges, becoming a political tool to achieve goals that bring benefits and challenges. The benefits pointed out by the literature are many, where even the problems faced by the complexity of the multiple levels become an opportunity for learning, in the search for the best strategy.[19,20] External players become a source for breaking dominant paradigms and end up promoting significant changes in the established patterns,[19] as these players provide more rational decisions, with higher quality information, favoring social learning, although other factors influence these results.[21]

Another benefit highlighted in the literature and associated with the integration promoted by the model is the mobilization of private resources (financial, human, technological) for the achievement of collective objectives,[22] which leads to a greater concern with legitimacy and transparency, since authority is decentralized and the multiple levels are in effective action.[4,5]

In contrast to the benefits listed, studies on MultiGov report that, in order to be absorbed, the benefits require robust institutions, management capacity, and collaborative networks at multiple levels.[23] That is, this governance establishes a highly complex environment where the possible coordination failures, common in this type of context, require a maturity of governance to address and eliminate, at all levels and stages of governance,[4,19] the sense of injustice, blockages of interaction,[20] conflicts related to lack of clarity of objectives, and inconsistencies in the rules of the common good.[4] Yang *et al.*[14] still highlight challenges regarding decentralization, related to insufficient transfer of power, lack of top-down accountability, exclusion of some stakeholders in decision-making processes, and inadequate integration of vertical and horizontal governance systems.

One of the elements of this complex context targets public–private dialogue. The need to maintain cohesion and coherence in the distribution of authority and responsibility then becomes a challenge and can lead to inefficient use of resources, increased transaction costs, and conflicts between different players and levels.[7,13]

3.4. Theoretical Elements for MultiGov Configuration: Approaches, Assumptions, Definitions, and Guidelines

MultiGov was underpinned in 1993 by Gary Marks to describe the dynamics of European Union integration during the 1980s and early 1990s, when the different national territories needed to restructure as a single bloc. In recent years, its concept has been expanded for use in other fields of study, and it has added non-governmental players to government players in a new arrangement for solving joint problems.[2,3,9,19,24–26]

The first MultiGov definitions, dating from the late 1990s, were intrinsically related to the territorialism of the European Union. In other words, the European context helped to form the term MultiGov, bringing to its conceptualization elements relating to the sharing of authority between different players, until then only governmental, for the formation of collaborative networks.[19]

Almost 20 years after the first discussions about the term, Newig and Fritsch[21] came up with a new perspective on MultiGov, perceiving it as political structures and processes that go beyond legal and administrative boundaries to deal with the interdependence of players in social development and in political decisions.

At the same time, Piattoni[27] began a series of studies that led her to propose a more comprehensive definition, delimiting the term to a diverse set of coordination and negotiation systems among formally independent but functionally interdependent players that establish complex relationships among themselves, and continue to redefine their interrelations through a continuous process of coordination and negotiation.

The contributions by Piattoni[27] go beyond the proposition of a definition for the topic. By pointing out that by moving and connecting to different analytical planes, the concept itself is multilevel, Piattoni allows us to use MultiGov in different contexts, not only territorial ones.

Thus, from this author's publications, studies have emerged that elaborate broader definitions, such as the one by Termeer *et al.*,[5] which conceive this governance as a process of relevant and continuous interactions between public and private players that act at different levels, in order to achieve collective objectives with greater efficiency, believing that these interactions have greater potential to act in complex situations.

Korhonen-Kurki *et al.*[28] adopt as definition the implementation of public policies, at different levels, by players with diverse influence and values, where the decision processes occur at various levels and scales, which requires horizontal, vertical, and crossed links among the players themselves. This definition is retrieved and better specified by Alcantara *et al.*,[3] who describe it as policy formulation through a collaborative decision-making process involving a variety of governmental and nongovernmental players, at different levels and instances, with the objective of producing the collective good.

Vaz and Reis[1] can be considered representative of a new approach that adds to the five ones defined by Stephenson[8]: the approach focusing on inter-organizational networks. The authors point out that MultiGov is a formation of networks in which horizontal cooperation enables the organized operation of different players, which are valorized at all stages of the decision-making process.

Nowadays, the model also begins to be understood in the light of the Commons Theory.[11] Snower[6] and Monios[7] are representatives of this view that consider MultiGov as a system that respects most of the eight Fundamental Design Principles by Elinor Ostrom.[11] According to these authors, these principles promote the interaction and cooperation necessary to act at the different levels of governance.

Consistent with the previous authors, Marti[29] seems to be part of the school that perceives MultiGov as a set of interactions. This author defines it as a model of governance for multilevel contexts, characterized by vertical, horizontal, and transversal interactions of public and private players engaged in collective solutions. According to him, it involves more than territorial jurisdictions and their governments, civil society, and private organizations, since it transcends the boundaries between these players.

When trying to define the model, Henrichs and De Meza[9] present MultiGov as a new perspective to understand the different relationships between all different levels, expanding the vertical and horizontal structures, public and private, providing them with a cooperative, cohesive, and transparent decision-making process that leads to the collective development of the network that comprises it.

Without conflicts with the definitions exposed so far, Yi *et al.*[12] promote dialogue between the vision of networks and that of the common good. For them, MultiGov is a model of collaborative governance in which public and private players are involved in a complex network of different levels, maintaining their vertical or horizontal independence, which differentiates this model from the traditional hierarchy.

In turn, the definition proposed by Alcantara and Morden[30] brings the vision of a system within other systems, a model with specific instances of decision-making that appear sporadically or regularly over time, systems, and space. If the instances of this governance appear frequently and remain stable, the set of these instances becomes a MultiGov system, which can follow the territorial logic or the contextual logic, as stated by Sandström *et al.*[4] Adding to what Monios[7] contextualizes, this system incorporates multiple levels of governmental, non-governmental organizations, and individuals, in a process of decentralization and deconcentration that not only transfers power but also leads to qualitative restructuring. Also, as a system, MultiGov is defined by Thomann *et al.*[25] as a continuous negotiation system, where decisions are shared with public and private players that are at different levels.

After understanding the approaches used for the study of MultiGov, as well as the timeline for the construction of its definitions, it was possible to identify the most contemporary approaches to the term, which dialogue with the theories of inter-organizational networks,[1] common good,[3,8] and system.[4,7,25,30] Based on the analysis of the authors' discourses, it was possible to highlight the key terms they bring and propose a definition that encompasses them.

In short, from a literature review, Stephenson[8] succeeded in listing five different approaches to the term MultiGov: (1) original approach; (2) functional approach; (3) combined approaches; (4) normative approach; and (5) comparative approach.

Advancing on this study by Stephenson,[8] the review carried out by this research identified other more contemporary approaches to the studies on MultiGov. To the five approaches identified by Stephenson,[8] three more can be added: (6) inter-organizational network approach[1,26,28]; (7) common good approach[3,6,7]; and (8) system approach.[25,30]

Thus, as if a dialogue between the authors representing the three new approaches to research on MultiGov and more current studies[6,7,9,12,29] were promoted, a definition of the term proposed by this research emerges: **MultiGov is a complex system of governance of multilevel and multidimensional networks of interactions and collaborations, which transcends borders between internal and external entities, public and private, recognizing them as autonomous, responsible, and engaged in collaborative, cohesive, and transparent decision-making processes, in the search of collective solutions for the common good.**

In addition to the definition and the eight approaches to the configuration of MultiGov, the analyzed publications provided the identification of extensive theoretical assumptions for the model, which, being consensual, were classified into seven categories to support research on the term, as follows.

(1) **Composition:** The inclusion of various stakeholders that, together, evaluate and make decisions, taking into account different interests,[31] contributing to the prior acceptance of decisions and to a more effective implementation.[21]

(2) **Diversity:** The diversity of players and levels of action enables multiple visions that complement each other in the decision-making process, providing a more complete and comprehensive solution.[20,21]

(3) **Coupling:** The quality of MultiGov's results has a strong correlation with the number of levels of governance involved, and a weaker but clearer correlation with the number of players.[21] However, the quality of the coupling — rigid or more flexible — reinforces the players' interest in collaborating and interacting, seeking optimal solutions.[32]

(4) **Interaction:** The interaction between the players promotes learning and empowerment of the interested parties.[2,7,31] In the view of Thomann *et al.*,[25] MultiGov systems vary in degree of institutional and political integration, as well as in functional differentiation — the delegation of authority to deal with specific challenges.

(5) **Flexibility:** The flexibility of decentralization into multiple levels provides greater adaptability and more sustainable use of resources.[20]

(6) **Common Good:** What prevails is the common good against the distinction between internal and external policies.[3] Legitimacy is characterized by the MultiGov players' acceptance and agreement with the system, rules, decentralization, and coordination of the entire process and, for this purpose, transparency, inclusive and participatory decision-making, accountability, equity, and security are essential.[20]

(7) **Responsibility, Autonomy, and Power:** The players' power is no longer concentrated in institutional positions (positional) but also in reputations and networks of resources (relational),[25] which promotes the division of responsibilities, distributing them at all levels and encouraging actions of collective interest.[33]

In addition, regarding the theoretical assumptions, the studies published so far establish guidelines for the configuration of MultiGov, which, even with different approaches, are complementary. For example, in the works by Piattoni,[27] by the political dimension of MultiGov, three frequently interconnected and interdependent guidelines are described, which makes multilevel arrangements inherently dynamic: (1) political mobilization toward decentralization of authority and responsibilities; (2) policy formulation in more structured arrangements for coordination and regulation among the different players; and (3) restructuring of public and private roles. In turn, Korhonen-Kurki *et al.*[28] conceptualize that, due to the dimension of multiple levels, this model of governance is based on three guidelines: (1) players at one level participating in processes at another level; (2) institutions created at one level can influence processes or institutions at another level; and (3) knowledge produced at one level can influence processes at other levels.

Gänzle[33] reinforces that the simultaneous activation of public and private players at different levels is a dominant feature of this governance. In more detail, Potluka and Liddle[34] point out four changes, here understood as MultiGov's guidelines, in the dimension of integration and collaboration between the authors: (1) participation of non-governmental players; (2) decision-making no longer based on single territories; (3) transformation of the government's role into new coordination and networking strategies; and (4) breaking paradigms in the traditional distribution of authority and responsibility.

The multiplicity of players involved is sometimes considered a problem[19,21] because it involves a greater complexity and difficulty in decision-making. Thus, reducing the complexity at some points in the decision-making process can be a strategy to be used.[19] Complexity can be resolved through self-regulation, with the players deliberating and establishing criteria to govern common resources without a top down mandate, resulting in more effective organic solutions.[7]

That is, MultiGov minimizes and overcomes the complexity of the context by organizing it in arrangements that can be understood[9] and by adopting adequate control and feedback instruments.[19,23] In these cases, Yang *et al.*[14] still define some guidelines to solve these challenges, such as mediation, that encourages participation and reinforces efficiency through community actions; the establishment of goals that balance and integrate priorities; financial help; a flexible system that allows participation in decision-making to be incorporated; and structures of consistency, transparency, and accountability.

Some relationships are evident, such as the assumptions of Interaction and Flexibility recognized by several authors in the collaborative strategic planning guideline. As the literature states, in order to respect MultiGov's theoretical assumptions, strategic planning must occur at all levels of governance, ensuring that the interaction of players in the decision-making process is flexible and favors consensus for the development of proposed solutions and, when consensus is not possible, that there is acceptance of the arguments presented.[9,24] Decentralization must be sufficient to generate a synergy that promotes learning and initiative at the different levels of the governance structure, supporting the development of collective thinking.[19,24]

In accordance with Alcantara and Morden,[30] to some extent, the hierarchy is not entirely absent, but supports fluid cooperative arrangements that lead to co-production and results. Conteh[22] says that the implementation of the MultiGov system requires a mixture of hierarchy and collaboration so that the different levels can adapt. It is necessary to be aware that each organization has a structure and a hierarchy that need to be adjusted so that the integration occurs and works. The effort for this adaptation is strategic for the success of decisions and actions of the network.

Therefore, the relationships of collaborative networks are characterized by mutual interdependence, and no longer by competition, which requires structural and procedural adjustments regarding the interaction between the different levels. According to Lion *et al.*,[32] this governance model guarantees an egalitarian institutional classification, respecting the autonomy of the command center, to promote the division of responsibilities among the players, assigning responsibilities at all levels and encouraging actions of collective interest.

Alcantara *et al.*[30] emphasize that co-production must take place at multiple levels, where public and private players make simultaneous efforts to achieve collective results. Players must share authority equally to qualify as a MultiGov instance, and consensus is not an obligation, but decision-making must be collaborative and not hierarchical.[30]

MultiGov, as highlighted by Henrichs and De Meza,[9] involves the keywords "power" and "management sharing" and dynamic balance between autonomy, insertion, and coordination of multiple governmental and non-governmental players, materializing in fluid and flexible negotiation spaces for conducting collective interests.

Another key argument for the model's guidelines comes from Bance and Chassy[31]: processes must focus on a participatory approach that involves collective learning.

Marti[29] confirms that the term MultiGov can be used in different contexts, as long as it fulfills the following conditions: (1) it challenges formal vertical hierarchies; (2) players are interdependent to develop collective solutions; and (3) the interaction must imply negotiation between the players involved.

Seeing MultiGov as a system,[4,13] it is defined the importance of decentralizing authority and responsibilities from a central government to vertically, horizontally, and transversally distributed centers of authority, where different players at different levels must find new forms of coexistence, with the objective of the common good.

In this way, seven theoretical assumptions and six guidelines to be respected in the configuration of the model were identified in the scientific literature. The guidelines orientate the instantiation of theoretical assumptions in practice.

3.5. MultiGov: Interrelation of Theoretical Elements

After the identification and description of the theoretical elements of the MultiGov model, it is possible to establish a summary table that presents the interrelationship between the theoretical elements to support the configuration of the model in organizations (Table 3.1).

In short, to configure MultiGov as a complex system of governance of multilevel and multidimensional networks of interactions and collaborations, which transcends boundaries between autonomous and responsible players engaged in collaborative, cohesive, and transparent decision-making processes in the search for collective solutions for the common good, the seven theoretical assumptions and six guidelines arising from the most contemporary theoretical approaches based on the theories of inter-organizational networks, common good, and system must be respected.

In the sequence, as Yang *et al.*[14] point out, MultiGov can be adapted to different contexts, and the success of the implementation will be determined by the energy distributed to the authorities located at the different levels and by the identification of the applications of this governance system. The mechanisms and components are decisive, as they make it possible to respect the guidelines for operating in multilevel environments.

The warning is that organizations need to reorganize their **processes and structures** so that they can act at multiple levels, developing **ability to**

Table 3.1. Summary of the theoretical elements of the MultiGov Model in organizations. Multilevel Governance (MultiGov).

Theoretical Assumptions		Guidelines	
		Guideline	Description
1 Composition	1	Multilevel learning	Decision-making no longer based on single territories[34]
			Different players at different levels[4,13]
2 Diversity			Restructuring of public and private roles with the participation of non-governmental players[26,33,34]
			Co-production must occur at multiple levels, where public and private players make simultaneous efforts to achieve collective results[3]
3 Coupling	2	Collaborative intra- and inter-organizational networks	Transformation of the government's role into new strategies for coordination and networking[34]
			Organization in arrangements that can be understood[8]
			Mediation for financial aid[14]
4 Interaction	3	Integration	Knowledge produced at one level can influence processes at other levels[28]
			The interaction must imply negotiation between the players[29]
			Search for consensus for the development of solutions and, when consensus is not possible, there must be acceptance of the arguments presented.[9,24] Consensus is not mandatory, but decision-making must be collaborative and not hierarchical[3]
			Adoption of adequate control and feedback instruments[19,23]
			Setting goals that balance and integrate priorities[14]
5 Flexibility	4	Decentralization of authority	Players at one level participate in processes at another level; institutions created at one level can influence processes or institutions at another level[14,28]
			Collaborative strategic planning[24]

6	**Common good**	5	System self-organization	Policy formulation in the form of more structured arrangements for coordination and regulation among the different players[26]

6	**Common good**	5	System self-organization	Policy formulation in the form of more structured arrangements for coordination and regulation among the different players[26]
				Mediation that encourages participation and enhances efficiency through community action[14]
				Development of collective thinking[19,24]
				Players are interdependent to develop collective solutions[29]
				Finding new forms of coexistence, with the objective of the common good[4,13]
7	**Responsibility, Autonomy, and Power**	6	Distribution of power and responsibilities and respect for autonomy	Political mobilization towards decentralization of authority and responsibilities[34]
				Challenging formal vertical hierarchies[29]
				The hierarchy is not totally absent, but supports cooperative arrangements[30]
				Mix of hierarchy and collaboration, so that the different levels can adapt[22]
				Breaking paradigms in the traditional distribution of authority and responsibility[26]
				Equal institutional classification, respecting the autonomy of the command center, to promote the division of responsibilities among the players, assigning responsibilities at all levels and encouraging actions of collective interest[32]
				Sharing egalitarian authority so that players qualify as an instance of MultiGov[30]
				Self-regulation[7]
				Learning and initiative at all different levels of the governance structure[19,24]
				Structures of consistency, transparency, and responsibility[14]
				Decentralizing the authority and responsibilities of a central government into vertically, horizontally, and transversely distributed centers of authority[4,13]

operate in a network, share authority and knowledge, self-organization, and co-production.[22] That demands another challenge, which is the governance of components indispensable to MultiGov for maintaining an adequate degree of coherence and cohesion, since the multiple players at multiple levels make the environment even more dynamic and complex.[7,13]

Benz and Eberlein[19] point out three categories of mechanisms: (1) independent negotiation arenas, which foster cooperation and effective problem solving, while reducing complexity and broadening the adaptability of the players in the network; (2) effective communication to ensure that all players have the information necessary for good negotiation and decision-making; and (3) learning during all MultiGov processes, which leads the players and the network itself to innovation and flexibility, adapting structures for better results. In MultiGov, mechanisms can be more flexible than in traditional governance, using not only formal instruments, such as policies and measures, but also informal ones, such as social dialogue and coordination methods.[13]

Homsy *et al.*[35] tried to summarize a structure of five components of hierarchy and horizontal interactions: (1) a sanctioning and coordinating authority with a central role; (2) civil society engagement; (3) co-production of horizontal and vertical knowledge; (4) supply capacity; and (5) recognition of co-benefits.

This chapter will not deepen the mechanisms and components of the MultiGov model found in the literature but, as part of a doctoral research linked to the Laboratory for Integration and Knowledge Governance Engineering (ENGIN) of the Post-Graduate Program in Engineering and Knowledge Management (EGC) of the Federal University of Santa Catarina (UFSC), Brazil, the continuation of this research will be carried out and later published.

3.6. Final Considerations

By identifying MultiGov's contextual and theoretical elements and interrelating them, it was possible to identify that this governance model is interconnected to organizational knowledge, since its configuration requires the sharing of authority and knowledge,[7,13] understanding that knowledge produced at one organizational level can influence processes at other levels[28] and promote the co-production of knowledge in horizontal, vertical, and transversal networks within the organization.[4,13]

This chapter contributes to future academic research in governance and knowledge management, as well as in public and private corporate governance, leading other researchers to deepen the studies on this construct and its configuration for their areas of expertise. There is much to contribute to the evolution of this model, which is quite suitable to the context of the society in which we live.

The literature indicates research gaps that can be explored by academia, such as studying indicators and evaluation processes in MultiGov[32]; empirically testing MultiGov's development capacity; describing existing structures[26]; studying the adaptation of institutional and policy designs to operate effectively in the complexity of MultiGov[22]; studying the degree to which the complexity of the problem can determine or shape the arrangements, appropriating other constructs such as national relations, sociology and public administration to understand the complexity between the institution and the players that compose it[8]; investigating MultiGov from the perspective of the players, in order to understand the institutional complexity[23]; understanding the subsidiarity on the MultiGov network[13]; conceiving the institutionalization of a multilevel governance structure that tracks the various complex interactions[35]; and describing and applying the mechanisms and components necessary for MultiGov proposed by Homsy *et al.*[35] in other contexts.

References

1. D.M. Vaz and L. Reis. From city-states to global cities: The role of cities in global governance. *JANUS. NET, e-journal of International Relations*, **8**(2), 13–28 (2017).
2. J. Den Boer, C. Dieperink and F. Mukhtarov. Social learning in multilevel flood risk governance: Lessons from the Dutch Room for the River Program. *Water*, **11**(10), 2032 (2019).
3. C. Alcantara, J. Broschek J. and J. Nelles. Rethinking multilevel governance as an instance of multilevel politics: A conceptual strategy. *Territory, Politics, Governance*, **4**(1), 33–51 (2016).

4. A. Sandström, C. Söderberg, C. Lundmark, J. Nilsson, J. and D. Fjellborg. Assessing and explaining policy coherence: A comparative study of water governance and large carnivore governance in Sweden. *Environmental Policy and Governance*, **30**(1), 3–13 (2020).

5. J.A.M. Termeer, Catrien, A. Dewulf, and M. Van Lieshout. Disentangling scale approaches in governance research: Comparing monocentric, multi-level, and adaptive governance. *Ecology and Society* **15**(4), (2010).

6. D.J. Snower. Toward global paradigm change: Beyond the crisis of the liberal world order. *Economics*, **13**(1), (2019).

7. J. Monios. Polycentric port governance. *Transport Policy*, **83**, 26–36 (2019).

8. P. Stephenson. Twenty years of multi-level governance: 'Where does it come from? What is it? Where is it going?' *Journal of European Public Policy*, **20**(6), 817–837 (2013).

9. J.A. Henrichs and M.L F.G. De Meza. Multilevel governance in regional development: A case study of the Intermunicipal Consortium of Frontier. *urbe, Revista Brasileira de Gestão Urbana*, **9**(1), 124–138 (2017).

10. P.D. Tortola. Clarifying multilevel governance. *European Journal of Political Research*, **56**(2), 234–250 (2017).

11. E. Ostrom. *Governing the Commons: The Evolution of Institutions for Collective Action*. Cambridge, UK: Cambridge University Press (1990).

12. H. Yi, C. Huang, T. Chen, X. Xu and W. Liu. Multilevel environmental governance: Vertical and horizontal influences in local policy networks. *Sustainability*, **11**(8), 2390 (2019).

13. M. Dobbs. Attaining subsidiarity-based multilevel governance of genetically modified cultivation? *Journal of Environmental Law*, **28**(2), 245–273 (2016).

14. A.L. Yang, M.D. Rounsevell and C. Haggett. Multilevel governance, decentralization and environmental prioritization: How is it working in rural development policy in Scotland? *Environmental Policy and Governance*, **25**(6), 399–411 (2015).

15. G. Stoker. Urban political science and the challenge of urban governance. In *Debating Governance: Authority, Steering and Democracy*, J. Pierre (ed.), pp. 91–109. New York: Oxford University Press, 91–109, (2000).

16. G. Knopp. Governança social, território e desenvolvimento. *Perspectivas em Políticas Públicas*, **4**(8), 53–74 (2011).

17. L. Maillet, P. Lamarche, B. Roy and M. Lemire. At the heart of adapting healthcare organizations. *Emergence: Complexity & Organization*, **17**(2) (2015).

18. P.S. Freire, F. Kempner-Moreira and J.L. Hott Jr. *Governança Multinível Em Rede: reflexões sobre um novo modelo de governança para a segurança pública*. VII Encontro Brasileiro de Administração Pública (2020).

19. A. Benz and B. Eberlein. The Europeanization of regional policies: Patterns of multi-level governance. *Journal of European Public Policy*, **6**(2), 329–348 (1999).

20. N. Juerges, J; Leahy and J. Newig. Actor perceptions of polycentricity in wind power governance. *Environmental Policy and Governance*, **28**(6), 383–394 (2018).

21. J. Newig and O. Fritsch. Environmental governance: Participatory, multi-level–and effective? *Environmental Policy and Governance*, **19**(3), 197–214 (2009).

22. C. Conteh. Changing trends in regional economic development policy governance: The Case of Northern Ontario, Canada. *International Journal of Urban and Regional Research*, **37**(4), 1419–1437 (2013).

23. M. Dąbrowski. Engineering multilevel governance? Joint European Support for Sustainable Investment in City Areas (JESSICA) and the involvement of private and financial actors in urban development policy. *Regional Studies*, **48**(12), 2006–2019 (2014).

24. S. Rantala, R. Hajjar and M. Skutsch. Multilevel governance for forests and climate change: Learning from Southern Mexico. *Forests*, **5**(12), 3147–3168 (2014).

25. E. Thomann, P. Trein and M. Maggetti. What's the problem? Multilevel governance and problem-solving. *European Policy Analysis*, **5**(1), 37–57 (2019).

26. S. Piattoni. Multi-level governance: A historical and conceptual analysis. *European integration*, **31**(2), 163–180 (2009).

27. A. Benz and C. Zimmer. The EU's competences: The 'vertical' perspective on the multilevel system. *Living Reviews in European Governance*, **5**(1), (2010).

28. K. Korhonen-Kurki, M. Brockhaus, A.E. Duchelle, S. Atmadja, P.T. Thuy and L. Schofield. Multiple levels and multiple challenges for measurement, reporting and verification of REDD+. *International Journal of the Commons*, **7**(2), (2013).

29. G. Marti. The effects of multilevel governance on the rights of migrant domestic workers in Singapore. *Journal of Ethnic and Migration Studies*, **45**(8), 1345–1360 (2019).

30. C. Alcantara and M. Morden. Indigenous multilevel governance and power relations. *Territory, Politics, Governance*, **7**(2), 250–264 (2019).

31. P. Bance and A. Chassy. The rollout of the multilevel governance system: A source of reworking the contingent valuation method? **45**(6), 108–1107 (2017).

32. C. Lion, P. Martini and S. Volpi. The evaluation of European Social Fund programmes in a new framework of multilevel governance: The Italian experience. *Regional Studies*, **38**(2), 207–212 (2004).

33. S. Gänzle. The European Union's Strategy for the Baltic Sea Region (EUSBSR): Improving multilevel governance in Baltic Sea cooperation? *Journal of Baltic Studies*, **48**(4), 407–420 (2017).

34. O. Potluka and J. Liddle. Managing European Union structural funds: Using a multilevel governance framework to examine the application of the partnership principle at the project level. *Regional Studies*, **48**(8), 1434–1447 (2014).

35. G.C. Homsy, Z. Liu and M.E. Warner. Multilevel governance: Framing the integration of top-down and bottom-up policymaking. *International Journal of Public Administration*, **42**(7), 572–582 (2019).

Beyond Organizational Knowledge: Governance Mechanisms Applied to Knowledge-Intensive Organizations

Ricardo Pereira*, Sicilia Vechi, Rosane Malvestiti and Neri dos Santos

*Federal University of Santa Catarina,
Graduate Program in Knowledge Management and Engineering,
R. Delfino Conti, s/n, Trindade, Florianópolis —
SC, 88040–900, Brazil*

*rikardop@gmail.com

This chapter aims to verify how a knowledge-intensive organization could add value, moving from management to knowledge governance, and thus improve its performance and competitive advantage. In this sense, the most adequate mechanisms for the transition from management to knowledge governance are identified. The results of the research showed that the adoption of governance mechanisms makes it possible to improve the management of the organization's knowledge assets, implying cost reduction and fostering a collaborative culture and the creation of knowledge. Therefore, it can be noted that there was a theoretical and practical contribution to the improvement of the organization's knowledge management process and to the analysis of theoretical concepts in organizational practice.

4.1. Introduction

The biggest problems with knowledge management are that organizations ignore organizational people and cultures. In an environment where an individual's knowledge is valued and rewarded, establishing a culture that recognizes tacit knowledge and encourages employees to share it is critical (Ref. 1, p. 422).[1]

Nonaka and Takeuchi[2] point out that the knowledge that drives an organization has direct implications for management functions and its entire structure, i.e. its operating systems, technology, and organizational procedures. They also point out that all people who work in a particular organization are becoming knowledge workers. Therefore, people management is the specific practice required for knowledge creation.

Millar et al.[3] understand that people management can facilitate knowledge creation and sustain organizational competitive advantage if organizations transcend the boundaries between levels and functions. This change would guarantee the sharing of knowledge between employer and employee, considering knowledge as their main asset. For this to happen, it is necessary to involve knowledge management and its processes, such as creating, storing, sharing, and applying knowledge. In this perspective, people management increasingly requires the integration of organizational processes and technologies with people and with the leadership of the organization, mainly in the transfer of tacit knowledge, both internally and externally, which characterizes the need for a transition from knowledge management to knowledge governance.

Governance, then, appears as a solution to integrate individuals, cultures, and technologies in an indissociable whole, seeking fluidity in the knowledge management process.

In fact, knowledge governance accomplishes the necessary integration between the theory of the firm, strategic management, and knowledge management, related to knowledge processes and how they are influenced by governance mechanisms, both formal (information systems, rewards, decision-making), as well as informal (culture, networks, and communities of practice). Knowledge governance means implementing governance mechanisms that reduce the costs of knowledge integration, sharing, and creation and maximize the net benefits of the knowledge transfer, sharing, and creation processes.[4]

An example that corroborates the above is the study by Huang *et al.*,[5] which explains the mediating roles of motivation and opportunity, provided by formal and informal mechanisms, in knowledge sharing.

The Asian Productivity Organization (APO) is an inter-governmental organization committed to improving productivity in the Asia-Pacific region. Founded in 1961, it has been contributing to the sustainable socio-economic development of the region through consultancy services in policies and institutional initiatives in capacity building. It aims to become a leading international organization in increasing sustainable productivity by 2020. The APO has developed a framework common to all member countries (Bangladesh, Cambodia, China, Fiji, Hong Kong, India, Indonesia, Iran, Japan, South Korea, Laos, Malaysia, Mongolia, Nepal, Pakistan, Philippines, Singapore, Sri Lanka, Thailand, and Vietnam) structured in three axes: knowledge accelerators, knowledge processes, and results, in terms of productivity, quality, profitability, and growth.[6]

This framework emphasizes the importance of knowledge management for organizational success. Therefore, it is self-explanatory and easy to understand and apply, in addition to highlighting the steps to be followed and the critical factors of its implementation. The instrument was created to boost small and medium-sized companies in the member countries, with the intention of maximizing the most of its benefits by providing a quick start, but that could be used by any organization.

In summary, the APO framework is an integrated approach to identify, create, store, share, and apply knowledge, with the aim of enhancing productivity, quality, profitability, and growth in a multidisciplinary system.[6]

Used as a reference in this work, the APO knowledge management framework, in order to facilitate its interoperability and application, follows the knowledge processes described in five steps: identify, create, store, share, and apply.[2,6]

4.2. Theoretical Foundation

4.2.1. *Knowledge management and processes*

Several authors[7,8] emphasize that knowledge management is the organization's ability to identify, create, store, distribute, and use knowledge and to incorporate it into its products, services, systems, and to innovate. APO reinforces these definitions, stating that, in the era of the knowledge-based economy, the key to success is knowledge management, a concept that is evolving rapidly in developing countries.[9]

Another aspect to be considered about knowledge management is that it is the result of individual experiences and perceptions, the cognitive processing of information, personal relationships, and the search for new information to solve new challenges. For this reason, knowledge management can ensure that learning and skills, both individual and organizational, are engaged and culturally promote knowledge sharing. Understanding that information leads to knowledge and generates new knowledge is a strategic resource of competitive advantage.[10]

With this conception, organizations tend to manage knowledge effectively. One of the means of production is the conversion of tacit (subjective) knowledge into explicit (objective and codified) knowledge as something continuous. The knowledge spiral proposed by Nonaka and Takeuchi (1995) presents this conversion in four conversion modes: (1) socialization: from tacit to tacit, directly sharing and creating, person-person; (2) explicitation: from the tacit to the explicit, exchanging tacit knowledge through narratives and reflection, person-group; (3) combination: from explicit to explicit, systematizing and applying explicit knowledge, group-organization; and (4) incorporation: from explicit to tacit, acquiring new tacit knowledge, organization-person.

Organizations can also implement knowledge management, whether internal or external. Redundantly, the acquisition of knowledge has a positive impact on knowledge sharing and has positive effects on people, the organization, and the production process, which in turn generates a continuous flow of improvement and knowledge creation.[7,11]

According to the APO, this knowledge flow occurs through three levels represented in its framework: the knowledge accelerators, the knowledge management processes, and the results achieved. Accelerators drive the knowledge management initiative, through leadership, technology, people and processes. Leadership ensures strategic and project alignment with the company's mission and vision, in addition to providing support and resources for the implementation of knowledge management projects. Technology enables the implementation and provides the organization with adequate and effective tools. For acceleration to occur, these tools collaborate to enable the participation of those involved by means of time and distance. They also favor the retention of organizational knowledge, assisting in its creation, storage, sharing and application.[6]

Workers and users can be considered as storage and creators of knowledge, as well as a repertoire of tacit knowledge that can become knowledge available to all, once it is coded, documented, and transformed into explicit knowledge. The success of knowledge management is dependent on sharing all this knowledge.[2,6]

Processes are flows of events that describe the work activities to be performed in the organization and can be related to people or technological resources. They can highlight the contribution of organizational knowledge that, when systematized, can improve productivity, growth, profitability, and quality. Specifically, knowledge management processes refer to the development and conversion of knowledge. An effective design of a knowledge management system guarantees its proper flow. The faster the flow of knowledge, the greater the outcomes from learning and from knowledge itself. In the literature, five knowledge management processes are highlighted: identifying, creating, storing, sharing, and applying.[2,6]

The first knowledge management process, "identifying," is the initial and crucial step for all the next steps in the knowledge management processes and involves people with their daily searches for the information needed by the organization, with their strategic knowledge needs (what they want and how to achieve it), their business goals and objectives, customer requirements, and knowledge reuse. In this step, the "knowledge audit" can help to identify the existing knowledge and present the gap of what is critically necessary to build the necessary competences, in order, to create the knowledge that lacks.[6]

The second knowledge management process, "creating," comes after identifying the needs for new knowledge. Therefore, creation can happen through teams or individuals, training, executing, solving problems, and carrying out discussions and review activities. It can also occur through the departments or in the organization as a whole — e.g. innovation generates new knowledge for products and services, processes, and internal procedures. Another departmental way is in research and development (R&D), with its groups of specialists, communities of practice, and, more intensely, when mergers with other companies occur.[6]

In order, for the knowledge flow to exist, access to what has already been created is necessary, so the next knowledge management process, of equal importance, is "storing." When knowledge is stored, it can be accessed through organizational knowledge bases. When it is easy to access and easy to use, it starts to be incorporated by people, providing the company with a basis for organizational intellectual capital. There is a difficulty in this process when knowledge is tacit, since tacit knowledge is difficult to be coded and, therefore, to be stored. For this reason, it is important to know and retain expert people and make them accessible to other people. A tool that assists in this step is the information technology and documents.[2,6]

The fifth and final knowledge management process is "sharing," which promotes the flow of learning through socialization, collaboration, workshops, and coaching, making knowledge available at the right time, quantity, people, and quality. This facilitates access to organizational knowledge bases and documents. Technology can assist and allow improving knowledge sharing in the organization. An important fact to be mentioned in this process is that mutual trust is fundamental for sharing.[6]

4.2.2. *Knowledge-intensive organization and knowledge governance*

The term *knowledge-intensive* can be used in different contexts, such as knowledge-intensive work, knowledge workers, and knowledge-intensive organizations. Regardless of the type of organization or type of work, they all seem to involve knowledge: people need to "know what?" and "for what?" to create knowledge and promote competitive advantage. Therefore, knowledge-intensive organizations are characterized by having jobs of an intellectual nature, with a strong cognitive component, for which people must be qualified to produce qualified products and services.[12,13]

In this context, the skills of people engaged in research that drive product development in knowledge-intensive organizations are essential skills. It is believed that the tacit knowledge and local creativity of all members of the organization are the most important factors for the success of this type of organization.[12]

Therefore, knowledge-intensive organizations depend heavily on knowledge or professional experience related to a specific discipline or technique, or functional domain, to provide knowledge-based products and services. It is worth mentioning that there are several types of knowledge-intensive organizations, such as classic professional services, internal services unit, and organizations in which a proportion of highly qualified specialists to support and manage people is necessary — e.g. departments of research and development, healthcare, education, and government policies.[3]

Although the definition is described and types are mentioned, much remains to be done to develop a meaningful categorization, which will provide an in-depth view of the management of knowledge-intensive organizations, as well as their concept — e.g. to define a knowledge-intensive service in which knowledge is the main factor of production. As the types of knowledge and organizational forms are varied, there is a certain ambiguity among the concepts. In addition to the types of technical knowledge and data, it is necessary to pay attention to intangible knowledge assets, such as tacit knowledge.[3,14]

The concept of knowledge-intensive service recognizes the incorporation of knowledge into services with the ability to effectively share valuable business knowledge and is a crucial means of innovation, problem solving, and continuous improvement. Another interesting way of using knowledge intensively is gambling, but it is not seen as a category of knowledge-intensive organizations or professional services.[3]

Both knowledge-intensive services and organizations have multiplied. However, leadership and management are critical challenges in such organizations, as people are their greatest asset. Structures, processes, and practices have evolved to meet these challenges, different from the various areas of activity, which include not only intensive knowledge in business services, such as information technology, financial, planning and development (P&D), legal services, and companies, but also in non-commercial services, such as education, cultural organizations, and public service.[3]

Knowledge governance starts from the hypothesis that knowledge management processes can be influenced and directed through the implementation of governance mechanisms, in particular the formal mechanisms of the organization that can be managed, such as organizational structure, task design, systems reward systems, information systems, standard operating procedures, accounting systems, and other coordination mechanisms.[15]

Seeking an overview of the different processes and critical success factors provided by the use of knowledge, Diehr and Gueldenberg[16] found as results, in relation to the processes, the identification of knowledge assets, knowledge governance and coordination, construction of relationships, knowledge presentation, knowledge transfer, and knowledge protection. Concerning the critical success factors, they found the following themes: absorptive capacity, solving customer problems, reputation, rewards, incentives, trust, and reciprocity. It is emphasized that both the knowledge processes and these critical success factors are important for the competitive advantage of organizations.

Ali *et al.*,[17] in turn, claim that knowledge governance, as well as its sharing, are important factors for improving the performance of project-based organizations. They emphasize that social processes positively stimulate the relationship between knowledge sharing and the performance of these organizations. They also suggest that project-based organizations should invest in knowledge governance as it is a system that induces knowledge sharing.

The various relationships between the mechanisms of knowledge governance and knowledge sharing arouse the interest of several researchers, however, the relationships between the mechanisms of knowledge governance and knowledge transfer processes are rarely considered in academic studies. However, the relationships between knowledge governance mechanisms, motivations for sharing knowledge, and knowledge-sharing behavior are not yet fully understood. Informal and formal knowledge governance mechanisms have a significant influence on knowledge sharing, motivation, and opportunities. However, even when employees are encouraged and rewarded for sharing knowledge, effective sharing is not necessarily guaranteed.[18]

Dávila *et al.*[19] suggest that the various governance mechanisms discussed in the literature can be divided into mechanisms focused on people and mechanisms focused on processes and infrastructure. The first group of mechanisms is based on the idea that people are the main holders of knowledge in organizations and the main agents of knowledge management processes. Therefore, knowledge management processes are carried out efficiently if people are willing to be involved in them. Rewards and organizational culture are widely discussed as key mechanisms for addressing this motivational challenge. These authors also emphasize that the approach behind the second group of practices suggests that organizations need to have an appropriate infrastructure and that organizational processes need to be adjusted in order to allow support for knowledge management processes. Among the mechanisms focused on processes and infrastructure, two received the most attention: methods of organizational design, and information and communication technologies, which facilitate knowledge management processes.

4.3. Organizational Knowledge Management Processes

Next, the stages of the knowledge management process are described, as provided for in the APO framework,[6] from the perspective of the analyzed company.

4.3.1. *Knowledge identification*

The APO framework[6] establishes as drivers of the "Knowledge Identification" process:

- the recognition of available sources of knowledge (tacit/explicit), based on the organization's core capabilities;
- the identification of knowledge necessary for the company to reach the solution;
- the definition of initiatives involving people, processes and technologies, for the identification of knowledge; and
- the identification of the existing knowledge gap.

In relation to the process "identification of knowledge," the studied company explores its knowledge demands based on market research. Thus, the demands and problems to be solved in the civil engineering structures sector are identified, as well as the software user's needs in this segment. The search for a business opportunity for the company precedes the search for the necessary knowledge to implement the solution.

The second step is the identification of internal employees in the organization with technical expertise to meet the demand from product development. The necessary knowledge is not always found in the employees. So, the company seeks market references that work in the area, seeks to talk to these people, and hires external consultants to define the key points to be developed to obtain the new needed knowledge.

4.3.2. *Knowledge creation*

The drivers extracted from the approached framework point to the "knowledge creation" process:[6]

- conversion of knowledge to fill in the gaps;
- activities at individual and team levels, such as structuring groups and defining activities to promote learning;
- creation of the new knowledge demanded to reach the solution; and

- activities at the organizational and departmental level, such as changes in processes, in internal procedures, and the creation of expert groups.

To create knowledge, the studied organization seeks to train internal employees through courses, based on the provision of validated academic materials, which provide input for research and product development within the company. Bibliographical references and surveys provide theoretical support for specialists to develop new specifications for the software to be created.

4.3.3. *Knowledge storage*

The drivers of the APO framework for knowledge storage are:[6]

- maintaining the organization's sources of tacit and explicit knowledge;
- establishment of bases to store the created knowledge, with form, content, access, and means of interaction; and
- plan for the stored knowledge to be incorporated into the organization's routines.

All content created by the studied company is stored on a project management platform, aiming at the storage and availability of all information about products, software modules, and study groups. This is the beginning of knowledge capture by the product team, which will feed the entire system from knowledge sharing. The support knowledge base, open to the software users, is another source of the created knowledge in the company.

4.3.4. *Knowledge sharing*

For the "knowledge sharing" process, the framework drivers point to:[6]

- creation of databases/document bases or inventory approach so that other people can find and access knowledge;

- transfer by collaboration, from person to person, by training, with the use of technology.

In addition to the internal sharing of information and knowledge through the project management platform, the organization fosters the sharing of technical knowledge with its external publics, in an open knowledge base on the web as support. The more than 1,400 available technical articles address recurring questions from users and customers or even fundamental engineering concepts for the development of good projects. This sharing with the entire construction chain and designers also allows the company to improve its processes and products, based on the questions, requests, and feedbacks received.

As indicators of the interaction with users and the update of the support knowledge base, it should be noted that the organization receives, on average, 2,200 online calls per month. The index of new doubts recorded in 2018 showed that 17% of the questions received by the support were new and that 83% have already been answered and made available in the databases, in the format of articles, question and answer section, and videos.

4.3.5. *Knowledge use*

The drivers of the "knowledge use or application" process in the framework are:

- transforming knowledge into actions, product improvement, and decision making;
- alignment and integration of knowledge to organizational processes and to daily tasks;
- how to learn before, during, and after knowledge conversions, in a cycle of tacit-explicit-embedded knowledge; and
- determination of the knowledge assets discovered.

The transformation of knowledge into value is successful when the company is able to identify the unmet market demand and, accomplishes to cross it with the intellectual potential of its collaborators, transforming the needs of customers or potential customers in the market into solutions.

4.4. From Management to Governance: The Next Stage in the Organizational Knowledge Process

4.4.1. *Evolution of management processes to knowledge governance*

One of the major barriers to implementing an organizational knowledge management system is to reconcile the stages of the knowledge management process in order to integrate the entire organization, including people, technology, and organizational processes, taking into account the organizational culture, strategy, and all institutional levels. As a way of minimizing these difficulties, knowledge governance can be a viable alternative for organizations.

As previously mentioned, knowledge governance integrates strategic management, firm theory, and knowledge management related to knowledge management processes and how they are influenced by formal mechanisms (information systems, rewards, decision-making) and informal (culture, networks, and communities of practice) governance. In fact, knowledge governance means implementing mechanisms that reduce the costs of sharing, integrating, and creating knowledge, maximizing the net benefits of the processes of transferring, sharing, and creating knowledge.[4]

Therefore, knowledge governance makes it possible to explore the competitive potential of knowledge as a strategic resource. Through their managers, organizations need to direct their intra-organizational knowledge management processes by means of the implementation of various governance mechanisms.[20]

The mechanisms proposed for this research contribute to innovation based on knowledge governance, and, according to Dávila *et al.*,[19] comprise three categories: focused on people, focused on infrastructure, and focused on organizational processes, and of four types: information and communication technologies (ICTs), organizational design, organizational culture, and rewards focused on knowledge.

Knowledge governance applied to the organization's knowledge management processes takes place through the convergence of the people, processes, and technology mechanisms, each of which predominates in the different phases.

In the Knowledge Creation Phase, the importance is given to individual and group learning, and the mechanisms focused on people and the use of rewards that motivate interaction provide incentives for the generation of ideas and the creation of new knowledge. This vision changes the scenario in which the company's current performance prioritizes the combination and incorporation of knowledge, while it can increase the frequency of exchanges between specialists, the generation of ideas, and, consequently, business opportunities.

In the Knowledge Storage Phase, the use of structural mechanisms, represented by the systems, ensures saving and facilitates access to information and created knowledge. The updating of the knowledge bases reflects the predominance of the combination of knowledge, which is the most appropriate mode of conversion at this stage. Likewise, the maintenance of a unified, open, and constantly updated database on the web for users to consult denotes the company's competence to promote the incorporation of knowledge by its internal and external customers. A system improvement, such as a structural mechanism, could be the implementation of artificial intelligence, given the volume of data already available in the company's bases.

In the Knowledge Sharing Phase, the bases already established meet the needs of structural mechanisms, while the use of knowledge rewards is essential to sharing. The existing rewards for the external public or users of engineering software are guarantees that their questions will be answered by the company in the form of personalized support and in the form of an article with a tutorial function on the website, which will allow autonomy, agility, and quality information for future consultations on the same issue. A knowledge reward for employees is the users' feedback via support channels, which generates reliable data for corrections, system improvements in software, insights, and future opportunities for service innovation. Still regarding communication sharing, internal communication in flow with a reduction in hierarchical levels, with greater horizontality, is another way of stimulating the sharing of knowledge favorable to the company's performance.

In the Knowledge Application or Use Phase, the mechanisms focused on structure and processes should excel by acting on changes in organizational culture, in reinforcing values, and in renewing concepts and validated beliefs that add value to the business or the company. Such changes increase acceptance and resilience about necessary improvements in services and drivers of knowledge creation and innovation. The structural mechanisms focus on systems that continuously support the knowledge processes.

4.4.2. *Practical implications and challenges of knowledge governance*

Organizations, when migrating from management to knowledge governance, will have maximized the benefits of knowledge transfer, sharing, and creation processes, with the adoption of mechanisms that aim to reduce the costs inherent to knowledge processes.

The adoption of governance mechanisms will improve the management of an organization's knowledge assets, in particular, minimizing some difficulties/deficiencies found in knowledge management. These mechanisms make it possible to integrate strategic management, firm theory, and knowledge management.

The mechanisms of governance can be subdivided into three genres, which encompass people, technology, and organizational processes. The first genre possesses fundamental importance to the organization, considering that people comprise the main organizational asset, and knowledge can be identified, created, transferred, used, and incorporated by individuals as part of the organizational culture.

The second genre, technology, from the perspective of knowledge governance, has its mechanisms benefited from the better integration of processes, sharing of tacit knowledge and, as a consequence, cost reduction and acceleration of the cycle of creation of knowledge assets for the organization.

The third genre, organizational processes, is valued in the governance of knowledge based on the integration of flows and technologies, with people and with the leadership of the organization, mainly in the transfer of tacit knowledge.

The transition from management to knowledge governance is relevant to mitigate the challenges encountered in knowledge management. One of the main ones is to motivate people to share knowledge in the organization.

Based on knowledge governance, it is possible to rely on formal and informal mechanisms, such as a culture of collaboration and reward, to promote changes that may impact the organizational culture.

The challenges of implementing knowledge governance mechanisms are manifested, initially, in the difficulties encountered by companies for socialization and explicitation from the sources of tacit knowledge.

Another challenge is the absence of a collaborative culture in companies, which blocks knowledge flows. Finally, there is still a gap about investments in management and governance so that knowledge-intensive organizations can evolve and generate assets.

Finally, it is worth noting that the management process is intra-organizational, turned inward, and for this reason, specific to the people allocated to the organization. Regarding governance, its perspective is inter-organizational, i.e. given the external scope. The greatest gain for organizations in this transition is that it alone cannot survive considering the current rapid changes. Therefore, your network, be it with suppliers, with customers, with the environment, and with the community in which it is part of, needs the participation of everyone in a co-production process, maximizing performance, billing, and scalability, for the organization and stakeholders.

4.5. Final Considerations

Knowledge governance can add value to the production chain of knowledge-intensive companies. The inter-operability among the various mechanisms of formal (information systems, rewards, decision-making) and informal (culture, networks, and communities of practice) knowledge governance and the strategic management and knowledge management reduce risks and uncertainties and promote the creation of new organizational knowledge and, therefore, maximize productivity, in addition to keeping the company active in its kind of market, with competitive advantage.

The research showed that the knowledge management processes (identify, create, store, share, and apply), as highlighted in the APO framework, are important steps for the success of any company and, particularly, for those intensive in knowledge, because the knowledge flow is more intense and requires a greater sharing of knowledge and experiences from the people involved, which can be achieved through the mechanisms of knowledge governance.

Based on the study, we came to some findings:

(1) as a contribution to the identification of knowledge, it is suggested that organizations encourage the socialization and the explicitation of its technical personnel's knowledge and the use of systems for the agile identification of the available information and knowledge;

(2) as a contribution to the creation of knowledge, it is suggested that organizations make use of motivating rewards for the interaction between its technical personnel to generate ideas and create new knowledge, through opportunities for knowledge socialization and explicitation, instead of the current priority given to combine and incorporate knowledge;

(3) as a contribution to the storage of knowledge, a possible structural improvement is the implementation of an artificial intelligence system, if there is a volume of data available in the organizations' databases;

(4) as a contribution to knowledge sharing, it is proposed to maintain knowledge rewards, such as user feedback to improve systems and tutorials for those who use the software, along with an increasingly less hierarchical and more horizontal communication flow within companies;

(5) as a contribution to knowledge use, changes are proposed in the organizational culture, in reinforcing values, in renewing concepts and validated beliefs that add value to the business or company and increase resilience for necessary changes, in addition to the renewal of the knowledge processes.

It is important to note that this is an emerging topic and, therefore, there are still many opportunities for empirical and relevant studies. For future work, we suggest the adoption of the mechanisms identified in this study and their verification in the reality of knowledge-intensive organizations, as well as the possibility of integrating people, processes, and technology.

Acknowledgments

This study was financed in part by the Coordenação de Aperfeiçoamento de Pessoal de Nível Superior – Brasil (CAPES) – Finance Code 001.

References

1. K. Dalkir. *Knowledge Management in Theory and Practice*, 3rd ed. Cambridge, MA: MIT Press (2017).
2. Nonaka and H. Takeuchi. *The Knowledge-Creating Company: How Japanese Companies Create the Dynamics of Innovation*. New York: Oxford University Press (1995).
3. C. Millar, M. Lockett and J. Mahon. Knowledge intensive organizations: On the frontiers of knowledge management. *Journal of Knowledge Management*, **20**(5), 845–857 (2016).
4. N. Foss. Knowledge governance: Meaning, nature, origins, and implications. SMG Working Paper 12/2011, December 2011. In *Handbook of Economic Organization,* A. Grandori (ed.), Denmark: Edward Elgar, pp. 5–45 (2012).
5. M.C. Huang, Y.P. Chiu and T.C. Lu. Mecanismos de governança de conhecimento e compartilhamento de conhecimento do repatriado: os papéis mediadores de motivação e oportunidade. *Journal of Knowledge Management*, **17**(5), 677–694 (2013).
6. P. Nair and K. Prakash. *Knowledge Management: Facilitator's Guide*. Tokyo: APO (2009).
7. R. Gonzalez and M. Martins. O Processo de Gestão do Conhecimento: uma pesquisa teórico-conceitual. *Gestão and Produção*, **24**(2), 248–265 (2017).
8. J. Tidd and J. Bessant. Innovation management Challenges: From fads to fundamentals. *International Journal of Innovation Management*, **22**(05), 1–13 (2018).

9. D. Rohajawati. Knowledge management: Workshop APO framework. *International Journal of Computer Science Issues*, **11**(19), 27–28 (2015).
10. C. Jannuzzi, O. Falsarella and C. Sugahara. Gestão do conhecimento: um estudo de modelos e sua relação com a inovação nas organizações. *Perspectivas em Ciência da Informação*, **21**(1), 97–118 (2016).
11. S. Aydin and M. Dube. Knowledge management, innovation, and competitive advantage: Is the relationship in the eye of the beholder? *Knowledge Management Research & Practice*, **16**(3), 402–413 (2018).
12. M. Alvesson and S. Sveningsson. Good visions, bad micro-management and ugly ambiguity: Contradictions of (non-) leadership in a knowledge-intensive organization. *Organization Studies*, **24**(6), 961–988 (2003).
13. J. Swart, and N. Kinnie. Organizational learning: Knowledge assets and HR practices in professional service firms. *Human Resource Management Journal*, **20**(1), 64–79 (2010).
14. I. Nonaka, and G. Von Krogh. Perspective tacit knowledge and knowledge conversion: Controversy and advancement in organizational knowledge creation theory. *Organization Science*, **20**(3), 635–652 (2009).
15. A. Grandori. Neither hierarchy nor identity: Knowledge-governance mechanisms and the theory of the firm. *Journal Management Government*, **5**(3), 381–399 (2001).
16. G. Diehr and S. Gueldenberg. Knowledge utilization: An empirical review on processes and factors of knowledge utilization. *Global Business and Economics Review*, **19**(4), 401–419 (2017).
17. I. Ali, A. Musawir and M. Ali. Impact of knowledge sharing and absorptive capacity on project performance: The moderating role of social processes. *Journal of Knowledge Management*, **22**(2), 453–477 (2018).
18. M. Huang, Y. Chiu and T. Lu. Knowledge governance mechanisms and repatriate's knowledge sharing: The mediating roles of motivation and opportunity. *Journal of Knowledge Management*, **17**(5), 677–694 (2013).
19. G. Dávila, T. Andreeva and G. Varvakis. Knowledge management in Brazil: What governance mechanisms are needed to boost innovation? *Management and Organization Review*, **15**(4), 857–886 (2019).
20. N.J. Foss and S. Michailova. *Knowledge Governance: Processes and Perspectives*. Oxford Scholarship Online (2009).

© 2022 World Scientific Publishing Company
https://doi.org/10.1142/9789811224119_0005

Framework for Knowledge Governance and Organizational Learning: The Interrelationship of Constructs

Giselly Rizzatti* and Patricia de Sá Freire

*Graduate Program in Knowledge Management and Engineering,
Federal University of Santa Catarina,
R. Delfino Conti, s/n, Trindade, Florianópolis —
SC, 88040–900, Brazil*

*girizzatti@gmail.com

In the organizational context, in order to support Knowledge Management, implementing mechanisms and procedures of governance are needed. Besides Corporate and Knowledge Governance, a *governance* that recognizes the knowledge, its mechanisms, and the processes that favor the learning, from the individual to the organizational level, called Organizational Learning Governance (LGov), is indispensable. Thus, this chapter's goal is to present a framework that points out the definition and the interrelationships between the mechanisms, components, and environment to govern knowledge and organizational learning. To this end, a qualitative, applied, theoretical, propositional research was carried out with exploratory and descriptive steps by bibliographic means, using an integrative analysis of publications raised after a narrative review and systematic search of international and interdisciplinary electronic databases. In conclusion, it can be stated that the processing of LGov requires four mechanisms (Knowledge Management, Knowledge Cycle, Learning Cycle, and Knowledge Governance), four components (Dynamic and Self-Organizing Capacity, Reliable Information, Shared Mental Model, and Shared Vision and Common Goals), and two Learning Environments (BA and 8Cs).

5.1. Introduction

Learning Organizations are made up of individuals who continually develop their abilities to create results, are stimulated by new patterns of behavior, and primarily seek to learn together to create, acquire, and share knowledge.[1] In this way, the management of this knowledge becomes fundamental, as it involves the collection and sharing of data and information for the creation of new knowledge[2] and, consequently, promoting Organizational Learning. Because it involves the complexity of learning at multiple levels, the need arises to implement mechanisms and procedures of governance that encompass Knowledge Management (KM)[3] and advance on the traditional model of Corporate Governance (CGov), called Knowledge Governance (KGov).[4–8]

Going beyond, more recently, a new approach has emerged as a way to understand the mechanisms and processes of knowledge, from the individual, group, and organizational levels, i.e. Learning Governance (LGov).[9,10] This emerging, important, and necessary model of Organizational LGov aims to meet the challenges imposed by today's disruptive transformations, generating adaptive and resilience capacity through assimilation, accommodation, and balance of new knowledge continuously to improve performance and differentiate itself from other organizations.

This chapter aims to present a framework that points out the definition and the interrelationships between the mechanisms, components, and environment to govern organizational knowledge and learning.

5.2. Methodological Procedures

This research can be considered as qualitative,[11] applied,[12] theoretical,[13] propositional with exploratory stages,[14] and descriptive[11] by bibliographic means, using an integrative analysis of publications raised after a narrative review and systematic search in international and interdisciplinary electronic databases.

In total, 112 publications were identified in the databases consulted — 65 in Scopus and 47 in Web of Science. An integrative analysis was carried out on the selected publications. Among the documents returned, 35 duplicates were excluded, resulting in 77 eligible for analysis; however, applying the exclusion criteria of non-adherence to the subject, 7 documents remained for analysis of the research.[9,10, 15–19]

The validation of the identified elements and their interrelationships was developed in three moments, according to Ollaik and Ziller[20]: (1) previous validation, by the conceptions related to the elaboration of the research, i.e. the literature review; (2) internal validation, with the development of the research, i.e. the construction of the Dimensions and interrelationships of the proposed elements; and (3) external validation, with the results of the research for consistency verification and validation with professional experts from the chosen Public Organization and theoretical experts from LGov areas.

5.3. Governance of Organizational Learning

To understand the term LGov, it is necessary first to approach the conceptualization of "Organizational Learning" (OL), which can be conceived as a main means to achieve renewal or strategic change of an organization,[10,21] requiring, as Crossan *et al.*[21] point out, that it learns new knowledge (exploration), while at the same time exploiting the knowledge already learned (exploitation). Including perceiving the organization as an open system, this process must encompass the entire organizational eco-system, not just a specific group or the individual.

The OL process is dynamic and occurs over time and between different levels of analysis: individual, group, and organization. To reach the organizational level, the OL occurs through four subprocesses — intuition, interpretation, integration, and institutionalization (4I Model). During the OL processes, there is a tension between the assimilation of new learning (feedforward) and the use of everything that has already been learned (feedback).[21]

The *intuition* happens only at the individual level and is based on experiences, images, and metaphors. This process can influence the individual's intuitive insights and, because it is subjective and tacit, it only affects other people when there is interaction. *Interpretation* deals with the explanation of insights for the individual himself and for others to whom he relates. It occurs through the use of language, cognitive maps, conversation, or dialogue. *Integration* comes from coordinated actions by the members of a group for dialogue, sharing of ideas, definitions, under-standing, and mutual adjustment, developing languages and systems of interaction. Finally, *institutionalization*, the result of transferring the learning of individuals and groups to the organization, affects only the organizational level. At this level, learning is implemented through sys-tems, structures, routines, and procedures.[21]

To propose a conceptualization for LGov, Vitry and Chia (Ref. 10, p. 281) understand OL as a process of change: change in behavior, change in objectives, and change in the way actions are perceived. However, it is also a reaction to change: learning to adapt to new and uncertain situa-tions. Therefore, LGov consists of the ability to learn to work together, share values, define collective goals, generate a shared mental model, and establish a common language and the ability to participate in meetings, polls, and discussions, among other moments of dialogue and seeking col-lective consensus.[10]

Considering the definition of Vitry and Chia[10] and dialoguing with the other authors, Rizzatti (Ref. 22, p. 204) defines **Organizational Learning Governance**:

> … as an organizational system for the development of dynamic and self-organizing capacity, which directs collective cognitive and behavioral

processes through an interrelated set of mechanisms, components, and learning environments for coping with and promptly responding to changes.

Once the concept of LGov is understood, to process them it is necessary to present the cycles of organizational learning.

5.3.1. *Organizational learning cycles for LGov*

Three organizational learning cycles can be considered that should be governed in the organization.

The first type is simple cycle learning, which is based on the results of previous behaviors and experiences, where practice is improved without questioning the objective of the organization. This cycle focuses on "error detection and correction" (Ref. 23, p. 3) in organizational routines, without changing the objectives, culture, or structure of an organization, i.e. "the organization adjusts to environmental factors, but existing norms and values are not questioned" (Ref. 24, p. 33). Thus, the organization learns without a significant change in its basic assumptions, i.e. the organization learns and adapts to new routines to improve its processes.[19]

The second type is the double-cycle learning, which questions the appropriation of previous behaviors, simultaneously with principles, assumptions, and threats, which makes the organization flexible and capable of solving its problems.[19] In other words, it covers "the modification of an organization's underlying norms, policies and objectives" (Ref. 23, p. 3), where there is questioning of the current principles and rules, which are changed if necessary. It involves changes, such as the reversal of systems and procedures and changes in strategies. The organizational culture will need to change due to the fact that the organization "learns to learn," i.e. there is the transformation of mental models for the generation of new meanings and actions.[18,24,25]

The third type is the triple-cycle learning[18] based on the governance process that creates a new mental model in the members of the organization,[26] with leadership and shared visions for the collective implementation of individual and group learning, structures that include informal networking and socialization and understandings of implicit mental models. There is, therefore, the understanding and creation of new processes of mental model generation,[24,25] which is a learning orientation.

5.3.2. *LGov mechanisms*

LGov is dependent on mechanisms that lead the genesis and the evolution of the governance and knowledge management capacity to the orientation of the need for a standard to be learned for the improvement processes in organizations.[9,27]

In order to govern learning, organizations have to take into account four theoretical perspectives: knowledge-based vision, dynamic capacity vision, knowledge governance approach, and strategic learning.[9]

Learning mechanisms constitute a cycle of knowledge evolution in such a way as to accumulate and renew knowledge as well as establish new knowledge for organizational routines. To this end, this cycle seeks solutions to needs unknown by the organization and converts these solutions into routines.[27]

Based on the literature studied, four mechanisms are necessary for LGov to process, leading to the learning necessary for the development of the organization[22] (Table 5.1).

Table 5.1.   LGov mechanisms.

LGov Mechanisms	Definition
Knowledge Management	Use a combination of sources (human and non-human) and types of knowledge (tacit, implicit, and explicit) in decision-making (strategic, tactical, and operational) that can add value to the products (goods and services), in order to create wealth and increase competitiveness.
Knowledge Cycle	Cycle of knowledge accumulation and renewal, as well as the establishment of new knowledge in organizational routines.
Organizational Learning Cycle	Cycle that involves the acquisition of new knowledge (exploration), while at the same time exploring what has already been learned (exploitation) throughout the organizational ecosystem, resulting in adaptation, transformation, or creation of new mental models.
KGov	Set of formal, informal, and relational mechanisms generated by the processes of corporate governance and knowledge management, in order to optimize the economic results of the organization.

Source: Rizzatti (Ref. 22, p. 68).

It should be explained that Fong and Chen[9] have formulated a structure called the Framework of statements of the vision of dynamic capabilities and strategic learning about the genesis and evolution of knowledge management capacity that is formed by the relationships of knowledge governance mechanisms, knowledge processes, and organizational performance results, which highlights the effectiveness of learning mechanisms and knowledge management capacity in creating value and sustaining competitive advantages over time. The Framework[9,28] illustrates the connection and interaction between Knowledge Governance mechanisms[7] and knowledge processes[27,29] for the formation of learning mechanisms[7,27,30] that conduct such mechanisms and the constitution and evolution of knowledge management capacity in a special dynamic capacity of an organization[30] to modify operational routines over time.[28]

In this framework,[9,28] the mechanisms of KGov have two approaches — one focused on people (organizational) and the other on technology. The organizational mechanisms represent the mechanisms that encourage innovation, leadership, strategic orientation, and communication. The technological mechanisms represent the mechanisms that help develop and use information and communication technology (ICT) systems. It is important to highlight that, although technological mechanisms perform an increasingly important function for knowledge acquisition, the level at which the knowledge acquired is shared depends especially on the cognitive context produced by organizational mechanisms.[9,28]

Another learning governance mechanism is the knowledge process,[9] which consists of four cyclical processes: ability to respond to knowledge, knowledge acquisition, knowledge dissemination, and knowledge use.[29]

Zollo and Winter[27] also state that organizational improvement processes are related to a cycle of knowledge evolution, which makes use of three learning mechanisms: accumulation of experience, articulation of knowledge, and codification of knowledge through routines, sharing, and documentation of knowledge. The descriptions of these mechanisms make it possible to establish how dynamic capacities and operational routines develop over time. Organizational knowledge adopts an evolutionary pattern through a series of linked stages in a recursive cycle. In this perspective, the evolutionary model of knowledge is based on the quadruple variation, selection, replication, and retention of the classic evolutionary paradigm composed of five phases:

(1) An external stimulus (or feedback), with internally generated information derived from the organization's existing routines, gives rise to the possibility of generative variation to solve a given problem.

(2) This generative variation of solutions thus goes through an internal selection process, aimed at assessing their potential to improve the effectiveness of existing routines, or the opportunity to form new ones, in which the solution will be evaluated and legitimized.

(3) Once it is legitimated, there is the phase of knowledge replication through the diffusion of approved changes within the company, in which there is knowledge transfer through knowledge management mechanisms and adaptations to solve problems, thus generating new solutions.

(4) Properly replicated, the solution is routinized (retention), through new routines or modification of existing ones.

(5) Routines vary over time and feed back into the knowledge process.[27]

In short, as one of the main results of Rizzatti's[22] research, one can point out that KGov is one of the mechanisms for the governance of learning and therefore deserves a special section in this chapter.

5.3.3. *KGov mechanisms*

KGov implies being able to engage in dialogue with three areas: KM, organizational studies and strategy, and people management, as it is about how and what strategies, structures, and shared values are indispensable to manage Knowledge Assets.[7,8]

Regarding the KGov categories, Pemsel and Müller[3] explain that they can be seen in three ways: (1) KGov in organizations; (2) KGov creating processes; and (3) KGov in inter- and intra-organizational relationships.

In order to establish a relationship between internal and external stakeholders, it is necessary first to identify and analyze their influence and interests in the organization. Uzzi[31] points out that the types of intra- and inter-organizational relationships impact the performance of the organization, because the source of trust and sharing is the fact that individuals establish transactions with other individuals and organizations.

KGov means choosing governance structures (e.g. markets, hybrids, hierarchies) and governance and coordination mechanisms (e.g. contracts, policies, reward schemes, incentives, trust, management styles, organizational culture, etc.), in order to maximize the benefits of the knowledge transfer, sharing, and creation processes.[32,33] Governance structures and governance mechanisms are important because they define incentives and coordinate the actions of members of the organization in knowledge processes.[34]

Thus, **KGov** can be defined as a set of formal, informal, and relational mechanisms generated by corporate governance and management of knowledge processes, in order to optimize the organization's economic results.[7,8] In other words, it aims to implement governance mechanisms that reduce the costs of sharing, integrating, and creating knowledge, which, in essence, promotes the development of organizational capacities.[33]

As for the mechanisms, Grandori[5] states that they can be evaluated on two criteria: (1) focused on the cognitive possibility of sustaining certain exchanges of knowledge; and (2) represented by the costs attributed to the mechanisms, mainly in cases where more than one is applicable.

According to Freire *et al.*[8] there are 10 mechanisms of KGov from the principles of Corporate Governance, presented in Table 5.2.

For Foss,[32] the mechanisms of KGov are the costs and risks of knowledge transfer transactions, such as the frequency of use, the uncertainty, and the specificity of Knowledge Assets, in addition to the expenses with inspection, monitoring entry performance, and other costs of transformation and application of this asset.

Ali *et al.*[35] explain that KGov consists of stimulating knowledge sharing through various formal mechanisms, such as organizational structures and reward systems, relational mechanisms, such as steering committees and specialists' panels, and informal mechanisms, such as trust and organizational culture.[36]

Grandori[37] points out the need for a combination of different governance mechanisms related to the structure and incentives for knowledge

Table 5.2. KGov mechanisms.

CGov Principles	KGov Mechanisms
Transparency	1. Formation of internal and external partnerships based on a culture of transparency.
	2. Formation of intra- and inter-organizational networks with effective communication in order to reduce cognitive distances and potentialize new relationships.
	3. People management practices to build psychological bonds of trust and sharing that facilitate approximation and understanding of the other by increasing the level of empathy.
	4. Formal incentives to KM.
Equity	5. Sharing of property rights.
	6. Promotion of organizational absorptive capacity.
Accountability	7. Performance and monitoring measures to control costs and risks of exit transaction and knowledge transfer.
Responsibility	8. Decentralized management, coordinated by communities and project teams.
	9. Promotion of inclusion for participation and collaboration.
	10. Systems of authority and leadership, with the hierarchy based on consensus with the social construction of meaning for decision-making.

Source: Freire *et al* (Ref. 8, p. 33).

sharing and participation in learning networks. For the governance of these networks to promote learning, Grandori[37] highlights the importance of mechanisms that enhance organizational absorptive capacity; the formation of partnerships; the construction of bonds of trust to facilitate approximation and understanding of the other, increasing the level of empathy; and attention to common language, for communication to be effective in reducing cognitive distances and enhancing new relationships.

5.3.4. *LGov and KGov components*

Among the organizational components that relate to the mechanisms of KGov and OL, the following were identified: **dynamic and self-organizing capacity**,[30,38] **reliable information**,[39–41] **shared vision and common goals**,[1,10] and **shared mental models**.[1,10]

Table 5.3. Learning and knowledge governance components.

Components	Definition
Dynamic capacity	The company's ability to dynamically manage its knowledge base over time, reconfiguring and realigning the processes of investigation and prospection of new knowledge (exploration), and the use and retention (exploitation) of this knowledge in the organization and in its network.
Self-organizing capacity	The organization's ability to be creative and innovative by itself, i.e. to be an autonomous agent of its own learning.
Reliable information	Information that serves as a basis for decision-making, generates new knowledge, and leads to the achievement of the organization's objectives.
Shared vision	Establishment of common goals to align personal and organizational goals, in order to carry out the collective work to reach the organization's future vision.
Common goals	After the exchange of ideas, sharing the same understanding in order to reach a consensus.
Shared mental models	It is an organizational understanding, i.e. the way members view the organization from their beliefs, values, points of view, and perception of reality, seeking to understand the common goals to be achieved and to implement the shared vision.

Source: Rizzatti (Ref. 22, p. 84) and Freire *et al.* (Ref. 8, p. 33).

In this way, the four components of LGov and KGov that should be governed can be defined according to Table 5.3.

From the dialogue between the several authors' works found in the literature, one can understand the mechanisms and components of LGov and KGov for improving organizational performance. It is important to point out that, besides the mechanisms and components, it is necessary to identify the facilitator environments to govern organizational knowledge and learning.

5.3.5. *Learning environments for LGov and KGov*

Regarding environments of knowledge creation and learning processes, this chapter retrieves the seminal Knowledge Management publications that deal with the physical, virtual, individual, and collective environment

(BA) as drivers of OL.[42–47] In addition to these, Freire and Silva[48] identified eight elements that must be managed in order to constitute a learning environment.

To create these environments, motivation to participate[49] and change of mental model[18,10] to facilitate organizational learning are necessary.

The BA environment encompasses two dimensions of interaction (individual and collective), and of communication medium (face-to-face or virtual), forming four environments: origin (*originating BA*), interaction (*interacting BA* or *dialoguing BA*), systemic (*systemizing BA* or *cyber BA*), and exercise (*exercising BA*).[42–47]

Besides the learning environment BA,[42–47] there is also the collaborative environment 8Cs[48] with organizational culture[50] for sharing knowledge,[2,51,52] collaboration,[53] and raising the level of awareness[44,54] of employees, so that they realize the importance of their role in the value chain and growth of the company; gaining the trust[55] of employees in the organization and in peers; open communication[56] to listen and be heard; and creating skills[57] that will lead the organization to sustainable development.

Table 5.4 presents all the environments and their definitions for LGov and KGov.

According to the dialogue between different authors identified in the literature, one can understand the process of mechanisms, components, and environments of LGov to improve organizational performance.

5.4. Analysis of Results: LGov Framework

Rizzatti and Freire[58] formulated a conceptual model with the dialogue of all the mechanisms, components, and environments pointed out by the literature.

In 2020, Rizzatti[22] extrapolated the model to a framework validated for the scope of public security.

According to the model and framework, it is understood that in order to achieve the intended objectives, one of the Organizational Learning Cycles can be adopted. However, to process it, it is necessary to have certain interconnected components and environments that need appropriate mechanisms that make LGov effective in organizations.[58]

Table 5.4.   LGov and KGov learning environments.

Environments	Definition
Originating BA	Meeting of individuals in a physical space where they exchange feelings, emotions, experiences, and mental models, thus removing the barriers that hinder the exchange of tacit knowledge, through empathy, commitment, and trust.
Interacting BA or Dialoguing BA	Place for dialogue, where individuals share their experiences and skills, converting them into common terms and concepts
Systemizing BA or Cyber BA	Place for combining new explicit knowledge generated from the existing knowledge in the organization, in order to reach a large number of people, through ICTs, as occurs in virtual learning environments.
Exercising BA	Place for individual and virtual interactions, where socialized, externalized, and combined knowledge is again interpreted and internalized by the individuals' cognitive system.
Knowledge	Combination of experiences, values, information, and insights that provides a framework for evaluating and incorporating new experiences and information.
Trust	Expectation that others will act in a compatible, favorable, and credible manner, without the intervention of other individuals.
Sharing	Exchange of knowledge, information, and experiences among members of the organization, resulting in the creation of new knowledge and learning.
Awareness	Developed through actions and interactions of individuals with the organizational environment, which result in the creation and expansion of knowledge and learning.
Collaboration	Process where members of the organization with complementary skills work together to achieve a common goal and share knowledge.
Communication	Exchange or sharing of information and knowledge among individuals, in a bidirectional way and through dialogue.
Culture	Set of rules, values, beliefs, principles, knowledge, and accumulated and shared learning that guides organizational behaviors.
Competency	Demonstration, by the individuals or the organization, of the disposition and characteristics necessary to carry out a certain activity.

Source: Rizzatti (Ref. 22, pp. 121–122).

The conclusion is that, for the processing of LGov, the interrelationship and governance of the interdependence of four mechanisms (KM, Knowledge Cycle, OL Cycle, and KGov), four components (Dynamic and Self-Organizing Capacity, Reliable Information, Shared Vision and Common Goals, and Shared Mental Model), and two Learning Environments (BA and 8Cs).[22]

In the framework to process LGov, it is necessary to implement learning environments (BAs), which involves the creation and sharing of knowledge through individual and collective interaction, and face-to-face and virtual means of communication, and the 8Cs, with the development of knowledge, trust, sharing, awareness, collaboration, communication, culture, and competency.[22]

By creating these environments, the objectives are to motivate individuals to participate in the process and to promote a change in the mental model.

Once the environments conducive to learning are established, it is necessary, from internal and external feedbacks, to check if there is already a standard response to the information, i.e. if the knowledge is already institutionalized, or, if not, through one of the cycles of learning, to check if it is necessary to use the single loop (organizational adaptation), where the organization learns and adapts to new routines to improve its processes; OR the double loop (organizational transformation), in which mental models are transformed to generate new meanings and actions; OR the triple loop (new mental models), where there is the understanding and creation of new processes for generating mental models.[22]

Once the information is understood and the learning cycle necessary for the situation is used, it is possible to start the knowledge cycle, with generative variation, with the exposition of ideas or new ideas that are debated and explained, through knowledge processes; perform selection, to identify the most appropriate idea for the situation; conduct replication, with KM for the adaptation in problem solving and new solutions; and ensure retention, to accumulate and renew the knowledge to be institutionalized.[22]

Once the Knowledge Cycle is concluded, these data, information, and knowledge generated result in the improvement of the organization's routines, processes, results, and performance and in the generation of knowledge assets that need to be governed and transferred, in order to add value to the organization.[22]

The knowledge assets, in turn, need and depend on KGov for the identification of internal and external partnerships, mitigation of costs and risk of knowledge transfer, definition of structures (market and hierarchy) and governance mechanisms (reward systems, trust, directives, culture, contract).[22]

The transfer of knowledge is carried out through intra- and inter-organizational relationships, with the identification of internal and external stakeholders and internal and external feedbacks channels that will be incorporated into human assets to foster mutual learning and generate new knowledge to govern the OL.[22]

Once the knowledge transfer is governed, the knowledge is incorporated into the intellectual and relational capital of the organization to foster intra- and inter-organizational learning, generating the capacity to adapt to new and uncertain situations (organizational change).[22]

As for feedback or feedforward, the LGov framework establishes that feedbacks and feedback channels are essential to generate OL. The feedforward, which refers to the assimilation of new learning,[21] can be identified in the LGov Framework, in the Dimension of the Organizational Learning Cycle, with the elements: OL cycles ([single loop: Organizational Adaptation], double loop [Organizational Transformation], and triple loop [New Mental Models]); generation of knowledge assets; and improvement of routines, processes, performance, and results.[22]

Once the OL is governed, the essential components for change in the organization are achieved, such as shared mental model (beliefs, values, same way of seeing and doing things); shared vision (where organization members want to reach together and collectively) and common goals (sharing the same understanding); reliable information; and a dynamic (able to manage the knowledge base dynamically over time, realigning and reconfiguring its processes) and self-organizing (able to learn autonomously) capacity (organization's ability to learn autonomously).[22]

5.5. Conclusion

This chapter presented the definition and the inter-relationships between the mechanisms, components, and environment to govern knowledge and organizational learning. For the studies of KM, it is important to highlight that KGov is one of the mechanisms of LGov and, this establishes itself as the value chain of knowledge generated by KGov.

Through the LGov Framework proposed by Rizzatti,[22] identified as the most contemporary and empirically validated, it is concluded that LGov is fundamental to continuously improve the processes of OL, corporate governance, KGov, and KM in order to generate individual, group, and organizational learning and knowledge for the improvement of organizational performance. This requires the governance of a series of inter-related elements, being the four mechanisms (Knowledge Management, Knowledge Cycle, Learning Cycle and Knowledge Governance), four components (Dynamic and Self-Organization Capacity, Shared Vision and Common Goals, Reliable Information and Shared Mental Model) and two Learning Environments (BA and 8Cs).

It is suggested to continue this study, deepening this research with the elaboration of a tool to define strategies and action plans to develop organizational learning governance; the definition of indicators for the monitoring and control of the proposed Framework; the identification and description of methods, techniques, and tools to be used by each mechanism, component, and environment of the LGov Framework, in order to treat the knowledge generated by internal and external feedbacks and to identify the way they should be conducted, and to deepen governance of Learning Environments, which are gaps that still need to be studied.

References

1. P.M. Senge. *A quinta disciplina*: a arte e prática da organização que aprende. 29th ed. Rio de Janeiro: Best Seller (2013).
2. I. Nonaka and H. Takeuchi. *Criação de conhecimento na empresa*: como as empresas japonesas geram a dinâmica da inovação. 18th ed. Rio de Janeiro: Campus (2004).
3. S. Pemsel and R. Müller. The governance of knowledge in project-based organizations. *International Journal of Project Management*, **30**(8), 865–876 (2012).
4. A. Grandori. Governance structures, coordination mechanisms and cognitive, models. *Journal of Management and Governance*, **1**(1), 29–47 (1997).
5. A. Grandori. Neither hierarchy nor identity: Knowledge governance mechanisms and theory of the firm. *Journal of Management & Governance*, **5**(3), 381–399 (2001).

6. B. Nooteboom. Learning by interaction: Absorptive capacity, cognitive distance and governance. *Journal of Management and Governance*, **4**(1–2), 69–92 (2000).
7. N.J. Foss. The emerging knowledge governance approach: Challenges and characteristics. *Organization*, **14**(1), 29–52 (2007).
8. P.S. Freire, G.A. Dandolini, J.A. Souza, T.C. Silva and R.M. Couto. Knowledge governance (GovC): The state of the art about the term. *Biblios*, **69**, 21–40 (2017).
9. P.S.W. Fong and L. Chen. Governance of learning mechanisms: Evidence from construction firms. *Journal Construction and Engineering Management*, **138**(9), 1053–1064 (2012).
10. Vitry and E. Chia. Governance learning: Building a network around managerial innovations. *Studies in Public and Non-Profit Governance*, **4**, 275–302 (2015).
11. N.S. Triviños. Introdução à pesquisa em ciências sociais. São Paulo: Atlas (1995).
12. S.C. Vergara. *Projetos e relatórios de pesquisa em administração*. 14th edn. São Paulo: Atlas (2013).
13. P. Demo. *Metodologia do conhecimento científico*. São Paulo: Atlas (2000).
14. A.C. Gil. *Como elaborar projetos de pesquisa*. 4th ed. São Paulo: Atlas (2002).
15. M. Gnerre. Literacy, Power and democracy in Mozambique: The governance os learning from colonization to the present Marshall, J. *American Ethnologist*, **23**(4), 908–909 (1996).
16. R. CarrHill. Literacy, power and democracy in Mozambique: The governance of learning from colonization to the present. *International Journal of Educational Development*, **16**(1), 103 (1996).
17. B. Nooteboom, *A Cognitive Theory of the Firm: Learning, Governance and Dynamic Capabilities*. Cheltenham: Edward Elgar Publishing (2009).
18. A. Löf. Exploring adaptability through learning layers and learning loops. *Environmental Education Research*, **16**(5–6), 529–554 (2010).
19. R. Rządca and M. Strumińska-Kutra. Local governance and learning: In search of a conceptual framework. *Local Government Studies*, **42**(6), 916–937 (2016).
20. L.G. Ollaik and H.M. Ziller. Concepções de validade em pesquisas qualitativas. *Educação e Pesquisa*, **38**(1), 229–242 (2012).
21. M.M. Crossan, H.W. Lane and R.E. White. An organizational learning framework: From intuition to institution. *Academy of Management Review*, **24**(3), 522–537 (1999).

22. G. Rizzatti. *Framework de Governança da Aprendizagem Organizacional.* 283 f. Tese (Doutorado em Engenharia e Gestão do Conhecimento). Universidade Federal de Santa Catarina, Florianópolis (2020).

23. C. Argyris and D. Schon. *Organizational learning.* Reading, MA: Addison-Wesley Publishing Company (1978).

24. G. Probst and B.S.T. Buchel. *Organizational Learning.* London: Prentice Hall (1997).

25. R. Snell and A.M. Chak. The learning organizations: Learning and empowerment for whom? *Management Learning,* **29**(3), 337–364 (1998).

26. M. Keen and S. Mahanty. Learning in sustainable natural resource management: Challenges and opportunities in the Pacific. *Society and Natural Resources: An International Journal,* **19**(6), 497–513 (2006).

27. M. Zollo and S.G. Winter. Deliberate learning and the evolution of dynamic capabilities. *Organization Science: Journal Management Science,* **13**(3), 339–351 (2002).

28. L. Chen and P.S.W. Fong. Visualizing evolution of knowledge management capability in construction firms. *Journal of Construction Engineering and Management,* **139**(7), 839–851 (2013).

29. L. Chen and S. Mohamed. Empirical study of interactions between knowledge management. *Engineering, Construction and Architectural Management,* **14**(3), 242–260 (2007).

30. U. Lichtenthaler and E. Lichtenthaler. A capability-based *Framework* for open innovation: Complementing absorptive capacity. *Journal of Management Studies,* **46**(8), 1315–1338 (2009).

31. B. Uzzi. The sources and consequences of embeddedness for the economic performance of organizations: The network effect. *American Sociological Review,* **61**(4), 674–698 (1996).

32. N.J. Foss. The knowledge governance approach. *SSRN Electronic Journal,* **1**, 1–32 (2005).

33. N.J. Foss and J.T. Mahoney. Exploring knowledge governance. *International Journal Strategic Change Management,* **2**(2/3), 93–101 (2010).

34. N.J. Foss and V. Mahnke. Knowledge management: What can organizational economics contribute? DRUID Working Paper No 03–02, DRUID, Copenhagen Business School, Department of Industrial Economics and Strategy/Aalborg University, Department of Business Studies (2003).

35. I. Ali, A. Musawir and M. Impact of knowledge sharing and absorptive capacity on project performance: The moderating role of social processes. *Journal of Knowledge Management,* **22**(2), 453–477 (2018).

36. S. Pemsel, R. Müller and J. Söderlun., Knowledge governance strategies in project-based organizations. *Long Range Planning*, **49**(6), 648–660 (2016).
37. A. Grandori. Poliarchic governance and the growth of knowledge. In *Knowledge Governance: Processes and Perspectives*, N.J. Foss and S. Michailova (eds.), Oxford: Oxford Scholarship Online (2009).
38. L. Maillet, P. Lamarche, B. Roy and M. Lemire. At the heart of adapting healthcare organizations: Developing a multilevel governance framework. *Emergence: Complexity and Organization*, **17**(3), 1–11 (2015).
39. L. Kahaner. *Competitive Intelligence: How to Gather, Analyze, and Use Information to Move Your Business to the Top*. New York: Touchstone (1996).
40. J. Pierre and B. Peters. *Governing Complex Societies: Trajectories and Scenarios*. Basingstoke: Palgrave Macmillan (2005).
41. K. Sawka. Whither analysis? *Competitive Intelligence Magazine*, **9**(2) (2006).
42. I. Nonaka and N. Konno. The concept of "BA": Building a foundation for knowledge creation. *California Management Review*, **40**(3), 40–54 (1998).
43. I. Nonaka, R. Toyama and N. Konno. SECI, BA and leadership: A unified model of dynamic knowledge creation. In *Managing Knowledge: An Essential Reader*, S.E. Little and T. Ray (eds.), London: Sage Publications (2002).
44. I Nonaka and R. Toyama. The knowledge-creating theory revisited: Knowledge creation as a synthesizing process. *Knowledge Management Research e Practice*, **1**(1), 2–10 (2003).
45. I. Nonaka and R. Toyama. The theory of the knowledge-creating firm: Subjectivity, objectivity and synthesis. *Industrial and Corporate Change*, **14**(3), 419–436 (2005).
46. I. Nonaka and H. Takeuchi, Teoria da criação do conhecimento organizacional. In *Gestão do conhecimento*, H. Takeuchi and I. Nonaka (eds.), Porto Alegre: Bookman, (2008), pp. 54–90.
47. I. Nonaka, G.Von Krogh and S. Voepel. Organization knowledge creation theory: Evolutionary paths and future advances. *Organization Studies*, **27**(8), 1179–1208 (2006).
48. P.S. Freire and S.M. Silva, Modelos de Gestão Organizacional para a sustentabilidade, da participação à colaboração. In *Gestão Empresarial para Sustentabilidade*, Jr Philippi, A, Sampaio, CAC, Fernandes, V. (org.), São Paulo: Manole, pp. 595–612 (2016).
49. W.R. King. *Knowledge Management and Organizational Learning: Annals of Information Systems*. New York: Springer Publishing Company (2009).

50. M. Alavi and D.E. Leidner. Review: Knowledge management and knowledge management systems: Conceptual foundation and research issues. *MIS Quarterly*, **25**(1), 104–136 (2001).
51. H.F. Lin. Knowledge sharing and firm innovation capability: An empirical study. *International Journal of Manpower*, **28**(3–4), 315–335 (2007).
52. T.H. Davenport and L. Prusak. *Conhecimento empresarial: como as organizações gerenciam o seu capital intelectual.* 8th ed. Rio de Janeiro: Campus (2004).
53. N. Hara, P. Solomon, S.L. Kim and D.H. Sonnenwal. An emerging view of scientific collaboration: Scientists' perspectives on collaboration and factors that impact collaboration. *Journal of the American Society for Information Science and Technology*, **54**(10), 952–965 (2003).
54. D. Heaton. Consciousness development for the learning organization. *The Learning Organization*, **24**(6), 401–407 (2017).
55. T. Peeman. *I Trust U. Managing with Trust.* Amsterdam: Pearson Education Benelux (2009).
56. T. Reich and S. Hershcovis. Interpersonal relationships at work. In *Handbook of Industrial and Organizational Psychology*, S. Zedeck, H. Aguinis, W. Cascio, M. Gelfand, K. Leung, S. Parker and J. Zhou (eds.), Washington: American Psychological Association (2011), pp. 223–248.
57. T.L. Fleury and A. Fleury. Construindo o conceito de competência. *Revista de Administração contemporânea*, **5**, 183–196 (2001).
58. G. Rizzatti, and P.S. Freire, Governança da Aprendizagem Organizacional (GovA): o estado da arte sobre o termo, *Revista Espacios*, **41**(3) (2020).

https://doi.org/10.1142/9789811224119_0006

Discovery, Entropy, Organization, and Trust

Bart Nooteboom

Tilburg University,

Tilburg, Netherlands

bart.nooteboom@gmail.com

This chapter discusses the dynamics of knowledge — specifically, how do ideas develop, and how does innovation take place? Here, the "cycle of discovery" that was presented earlier in Nooteboom[1] is discussed: it is a theory of discovery at the individual and at the collective, organizational level. Can it be compared to the ancient cycle of *yin* and *yang* from Taoism? How does it relate to another principle that was proposed by the author, of the organization or communities within them as "focusing device?" Can the notion of "entropy" help in the analysis? Here, connectedness is added to entropy. Then, trust can be added to that.

6.1. Individual and Organizational Discovery

In Nooteboom,[1] the author presented a "cycle of discovery": a cyclical process of the development of intelligence and cognition. Here, the question is whether it is at the individual or organizational level or both. Originally, it was a model for the individual development of ideas, inspired by the work of the developmental psychologist Jean Piaget. The arguments and evidence are discussed in Flavell.[2] The reasoning is largely qualitative, as it usually is in a process theory, however, process is often difficult to measure. It was mainly oriented at the qualitative development of intelligence in children in different stages.

The author has developed and applied it on the level of the organization. Here again, the evidence was casuistic, concerning the internationalization of business firms. A central feature of the process is "generalization," which, in evolutionary terms, serves to subject a given idea, practice, or product to a new "selection environment," where it is subjected to unfamiliar challenges to its survival. For a firm, this can be export to a new market, with different demands and competitors. For science, it can be a new field of application. This forces adaptations to the product. First, as the easiest change, this can be a modification of the composition of familiar elements, in "differentiating assimilation." When that does not work, one adopts and assimilates elements from local practices that succeed where one's own practice does not, in what is called "reciprocation," in hybrids of familiar and new elements. This often yields inefficiencies, complications, duplications, and bottlenecks or inconsistencies that need to be circumvented in "workarounds," which give the incentive for a new structure of the whole, in "accommodation." The reciprocation stage gives the opportunity to find out where the real strength of new and old elements and design principles lies and hints of where in the structure, and how, one might do things differently. This then leads to trials with new designs that may yield something more radically new. In the beginning that is still hesitant and tentative, with alternative forms, to settle in a new "dominant design." Then we are back at the beginning of the cycle.

At both the individual and the organizational levels, learning is here seen as an alternation of "assimilation" — absorption of perceptions in the existing frames of mind or practice, and in the process, when that fails, "accommodation" of the framework. This is consistent with the idea of Thomas Kuhn in the philosophy of science, and the economic principle, that one does not surrender something until the weight of anomalies becomes "excessive." Generalization, i.e. the shift of the environment of application, is consistent with the principle of "allopatric speciation" in evolutionary theory, wherein a novel "species" develops in a new "selection environment." It is also reminiscent of the idea of the philosopher Hegel that one learns by one's failure.

Initially, the move to a new market was intended to escape from the saturation of a home market and to find new sales in an export market, but later was used as a deliberate innovation strategy. This came out in a conversation with a former CEO of Shell. This recognition is important, because the adaptation of a product to a new market disturbs the economies of scale of familiar practice, and the home office of the multinational may block that, until the procedure of adaptation is recognized as an innovation strategy.

The point the author now wants to make is that this procedure has similarities to the ancient cycle of *yin* and *yang* from Taoism.[3] That also is circular, with an alternation of the two principles of *yin* and *yang*. The "feminine" principle of *yin* is associated with softness and darkness — the defensive, yielding to the present order — and the "male" principle of *yang* is associated with hardness and light — the aggressive and the enterprising. In the cycle of discovery, we find the subjection to the novel order, in the new environment, which may be seen as *yang*. Then, the assimilation, in differentiation and reciprocation, can perhaps, be seen as *yin*. The action of more radical renewal, in accommodation to a new order can perhaps be seen as *yang*. The settling of the novelty in a "dominant design" can perhaps be seen as *yin*. Is it legitimate to compare assimilation to *yin*, and accommodation to *yang*?

6.2. Entropy

Let us consider the notion of entropy. Entropy is the number of alternative compositions of components that a system with given properties can have. The mathematical formula for entropy E of a system of n elements i of probability pi is $E = \sum_i^n pi \cdot logpi$. For a system of 2 units of equal probability ½, $E = 1$, called a "bit." For a system of four elements of equal probability, $E = 2$ or two bits. For a system with eight elements of equal probability $E = 3$, or three bits. For a system with n states of equal probability, $E = \log n$. A computational advantage of the log function is that $\log 1/n = $ minus $\log n$.

E increases with the number of elements n and with their "evenness," equality of pi, which is their probability of occurrence, prominence, weight, or legitimacy. The effect of the number of elements is illustrated above, with n ranging from two to eight elements The decrease of E with the "unevenness" of pi is as follows. For the case with three elements n with equal $pi = 1/3$, $E = 1.58$ with $p1 = 2/4$, $p2 = 1/4$, $p3 = 1/4$, $E = 1.50$, This appeals to the intuition that, in an organization, not everything has the same importance or "weight."

Theil[4] used the entropy measure as a measure of concentration of sales in markets or production in industries. Pi here is the share of seller or producer i. If there is only one seller or producer, there is maximum concentration, $E = 1$, i.e. least entropy

The log function $\log n$ increases less than proportionally with n: it increases at a decreasing rate, and its derivative is $1/n$. The increase in entropy has "decreasing returns." As disorder increases, the resistance to further rise increases. Further increase of "evenness" becomes more difficult.

A puzzle then is the following. Nature and culture are rife with Complex Adaptive Systems (CAS) — systems that are composed from subsystems, such as: neutrons, protons, and electrons composing atoms; atoms composing molecules; molecules composing organs; organs composing bodies; bees composing colonies; people composing organizations, firms, and consumers; institutions composing markets, people, and nations; and nations composing supranational entities like the EU.

The puzzle is identified as follows. On one hand, CAS creates order and organization ("complexity") in the coherence of subsystems and thus they decrease entropy. On the other hand, they constitute new units of the system and thereby increase entropy. How can that be? The solution to the puzzle is that while the subsystems integrate into a new order, they lose autonomy. To create the unity or coherence of the higher system, with its new functions, the subsystems are constrained in their operation, losing some functions or narrowing their range, and that constitutes less entropy. In a bee colony, bees are highly specialized as food seekers, gate keepers, soldiers, and feeders of the queen bee.[5]

The formula of entropy is incomplete. One should consider not only the number and "unevenness" of units, but also their relations. It is through internal and external relations that identity is constituted and order is created. If relations break down, this is also a feature of decay, of entropy. The formula for entropy could be extended as follows:

$E = - \sum_{i=1}^{n} pi, logpi + |1 - C/M|$, where C is the number of direct connections between units, and M is its optimum, and the vertical slashes indicate absolute value. That depends on the purpose of the system. The maximum number of connections is $n(n - 1)/2$. That is not necessarily optimal, as in an organization, where if all people connect with all, there is noise that distracts from work. If $C = M$, i.e. the number of connections is at its optimum, the addition to entropy is 0. If $C = 0$, i.e. if there are no connections, the addition is 1. If the number of connections is lower or higher than the optimum, there is addition to entropy. One can picture this as an $n \times n$ matrix with along both axes the n units, and a surface above the matrix that represents the value of interaction. It is likely to have a bulge, at the optimum. It can also have several bulges and multiple optima.

Entropy yields a way of observing the issue of authenticity and conformism: people lose some freedom of action for the sake of the coherence of a community or nation. It applies also to language: in the order of a sentence, the disorder of potential meanings of a word shrinks to a specific meaning determined by the sentence and its context. In addition, when people get disconnected, as is the case in current society, entropy increases.

In the literature on freedom, a distinction is made between "negative" freedom, in the absence of external constraint, and "positive freedom," in access to resources. Here, the subsystem loses negative freedom in constraints of fitting in the higher system, but gains positive freedom in access to new functions offered by the higher system. There is loss of one freedom, and gain of the other.

6.3. Politics

In politics, the trade-off between positive and negative freedom is a big issue. Formerly colonized countries are eager to establish a homogeneous, more equal nation and remove the former colonizers, but thereby they lose the resources built by them. Maalouf[6] gives examples, such as Egypt under Nasser, in the 1950s. An exception was Mandela, who did not chase out the former oppressor, and even asked him to stay in order to contribute. An example of a non-colonized country is France in 1685, where in an attempt to establish a more homogenous religious society, Louis XIV renounced the Edict of Nantes, in which Henri IV had accorded liberty of religion to Protestants, besides Catholicism. This renunciation of the edict led to a massive move of Protestants (Huguenots) to Amsterdam and other places to the North of France, which enriched the culture and economy there, to the detriment of France.

If the bane of nature is the thrust to evenness, the bane of society is the opposite: the push toward more unevenness. In capitalism, the ideal is "perfect competition," with many small competitors, but it led to an inexorable march toward inequality, dominance, and concentration in monopolies, oligopolies, and increasing inequality of income and wealth. As Maalouf shows, this occurs repeatedly in political history.

Like many others, Maalouf narrates the conservative revolution that started, in the West, with Margaret Thatcher, followed by Ronald Reagan in the US in 1978–1979. It was motivated by resistance and revulsion with respect to excesses of socialism, exhibited by the miners' strike that caused a blackout; feelings that the indigent were being "pampered" by social security, while being "shy of work"; and loss of traditional values of family and nation. The conservative revolution sought more "evenness," in the sense of self-sufficiency, less dependence, less government intervention, less social security, and more market freedom, in liberalization and privatization. Politically it was engendered by the collapse of the Soviet Union and communism, which discredited the socialist drive toward egalitarianism. The Soviet Union combined evenness of ownership, access, and rights, formally at least, with evenness also in ideas, lack of variety and freedom of initiative, and lack of opportunity for connecting them. That prevented dynamism and innovativeness, which broke up the union.

The Iranian Revolution, at the same time, was anti-communist but also anti-capitalist, and was conservative in seeking a return to traditional religion, values, and habits. This spread to other Muslim countries.

The best society has a combination of evenness and egalitarianism, in access, rights, and legitimacy, with unevenness in ideas, allowing for diversity of views and initiative, and connectedness to produce cross-fertilization of those ideas, enabling further cognitive and spiritual development. The first two have been characteristic of liberalism, but with the conservative revolution, the connectedness of people unraveled. Maalouf traced that to the revival of Adam Smith's "invisible hand," which led to a surge of disconnection and egoism. This was not only a matter of greed for possessions, entertainment, power, and attention, but also an urge to ensconce oneself in a fort of identity and fight others. It is also due to a lack of external threat that unifies. During the initial wave of the corona-virus, people came together, to some extent, in conformance to shared order, but now that the virus is receding, in some places, people revert to their urge for individuality and diversion. What to think of Dutch young-sters who seek diversion in the Belgian resort of Knokke, and create ruckus by violating the distancing imposed because of COVID-19 restrictions, and engage in scuffles with the police, in protest against the closure of pubs at one 'o clock at night?

Suppression by authorities of diverging ideas and their dissemination has gained enormous power with the use of new technologies of surveillance, for monitoring phones and hacking computers, desirable to fight terrorism and crime, but threatening privacy and opening up opportunities for the control of thought and behavior. More heinous even, is the disarming of diverging ideas by breaking down ideas in general, after the crumbling of truth, with fake news. Control is hardly needed then.

6.4. Knowledge

The second law of thermodynamics says that the entropy of a closed system can only increase, such as in the cooling off of a container of hot water in a cool environment: the movement of molecules, which constitutes temperature, becomes more equal, in the transfer to molecules in the environment, and the energy gets distributed. Energy dissipates.

An organism can only survive and stay alive when it is not a closed system, combating the process of increasing entropy by taking in energy in the form of food and excreting refuse. Increasing entropy has been seen as loss of order, as when a body decays when no longer being fed. When left alone, an organization also dissipates, descending into chaos and resulting in dissolution of order, with information being misunderstood and ties falling apart. One task of management is to prevent this from occurring and maintaining some order. Scientists try to create order by reducing rich phenomena to a few principles.

A question the author has in the theory of knowledge is this: does new knowledge increase or decrease the entropy of a stock of knowledge? At first thought, one may think that it increases entropy because it adds to the stock of possibilities. However, this is not so if, in fact, the new knowledge invalidates much of existing knowledge, reducing the number of relevant elements, yielding integration and unification, reducing the number of laws, which is what physics, for example, is continually trying to do, to increase order. The endeavor of the present book may be seen in that way. In trying to find connections, similarities, and underlying fundamental principles, the author tries to reduce entropy. This does not apply to cultural products such as literature, music, and pictorial art. We still marvel at old cultural productions and treasure them.

In turning to a knowledge system, such as an organization, let us distinguish the use of existing knowledge and the production of new knowledge. When the number of people n in an organization increases, the totality of knowledge produced and used by all people has decreasing returns to scale, as in the log function of entropy, due to information overload, gradually exhausting individual absorptive capacity, especially in present times, with a diversity of media, including social media, and explosion of content, sources, and channels, due to ease of access, so that the efficiency of information use increases less than proportionally to n. As according to the logarithm of n, in the formula for entropy.

The production of new knowledge, on the other hand, arises from the interaction between people, so what counts is the number of connections between them. The number of possible direct connections between n components, is $C = n(n - 1)/2$. On the one hand, this may *clog* up communication to the detriment of action and decision-making, but that may already be included in the increase of entropy. On the other hand, the number of possible connections increases the potential for novelty by interaction.

The derivative, a measure of the increase of the number of possible connections, is $n - 1/2$. Beyond the minimum of $n = 2$, the increase of potential combinations is greater than the increase of entropy, whose derivative is $1/n$. Thus, innovation potential increases faster than entropy and the loss of order. Chaos gives rise to opportunities. Perhaps this is a way to look at the difference between democracy and authoritarianism. In the latter, order is greater, but opportunities for renewal are smaller. The price for the higher order is more rigidity.

The model should be further refined. In other research, the author proposed "optimal cognitive distance." Higher cognitive distance increases misunderstanding, but at the same time increases the potential for innovative "novel combinations." The conclusion is that, for innovation, one should seek an "optimal" distance: large enough to yield innovative potential, but no too large to realize it, due to lack of understanding. If understanding decreases linearly with distance d, and novelty potential increases linearly, productive outcome is a quadratic, inverse-u–shaped function of distance. If understanding decreases according to $1 - ad$, and novelty potential increases with bd, then optimum innovative performance I is achieved when $d = 1/2\ a$, and $I = b/2a(1 - 1/2a)$.

If we take this into account an increased number of potential combinations at too high a distance, in a fragmented society of people thinking differently too much, holes will arise in the fabric of society, innovative potential will decreases, and democracy will not realize its potential.

6.5. Organizational Focus

The author now further applies the notions of cognitive distance and entropy to organizations.

Tsoukas and Chia[7] take a process view of an organization as a continual process of change, in interaction with its environment. Organizations are not to be seen as static objects that change, but, on the contrary, as constructs to stabilize change and reduce decay, which occurs continually anyway, such as in organizational structure and procedures. This stabilization often overshoots in organizational inertia and institutionalized myopia.

Organizational purpose is said to require "organizational culture." However, it is a bit too vague. The author proposes[8] that purpose is achieved by means of an organizational "cognitive focus," which has both intellectual and moral/emotional features, concerning how to deal with the dissolution of order, uncertainty, or risk of relations and how to deal with each other. It plays the same role as a "paradigm," directing thought and action in science To function as a coordinated system of actions, organizations need some more or less specialized shared language or jargon, perceptions, understanding, and morality, as part of organizational culture.[9] Without such focus of shared perceptions, meanings, understandings, and values, too much effort, time, and aggravation would have to be spent to disambiguate meanings, eliminate misunderstanding, set priorities, establish directions, coordinate activities, align incentives, and negotiate the terms of collaboration. This is the view of organization as a system for "sense-making,"[10] "collective mind,"[11] and system of "shared meanings."[12] Witt[13] offered a related view of entrepreneurs and managers as providing "cognitive leadership."

The focus includes fundamental assumptions concerning the human being and its environment, concerning, for example, whether the human being is more self-centered or altruistic, risk is seen as a threat or opportunity, the world is to be mastered or submitted to, is predictable or uncertain, nature is to be exploited or saved.

A wider organizational focus, with more cognitive distance, has greater entropy. This is another puzzle: a wider focus entails more "evenness" in the sense of less concentration in a dominant perspective or practice, and hence larger entropy. On the other hand, there is more variety of perspective, which seems to indicate less evenness, and hence less entropy. Apparently, we should distinguish between difference in "content" and difference in "weight," "dominance," access, or "legitimacy." With wider focus, there is less dominance of one or a few perspectives, and a wide variety, but with more variety of content. With more different perspectives of equal weight, or "legitimacy," hence higher entropy, there are more possibilities of achieving "novel combinations," and hence higher innovation potential. Moreover, when new knowledge is produced, in interaction, and through "novel combinations," entropy is reduced again, through invalidating old knowledge and "creative destruction." In other words, the higher entropy of more elements can yield novel combinations that, when successful, reduce entropy.

In the system of many small, independent firms, i.e. "the industry" or "the market," entropy is large, and in a production department within a firm, oriented at efficient production, focus is tight and entropy is small. Within the firm, one can have different communities, some with narrow focus (production departments), and some with relatively wide focus, constituting "corporate entrepreneurship" (in marketing or R&D). It has the advantage of using the resources of the large firm, where risks are spread, but is more constrained in its scope than an outside, independent entrepreneur.

There is a stream in the literature of viewing entropy as an overload of communication between units, crowding out work, and increasing with the number of units n of an organization.[14] The author thinks this requires a different model than that of entropy.

With n units, the number of potential bilateral links between them is $n(n - 1)/2$, which increases quadratically with n, thus more than proportionately with n, while log n increases less than proportionately. As the number of links increases, communication explodes and may crowd out work. That is why communication has been constrained by inserting hierarchical levels, restricting communication to the next higher and lower levels, at the price of less contact between top and bottom of an organization, and higher management becoming "footloose." An alternative is the "hub and spoke" structure, with all communication going through the hub, apportioning only relevant information to others, not to unduly disturb work, in the spokes. That has the drawback of potential information overload in the hub.

If entropy does not include this effect of ties, is it sufficient? As discussed, it results from an overload of information throughout the system, exceeding the absorptive capacity of its units, creating missed information and misunderstanding and distortion of work.

Now, if we weigh the cognitive distances between any pair of links with a quadratic, inverse-u–shaped function of the cognitive distance, we might obtain a measure of innovative potential.

How does focus work, and how is it implemented? On the competence side, focus is needed to enable people to understand each other and connect complementary knowledge, without unduly restricting variety and creativity. On the governance side, focus is needed to motivate people to collaborate, share, and connect knowledge, without unduly limiting autonomy, ambition, and competitive spirit. Organizational focus also has a function of both selection and adaptation of people. Selection occurs by way of recruitment of people, but often based on self-selection of personnel joining the organization because they feel an affinity to it, and adaptation occurs through socialization into the firm and training of incoming personnel. To facilitate these functions, focus must be embodied in some visible form. Such form is needed for several reasons. One is to function as a signaling device to outsiders. That is needed as a basis of the (self) selection process of incoming staff, and for recognition and identification by other stakeholders, such as customers and suppliers. Organizations develop their own specialized semiotic systems, in language, symbols, role models, metaphors, myths, and rituals. This is what we call organizational culture. It differs between organizations to the extent that they have different goals and have accumulated different experiences, in different industries, technologies, and markets. The central difference between firm and market is that in the former such focus is made and in the latter it is not, or to a much lesser extent (there still is a remaining, shared cognitive focus from shared industrial and market structure, and national or regional culture), or to some extent in forms of collaboration with some shared understanding. Thus, the market has the higher potentiality of variety of performance, and the firm has the higher actuality of performance.

Cognitive activities in an organization require some embodiment to crystallize, and to direct and stabilize cognition and communication within the organization. Here we find symbols, such as logos and style of advertisement and external communication. With regard to the internal function of coordination, we find the exemplary behavior of organizational heroes, often a founder of the organization, and corresponding myths and rituals. More formalized forms of organization are procedures, for reporting, decision-making, recruitment, contracting, and the like.

6.6. Science

Biological evolution entails carriers of genes. These carriers are called "interactors" because they interact with a selection environment on the basis of properties, derived from the genes, called selectors because they generate properties on the basis of which the interactor is selected or not

Concerning the evolution of knowledge, in particular science, there are problems for evolutionary theory. It is not directly clear what the success criterion of evolutionary selection is for knowledge. In biology, it was survival. What does that mean in science? Do knowledge workers die when their ideas fail? No, rather the ideas die out. Therefore, if ideas are selectors, they are also interactors.

How does entropy work here? When interactors are selected out, this decreases entropy. Replication initially increases entropy, but enables novel combinations that may again reduce entropy. In sexual reproduction in biology, these combinations are chromosome crossovers.

Kuhn[15] famously claimed that scientists do not seek falsification of theory, as Popper[16] said they should. That is too much to expect. Their scientific achievements form the basis for reputation and rewards in the form of further careers and room for further research, and they often seek to protect that by trying to confirm rather than falsify their theories. Falsification is more a matter of competition between scientists in the "forum" of a scientific community, mostly via journals. Popper later granted that it is rational to hold on to theories and milk them for all they are worth and to find out where their real limitations lie.[17]

In evolutionary terms, communities of scientists, in "research programs," proposed by Lakatos,[18] would be "species," and, for evolutionary theory to work, there must be "isolating mechanisms" between them to prevent the species from mixing. In industries, there is some evidence of that, with distinctive industry structures and logics. However, it is a known source of innovation when boundaries between industries are crossed, in "novel combinations," as professed by Joseph Schumpeter. A prime example is the Internet, as a combination of the formerly separate industries and technologies of computing and communication.

Here also, replication in communication, in publications, meetings at conferences and seminars, and PhD training is more a matter of cognitive reduction, amplification, and reconstruction than a matter of replication. As in the case of organizations and their capabilities, the survival and replication of purported replicators is not entirely dependent on success of interactors under selection. Here, in some disciplines, more than in others, (even) more opportunities exist to mold the selection environment than in the case of firms in markets, in opportunities to create a selection environment of dedicated scientific associations with their proprietary journals.

Scholarly societies or disciplines, schools of thought, or research programs may perhaps be seen as species. What, then, would be the "isolating mechanisms" here? Like organizations in general, scientific societies have a shared cognitive focus of basic assumptions and views. Different research programs do seem to have such mechanisms, in "protective belts," and this generates misunderstanding and disagreement concerning what is relevant between such programs. That is an effective isolating mechanism. Scientific journals are often attached to such schools and are not open to submissions from rival schools. Rejected or ignored groups then often institute their own proprietary journals. In this way, there are obstacles to interdisciplinarity. From an evolutionary perspective, that is a good thing, in the separation of species. However, this is perhaps one of the reasons to doubt the validity of evolutionary theory concerning science. There is symbiosis between species, but in science it is rare. Scientists want to tender to their turf.

A case that the author knows of is "behavioral economics," which employs insights concerning unreflected, subconscious choice on the basis of non-rational behavioral heuristics. However, the author has heard from applied psychologists that they turn away, because there also economists want to force everything into the framework of rational optimizing choice, while the point is that this is not and cannot be done.

6.7. Trust

Fruitful relations require trust. Trust is a complex notion and cannot be fully treated here.[19] A survey of some crucial, notions, and the sources of trustworthiness is provided here. Trust is a disposition to trusting behavior, which entails giving room for the conduct of another, and that gives risk or uncertainty to the extent that you are dependent on that other. Trust then is being vulnerable.to the conduct of another, and yet believing that "it will be all right."

There is positive and negative freedom. In negative freedom, there are no outside constraints to action, in a hierarchy or contract, so that one can "go one's own way." Trust gives negative freedom to the other. That creates risk, which requires the virtue of courage. Without risk, there are no relations. Positive freedom goes further than the absence of constraints, in giving means and access to resources. Fruitful relations give both negative and positive freedom.

There are corresponding notions of negative and positive power. In negative power, one limits negative freedom, constraining the other's choice. Positive power gives more freedom and options of choice, enhancing both negative and possibly positive freedom.

Power depends on the capital one has. That can be economic capital, or social, cultural (including intellectual, technological), or symbolic capital (Bourdieu). An example of social capital is reputation or authority arising from position or connectedness in networks.

There is a difference between trust in competence, the ability to execute an agreement, and intentional trust, in the intention and commitment to execute the agreement to the best of one's ability. Also, there are different levels of trust: one can have trust in things, e.g. individuals, organizations, and wider systems, such as the economy or the political system. One must have trust on all levels. Trust in an individual who is not supported by his boss or organization is risky. The same goes for trust in an organization with internal violation of rules or principles. Trust in an organization at odds with its institutional environment is not reliable.

The problem is that when something goes wrong, one does not directly know the cause. It can be due to an accident that is no one's fault or it can be due to carelessness, lack of attention, or outright opportunism. Especially the cheater will claim that it was an "error." In other words, there is "causal ambiguity." That uncertainty is of fundamental importance. One must now also trust someone's openness about what is going on. That uncertainty is of fundamental importance. One must now also trust someone's openness about what is going on in communication. Trust also depends on circumstances. One is more competent in some things than in others, and cheating depends on the extent of temptation. What is the pressure of punishment and moral dedication? What restrictions are there in the form of multiple roles and obligations to family, the community, and friends? What loyalty will take precedence?

Table 6.1.   Sources of (intentional) trustworthiness.

	In the Environment of the Relation	Inside the Relation
Control on the basis of self-interest	Contract, institutional oversight, reputation	Hierarchical oversight, dependence, incentives, hostages
Ethics, altruism	Norms, values, habits	Empathy, identification, friendship, routine

Source: Nooteboom.[19]

In short, trust is a predicate with four "places": someone (subject) has trust in someone (object, person, organization, system) in some respect (competence, intention) under some conditions. Trust is also both the cause and the consequence of a relation. It functions as the basis for the relation, but must also be built up in it. Intentional trust has several sources,[19] as shown in Table 6.1.

This is about intentional trustworthiness, not competence. There is a distinction between trust and control. There are sources of both, inside and outside the relation, in the institutional environment.

One can control a relation with means outside the relation, such as a legally enforceable contract, institutional supervision, and reputation. Reputation depends on the involvement of a community. Within a relation, there can be hierarchical supervision and dependence.

Beyond control, there can be trust outside the relation institutional trust in people in general, based on morality and ethics, associated with culture. Ethics is theory about good and bad, and morality is specific rules. Within the relation, there can be a more personal bonding on the basis of family and friendship, or tribe or clan and in experience of people with each other, that may be routinized or no longer reflected.

Table 6.1 can be used as a diagnostic tool to analyze what sources might be present and as a therapeutic instrument to craft or elicit a source.

References

1. B. Nooteboom. *Learning and Innovation in Organisations and Economies*. Oxford: Oxford University Press (2000).

2. J.H. Flavell. *The Developmental Psychology of Jean Piaget*. Princeton, NJ: Van Nostrand (1967).
3. Wilhelm, R. *I Ching or Book of Changes*. London: Penguin (2003).
4. H. Theil. *Economics and Information Theory*. Chicago: Rand McNally (1967).
5. B. Testa and L.B. Kier. Emergence and dissolvence in the self-organization of complex systems. *Entropy*, (2), 1–25 (2000).
6. A. Maalouf. *Le naufrage des civilisations*, Paris: Grasset (2019).
7. H. Tsoukas and R. Chia. On organizational becoming: Rethinking organisational change. *Organization Science*, **13**(5), 567–582 (2002).
8. B. Nooteboom. *A Cognitive Theory of the Firm; Learning, Governance and Dynamic Capabilities*. Cheltenham UK: Edward Elgar (2009).
9. E.H. Schein. *Organizational Culture and Leadership*, San Francisco: Jossey-Bass (1985).
10. K.F. Weick. *Sensemaking in Organisations*. Thousand Oaks, CA: Sage (1995).
11. K.F. Weick and K.H. Roberts. Collective mind in organizations. *Administrative Science Quartery*, (1993), reprinted in M.D. Cohen and L.S. Sproull (eds.), *Organizational Learning*, London: Sage (1996), pp. 330–358.
12. L. Smircich. Organization as shared meaning. In *Organizational Symbolism*, L.R. Pondy, P.J. Frost, G. Morgan and T.C. Dandridge (eds.), Greenwich, CN: JAI Press, (1983), pp. 55–65.
13. U. Witt. On the proper interpretation of 'evolution' in economics and its implications for production theory. *Journal of Economic Methodology*, **11**, 125–146 (2004).
14. R. Janow. Shannon entropy applied to productivity of organisations. *IEEE Xplore* (2003).
15. T. Kuhn. Trust also depends on conditions. In *The Structure of Scientific Revolutions*, 2nd ed. London: University of Chicago Press (1970).
16. K.R. Popper. *The Logic of Scientific Discovery*. London: Hutchison (1959).
17. I. Lakatos and A. Musgrave. *Criticism and the Growth of Knowledge*. Cambridge: Cambridge University Press (1970).
18. I. Lakatos. *The Methodology of Scientific Research Programmes*. Cambridge: Cambridge University Press (1978).
19. B. Nooteboom. *Trust: Forms, Foundations, Functions, Failures and Figures*. Cheltenham, UK: Edward Elgar (2002).

Part II

Organizational Learning

The Learning Process of Project Teams: An Experience-Based Approach

Ana María Ortegón*,‡ *and Andrea Valéria Steil*†,§

**Empreser Tejido Empresarial, Consultora*
Cr 44b 22–23, Bogotá 111321275, Colombia

†*Department of Psychology,*
Federal University of Santa Catarina,
Trindade University Campus, Florianópolis 88040970, Brazil

‡*aortegon@empreser-te.com*
§*andrea.steil@ufsc.br*

Existing evidence associates team learning and project-based work with competitive advantages within organizations. However, few studies describe how the learning process of project teams occur and its implications on organizational governance. This chapter describes the learning process of a project team in a company in the industrial infrastructure sector from the theoretical perspective of group processes, which aims

115

to analyze teams within a real context. Evidence was drawn from primary sources, through interviews with the team and some of its stakeholders, as well as from secondary sources such as institutional documents. Conclusions indicate that the dynamic components of the team setting and the learning behaviors that take place under a temporal perspective are relevant to learning, according to Gersick's Punctuated-Equilibrium Model. Results also point to the dynamic nature of the team's learning goals.

7.1. Introduction

Organizational theories have adopted the learning metaphor to understand how organizations acquire, use, and expand their knowledge to develop competencies, innovate, improve performance, or develop human capital. Organizations that perform project-based work prove to organize knowledge resources[1] with speed and flexibility to meet market demands in a personalized and differentiated manner.[2]

Projects pursue objectives through collaboration. Members of a project team have complimentary experiences, profiles, and perspectives, turning projects into environments conducive to learning and knowledge sharing.[3–5] Team learning depends on the harmonious interaction of its members so that reflection and action are made possible.[3,4] Harmonious interaction is a challenge for project teams, where the loss of knowledge is one of the main issues.[5] Therefore, this chapter presents a qualitative longitudinal case study with the aim to comprehend the learning process of the project team.

Comprehending the learning process of project teams within real settings directly contributes to the governance of organizations that are project-based and to the governance of the projects themselves. Within the organizational context, governance focuses on strategic issues, control issues, and issues of managing relations among different stakeholders.[6] Project governance understands this to be "the use of systems, structures of authority and processes to allocate resources and coordinate or control activity in a Project."[7] Given the fact that project governance regulates the establishment of goals through responsible decision-making processes and supports reaching these goals, a better understanding of the learning process of the team responsible for executing the project promotes better decision-making at the project level.

In addition to helping the governance of projects themselves, comprehending the longitudinal process of team learning during a real project helps organizational governance as it adds meso-level information to a macro-governance perspective.[6] Increasing information at a meso-level amplifies knowledge of the systemic nature of organizational functions, their culture, and real decision-making processes.

7.2. Conceptual Bases

7.2.1. *Team learning*

A work team is a combination of two or more people who interact to reach common goals through actions and interdependent workflow, relevant tasks, and the fulfillment of specific rolls and responsibilities.[8] There are at least two perspectives of analysis for team development[9,10]:

(1) one that presupposes a team goes through sequential steps of development, conflict, normalization, and performance, denominated as the traditional approach; and

(2) one that indicates a team alternates between phases of inertia and transition, denominated as the punctuated-equilibrium model, typical of temporary teams. Under this perspective, inertia is characterized by patterns of interaction established during team formation, which remains until around the half-mark of the final deadline of the project. From the half-mark until the end of the project, significant changes begin to take place in the patterns of team interaction in a short amount of time.[11]

Regardless of the perspective, team development brings to light its adaptability and entails learning.

In this chapter, team learning is defined as the iterative process of reflection and action behaviors servicing an organizational goal.[3,12,13] Reflective behaviors are those that help to develop new ideas within the team — i.e. behaviors such as requesting feedback, exchanging information, asking for help, discussing mistakes and problems, and analyzing prior experiences. Reflective behaviors involve collaborative development of ideas originating from agreements between team members. Action-focused behaviors are those that put new ideas into practice. Examples of action-focused behaviors are decision-making, changes, improved performance, plans of action, problem resolution, and experimenting with and transferring knowledge. The definition of learning adopted in this chapter is in line with the group processes research perspective,[14] as our objective is to comprehend work teams within real settings.

7.2.2. Projects

Projects represent an organizational format that is flexible, temporal, restricted in resources, and where teams are responsible for its execution. These teams are formed by people with diverse profiles that bring together knowledge and experiences to reach the objectives of the project.[15]

Different from traditional teams, project teams face settings with a high risk of failure[16] due to the singularities of their work. The characteristics of project settings are[17,18]: the provisional nature of both the projects and members of the executing team[15,19] as well as their unique nature[1,17,20]; project life cycle[20]; and a potential barrier to team learning.[19] Situations that affect project team learning were identified in this research. Among these are contextual and managerial factors at organizational level, contextual factors at team level, and learning processes.

7.3. Method

The study focused on comprehending the reality of a project team through observation and data collection that demonstrated how team learning occurs from the participants' perspective. Therefore, a single case study was developed under the constructivist and qualitative approach.

7.3.1. Study design

The case was developed based on two aspects: the constructs that help comprehend the phenomenon and the description of the work setting of the team. The constructs were: (1) learning behaviors focused on reflection, (2) learning behaviors focused on action, (3) project team, and (4) member interaction. The research setting was a large Colombian company from the construction sector (Ingenio, a fictitious name).

A team with the following characteristics was intentionally selected such that it: (1) operated with defined beginning and end; (2) faced problems due to the complex nature of the project; and (3) had advanced 60%–70% into activities. The chosen team realized the assembly of oval tanks for a residual water treatment station in Colombia. When the investigation began, the team comprised 15 people.

7.3.2. Participants

The participants in this study were all the team members — staff with administrative responsibilities, supervisors, and two executives from the Bogotá central office. All members participated voluntarily and signed an informed consent form.

7.3.3. Sources of evidence

Four sources of information were used[21]: (1) Interviews: five in depth[21] and six short ones; (2) Focal groups — two focal groups were developed; (3) Participation in meetings — interaction and exchange of ideas were observed in four team meetings; and (4) Documentation — manuals and different kinds of reports were analyzed.

7.3.4. Data analysis

A thematic analysis was realized, which identified, organized, and articulated themes[22] about how learning behaviors are perceived by participants. Information was identified, encoded, and categorized. The process of analysis was supported by NVivo software.

7.4. Results

The structured of the thematic analysis is composed of two themes and subthemes, and four theoretical propositions (Table 7.1). This structure

Table 7.1. Topics, subtopics, and propositions of thematic analysis.

Topics	Subtopics	Propositions
Dynamic components connected to team learning	• Base conditions of the project: inheritance and challenges • Team configuration	**Proposition 1:** The plan of action presented to the team on the first project meeting defines explicit learning goals: routine tasks, basic norms for job execution, action strategies proposed by technical managers and transferred to other members of the team. **Proposition 2:** The performance gap of the team, identified in the transition period, propels it to reformulate learning tasks according to task complexity and goal realization within project time frame.
Team learning behaviors	• Emphasis on action behaviors • Iteration behaviors of reflection-action	**Proposition 3:** During the inertia phase, a learning pattern presents itself, directed by the team technical managers, and which emphasizes action-focused behaviors. These behaviors are changes in routine tasks, continuous improvement, transferring knowledge from managers with a technical profile to other members of the team, and the execution of plans of action according to decisions and the initial plan of project managers.
Team learning behaviors	• Iteration behaviors of reflection-action	**Proposition 4:** As the team reaches the midpoint of the project, its members become aware of an existing gap between their present reality and the expected results. This awareness moves the team to a complete iterative cycle of reflective behaviors (analysis of experiences, sharing information, requesting help, and individual learning as a driving force for team learning) and of action (experimenting, improved performance, changes, plans of action, decision-making, transfer of knowledge, and searching for knowledge outside the team) which involves all team members, in order to achieve project goals.

demonstrates that team learning has a temporal perspective: learning behaviors change throughout the project, according to the phases of inertia and transition proposed by the punctuated-equilibrium model.[11]

The theoretical propositions synthesize the direction of the team's learning process from the first meeting up to the transition phase. The case narrative is presented in the sequence, according to this thematic structure.

7.4.1. *A team that learns on the path to innovation*

The team was formed to finalize the assembly of six digester tanks of large dimensions and complex technologic characteristics. The team was assembled to finalize the building project that had been in progress for over a year and which had a nine-month deadline.

7.4.1.1. *Dynamic components connected to team learning: Inheritance and challenges*

The history of the Ingenio–Investor–Trust relationship, and the fact that it was a project already in progress, originated two components to be analyzed: the base conditions of the project and the configuration of the team.

Various issues marked the start of the project: (1) difficult relationship with the client; (2) technical challenges resulting from new tasks; (3) conflict among team members and the lack of task interdependence; and (4) profitability issues. These conditions generated the following explicit learning objectives for the team: "Reconstitute the relationship with the client" (Interview 1), gaining client confidence and demonstrating ability and technical quality[16]; and eradicate communication issues and poor work environment inherited from the prior contract. This meant improving the emotional and psychological climate of the team, considered to be learning antecedents.[13]

Team configuration throughout the project: This component allowed for a temporal perspective of team learning to be identified,[23] which can be explained through the punctuated-equilibrium model.[11] Changes in the inertia phase at the end of the project occurred as follows. In the first team meeting, the manager shared the performance strategy, the interaction patterns, and how to execute tasks and the setting of the project. Inertia phase 1 (Figure 7.1) occurred between month one and month six of the project. As soon as the team was formed, management defined its performance framework. However, building execution presented

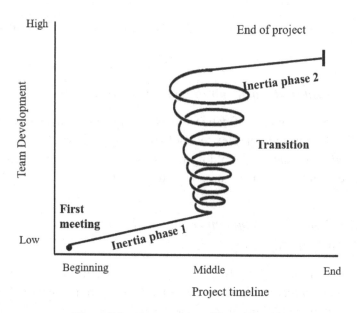

Figure 7.1. Punctuated-equilibrium model.

problems regarding realization of tasks and coordination between areas, hindering progress and learning. Tasks such as those described in Table 7.2 hampered team articulation due to lack of experience, technical knowledge, references for evaluating performance, and procedure standardization. As described by Savelsbergh *et al.*,[4] task demands may thwart learning within construction teams. If there is insufficient information, competition, or task overload, learning behaviors diminish.

The speeches in Table 7.2 suggest little clarity as to how to perform tasks and comprehend their connections, interfering with team learning behaviors.[13] Furthermore, the team was not perceived as a safe place for assuming interpersonal risks and exchanging ideas (Interview 7). This represented little psychological security and an adverse environment for learning. Problem resolution remained restricted to project managers, with little participation from the team members and insufficient meetings for sharing knowledge.

The transition began (spiral Figure 7.1) when the team noticed that it had reached nearly 80% of execution timeline and presented significant delays. The middle point (from the half-mark to the final deadline) of the

Table 7.2. Task characteristics.

	New Tasks	Interdependent Tasks	Risky Tasks
Sample speeches	"[We] have to install scaffolding. The planned timeline for installation was 5 days and increased to 20 days" (Interview 1)	"[...] installing the superior cone had to be done with precision so that it might adjust to the digester [...]. Jobs with more resources had to be done [...]" (Interview 4)	"Such a project has a high level of risk [...] to enter the digester. There obviously were controls, but at a certain point it was uncontrollable" (Interview 9)

Box 7.1. Speech that expresses the beginning of the transition.

I think the alarms sounded around May or June, when we realized we had a significant delay and many problems [...]. [...] the pressure began in June [...]. We knew we wouldn't be able to meet the deadline. We needed to develop a plan of action, that's when the heavy work began. (Interview 7)

[...] I think the meetings first thing in the morning were a huge improvement in how the project was managed. At the meetings, people such as the foremen, the surveyor, other leaders started to come. So, people with qualities that were not being explored started to be seen, day-to-day issues of the project came to light, and solutions started to emerge [...] (Interview 7)

---

project raised the alert about the nearing final date (Box 7.1).[11] From the point of the schedule alert forward, management implemented new actions, holding monitoring meetings that were more frequent and interactive. Additionally, the vice-president of operations of the company came on site to the plant, and a few technical managers left the project. Team management changed. The sharing of information improved the comprehension of objectives and critical issues, and team members engaged in the analyses of project challenges and solidified ideas to efficiently advance results.

The new action framework changed team structure and communication, contributing to psychological security, favorable emotional climate, and learning behaviors. The second phase of inertia began as of September 26, when the team delivered the products for which it was responsible, according to project execution deadline, and staff naturally began to leave.

The reduced team continued to execute tasks that depended on client input. The contract was extended until December 2017. During this period, time pressure diminished, and the daily meetings ended. The second phase of inertia was maintained until the end of the project.

7.4.1.2. *Team learning behaviors*

Team development during the inertia and transition phases made it possible to observe differences in learning, i.e. the iterative process of reflection–action behaviors.

Figure 7.2(a) illustrates the learning process of the studied team, considering: (1) the base conditions of the project (left side, gray strips); (2) team configuration (straight and spiral lines, in the center); and (3) learning behaviors (icons in the center). In the inferior horizontal axis is described the situations or circumstances typical of each moment. Figure 7.2(b) presents the captions that describe icons on Figure 7.2(a).

Emphasis on action behaviors: The first inertia phase had a misaligned pattern of reflection–action behaviors, with more emphasis on action than on reflection (Figure 7.2(a)). Decisions and execution of actions were poorly reflected upon (Speech 1, Table 7.3), and planning was rushed or performed based on previous experiences that were irrelevant to current task characteristics. Analysis of prior experiences (Speech 2, Table 7.3), which were focused on their similarities to previous projects, restricted the team's ability to create new ideas.

However, in the face of the complex characteristics of the tasks, this knowledge was insufficient for achieving expected results, limited the intensive use of the team's knowledge, and delayed problem resolution. During this phase, reflection was of little use in directing the team toward a performance that was efficient and productive.[24]

Emphasis on action behaviors: The first inertia phase had a misaligned pattern of reflection–action behaviors, with more emphasis on action than

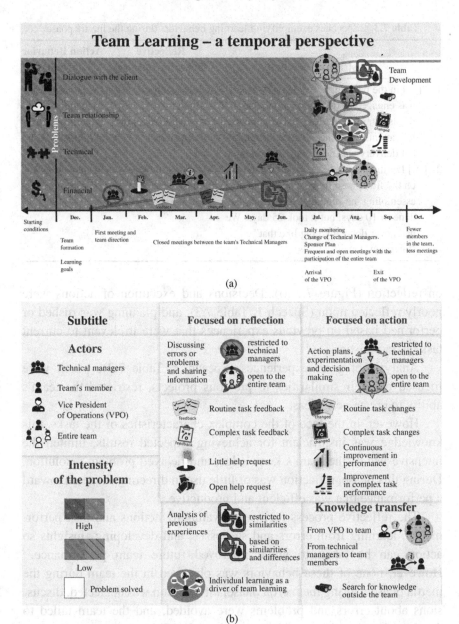

Figure 7.2 (a) Team learning: A time perspective based on the punctuated-equilibrium model. (b) Description of icons in Figure 7.2(a).

Table 7.3. Speeches exemplifying learning behaviors during the inertia phase.

Illustrative Speeches	Reflective Behavior (or not)	Action Behavior (or not)
1 "[…] in the beginning, the delivery group was engaged to fill the personnel gap in the assembly activities. Delivery received less attention, so the advanced assembly, but delivery was not done" (Interview 6)	Little feedback about consequences of decisions	Decision-making changes Experiments that hindered cash flow
2 […] During planning, we predicted, based on the first phase [prior contract], that assembling the superior cones could be done in 10 days, but it took 25 days. We had never done anything like that" (Interview 1)	Analysis of prior experience of little relevance	Inadequate plans of action

on reflection (Figure 7.2(a)). Decisions and execution of actions were poorly reflected upon (Speech 1, Table 7.3), and planning was rushed or performed based on previous experiences that were irrelevant to current task characteristics.

Analysis of prior experiences (Speech 2, Table 7.3), which were focused on their similarities to previous projects, restricted the team's ability to create new ideas.

However, in the face of the complex characteristics of the tasks, this knowledge was insufficient for achieving expected results, limited the intensive use of the team's knowledge, and delayed problem resolution. During this phase, reflection was of little use in directing the team toward a performance that was efficient and productive.[24]

The reflective process facilitates evaluating actions and past performance, learning from errors and successes, and developing insights so action can be taken to guide improved future team performance.[24] However, none of these behaviors was observed in the team during the inertia phase. During the inertia phase, information was neglected, discussions about errors and problems were avoided, and the team failed to develop plans consistent with expected results (Table 7.4).

Iterative behaviors of reflection–action: During the transition phase, the pattern was that of an iterative cycle of reflection–action behaviors.

Table 7.4. Speech that expresses difficulties in the process of iteration of action–reflection behaviors.

Illustrative Speech	Behavior Focused on Reflection (or not)	Behavior Focused on Action (or not)
1 "[…] there was a moment when the head chief, together with the planner, closed themselves off. They did not allow anyone outside the operational team to express an opinion" (Interview 1)	Discussion of errors and problems was restricted to the discretion of experts, little feedback, few requests for help, little sharing of information	Plans of action that did not meet expected results
2 "[…] It would have been possible to do much more when we noticed that project deviations were going to happen that they would increase. This is because the reports said that we would use more resources than we were using. […] However, it seems [the managers] did not pay attention or think 'this is terrible' and later forgot about it […]" (Interview 2)	Little attention to report analyses that pointed to budget deviation	Plans of action did not meet expected results, delay in making changes

During this phase, the development of insights (reflection) was followed by the application of these insights (action), as illustrated in Figure 7.2(a). This pattern was established with the goal of reaching project results according to the established deadline. Due to the urgency of the project deadline, daily monitoring meetings began and the Vice President of Operations offered support. This scenario motivated and intensified learning behaviors based on agreements between team members (Table 7.5), as shown in prior research studies.[3,12]

The meetings allowed the entire team to participate in the evaluation of progress and problems of the project, share knowledge and experiences, offer insights for solutions, and implement actions of improvement and solutions. This facilitated team engagement with the final goal. According to Raes *et al.*,[3] the meetings promoted a cycle of sharing and collective development.

Table 7.5.   Speeches that highlight learning behaviors during team meetings.

Illustrative Speech	Behavior Focused on Reflection (or not)	Behavior Focused on Action (or not)
1 "In the meeting, we found a way to offer support to what was necessary. If personnel or equipment was needed, this became a priority. [...] All of this took place during the meeting; had we not held the meetings, I think it would have been difficult [to meet the demands of the project]" (participant from focal group 2)	Discussion of errors or problems Sharing of information Feedback Request for help	Decision making Changes Experiments that hindered cash flow Inadequate plans of action
2 "When the VPO arrived at the project, he discussed cases and examples from other projects with us. He asked us what was happening. We reached the conclusion that it was important to hold daily meetings with the people in charge of the people in the field — leaders, foremen, supervisors, and engineers" (Interview 5)	Sharing of information Feedback	Knowledge transfer Changes Decision making

The comprehensive participation of team resulted in "scaling the problems to the lowest levels" and allowed for "clearer communication and to speaking the same language." During the transition, "the team aligned itself very well, performed at 100% capacity, I believe it was the best moment of the project" (Interview 1).

The presence of the VPO meant to the team a new source of knowledge and ideas for problem resolution. He contributed to inciting more dynamic daily meetings and was the principal vehicle of communication between the project and the company.

7.5. Discussion

The structure described in the thematic analysis of this case endorses the affirmation that project team learning is an iterative process of reflection–action behaviors. Its dynamics change according to the members' perception of urgency regarding advances toward results and the final deadline of the project. The contributions to literature derived from this case study are the evidence of a temporal perspective of team learning and the identification of the flexible nature of learning goals throughout the project.

The reflection–action learning process of the team developed as a result of three aspects, which encompass the objective of this chapter. The directions given to the team during its first meeting, which resulted from the base conditions of the project, led the team to explicit learning goals of routine tasks, the appropriation of basic norms to perform the job, and the accession to action strategies proposed by the technical managers. The client relationship history focused on initial learning goals. This fact allows us to conclude on the importance of thinking about strategies that increase client participation in project governance. Such participation will help the team to draw learning goals that are potentially more congruent with the final goals of the project and its timeline.

The iterative process of reflection–action learning behaviors transformed itself at the rate that the final project deadline neared. During the inertia phase (from start up to 80% of the timeline), action learning behaviors of the members prevailed, guided by team technical managers, denoting some reflective behaviors involving these managers only. In contrast, during the transition phase, there were reflection–action behaviors that developed interdependently in an iterative process to reach objectives. This suggests that action–reflection learning behaviors do not always occur interdependently. The differences in learning patterns during the inertia and transition phases prove that routine tasks and complex tasks have different connections with learning behaviors. Complex tasks require greater interdependence from reflection–action behaviors and search for knowledge beyond the scope of the team.

The way the team was managed, the type of leadership, and the relationship among team members interfere with learning behaviors and development of project results. During the inertia phase, interaction between team members was limited, as most of the interaction took place among three or four members with a technical background who coordinated operational staff and transferred information to the rest of the team.

The remaining members of the team had little interaction or participation in problem resolution. Later, in the transition phase, team interaction was greater and involved members of different technical, administrative, and operational backgrounds. Interaction went beyond the scope of the team and involved other people in the organization. This change also proved that face-to-face exchange between team members: (1) improved understanding about goals, both of the project and of the company; (2) facilitated the appropriation of rules; and (3) improved team climate. Consequently, the team gained autonomy and awareness of the importance of the quality of delivered products and of the company's image before the client, resulting in the timely delivery of project results.

As prior research points to a lack of empirical studies that clarify such phenomena,[23] the identification of temporal dynamics of team learning is a contribution to literature. In this manner, the study contributes to literature about team learning and to literature on team processes.

Learning goals also responded to the temporal perspective previously described. During the inertia phase, these goals were explicitly directed to routine task learning, which contributed to immediate enhanced performance of the team aiming to regain client confidence. It could be said that the learning goals had a political role, that of "reconciling relationships with the client" (Interview 1). This choice left complex task learning in the background. This means the learning processes of team work allowed it to structure collective efforts to reach project results as well as learn about knowledge and skills of other team members that had not been considered at that time.

The alert about project delays lead to changes in the learning goals, but there was no evidence that these goals had been explained. During the transition, priority was given to learning complex tasks and teamwork processes (empowerment, participation, and ability to listen). As a result, the team learned to structure collective efforts to overcome project challenges, and comprehension of complex tasks improved.

The learning goals, therefore, were dynamic, and not always explicit. They may emerge naturally in schedules and proposed work strategies for project execution without being formally declared. This aspect builds evidence on a theme with little study, as previously mentioned.[14]

The challenge remains to understand the pertinence of having explicit learning goals from the beginning of the project, which may be revised and adjusted as the project evolves.

Different perspectives have already been applied to study the relation between learning, knowledge processes, and the promotion of innovation.[14] The existing link between learning and knowledge management has long been evident in scientific literature and under different approaches.[25] In attempting to understand how knowledge is acquired, accumulated, and used, organizational learning supports skills acquisition, management of organizational changes based on existing knowledge, and/or the development of skill and resources. Further, it could be said that team and organizational learning and knowledge management act to value, provide visibility, and improve the creation and use of permanent relevant knowledge to reach the objectives of organizations.

Consequently, the issue discussed in this chapter contributes to the organizational knowledge management field as it addresses theoretical and practical studies on the use of knowledge as a strategic production factor in business management. Some determining elements in organizational knowledge management worth recognizing are organizational learning and its processes of knowledge creation (identification, integration, socialization, reflection–action and determination of cognitive and behavioral changes of teams and individuals), where the focus falls on how knowledge governance is conceived and how this drives learning goals.

Finally, this chapter demonstrated how learning behaviors and conditions at a meso-level (project team) occur within a real setting. The dynamics between conditions and behaviors result in contextualized knowledge. Understanding this dynamic at a meso-level helps both researchers and managers in the management and governance of this knowledge at a strategic level. Project-based structures promote the creation of knowledge, but without adequate governance of this knowledge, it could hinder knowledge retention and sharing. By describing how the learning process of a project team occurs in a real setting, this chapter presents evidence for building governance mechanisms that will help the organization to reach both its strategic objectives and its knowledge-based objectives more in line with organizational reality.

References

1. J. Sydow, L. Lindkvist and R. De Fillippi. Project-based organizations, embeddedness and repositories of knowledge. *Organizational Studies London*, **25**, 1475–1489 (2004).
2. K. Artto and K. Wikström. What is project business? *International Journal of Project Management Netherlands*, **23**, 343–353 (2005).
3. E. Raes, A. Boon, E. Kyndt and F. Dochy. Exploring the occurrence of team learning behaviours in project teams over time, *Research Papers on Education UK*, **32**, 376–401 (2016).
4. C. Savelsbergh, J. Gevers, B. Heijden and R. Poell. Team role stress: Relationships with team learning and performance in project teams. *Group Organization and Management USA*, **37**, 67–100 (2012).
5. J. Swan, S. Harry and S. Newell. Why don't (or do) organizations learn from projects? *Management Learning*, **41**, 325–344 (2010).
6. J. Mair, J. Mayer and W. Lutz. Navigating institutional plurality: Organizational governance in hybrid organizations, *Organizational Studies*, **36**, 713–739 (2015).
7. J.K. Pinto. Project management, governance, and the normalization of deviance, *International Journal of Project Management Netherlands*, **32**, 376–387 (2014).
8. S.W. Kozlowski and D.R. Ilgen. Enhancing the effectiveness of work groups and teams, *Psychological Science in Public Interest USA*, **7**, 77–124 (2006).
9. E. Salas, G. Goodwin and S. Burke (eds.). *Team Effectiveness in Complex Organizations: Cross-disciplinary Perspectives and Approaches*. New York: Routledge, Taylor & Francis Group, (2009).
10. S.W. Kozlowski, D.J. Watola, J.M. Jensen, B.H. Kim and I.C. Botero. Developing adaptive teams: A theory of dynamic team leadership. In: E. Salas, G. Goodwin and C. Burke (eds.), *Team Effectiveness in Complex Organizations*. New York: Routledge, 113–155 (2009).
11. C. Gersick. Time and transition in work teams: Toward a new model of group development, *The Academic Management Journal USA*, **31**, 9–41 (1988).
12. A.C. Edmondson. The local and variegated nature of learning in organizations, *Organizational Science Maryland, USA*, **13**, 128–146 (2002).
13. C. Savelsbergh, R. Poell and B. Heijden. Does team stability mediate the relationship between leadership and team learning? An empirical study among Dutch project teams, *International Journal of Project Management Netherlands*, **33**, 406–418 (2015).

14. A.C. Edmondson, J.R. Dillon and K.S. Roloff. Three perspectives on team learning, *Academic Management Annals London*, **1**(1), 269–314 (2007).

15. K. Koskinen and P. Pihlanto. *Knowledge Management in Project-based Companies*. New York: Palgrave Macmillan (2008).

16. A.C. Edmondson and I. Nembhard. Product development and learning in project teams: The challenges are the benefits. *Journal of Product Innovation Management USA*, **26**, 123–138 (2009).

17. K. Koskinen. *Autopoietic Knowledge Systems in Project-based Companies*. New York: Palgrave Macmillan (2010).

18. A. Davies and M. Hobday. Learning in the project business. In: *The Business of Projects: Managing Innovation in Complex Products and Systems*. Cambridge, UK: Cambridge University Press (2005), pp. 184–214.

19. A. Alashwal, H. Rahman and A. Beksin. Knowledge sharing in a fragmented construction industry: On the hindsight. *Scientific Research and Essays*, **6**, 1530–1536 (2011).

20. PMI PMBOK. *Um guia do conhecimento em gerenciamento de projetos*. Guia PMBOK. 6th ed. Pensilvania: Project Management Institute (2017).

21. S. Taylor and R. Bogdan, *Introducción a los métodos Cualitativos*. Pensilvania: Paidós (1994).

22. V. Braun and V. Clarke. Thematic analysis. In: *APA Handbook of Research Methods in Psychology. Research Designs: Quantitative, Qualitative, Neuropsychological, and Biological*. 2nd ed. Washington, DC: American Psychological Association, (2012), pp. 57–71.

23. N. Lehmann-Willenbrock. Team learning: New insights through a temporal lens. *Small Group Research USA*, **48**, 123–130 (2017).

24. M. Schippers, A.C. Edmondson and M. West. Team reflexivity as an antidote to team Information-processing Failures. *Small Group Research USA*, **45**, 731–769 (2014).

25. W. King. Knowledge management and organizational learning. *Annals of Information Systems USA*, **4**, 3–13 (2009).

© 2022 World Scientific Publishing Company
https://doi.org/10.1142/9789811224119_0008

Knowledge Governance to Create Socially Understanding Communities

Muhammad Asim Qayyum* and Arif Khan†

School of Information Studies,

Charles Sturt University, Australia

*aqayyum@csu.edu.au

†akhan@csu.edu.au

This chapter discusses the knowledge governance mechanisms and approaches in formal and informal group settings, with a particular focus on the motivation structures that can make knowledge sharing and creation successful. Physical and virtual settings are reviewed as part of this discussion because the work procedures have increasingly become remote, and geographical isolation is growing. It is proposed that the knowledge work and its governance should be about achieving a good for the community at large even in virtual and geographically dispersed work settings, and this can be done by inducing appropriate desired incentives within group members. Along with those incentives, ethical working procedures should encourage moral principles to help build trustworthy relationships among group members, and with community stakeholders, as the latter are recognized and consulted. Inducing such pro-social extrinsic or intrinsic motivations as part of knowledge governance procedures will help build a socially understanding community, or communities, leading to wise decisions and creating a world worth living in.

8.1. Introduction

Information abounds in the world nowadays, thus increasing an individual's potential to create knowledge from that information and use it in everyday work tasks. However, is that knowledge creation happening for the sake of improving efficiency and effectiveness of immediate work processes, or is it also focused on the generating beneficence for the communities in which one lives and works? No doubt the communities themselves are transforming from physical to virtual as the knowledge sharing activities move from face-to-face interactive modes of storytelling, lullabies, songs, and news sharing[1] to doing all of these activities in an online environment (e.g. blogs, video sharing, etc.). The switch also means that individuals work in physical isolation at times, more so as witnessed after the recent COVID-19–enforced social distancing rules. Such work habits may make workers feel disconnected from their immediate communities as they lose themselves in the geographically neutral isolation of the Internet and their work tasks. Lost is that respect is rich factual knowledge and wisdom handed down about the pragmatics of life.[2] Lost also are life truths and experience, or the wisdom of community elders, which lends strength to individual members of the community.[1] Therefore the question of creating good for a community may lose itself in the definition of a community, and instead be absorbed in improving the efficiency of the organizational work process.

As for the functioning of today's corporate work environment, the use of principles of knowledge governance mechanisms gains importance as they can be used to influence the behaviors of employees undertaking knowledge processes.[3] The pioneering work of these authors suggests that governance mechanisms can be used to develop employee trust in the work and improve knowledge sharing performances by influencing them with some motivation. The motivations that immediately come to mind are the extrinsic ones that may be monetary or worldly recognition based. Such extrinsic motivations can be assumed to provide an organizational employee with the required incentive to undertake knowledge processes. The premise of this current study is that the motivation structures within knowledge governance mechanisms need to focus on achieving a good for the community to create the desired incentive and trust required, or a type of pro-social intrinsic motivation. Only then an organization can help create an understanding and social community that functions, thrives, and creates a world worth living in. Therefore, the purpose of this study is to identify and describe the knowledge governance approach that organizations can adapt to help create a socially understanding community.

We feel that this work is significant because current organizational thinking is focused on ensuring modern ethics within its operating structures, leading to adoption of practical means of creating a profitable organization while ignoring the incorporation of much-needed philosophical underpinning of wisdom.[4] Lost in the corporate culture is the need to disregard greed and excess and strive instead for achievement of moral excellence within its employees to pursue a common good.[5] The organizations need to go beyond simply creating a knowledge society and replace profit maximizing with the larger mission of social benefits maximization.[6] Using a knowledge governance approach based on the use of socially responsible intrinsic motivation factors may be a solution, as will be discussed among other relevant themes covered in this chapter.

8.2. Principles of Knowledge Governance Mechanisms

Knowledge governance has developed across the fields of strategic management, economics, and organization theory to explain the complexities of various knowledge-related phenomena, and this becomes part of knowledge management.[7] In order to understand how knowledge governance helps organizations achieve their knowledge-related goals, it is pertinent to go through the research that focuses on the interplay between macro-level constructs, such as communities of practice and interest, and micro-level constructs such as individuals' motivation, beliefs, and behaviors. At both these levels, an organization's knowledge-related goals can be achieved by deploying various formal and informal strategies to influence behavior of employees and their contribution to knowledge creation and sharing processes.[8]

Information, knowledge, and understanding may be critical to enable increased efficiency, but perhaps not effectiveness. To understand this effectivity versus efficiency in an organizational context, it is important to differentiate between them. Generally, effectiveness is evaluated efficiency,[9] and the difference between effectiveness and efficiency could be regarded as difference between wisdom and understanding. As mentioned by Ackoff,[10] knowledge and intelligence increase efficiency, while wisdom increases effectiveness. Therefore, in organizational contexts as per Ackoff, these terms can be understood in terms of development and growth. Information and knowledge may contribute to the growth of an organization but development relates to an increase in value which, therefore, requires an increase in the understanding of information and knowledge leading to wisdom. Efficiency is then a measure of how well resources are used to achieve a goal, while effectiveness is the efficiency considered by the value of goals achieved. Thus, efficiency is value-free while effectiveness is value-full because effectiveness reflects the utilization of knowledge that has been transferred to a receiving unit.[11] This difference between effectiveness and efficiency leads to the importance of understanding governance mechanism in virtual communities because it will further facilitate researchers and the community to understand and use the governance mechanism of virtual communities in a more systematic manner.[12]

Knowledge management processes are usually associated with enabling organizations to capture, reconcile, transfer, and create knowledge in an efficient manner. However, Bharadwaj *et al.*[13] argued that the organizational processes together with a sound infrastructure provide a useful foundation for knowledge effectiveness, which in turn may contribute to ethical and efficient working in organizations. Growing literature on knowledge management acknowledges that knowledge governance, or mechanisms to oversee the knowledge processes, is important to coordinate the actions of organizational members during the knowledge creation process. The use of principles of knowledge governance mechanisms gains importance as they can be used to influence the behaviors of employees undertaking knowledge processes.[3] However, generating a sound understanding from the knowledge systems still needs to be done by socially and cognitively capable humans[14] because the ability to develop computerized information, and then try and generate knowledge from such systems, does not necessarily lead to wise actions. Ackoff[10] termed this capability as an attribute that "differentiates man from machines."

In an organization, Schopflin and Walsh[15] assert that central control is not a good answer to information and knowledge governance, and corporate policies still need to be put into place for good governance. In smaller project-based units, the policy of one strategy per unit may work best if the executives of each unit follow pragmatic mechanisms rather than try to be innovative and employ naïve and authoritative strategies.[16] These authors also state that trying to implement knowledge-creating processes across units may not work due to differing cultural and work practices, and therefore any governance strategy considered should consider both holistic and narrow knowledge systems implementation perspectives to ensure a contingency plan is in place.

Other than using policies and audit procedures for governance, a people-centric approach is also encouraged, especially engagement with people through communities of practice (CoP) or communities of interest/purpose as most knowledge resides in people's heads. Schopflin and Walsh.[15,17] These sometimes ad hoc and informal communities can especially be useful in knowledge creation and its understanding as they may exist beyond organizational boundaries, and workers can access support that may not be available from within their own team. The addition or consultation with stakeholders who are impacted by the resultant action is a necessary aspect that must not be ignored.[18] Governance mechanisms of such practice communities are still evolving, and most people may point to the knowledge champion(s), or the person(s) organizing the community to organize, facilitate, record the happenings and its outputs, and develop recommendations accordingly. A knowledge verification layer, as proposed by Karvalics and Dalal,[17] may be added to ensure that all in-flow of information is verified at source. In case of community members converging from different organizations, the takeaway for each of those members will be different, and hence minimal governance may be required to bring down any barriers to free exchange of ideas.

8.3. Motivationally Inspired Knowledge Sharing in Governance Mechanisms

Researchers agree that the knowledge-sharing process requires a positive attitude and aptitude of employees toward adapting a sharing behavior.[19] Hence, a knowledge-sharing culture motivates individual employees in an organization to communicate openly with others, and a knowledge governance mechanism is vital to promote knowledge sharing within organizations. However, recent research shows some inconsistency in results from studies on relationship among knowledge governance mechanisms and motivations to share knowledge.[20] For example, research from Crowne,[21] Liu and Liu,[22] and Furuya *et al.*[23] showed that knowledge governance mechanisms facilitate knowledge sharing, whereas, other studies such as Lin[24] and Bock *et al.*[25] reported that presence of motivation had insignificant impact on knowledge sharing.

Another line of research shows that knowledge creation and sharing requires motivation, and organizations need to step forward to include this aspect in their governance strategy. In this regard, various knowledge governance mechanisms have been proposed by the researchers to influence and manipulate employees' behavior.[26–29] Such strategies may include formal mechanisms, e.g. reward system, job design, etc., or mixed approaches such as networking, project groups, and steering committees. Some of these researchers have also suggested informal mechanisms, such as enhancing reputation and building trust and professional ethos. These and other studies have explored multiple dimensions of knowledge governance mechanisms and their relationship with knowledge sharing, but the relationship between knowledge governance mechanisms and motivations of employees within an organization to share knowledge remains under-researched. However, we argue that knowledge governance mechanisms not only promote motivation to share knowledge but also provide opportunities for knowledge sharing.

Osterloh and Frey[30] argued that organizations can enable different types of motivations to generate and share knowledge because knowledge generation and transfer is a vital source to maintain a sustainable competitive advantage of any organization. It is appropriate here to distinguish between tacit and explicit knowledge when it comes to understanding the kind of worker motivation required to achieve knowledge-related goals in an organization. It is likely that employees cannot be sanctioned for holding back tacit knowledge and that transfer of such knowledge cannot be accomplished by contracting; therefore, properly motivating members to share knowledge becomes a central factor in the knowledge management strategy employed by a group or an organization.

According to Osterloh and Frey,[30] some researchers agree that employees can be motivated intrinsically when tacit knowledge in-between teams is transferred, whereas employees are extrinsically motivated when they are able to satisfy needs, such as monetary compensation. Hence, pay-for-performance mechanism may be an effective governance strategy to manage the motivation of employees within an organization. Similarly, human resource management (HRM) strategies and practices that relate to retention of knowledgeable employees with compensation and remuneration can also be a management strategy to acknowledging intangible and tangible motivations.[31] Finally, Wang[32] argued that learning-related knowledge governance practices enable increased performance, and by legitimizing learning such as opportunities for mentoring, coaching, and learning-by-doing, organizations can increase employees' motivation to create and share knowledge.

Researchers such as Foss[8] and Gagné[33] state that employees may have some differences in their motivations to share knowledge. However, organizational design and HRM policies can influence their motivation to share knowledge in return for some award and monetary benefits. Hence it can deduced that formal knowledge governance mechanisms such as incentives, reward system, performance evaluation, training, etc., can motivate employees and support a knowledge-sharing culture. Therefore, Huang *et al.*[20] stated:

> Formal KGMs [knowledge governance mechanisms] provide excellent opportunities for organizations to communicate and create norms... and enhance the knowledge sharing willingness.

It is likely that knowledge governance mechanisms not only influence personal motivation but also enhance knowledge-sharing opportunities among employees.

8.4. Knowledge Creation and Governance in Virtual and Physical Communities

The Internet and the World Wide Web have fostered the opportunities for information exchange and expertise to cross geographical and political boundaries. A stream of research has shown significant growth of literature around knowledge creation embedded in various forms of virtual communities,[34] and generally focuses on contributing or co-creating knowledge using a virtual platform. The virtual platforms used for co-creation of knowledge are usually Internet-based communication platforms, which are spread across space and time. The design of knowledge governance mechanism for such virtual communities is typically always a challenge for organizations, and any governance mechanism that leads to generation of wisdom in all such efforts will only materialize when the common goals are shared and understood by all community members. Only then the interests of the community will be preserved. Since 2006 onward, many issues concerning the governance of virtual communities have been discussed in the literature,[35-38] encompassing motivation, participation, control, ownership and appropriation of intellectual property, and goal setting.

For organizations operating in a sharing economy, setting up virtual communities of practices is core to knowledge creation. However, research on design of governance in such virtual communities is minimal, thus, making it difficult to structure a particular governance design. For example, Li–Ying and Salomo[39] argued that little is known about organizational practices used to govern virtual communities, and issues such as encouragement, motivation, coordination, and strategic interactions control need more focus. There are some encouraging signs within the governance practices research as mentioned by Li-Ying and Salomo[39] — e.g. there is some research on encouraging participation in virtual communities by demarcating the perimeters of interaction and defining online communities, where an organization facilitates the establishment, operation, and development of virtual communities and provides them the required resources. Knowledge governance in virtual communities has drawn some attention from other knowledge management researchers in the past. For example, Lampe and Johnston[40] examined how feedback can motivate new members to contribute information in a virtual community such as news forums.

O'Mahony and Ferraro[41] discussed the effect of different electronic forums in helping open-source communities to coordinate and co-produce software and deduced that the governance system evolves with changing perceptions of authority among its group members. Similarly, Forte *et al.*[42] focused on the evolution of Wikipedia contributors' social norms and policies that help with conflict resolution and noted that the growth of community led to increasing decentralization, which allowed communal work to flourish. Fairfield[43] discussed contract law replacement by common law to protect fundamental rights necessary for the public within the virtual communities. Finally, Leug[14] argued that governance in virtual communities must explicitly recognize what people are exchanging is information and knowledge that they understand over time, and that understanding may evolve. However, most research on the knowledge of virtual knowledge sharing and collaboration is conducted within the boundaries of the organization and usually for members/employees of the organization. Hence, the question remains that, in such scenarios, does knowledge creation happen for the sake of improving efficiency and effectiveness of immediate work processes, or is it also focused on generating social and beneficence for the communities in which one lives and works?

Social networks are also said to facilitate creation and sharing of new knowledge within organizations; however, the concept of "knowledge networks," illustrated by Bradshaw *et al.*[44] explains how business units take advantage of knowledge that reside in different parts of an organization. There is also a growing realization that knowledge plays a vital role in shaping and identifying contemporary societies, both physical and online.[45] The knowledge can flow within a wide variety of different virtual communities that exist on the web, such as newsgroups, social networks, and weblogs, to name a few. In the context of virtual communities existing outside the organization, the governance mechanisms face different challenges as people from various countries and cultures come together to share similar interests and exchange ideas, thus co-creating knowledge. These challenges may be considered in terms of supporting international crosslinks to enable or facilitate knowledge creation and minimize geographical distances, intercultural barriers, and other language and communication problems. These problems can be addressed technically through the use of information and communication technology tools and techniques that facilitate the process of knowledge creation in the online environment — e.g. Web 2.0 now allows networking via social media platforms, thus opening promising trends in knowledge creation. However, in order to align virtual communities and the knowledge creation process, a sound governance mechanism of online communities is critical. Further investigation into social media control mechanisms and governance systems may contribute to resolving the dilemmas arising from differential roles and interests of members within formal and informal virtual communities.

Other key characteristics and mechanisms of governance in virtual communities outlined by researchers include ownership of assets, goal settings, development process, conflict resolution, community management, and use of information tools.[46] Dutton[35] also discussed goals settings, control modularization, and performance evaluation. However, approaches of defining governance mechanism in virtual communities should be based on the premise the governance is not only a structure but also a process,[39] because governance is also relevant to the outcome of exchange relationships.

8.5. Governance to Create "Good for the Community"

All types of organizationally inspired communities discussed above will probably include very smart and intelligent people, and the knowledge they create will be useful for the respective organizations they work for. However, is that generated knowledge useful for the conventional communities also in which those organizations operate? Sternberg[47] refers to the moral-equivalence fallacy, "the belief that to be smart is to be good," and asserts that being smart does not mean that those people are also good for the community. Just a focus on improving the organization accounting bottom line can lead one to fall into such a fallacy and display just intelligence with little wisdom. As a review of wisdom literature by Qayyum[18] indicates, the existence of moral and social values (ability to distinguish right from wrong) in organizational decision-makers is essential to overcome greed and focus instead on achieving good for the community. Such values help guide the leaders to recognize, remember, and consult stakeholders within and external to the organization in pursuit of achieving a common good or to display practical wisdom. The moral values then go beyond simple ethical working standards (commonly found in most modern organizations) to include traits such as compassion, forgiveness, justice, etc. The creation of socially understanding communities may not be possible without having at least some members who possess these morally binding traits and are able to include voices of the stakeholders.

While information governance focuses on how information is controlled, accessed, used, and disseminated using mechanisms and policies,[17] Foss and Michailova[3] focus on knowledge processes happening in an organization and state that governance influences all aspects of knowledge management, including sharing, retention, and creation. Therefore, knowledge governance uses control mechanisms to reduce knowledge management costs and focuses on organizational/market structures and coordination mechanisms such as incentives, reward schemes, and trust. Extending this definition to informal communities based on common interest, we find that internal operating structures of these informal groups will be loose as the focus is now on a task rather than achieving organizational efficiencies. Such a structure can be equated to a standalone project unit that strives for excellence rather than just being good enough.[16] Thus, governance of information and knowledge flowing in such a task-based group will depend on motivations of individual members feeding into the whole, and the strength of trust and bond between them should create the desired excellence. Incentives or reward schemes can be mutually decided between members to ensure that motivation remains on track for most, and the required knowledge is created. The incentives may be the same for all processes and individuals, or may differ in shape and intensity depending on the knowledge process,[48] but the primary desired outcome of knowledge governance process is that there should be shared learning leading to a satisfactory solution for most members.[1]

8.6. Concluding Words for a Community-Focused Governance

After all the virtual group work discussion, let us take a final look at traditional communities living in close geographical proximity, where the knowledge structures may range from word of mouth to some specialized Internet sites. Information flows happening in these communities depend on prevailing culture, educational, legal, and health systems, and are very much respect-based family and community focused.[1] It is said the best way for wisdom to prevail is when there is an independence of thought to allow an individual to reflect upon and integrate the various pieces of information, and the principles of morality and the natural environment surrounding the communities are carefully deliberated to create common benefits and good for the community. We believe that these principles can also be incorporated in virtual group work environments, and wisdom may be generated by including in the governance process the experienced workers and "community elders" as knowledge of matters is mutually shared with the stakeholders to settle issues. Mungmachon[1] characterizes this situation as an ideal form of knowledge management, and we concur because daily interactions and information sharing lead to stronger relationships among stakeholders, and the resulting wisdom that prevails values morals over material things. Reliance on electronic governing mechanisms will continue to complicate the process in future with reduced use of human cognitive skills, but the bottom line to all knowledge governance mechanisms lies in achieving a successful knowledge transfer and sharing among community members. This sharing process must be accompanied by a good and enjoyable learning process, an understanding gained directly from experienced workers and elders, and finally an action that can be termed as being wise because it achieves good for all stakeholders and community.

References

1. R. Mungmachon. Knowledge and local wisdom: Community treasure. *International Journal of Humanities and Social Science,* **2**(13), 174–181 (2012).

2. P.B. Baltes and U.M. Staudinger. Wisdom: A metaheuristic (pragmatic) to orchestrate mind and virtue toward excellence. *American Psychologist,* **55**(1), 122–136 (2000).

3. N. Foss and S. Michailova (eds.). *Knowledge Governance: Processes and Perspectives.* Oxford: Oxford University Press (2009).

4. L. Prusak. A handbook of practical wisdom: Leadership, organization and integral business practice. *Academy of Management Learning & Education,* **12**(2), 312–313 (2013).

5. I. Nonaka and H. Takeuchi. The wise leader. *Harvard Business Review,* (5), 58–67, 146 (2011).

6. M. Goede. The wise society: Beyond the knowledge economy. *Foresight,* **13**(1), 36–45 (2010).

7. S. Pemsel, R. Müller and J. Söderlund. Knowledge governance strategies in project-based organizations. *Long Range Planning,* **49**(6), 648–660 (2016).

8. N. Foss. Alternative research strategies in the knowledge movement: From macro bias to micro-foundations and multi-level explanation. *European Management Review,* **6**(1), 16–28 (2009).

9. D. Muller. Economics of human-AI ecosystem: Value bias and lost utility in multi-dimensional gaps. arXiv preprint arXiv:1811.06606 (2018).

10. R.L. Ackoff. From data to wisdom. *Journal of Applied Systems Analysis,* **16**(1), 3–9 (1989).

11. U. Andersson, P. J. Buckley and H. Dellestrand. In the right place at the right time! The influence of knowledge governance tools on knowledge transfer and utilization in MNEs. *Global Strategy Journal,* **5**(1), 27–47 (2015).

12. S. Nambisan. Designing virtual customer environments for new product development: toward a theory. *Academy of Management Review,* **27**(3), 392–413 (2002).

13. S.S. Bharadwaj, S. Chauhan and A. Raman. Impact of knowledge management capabilities on knowledge management effectiveness in Indian organizations. *Vikalpa,* **40**(4), 421–434 (2015).

14. C. Leug. Information knowledge and networked minds. *Journal of Knowledge Management,* **5**(2), 151–159 (2001).

15. K. Schopflin and M. Walsh. *Practical Knowledge and Information Management.* Facet Publishing, London, UK (2019).

16. S. Pemsel and R. Müller. The governance of knowledge in project-based organizations. *International Journal of Project Management,* **30**(8), 865–876 (2012).

17. L.Z. Karvalics and N. Dalal. Beyond knowledge management: An extended model of knowledge governance. *International Journal of Knowledge Society Research* (IJKSR), **2**(4), 62–72 (2011).
18. M.A. Qayyum. Modelling wisdom in learning and decision making. *International Journal of Knowledge and Learning*, **12**(2), 146–166 (2018).
19. K. Husted, S. Michailova, D.B. Minbaeva and T. Pedersen. Knowledge-sharing hostility and governance mechanisms: An empirical test. *Journal of Knowledge Management*, **16**(5), 754–773 (2012).
20. M.C. Huang, Y.P. Chiu and T.C. Lu. Knowledge governance mechanisms and repatriate's knowledge sharing: The mediating roles of motivation and opportunity. *Journal of Knowledge Management*, **17**, 677–694 (2013).
21. K.A. Crowne. Enhancing knowledge transfer during and after international assignments. *Journal of Knowledge Management*, **13**(4), 134–137 (2009).
22. N.C. Liu and M.S. Liu. Human resource practices and individual knowledge-sharing behavior — an empirical study for Taiwanese R&D professionals, *The International Journal of Human Resource Management*, **22**(4), 981–997 (2011).
23. N. Furuya, M.J. Stevens, A. Bird, G. Oddou and M. Mendenhall. Managing the learning and transfer of global management competence: Antecedents and outcomes of Japanese repatriation effectiveness. *Journal of International Business Studies*, **40**(2), 200–215 (2009).
24. H.F. Lin. Effects of extrinsic and intrinsic motivation on employee knowledge sharing intentions. *Journal of Information Science*, **33**(2), 135–149 (2007).
25. G.W. Bock, R. Zmud., Y.G. Kim and J.N. Lee. Behavioral intention formation in knowledge sharing: Examining the roles of extrinsic motivators, social-psychological forces, and organizational climate. *MIS Quarterly*, **29**(1), 87–111 (2005).
26. A. Grandori. Neither hierarchy nor identity: Knowledge-governance mechanisms and the theory of the firm. *Journal of management and Governance*, **5**(3–4), 381–399 (2001).
27. G. Hoetker and T. Mellewigt. Choice and performance of governance mechanisms: matching alliance governance to asset type. *Strategic Management Journal*, **30**(10), 1025–1044 (2009).
28. G. Grabher. Temporary architectures of learning: Knowledge governance in project ecologies. *Organization Studies*, **25**(9), 1491–1514 (2004).
29. A. Wiewiora, G. Murphy, B. Trigunarsyah and K. Brown. Interactions between organizational culture, trustworthiness, and mechanisms for inter-project knowledge sharing. *Project Management Journal*, **45**(2), 48–65 (2014).

30. M. Osterloh and B.S. Frey. Motivation, knowledge transfer, and organizational forms. *Organization Science*, **11**(5), 538–550 (2000).

31. H. Inkinen, A. Kianto, M. Vanhala. Knowledge management practices and innovation performance in Finland. *Baltic Journal of Management*, **10**(4), 432–455 (2015).

32. D. Wang and S. Chen. Does intellectual capital matter? High-performance work systems and bilateral innovative capabilities. *International Journal of Manpower*, **34**(8), 861–879 (2013).

33. M. Gagné. (2009). A model of knowledge-sharing motivation. *Human Resource Management*, **48**(4), 571–589 (2009).

34. J. Nieves and J. Osorio. The role of social networks in knowledge creation. *Knowledge Management Research & Practice*, **11**(1), 62–77 (2013).

35. W.H. Dutton. The wisdom of collaborative network organizations: capturing the value of networked individuals, *Prometheus*, **26**(3), 211–230 (2008).

36. J. West and S. O'Mahony. The role of participation architecture in growing sponsored open source communities. *Industry & Innovation*, **15**(2), 145–168 (2008).

37. Y. Qiu, Y. Chui and M.G. Helander. A cognitive approach to understanding knowledge-based virtual team decision making in product design. *International Journal of Intelligent Enterprise*, **1**(1), 45–64 (2007).

38. T.W. Malone, R. Laubacher and C. Dellarocas. The collective intelligence genome. *MIT Sloan Management Review*, **51**(3), 21–31 (2010).

39. J. Li–Ying and S.R. Salomo. Design of governance in virtual communities: Definition, mechanisms, and variation patterns. *International Journal of Collaborative Enterprise*, **3**(4), 225–251 (2013).

40. C. Lampe and E. Johnston. Follow the (slash) dot: effects of feedback on new members in an online community. *In Proceedings of the 2005 International ACM SIGGROUP Conference on Supporting Group Work*, November, pp. 11–20 (2005).

41. S. O'Mahony and F. Ferraro. The emergence of governance in an open source community. *Academy of Management Journal*, **50**(5), 1079–1106 (2007).

42. A. Forte, V. Larco and A. Bruckman. Decentralization in Wikipedia governance. *Journal of Management Information Systems*, **26**(1), 49–72 (2009).

43. J.A.T. Fairfield. Anti-social contracts: The contractual governance of virtual worlds. *McGill Law Journal*, **53**, 427–476 (2008).

44. P. Bradshaw, S. Powell and I. Terrell. Building a community of practice: Technological and social implications for a distributed team. In *Knowledge Networks: Innovation through Communities of Practice*, P. Hildreth and

C. Kimble (eds.), Hershey, PA, USA; London, UK: Idea Group Publishing (2004) pp. 184–201.

45. H.A.K. Al-ghamdi and A.A.K. Al-ghamdi. The role of virtual communities of practice in knowledge management using Web 2.0. *Procedia Computer Science*, **65**, 406–411 (2015).

46. M.L. Markus. The governance of free/open source software projects: monolithic, multidimensional, or configurational? *Journal of Management and Governance*, **11**(2), 151–163 (2007).

47. R.J. Sternberg. *Wisdom, Intelligence, and Creativity Synthesized*. Cambridge, UK: Cambridge University Press (2003).

48. N.J. Foss. The emerging knowledge governance approach: Challenges and characteristics. *Organization*, **14**(1), 29–52 (2007).

Knowledge Governance as a Key Factor in Interorganizational Learning

Julieta K. Watanabe-Wilbert*, Carla S. Zandavalli and
Gertrudes Aparecida Dandolini

Federal University of Santa Catarina, Graduate Program in
Knowledge Management and Engineering,
R. Delfino Conti, s/n, Trindade, Florianópolis —
SC, 88040–900, Brazil

*researcher.wilbert@protonmail.com

Interorganizational learning (IOL) is a subject of growing interest in academia, since acquiring knowledge outside the boundaries of an organization improves its performance. This chapter presents IOL as a main research construct and presents some factors that influence it. As research method, a case study was used in a learning network, comprising organizations from different sectors. Among the presented results, the influence of knowledge governance (KGov) as a critical success factor for IOL stands out. The application of KGov to the factors that influence IOL helps its effectiveness for organizations seeking to learn from each other.

9.1. Introduction

Knowing how to manage knowledge is an organizational capacity enshrined in the literature. The COVID-19 pandemic, unexpected and crisis-generating in the 21st century society, reminds us of the importance of the exchange of available knowledge about a problem, and the collaborative creation of new knowledge for its solution. More than ever, it is palpable for an organization to give importance to knowledge and its processes, to create, share, and employ knowledge.[1]

In this sense, organizations learn from the knowledge stored in their organizational memory, through the analysis of what worked and what did not work in the past, to guide future actions.[2] There are situations, however, where organizations are faced with problems whose solutions are not found in their knowledge stocks. When organizations recognize this fact, there is a chance that they will seek new knowledge beyond their borders in order to enrich their learning processes.[3–5] In this scenario, learning networks can be formed, which can be defined as arrangements formally adopted by organizations, with explicit objectives of mutual learning.[6,7]

The literature defines interorganizational learning (IOL) as the process of organization learning from others,[8–14] also present in learning networks. IOL, associated with the acquisition, sharing, transmission, adaptation, and use of external knowledge, has attracted the attention of researchers. However, there are still few publications on the subject with an approach that considers IOL as the main focus. For being considered as a means to an end, such as better performance,[15] innovation,[8] and problem solving,[9,16] IOL ends up not being given a prominent role in the field of research.

The factors that promote IOL require investigation. With this subject in mind, the present study was conducted to provide answers to the following question: what factors influence IOL? A case study was chosen as the research method to identify factors of IOL in a learning network. Through interviews with its members, it was possible to identify the factors that influence the IOL on that network. Among them, knowledge governance (KGov) emerged prominently as an IOL facilitator. This aspect is explored and highlighted in a specific way in the analysis in this study.

This chapter presents, based on a literature review, the concepts and factors that influence IOL. Below, the research method used in this study is mentioned. Then, the case study is described. Finally, the results and discussions are presented regarding the case and the final considerations of this chapter.

9.2. IOL

IOL is the learning process that an organization performs from sources of knowledge external to it[6,17–19] with their peers.[10,20] IOL is a multidimensional concept,[21] composed of information sharing, memory of specific knowledge of the relationship between organizations, and shared development.[22,23] It is a learning process that occurs at the group level of organizations that cooperate proactively[11] and that fundamentally deals with the acquisition and use of external knowledge[3,24] from social interactions mediated by communication processes.[25] Some authors[12,13,26] recognize that IOL also includes interpretation, combination, and dissemination of knowledge by the interacting organizations. Therefore, IOL permeates the interorganizational and organizational levels. However, the scope of this study is limited to activities that occur at the interorganizational level. As already mentioned, a configuration frequently mentioned by authors about a structure that promotes IOL is an interorganizational network, which is defined as a group of autonomous organizations[27] that establish mutual relationships for different purposes.[28–30] When organizations form networks to learn, they are called "learning networks."[30–32] In learning networks, there are often formal and programmed situations that promote IOL[16] and result in the expansion of the knowledge base of each organization.[33]

9.3. Factors that Influence IOL

There are three dimensions in which the factors that influence IOL can be analyzed. The first one refers to the environment external to the network

(External Factors Dimension) in which the network is immersed. External factors often act as the main motivators both for the formation of learning networks and for their reconfiguration. The second dimension concerns the characteristics of the network of organizations (Network-Related Factors Dimension), e.g. size of organizations, forms of group decision, and other configurations that take into account the social interaction within the group. The third dimension is related to the influence of the participants' home organization in the context of the network, but this will not be addressed in this research, as explained above.

The main external factors that influence IOL as well as the factors related to the characteristics of the organizations' network are detailed in Tables 9.1 and 9.2.

It is observed that external factors are the scenario of the environment external to organizations, which lead them to seek other organizations in order to learn.

According to Choi and Ko,[21] interorganizational relations are the basis for IOL. Indeed, among the network-related factors, interorganizational relationships are the most cited by the authors mentioned in Table 9.2.

The reviewed IOL literature does not mention the term KGov. However, elements of network governance in IOL are in line with the concept of KGov. By governance, it is understood the set of policies that lead a business to success,[60] and network management mechanisms that promote IOL can be understood as KGov mechanisms. The absence of the term "Knowledge Governance" in the IOL literature may be due to the fact that it is a recent construct with conceptual variations.[61] Nevertheless, this chapter presents KGov in IOL in an exploratory way, from the emergence of the theme in the case study.

Table 9.1.   External factors — independent of the network or organizations.

Factors	Description
Environmental pressures	Market pressures represented by the demands of customers and stakeholders that implement external audits in organizations for the purpose of improvement.[34,35]
Crisis situations	Uncertainties, financial market crises, or social crises as reason for organizations to integrate networks for mutual learning.[9,34]

Table 9.2.   Network-related factors (manageable by the network).

Factors	Description
Network competence or know-how	A network composed of organizations with successful practices and varieties of experience attracts organizations to the exchange of tacit knowledge and the combination of knowledge.[10, 35–38]
Environment internal to the network	A large geographical distance between the organizations and the social interaction space can make interactions more difficult, if the network is very wide.[29,39]
Sense of unity	The existence of a feeling of belonging resulting from a common purpose or shared identity facilitates IOL.[40,41]
Interorganizational relationships	Trust between members of the network permeates aspects of competence related to knowledge, cognitive, and affective aspects. Previous relationships, social proximity, time of belonging to the group, and long-term relationships are promoters of IOL. The informality of relationships permeated by camaraderie and loyalty favors IOL.[10,20–22,29,39,40,42–50]
Collaboration	Organizations with interdependent or integrated processes tend to promote cooperative learning. Joint formal and informal actions on the network, joint projects, and sharing of resources among the network's organizations are factors that promote IOL. Relevant is also the network's support for its organizations in the IOL process.[5,14,16,29,30,34,40,43,47,49,51]
Network structure	The size of the network can influence the dynamics of IOL because the larger it is, the greater the complexity of interactions and the greater the need for more complex coordination mechanisms. This becomes very noticeable in virtual learning networks, which require a technological infrastructure corresponding to the needs. Network knowledge repositories for storing collective knowledge are mechanisms to promote IOL.[21,26,43,52–54]
Culture	Many interorganizational projects are carried out with organizations with different languages and national cultures,[16,12,39] which affect the interorganizational knowledge transfer. The different organizational cultures also provide the opportunity for actions of mutual understanding that help the integration of diversity on the network.[5,18,26,29,41,55,56]
Network individuals	The turnover of key people affects the IOL process, since they are people who may have cultivated a differentiated level of relationship with people from other organizations in the network.[47]

(Continued)

Table 9.2.   (*Continued*)

Factors	Description
Network objectives	Organizations with conflicting objectives hinder interactions and, therefore, IOL. Joint objectives promote the engagement of organizations in their mutual learning process.[11,43]
Intellectual property	The concern with the intellectual property of the knowledge that circulates in the network, especially when created from the contributions of its organizations, is a reality, mainly in innovation contexts.[48]
Type of organization	Non-competing organizations are more likely to operate in the same learning network; however, there is a need for similarity in the organizations with regards to the knowledge base, structures or technologies so that the exchange is possible.[3,14,44,50,51,57]
Network governance	The network coordination and management mechanisms (e.g. the existence of a central core of network coordination for relationship management) promote IOL.[10,14,49,58,59]

9.4. Research Method

This research is a case study[62,63] with a qualitative approach. Some authors[62,63] recommend the investigation of existing theory before data collection in case studies as a form of guidance, enabling to enhance the researcher's ability to interpret the data. For this reason, a systematic review of the literature was conducted, which provided the theoretical basis of the study. After that, seven semi-structured interviews with members of six organizations, from June 17, 2020, to June 30, 2020, were conducted, through virtual means, using the Zoom platform. Other data about the network were collected from websites (Facebook) and reading of documents made available by the participants. Thematic analysis[64,65] was employed for the data analysis.

Section 9.5 presents the results and discussions of the case study in the light of the researched literature.

9.5. Results and Discussion

The case of a learning network formed by organizations from different sectors is presented here, where factors that influence the organizations' learning on the network were identified. These factors can either promote IOL or serve as barriers to it. The approach will be to describe the factors that promote IOL identified in the case, since this is a successful IOL case. KGov is presented prominently on the researched learning network, given the relevance with which it emerged in the narratives of the interviewees.

9.5.1. *Case Study: BENCHNET*

The IOL network, here called BENCHNET, was formed with large organizations, which based their strategic management on MEG — the Brazilian Management Model from the National Quality Foundation. The organizations of the network belong to different sectors, and a remarkable fact that has attracted attention in the research is the longevity of the network, which is currently 15 years old. Its members formalized the creation of BENCHNET in mid-2005. Since then, some organizations have left the network and others have joined it. Currently, BENCHNET is composed of nine organizations, two from the education sector (one public and one private), two from the public sector (one from sanitation and one from the electricity sector), one from the research and technology public sector, one from the private food sector, one private social service entity, one public logistical services company, and a multinational company from the private technology sector.

BENCHNET's objective is mutual learning based on benchmarking practices on a given topic. The group meets monthly so that each organization can present its performance indicators and practices on a previously chosen topic, following the schedule established in the BENCHNET planning at the beginning of each year. The collected data revealed that there are factors that influence IOL on the studied network, which are presented in Section 9.5.2.

9.5.2. *Factors that influence IOL on BENCHNET*

Aligned with the researched literature (Tables 9.1 and 9.2), this section presents the factors that influence IOL on BENCHNET that emerged from the data (Figure 9.1), detailing each of them in sequence.

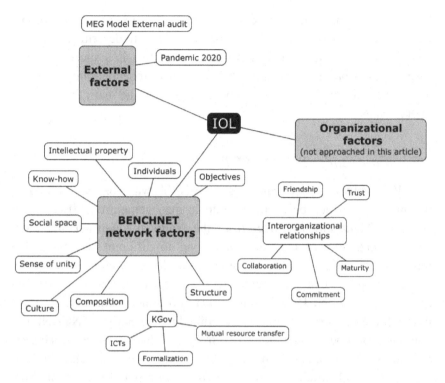

Figure 9.1.   Factors that influence IOL on BENCHNET.

9.5.2.1. *External factors (independent of the network or its organizations)*

The same factors that influence IOL in the investigated literature were verified in the case of BENCHNET, i.e. the pressures which originate from the environment and from crisis situations. Regarding environmental pressures, the interviewees highlight that the implementation of MEG in the network founding organizations acts as an external audit that promotes the search for external knowledge.[34,35] The MEG model ended up driving the organizations to seek benchmarking and thus the formation of a network beyond market competition in their respective sectors.

Regarding the crisis situation, Choi and Ko[21] and Jones and McPherson[34] explain that crises promote IOL. In the case of BENCHNET, the event mentioned by the interviewees was the COVID-19 pandemic. The social distancing measures generated the need to readapt the modality of network meetings, promoting learning both at the network level and within the organizations themselves. In this context, the exchange of knowledge about how each organization is trying to adapt to an unprecedented situation was enriched by inviting market analysts to the monthly meeting to discuss the pandemic scenario.

9.5.2.2. *Network-related factors (manageable by the BENCHNET)*

From the analysis of the interviews, 11 factors intrinsic to BENCHNET that influence IOL were identified, in line with those found in the studied literature, as described below:

(1) *Network know-how*: Organizations need to trust that their partners have knowledge and contributions to offer.[10,35–38,66] In the case of BENCHNET, there is a prerequisite for entering the network, which is that the organization has a systematic method of strategic organizational management. If, on one hand, the equivalent level of knowledge facilitates exchange,[50,51] on the other hand, there may be stagnation in the progress of aggregating new knowledge. A mechanism observed to minimize this risk in BENCHNET is the presence of universities in the network.

(2) *Social space internal to the network*: The social space influences interactions.[29] On BENCHNET, the representatives of organizations perceive the meetings as a place for discussions and reflections on common themes. This social space — a meeting room as a tangible representation — is provided by the organizations, alternating between them, for monthly meetings.

(3) *Sense of unity*: Members of the BENCHNET share an identity — that of organizations with systematic methods of strategic organizational management and that seek excellence through the exchange of practices and comparison of indicators. This shared identity facilitates IOL.[11,23,41,52]

(4) *Interorganizational relationships*: According to the interviewees, interpersonal relations on BENCHNET are based on trust, identity of objectives, commitment, maturity, frank communication, and friendship based on the time of existence of the network. The case ratifies the relevance of the interorganizational relationships materialized by the organizations' representatives and mentioned by several authors.[10,20,21,29,39–45,47–49] In this category of interorganizational relations, collaboration proved to be solid on BENCHNET. There is a sharing of resources and joint work in events, in addition to an exchange of resources (e.g.: the auditorium of one of the organizations) as a way for organizations to support the network.[14,16,29,30,40,43,47,49,51]

(5) *Network objectives*: BENCHNET aims to provide organizations with mutual learning, mainly through benchmarking processes. The clarity of this collective objective and the evidence of mutuality in learning reinforce the spirit of knowledge exchange.[11,15,23,43,45]

(6) *Network structure*: BENCHNET has a Dropbox repository and a WhatsApp group managed by the network coordinator. For events and meetings, the organizations provide places on a rotating basis, strengthening the bonds between them. The case presents a favorable structure for IOL, according to the authors mentioned in Table 9.1.[21,26,43,52–54] The small size of the network (nine organizations) facilitates management and interactions.[6]

(7) *Network composition*: BENCHNET's organizations are non-competitors, which minimizes conflicts of interest. They are of the same size and similar in the knowledge base on strategic organizational management, which allows mutual exchange of knowledge, confirming what was mentioned by several authors.[3,14,50,51,57]

(8) *Network individuals (organization's representatives)*: There are two representatives from each organization who are mostly strategic-level professionals in their organizations. The interviewees reported facts that showed the representatives' commitment to their organizations and to BENCHNET, as well as described their competencies and the collaborative way they have been working.[36,44,47,66]

(9) *Culture*: Because the network is composed of public and private organizations, there are cultural differences to be managed.[16,26,29,42,56,67]

However, on BENCHNET the cultural issue was perceived only in relation to the need to adapt the knowledge generated through the network and its application in the organizations of origin.

(10) *Intellectual property*: There is a formal recognition of the authorship of ideas or projects in the benchmarking processes, i.e. when an organization adopts practices from others, it gives credit to the origin of the knowledge in its reports and presentations. Thus, the concern of misappropriating knowledge from another organization is eliminated.[48]

(11) *KGov*: Network governance mechanisms in BENCHNET strongly emerged as the basis for sustaining the knowledge shared and created in the network for the success of IOL.

According to the interviewees, the network governance practices promote BENCHNET's knowledge processes. Such practices refer to KGov in the learning network.[68–70] The influences of the KGov in BENCHNET's network are presented in Section 9.5.2.3.

9.5.2.3. *KGov as a prominent factor that influences IOL*

Although there is no consensus regarding the definition of KGov in organizations,[61] there is, however, a convergence in the understanding that KGov deals with the unfolding of organization's corporate governance mechanisms related to knowledge processes.[1,68,70] For example, an organization's structures and trust-building, communication, and interaction practices that motivate people to engage in knowledge processes are components of KGov present in organizational learning.[25] KGov is also understood as knowledge production governance and involves the coordination of knowledge use, sharing, integration, and creation processes.[1,70] Therefore, in the case of BENCHNET, network governance coincides with KGov because it is a learning network that uses governance mechanisms that aim to improve knowledge processes. Thus, KGov on BENCHNET emerges as a prominent construct among the relevant factors that influence IOL, corroborating the statement by Ye *et al.*[71] that learning involves knowledge processes and KGov optimizes them and influences both organizational learning and IOL. As already mentioned, the literature

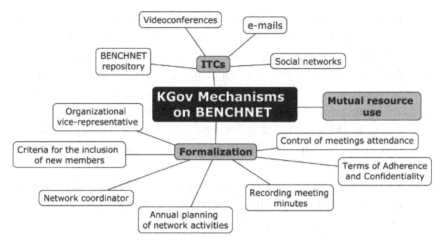

Figure 9.2.   KGov mechanisms on BENCHNET network.

so far brings the association of KGov with IOL,[69,71] and mechanisms of KGov that promote IOL have emerged with emphasis from BENCHNET, as shown in Figure 9.2.

KGov mechanisms to ensure the purpose of the network (mutual learning) between BENCHNET's organizations are based on formal instruments of interorganizational relationships. They are governed by formal knowledge transfer contracts and reinforce trust between organizations.[3,10,16,38,48] BENCHNET has three main documents that formalize the interactions:

(1) **Terms of adherence and confidentiality:** in which the organization's commitment appears through the names of the representatives. The terms are signed by the CEOs of the BENCHNET organizations.

(2) **Control of meetings attendance:** from the third consecutive absence without justification, the organization loses the right to participate in the network. This procedure prevents the group from losing continuity and pace of the activities proposed in the strategic planning of the network.

(3) **Recording meeting minutes:** the minutes, with the record of attendance and the topics worked, are shared with all organizations in the

group. Archived in the BENCHNET repository, the knowledge brought by the organizations is available for further consultation.

A formal network practice is the annual planning of network activities. According to some authors,[30,40,51] joint planning by several organizations generates learning through the exchange of diverse experiences. During the first meeting of the year, BENCHNET establishes its annual planning under the responsibility of the new coordinator. Thereafter, the organizations (which make an internal diagnosis each December) present topics that will be discussed and studied during the coming year in the monthly meetings. Lectures by specialists external to BENCHNET complement the network with knowledge not found internally. A schedule is then established. The annual planning is reviewed after one semester for occasional adjustments.

The most characteristic mechanism of KGov identified in BENCHNET is the coordination of the network taken as the network hub,[11] which acts as an interorganizational organizer.[14,21,40,41] BENCHNET's coordinator performs this role and encourages knowledge sharing. Each organization assumes this role for one year on a rotating basis and is succeeded by a vice-coordinating organization. This vice-coordinator works together with the coordinator to share the decisions and also to prepare itself to take up the coordination in the following year. The requirement to be coordinator is that the organization has been a member of the network for at least two years. Although the role of coordinator is voluntary, it is encouraged that all organizations go through the experience of coordinating. Even though there is no network hierarchy, the coordinator has the task of organizing the network in what concerns meetings, repositories, etc. In addition, the annual change of the coordinating person provides the group with experiences of differentiated directing styles, in the face of differences inherent to the diverse organizations.

At present, there is a movement in BENCHNET to bring new companies to the network to increase diversity. This concern of the network to oxygenate itself also demonstrates the commitment of the group members to recreate themselves so that BENCHNET continues to be a successful experience. In this sense, the rotation of the coordination could be one of the keys to the longevity of the network, since each organization that takes up the role of coordinator ends up printing a different management brand on the network.

There are criteria for the inclusion of new organizations onto BENCHNET. Whether due to the interest of an organization or the invitation by a BENCHNET organization, the applicant organization must demonstrate the use of a systematic management method, be similar in size to the existing members, and obtain the consent of all members, which analyze potential conflicts of interest (e.g. direct competition). All members must accept the entry of the applicant organization for its inclusion to take effect. Care is taken to check if an organization is only on the network to absorb knowledge, without making available to the network its own knowledge.

A mechanism to avoid the absence of an organization in the network's meetings is the presence of an organizational vice-representative. This avoids discontinuities in the functioning of the group, in addition to preventing a problem pointed out by Manuj *et al.*,[47] who report the issue of the turnover of the network's key people.

The mutual resource use, such as physical space for events, from one organization to another, strengthens the bonds of camaraderie, which in turn acts on interorganizational trust.

Finally, the use of information and communication technologies for administrative activities of the network has proved effective on BENCHNET, speeding up the flow of communication and coordination between the organizations of the group.

The network factors identified as promoters of IOL suggest that the network longevity is not the result of chance. The case suggested that, on BENCHNET, KGov creates favorable conditions for interorganizational knowledge flow and maintains long-lasting interorganizational bonds, and thus promotes IOL.

9.6. Conclusions

This study aimed to identify the factors that most influence IOL. The studied network (BENCHNET) has 15 years of existence and is composed of 9 organizations, of both public and private origins and from different economic sectors. The factors that influence IOL are external factors, network's factors, and organizational factors. The latter two factors were not examined in this article. One can perceive that both the interorganizational relations, based on trust, identity of objectives, commitment, maturity, friendship, and KGov are fundamental for the success and longevity of BENCHNET. KGov has shown to significantly contribute to ensure the purpose of the network — mutual learning among organizations — and to motivate and create mechanisms that help knowledge acquisition and sharing in the network's organizations.

Despite the limitations of this research — e.g. a single case study — the results are believed to contribute to knowing factors that influence IOL on a learning network. In future, researchers should identify practices that facilitate IOL at network and organizational levels. They also should identify the organizational factors that influence IOL in order to seek improvement for each organization of the network, resulting in improvement of the network itself. Furthermore, KGov associated with IOL opens up a wide field of research that requires deep study.

References

1. S. Pemsel, A. Wiewiora, R. Müller, M. Aubry and K. Brown. A conceptualization of knowledge governance in project-based organizations. *International Journal of Project Management*, **32**(8), 1411–1422 (2014).
2. K. Dalkir. *Knowledge Management in Theory and Practice*. Foreword by J. Liebowitz. Cambridge; London: The MIT Press (2011).
3. P.J. Lane and M. Lubatkin. Relative absorptive capacity and interorganizational learning, *Strategic Management Journal*, **19**(5), 461–477 (1998).
4. V.A. Gilsing and B. Nooteboom. Exploration and exploitation in innovation systems: The case of pharmaceutical biotechnology, *Research Policy*, **35**, 1–23 (2006).
5. H.L. Cheng. Effect of organizational politics on non-dominant firms: From interorganizational learning to intraorganizational learning. *The Journal of Applied Behavioral Science*, **48**(4), 463–494 (2012).
6. L. Knight. Network learning: Exploring learning by interorganizational networks, *Human Relations*, **55**(4), 427–454 (2002).
7. L.D. Peters, A.D. Pressey, and W.J. Johnston. Contingent factors affecting network learning. *Journal of Business Research*, **69**(7), 2507–2515 (2016).

8. Y.F. Badir and G.C. O'Connor. The formation of tie strength in a strategic alliance's first new product development project: The influence of project and partners' characteristics. *Journal of Product Innovation Management*, **32**(1), 154–169 (2015).
9. A. Halachmi and A.M. Woron. Spontaneous interorganizational learning. *International Journal of Organization Theory and Behavior*, **16**(2), 135–164 (2013).
10. S.S. Lui. The roles of competence trust, formal contract, and time horizon in interorganizational learning. *Organization Studies*, **30**(4), 333–353 (2009).
11. J. Gibb, A. Sune and S. Albers. Network learning: Episodes of interorganizational learning towards a collective performance goal. *European Management Journal*, **35**(1), 15–25 (2017).
12. I. Manuj, A. Omar and A. Yazdanparast. The quest for competitive advantage in global supply chains: The role of interorganizational learning. *Transportation Journal*, **52**(4), 463–492 (2013).
13. I.M. Nembhard. All teach, all learn, all improve? The role of interorganizational learning in quality improvement collaboratives. *Health Care Management Review*, **37**(2), 154 (2012).
14. S.M. Yang, S.C. Fang, S.R. Fang and C.H. Chou. Knowledge exchange and knowledge protection in interorganizational learning: The ambidexterity perspective. *Industrial Marketing Management*, **43**(2), 346–358 (2014).
15. A. Rajala. Examining the effects of interorganizational learning on performance: A meta-analysis. *Journal of Business & Industrial Marketing*, **33**(4), 574–584 (2018).
16. M. Janowicz-Panjaitan and N.G. Noorderhaven, Formal and informal interorganizational learning within strategic alliances. *Research Policy*, **37**(8), 1337–1355 (2008).
17. H.R. Greve. Interorganizational learning and heterogeneous social structure. *Organization Studies*. **26**(7), 1025–1047 (2005).
18. S. Melo and M. Beck. Intra and interorganizational learning networks and the implementation of quality improvement initiatives: The case of a Portuguese teaching hospital. *Human Resource Development Quarterly*, **26**(2), 155–183 (2015).
19. A.R. Mozzato and C.C. Bitencourt. Understanding interorganizational learning based on social spaces and learning episodes. *BAR-Brazilian Administration Review*, **11**(3), 284–301 (2014).
20. A. Leung, H. Xu, G.J. Wu and K.W. Luthans. Industry Peer Networks (IPNs): Cooperative and competitive interorganizational learning and network outcomes. *Management Research Review*, **42**(1), 122–140 (2019).

21. S. Choi and I. Ko. Leveraging electronic collaboration to promote interorganizational learning. *International Journal of Information Management*, **32**(6), 550–559 (2012).
22. D.S. Colet, and A.R. Mozzato. Proposal for a framework of the contribution of interorganizational learning for micro and small enterprises. *Navus*, **8**(3), 126–136 (2018).
23. T.V. Matheis and C. Herzig. Upgrading products, upgrading work? Interorganizational learning in global food value chains to achieve the Sustainable Development Goals. *GAIA-Ecological Perspectives for Science and Society*, **28**(2), 126–134 (2019).
24. T.J. Kull and S.C. Ellis. Coping with dependence: A logistics strategy based on interorganizational learning for managing buyer–supplier relations. *Journal of Business Logistics*, **37**(4), 346–363 (2016).
25. S. Michailova and E. Sidorova. From group-based work to organizational learning: The role of communication forms and knowledge sharing. *Knowledge Management Research Practice*, **9**, 73–83 (2011).
26. N.S. Levinson and M. Asahi. Cross-national alliances and interorganizational learning. *IEEE Engineering Management Review*, **25**(3), 32–41 (1997).
27. G. Müller-Seitz. Absorptive and desorptive capacity-related practices at the network level–the case of SEMATECH. *R&D Management*, **42**(1), 90–99 (2012).
28. E.B. Abbade. Interorganizational alignment of strategic orientations in supply chains. *Revista de Negócios*, **20**(2), 15–30 (2015).
29. A.R. Mozzato and C.C. Bitencourt. The process of interorganisational learning in the context of spatial agglomeration. *International Journal of Innovation and Learning*, **24**(2), 176–199 (2018).
30. P. Bergh. Swedish inter-organisational learning network: Outcomes in three dimensions. *International Journal of Business and Globalization*, **2**(1), 56–71 (2008).
31. D. Coghlan and P. Coughlan. Effecting change and learning in networks through network action learning. *The Journal of Applied Behavioral Science*, **51**(3), 375–400 (2015).
32. W.W. Powell, K.W. Koput and L. Smith-Doerr. Interorganizational collaboration and the locus of innovation: Networks of learning in biotechnology. *Administrative Science Quarterly*, **41**, 116–145 (1996).
33. A.R. Mozzato and C.C. Bitencourt. Understanding interorganizational learning based on social spaces and learning episodes. *BAR — Brazilian Administration Review*, **11**(3), 284–330 (2014).

34. O. Jones and A. Macpherson. Interorganizational learning and strategic renewal in SMEs: Extending the 4I framework. *Long Range Planning*, **39**(2), 155–175 (2006).

35. P.V. Bastos and H.R. Greve. Interorganizational learning and the location of manufacturing subsidiaries: Is chain migration also a corporate behavior? *Advances in Strategic Management*, **20**, 159–192 (2003).

36. J. Hartley and M. Allison. Good, better, best? Interorganizational learning in a network of local authorities. *Public Management Review*, **4**(1), 101–118 (2002).

37. R.B. Bouncken, R. Pesch and S. Kraus. SME innovativeness in buyer–seller alliances: Effects of entry timing strategies and interorganizational learning. *Review of Managerial Science*, **9**(2), 361–384 (2015).

38. M.D.M. Benavides-Espinosa. El conocimiento como recurso estratégico para el aprendizaje interorganizativo. *Revista Venezolana de Gerencia*, **16**(56), 564–577 (2011).

39. J.E. Scott. Facilitating interorganizational learning with information technology. *Journal of Management Information Systems*, **17**(2), 81–113 (2000).

40. Y.C. Kim, J.W. Lu and M. Rhee. Learning from age difference: Interorganizational learning and survival in Japanese foreign subsidiaries. *Journal of International Business Studies*, **43**(8), 719–745 (2012).

41. B. Uzunca. Biological children versus stepchildren: Interorganizational learning processes of spinoff and nonspinoff suppliers. *Journal of Management*, **44**(8), 3258–3287 (2018).

42. J. Downe, J. Hartley and L. Rashman. Evaluating the extent of interorganizational learning and change in local authorities through the English Beacon Council Scheme. *Public Management Review*, **6**(4), 531–554 (2004).

43. V. Eiriz, M. Gonçalves and J.S. Areias. Interorganizational learning within an institutional knowledge network. *European Journal of Innovation Management*, **20**(2), 230–249 (2017).

44. T. Schumacher. Linking action learning and inter-organisational learning: The learning journey approach. *Action Learning: Research and Practice*, **12**(3), 293–313 (2015).

45. H. Toiviainen. Interorganizational learning across levels: An object-oriented approach. *The Journal of Workplace Learning*, **19**(6), 343–358 (2007).

46. Q. Zhu, H. Krikke and M.C. Caniels. Supply chain integration: Value creation through managing interorganizational learning. *International Journal of Operations & Production Management*, **38**(1), 211–229 (2018).

47. I. Manuj, A. Omar and T.L. Pohlen. Inter-organizational learning in supply chains: A focus on logistics service providers and their customers. *Journal of Business Logistics*, **35**(2), 103–120 (2014).
48. G.A. Avalos-Quispe and L.M. Hernández-Simón. Open innovation in SMEs: Potential and realized absorptive capacity for interorganizational learning in dyad collaborations with academia. *Journal of Open Innovation: Technology, Market, and Complexity*, **5**(3), 72–86 (2019).
49. M. Mellat-Parast. Supply chain quality management. *International Journal of Quality & Reliability Management*, **30**(5), 511–529 (2013).
50. H. Schildt, T. Keil and M. Maula. The temporal effects of relative and firm-level absorptive capacity on interorganizational learning. *Strategic Management Journal*, **33**(10), 1154–1173 (2012).
51. A.H. Pratono, N.K. Darmasetiawan, A. Yudiarso and B.G. Jeong. Achieving sustainable competitive advantage through green entrepreneurial orientation and market orientation, *The Bottom Line*, **32**(1), 2–15 (2019).
52. S.L. Manring and S.B. Moore, Creating and managing a virtual interorganizational learning network for greener production: A conceptual model and case study. *Journal of Cleaner Production*, **14**(9–11), 891–899 (2006).
53. R. Grunwald and A. Kieser. Learning to reduce interorganizational learning: An analysis of architectural product innovation in strategic alliances. *Journal of Product Innovation Management*, **24**(4), 369–391 (2007).
54. L.K. Comfort. Risk and resilience: Inter-organizational learning following the Northridge earthquake of 17 January 1994. *Journal of Contingencies and Crisis Management*, **2**(3), 157–170 (1994).
55. D.N. Ammons and D.J. Roenigk. Benchmarking and interorganizational learning in local government. *Journal of Public Administration Research and Theory*, **25**, 309–335 (2014)
56. L.W. Busenitz, J.O. Fiet and D.D. Moesel. Reconsidering the venture capitalists' "value added" proposition: An interorganizational learning perspective. *Journal of Business Venturing*, **19**(6), 787–807 (2004).
57. C. Linder and S. Sperber. Towards a deeper understanding of the emergence of process innovations: Which role do inter-organisational learning and internal knowledge exploitation play? *Journal of Engineering and Technology Management*, **53**, 33–48 (2019).
58. B. Grüb and S. Martin, Evaluating communication as an essential precondition for inter-organisational learning in Governance Networks–The case of the Healthy Cities Network in Germany. *Health Services Management Research*, **32**(3), 130–145 (2019).

59. Y. Yang. Bilateral inter-organizational learning in corporate venture capital activity. *Management Research Review*, **35**(5), 352–378 (2012).
60. R. Gupta, S.C. Sharma and P. Gupta. "Corporate governance" importance, pillars and principle (Road to corporate transparency). *Journal of Critical Reviews*, **7**(12) 3917–3923 (2020).
61. P. De Sá Freire, G.A. Dandolini, J.A. De Souza, T.C. Silva and R.M. Couto. Governança do Conhecimento (GovC): o estado da arte sobre o termo. *Biblos*, **69**, 21–39 (2017).
62. R.K. Yin. *Qualitative Research from Start to Finish*, 2nd ed., New York: Guilford Press (2016).
63. S.B. Merriam and E.J. Tisdell. *Qualitative Research: A Guide to Design and Implementation*, 4th ed., San Francisco: Jossey-Bass (2016).
64. V. Braun and V. Clarke. Thematic analysis. Using thematic analysis in psychology. *Qualitative Research in Psychology*, **3**, 77–101 (2006).
65. V. Braun and V. Clarke. Thematic analysis. In *APA handbook of research methods in psychology*, Research designs: Quantitative, qualitative, neuropsychological, and biological, H. Cooper, P. M. Camic, D. L. Long, A. T. Panter, D. Rindskopf and K. J. Sher (Eds.). (2), 57–71 (2012).
66. M. Holmqvist. Intra-and interorganisational learning processes: An empirical comparison. *Scandinavian Journal of Management*, **19**(4), 443–466 (2003).
67. R. Beck and K. Schott. The interplay of project control and interorganizational learning: Mitigating effects on cultural differences in global, multisource ISD outsourcing projects. *Business & Information Systems Engineering*, **4**(4), 183–192 (2012).
68. N.J. Foss. The emerging knowledge governance approach: Challenges and characteristics. *Organization*, **14**(1), 29–52 (2007).
69. S. Pemsel, J. Söderlund and A. Wiewora. Contextualising capability development: Configurations of knowledge governance mechanisms in project-based organizations. *Technology Analysis & Strategic Management*, **30**(10), 1226–1245 (2018).
70. J. Zhao, X. Xi and T. Guo. The impact of focal firm's centrality and knowledge governance on innovation performance. *Knowledge Management Research & Practice*, **16**(2), 196–207 (2018).
71. X. Ye, Z. Wang, Y. Zhang and H. Li. How do knowledge governance mechanisms impact on repatriate knowledge transfer intention? The moderating role of perceived career and repatriation support and person-organization fit. *Management Decision*, **59**(2), 324–340 (2020).

Interorganizational Learning: The Central Role of Social Spaces and Learning Episodes

Anelise Rebelato Mozzato[*,‡] *and Claudia Cristina Bitencourt*[†]

[*]UPF Management School,
University of Passo Fundo,
190 Adolfo Loureiro Street,
Passo Fundo, RS 99010650, Brazil

[†]Unisinos Management School,
University of Vale do Rio dos Sinos,
40 Inácio Vasconcelos Street,
Porto Alegre, RS 90.480–160, Brazil

[‡]anerebe@upf.br

Different organizational configurations have been gaining ground in the world economy, involving interorganizational relationships with different agents. This suggests the need for more studies that deal with interorganizational relations and their governance, including interorganizational learning (IOL), reinforcing the relevance of the theme, which is the focus of this chapter. Thus, we seek a greater understanding of the IOL as a dynamic process found in interorganizational cooperation. We work from a practice-based perspective because we believe that it can be an alternative to contribute to the advancement of studies on IOL. Therefore, the IOL is understood as part of an organizational learning continuum and is analyzed within the scope of practical rationality in a less cognitive and more socio-behavioral approach. We understand that the proposition of the six constitutive elements of the IOL allows a better understanding of the IOL process in different interorganizational relationships. Thus, the IOL was analyzed as a dynamic process that takes place in cooperative interorganizational relationships found in different structured and unstructured social spaces in everyday life, providing learning episodes. It is worth noting that governance in different types of interorganizational relationships can facilitate the IOL process.

10.1. Introduction

Diverse organizational settings have been gaining ground in the world economy, with a growing number of different forms of strategic alliances.[1] As a result, organizations are increasingly introducing new settings involving interorganizational relationships with different agents such as organizations, universities, and trade associations, among others.[2,3]

In addition, the importance of organizations that work with collaborative perspectives is evident, exploring learning (situations) built on relationships between organizations. Reference 4 discuss different levels of learning and further, while Ref. 5 suggest new studies in the field of interorganizational learning (IOL), reinforcing the relevance of the theme, which is the focus of this chapter.

Despite its relevance, IOL is still poorly investigated and is best termed a field in progress.[4,6–14] Authors, including Ref. 15 in a recent bibliometric review, point out the need for further studies on the IOL. These authors claim that academic interest in the IOL has increased in the last decade, precisely because of its potential to absorb, transfer, and create valuable knowledge to improve the performance of those involved.

With this in mind, it is clear the need to put forward some theoretical and empirical reflections and afford greater depth to studies in the field of

IOL. This chapter is based on the assumption that IOL is understood as part of the continuum of organizational learning (OL) as it was proposed by Refs. 5, 8, and 16–19. Following this line of thought, IOL is understood as a dynamic process that occurs in interorganizational relations of cooperation, in different social spaces (structured and non-structured), stimulating learning situations referred to here as learning episodes.

In such interorganizational relations, governance facilitates the achievement of results and experiences in the interaction between different agents, including the IOL process. References 20 and 21 consider the IOL as a variable that can be affected by governance. Both the seminal work of Ref. 22 as the more current, as in the examples of Refs. 23 and 24, highlight the importance of more research on governance in interorganizational relations.

More specifically, we consider that the practice-based perspective extends the literature on IOL by advocating a fourth level of analysis (the interorganizational level) and a fifth process (cooperation) to be added to the three levels of analysis (individual, group, and organizational) and the four processes (intuiting, interpreting, integrating, and institutionalizing) of the OL framework proposed by Ref. 4. Therefore, our proposed model is based on new evidence gathered from practice-based approach in Refs. 25–29, taking Refs. 5 and 16 as a starting point.

10.2. IOL as Part of a Continuum of Organizational Learning

With the aim of achieving a clearer understanding, IOL is treated as part of a continuum of OL as identified by Refs. 4 and 16, even though this is not included in the corresponding frameworks presented by these authors. Reference 13 proposes the inclusion of the fourth level into the framework elaborated by Ref. 4, which refers to the analysis of IOL and deals with the fifth process on this level, namely cooperation. Figure 10.1[4] demonstrates its inclusion in the framework, which is presented by Ref. 13.

Figure 10.1 illustrates the multilevel structural characteristics of the learning process, exposing the intimate interconnection between all levels and the fact that they are pervaded by processes that reinforce the importance of approaching learning based on a social and behavioral view, from

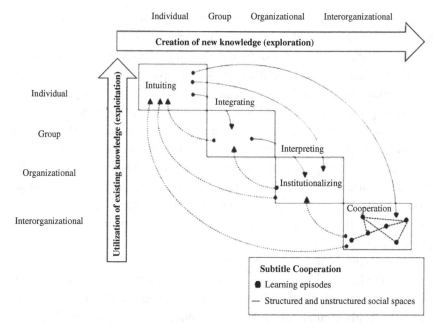

Figure 10.1.   IOL as a dynamic process through cooperation.

a practice-based approach. Having IOL as a process that occurs beyond organizational boundaries, it occurs in the interaction between different agents that cooperate with each other, generating episodes of learning. Thus, there is the incorporation of external knowledge from these interactions and cooperation between different agents.[4,13,14]

Thus, in interpreting the framework dynamics, the first three levels of learning and the four processes involved operate along the lines of the ideas espoused by Ref. 6. However, with respect to the fourth level and the resulting inclusion of a fifth level, despite following the same logic, it is worth noting that intuition intervenes in integration, which in turn intervenes in interpretation, and that interpretation intervenes in institutionalization. This in turn results in institutionalization interfering in cooperative processes. As a result, cooperation intervenes in institutionalization, which in turn interferes in interpretation. Sequentially then, interpretation intervenes in integration, which ultimately intervenes in intuition.

Faced with this dynamic, (movement in both directions), it can be observed that learning takes place over four levels: individual, group, organizational, and interorganizational.

However, inclusion on this fourth level means that the direct interference of intuition on institutionalization (as proposed by Ref. 6) is transferred to cooperation. Pursuing this line of thought, when the authors propose that institutionalization has a direct effect on intuition, it is understood that cooperation has a direct effect on intuition. Moreover, as they point out, such levels are permeated by social and psychological processes.

The interorganizational cooperation strategy is linked with several important results. It facilitates the production of new knowledge, fosters innovation and new solutions, and helps organizations achieve a more central and competitive position in relation to enterprises that work in isolation. Cooperation as the fifth process, included in the Ref. 6, is related to relational strategies established between the different agents that are external to the organization, facilitating IOL as a dynamic process.

Cooperation may be seen as stemming from collaborative actions established in interorganizational relationships, with mutual commitment. However, the idea of competition is not absent in this setting. Even within the logic of cooperation, the coexistence of cooperation and competition is accepted.[30–32] In interorganizational relationships, learning is often seems to be a natural result of cooperation.[33]

Reference 34 claims that IOL may be seen as the collective acquisition of knowledge between groups of organizations, in this way compassing the idea of interactions between organizations. Therefore, IOL is distinct from OL in that it includes the effects of interactions between organizations, which generates greater synergy and fosters learning.

It is precisely the synergy that results from interactions (cooperation) between organizations that distinguishes interorganizational from intraorganizational learning. Reference 35 believes that it is this interaction between agents, which is not limited to organizational boundaries, that give rise to a collective learning environment.

IOL is understood as a form of learning that takes place by means of cooperative relationships (interactions) between different agents. These interactions improve and expand each participant's knowledge base and boost the potential to create individual and collective comparative advantages. Given plurality and overlapping of the concepts and IOL's focus, we will draw on the concept outlined by Ref. 36:

> IOL is a distinctive form of learning because the organization learns from the experience of others rather than from its own experience. While distinctive in the source of learning, IOL is supported by intraorganizational processes of knowledge creation and retention, and some of its findings parallel those of research on intraorganizational transfer of knowledge.

In 2018, we presented six constitutive elements of the IOL, even though emphasizing that they can change according to the type of interorganizational relationships established. In Figure 10.2,[14] we demonstrate these constitutive elements of the IOL.

These six constitutive elements of the IOL illustrated in Figure 10.2 are in a dynamic interconnection process, allowing several relationships to be established in different interorganizational relationships. We understand that the proposition of the six constitutive elements of the IOL allows a better understanding of the IOL process. The meaning of each of the constitutive elements of IOL is showed in Figure 10.2.[14]

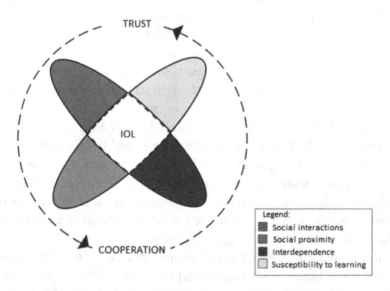

Figure 10.2. The dynamics of the IOL process with its constitutive elements.

10.3. Practice-Based Approach: Learning as a Process

We aim to understand IOL, based on a socio-behavioral view, within the logic of practical rationality, without remaining centered on cognitive approaches. With this in mind, we make use of the based-on-practice or practice-based approach. Reference 27 works on a practice-based approach, contemplating learning as a process and the different levels that occur within this process. Thus, despite the authors' primary concern being with OL, we feel that analyzing IOL through this theoretical lens is innovative, and it can result in worthwhile insights into the construction of referential concepts of IOL (Table 10.1).

Reference 26 argues that the practice-based perspective has been used as a theoretical lens for reinterpreting many organizational phenomena.

Table 10.1. Constitutive elements of IOL.

Constitutive Elements	Theoretical Proposals
Trust	Reflects the conviction that the partner's word will be kept, consequently ensuring that the obligations of the relationship will be performed directly influencing the IOL process.
Cooperation	Consists of collaborative actions between different interorganizational agents that have reciprocal commitments. Cooperative work assumes importance in view of the variety of positive effects of such work processes. However, it must be thought out in processes that can coexist with the competition.
Social interactions	Consists of social relations in interorganizational relationships. Facilitated communication and openness to connectivity. Power relations are not denied.
Social proximity	It concerns the largest identity between the different agents in interorganizational relations, facilitating the establishment of stronger social bonds, thus leading to greater social proximity.
Interdependence	It concerns the largest identity between the different agents in interorganizational relations, facilitating the establishment of stronger social bonds, thus leading to greater social proximity.
Susceptibility to learning	It is related to the possibility of learning by different agents, depending on both the willingness and the ability to learn.

This in turn leads to the idea that it is also possible to reinterpret IOL as an interorganizational phenomenon.

Pursuing this logic, the question of process-based learning[27,37] arises — returning to Ref. 38 on how learning occurs through relationships, which is interesting precisely for its process-based perspective of learning and rather than a descriptive perspective.

Reference 39 already understood learning to be a process rather than a product (or stock of knowledge), recognizing the value of interaction and personal contact. Considering that this study returns to a process-based vision of learning at an organizational level, it is necessary to understand action within the social context, in the sense highlighted by Ref. 40, reiterating that learning is inherently a relational activity.

Learning is an everyday action, a flow of activities that is part of the daily work routine, and an effect of a series of interrelated practices and operations that are carried out.[26,41,42] In other words, learning happens by means of practical rationality.

Studies making use of a practice-based approach can potentially go beyond a conventional organizational analysis.[43] The author, in addition to the cognitive view, highlights that the practice-based approach also came about as a critique of a positivist and rationalist view of organizations. The various interests and research traditions that are dubbed practice-based studies means that it is not easy to delineate a common perspective. We also adopt this perspective, with the aim of reaching a better understanding of the IOL process, just as Ref. 44 attempted to do in understanding OL.

In situating our work as an attempt to improve understanding of IOL in practice-based theories, we intend to focus our attention on socially constructed phenomena situated within the fifth process that is delineated in the framework proposed by Ref. 4 — that is to say, interorganizational cooperation. This agrees with Ref. 43 view that is oriented toward the subjective, emotional, and provisional, as the author considers that practice-based studies call into question the objective, cognitive, and abstract nature of knowledge. Also, according to Refs. 29 and 44–48, OL takes place in practice through participation.

This view of learning as a process at the interorganizational level sees everyday action as an element in the social setting; in the sense, as stressed by Ref. 40, learning is an inherently relational activity.

"Practice-based approaches conceptualize context not simply as a container within which activities occur, but crucially as enacted, whereby its elements are simultaneously influenced by mediums and outcomes of social activity."[49] Reference 27 suggests that "learning is integrated into individuals' daily lives, deriving from informal sources of social relations. It is therefore assumed that any activity can constitute an opportunity for learning and that casual social situations are as important as formal learning experiences."

Reference 50 states that behavioral issues have received insufficient attention despite the perception that they may help understand learning between different organizations. They refer: "integration of new information at the group level makes inter-OL possible. It is the individuals and the social processes and practices, such as dialogue, through which they develop shared understandings that facilitate inter-organizational learning."[50] In line with this view, these authors identify dialogue as a central element of IOL processes because dialogue creates a shared understanding that facilitates learning.

Reference 34 already advocated that IOL may be hindered by a lack of communication. Importance is given to dialogue and communication precisely because learning is seen as a process that involves issues of context and interaction. Such interactions, particularly cooperative ones, foster IOL, which takes place through a range of existing interorganizational relationships.

Our view follows the reasoning put forward by Ref. 49, who believes that cognitive theory is not opposed to the practice-based approach, but that it constitutes a limited approach when guided by positivism, tending towards reductionism. Reference 49 corroborates this in stating that, "socially shared cognitions plays a crucial part in guiding practices."

Given the fact that learning is an everyday action in the sense that it is the effect of a series of interrelated practices and operations,[25,26,28,41,42] it should be noted that learning is closely related to the social-behavioral view[50] and that this is a less cognitive approach.[8]

It is believed that viewing learning as a practice-based study greatly contributes to a better understanding and advancement of IOL theory, thus expanding the possibilities for analysis based on everyday practices. It is in this logic that we understand social learning spaces and learning episodes.

10.4. Social Learning Spaces and Learning Episodes

Interorganizational relationships are established in both structured and unstructured social spaces for learning,[51] providing learning episodes.[8] Reference 51 demonstrate that learning behaviors can be formal (taking the form of planned events) or informal (taking the form of spontaneous interaction), with different repercussions in the IOL process. These authors emphasize that IOL does not always occur spontaneously. As a result, IOL can be stimulated if structural measures are formalized.

Similarly, Ref. 52 has stressed that, in an ordinary interorganizational context, informal social interactions are supported by the formal structure. In agreement with this, Ref. 17 stated that studies on IOL require equal focus on the formal and informal aspects of learning, without privileging one over the other. Reference 53 highlighted formal and informal aspects as subtle elements that need to be thought out, given that neither information nor knowledge is easily transferred by way of license or purchase.

When these opportunities for social interaction are perceived as an obligation and not as a voluntary learning opportunity, people become less willing to interact and formality tends to inhibit informality, leading to a loss of spontaneity.[51] These authors assert that both formal and informal social interactions have a positive effect on IOL results, as Ref. 54 suggests. They also highlight the complementarity between formal and informal interactions. Even though formality and informality reinforce each other, these relationships cannot be said to be perfect complements, given that the positive effect of informalization tends to disappear as the degree of formality increases. Reference 8 identifies the central role of social interactions in the study of IOL in interorganizational relationships.

Therefore, while an increase in the extent of informal learning behavior will yield consistent positive effects on formal behavior, additional formalization will have a positive effect on informal learning mechanisms only up to a point.[51] The authors show that, as Ref. 55 advocated in the case of OL, excessive formalization (formal mechanisms), even when used with the intent of stimulating learning, can hinder both informal learning behaviors and IOL.

Therefore, it is clear that social spaces can foster interorganizational relationships, which, in turn, can lead to the occurrence of learning episodes in the flow of everyday activities that take place in formal and informal spaces. More specifically, it is understood that IOL should be analyzed in accordance with Ref. 8, when they refer to the importance of analyzing context (history, aims, and routine), content (changes that took place), and process (actions and intentions, leading to learning episodes).

According to the assumptions demonstrated by Ref. 51, these formal spaces in interorganizational settings are essential in fostering IOL, a process, which can also be stimulated by informal spaces. In this line of reasoning, IOL is understood as a process, a result of a flow of everyday activities, which is recurrent in horizontal relationships established between different agents, i.e. within the logic of practical rationality. Such activity flows are what Ref. 17 termed network learning episodes, which, according to the author, offer an appropriate unit of analysis for empirical research, thus improving the understanding of learning in interorganizational relationships.

These learning episodes, according to Refs. 8 and 17, are related to the flow of everyday activities that are found both in structured and unstructured spaces. In other words, learning episodes are actions and interactions that take place between different agents and which foster events and learning experiences (learning events), with a direct or indirect impact on different interacting agents.

Such learning episodes can be analyzed for their content, with a focus on what was learned (e.g. the research of Ref. 8). Alternatively, the focus can be on episode occurrences, in which case their importance to the agents involved is analyzed.

We understand that, in addition to cooperation and trust, the other four constitutive elements of AIO (social interaction, social proximity, interdependence, and susceptibility to learning) lead to episodes of learning. Moreover, each organization's internal dynamics, as well as the nature of the interorganizational dynamics, determine whether IOL will take place.[56]

Another important factor for the occurrence of the IOL is governance. As Refs. 20 and 21 indicate, many variables can be affected by governance, such as IOL. Interorganizational relations, including the IOL, can be more useful through governance, regardless of type, like the three basic ways of governance proposed by Ref. 22. Accordingly, governance favors

IOL and knowledge sharing, thereby improving the performance of those involved in cooperation.

As stated by Refs. 23 and 57, governance with its mechanisms promotes greater social and relational capital. Thus, governance facilitates the expected results achievement by the interaction between the different agents. However, we do not propose an in-depth study in network governance, although it is necessary, as pointed out by Ref. 24. To conclude, we emphasize that IOL was analyzed as a dynamic process that takes place in cooperative interorganizational relationships found in different structured and unstructured social spaces, which provide learning episodes.

10.5. Final Remarks

To conclude the proposal presented here, we should point out that IOL features were addressed according to social-behavioral views more than cognitive approaches, emphasizing the practice-based approach. We understand that the practice-based perspective can be an alternative ontological and epistemological basis to contribute to the advancement of studies on IOL.

As Ref. 29 highlights, practice-based studies can make a significant contribution to link the analysis of working, learning, and organizing because they enable contextualization of organizing within a circumscribed empirical context, define them as a collective practical accomplishment, analyze the activities that contribute to the stabilization and performativity of organizing, and examine knowledge in knowing.

IOL is viewed as part of a continuum of OL, thus enlarging the scope of analysis. Additionally, IOL was analyzed as a dynamic process that takes place in cooperative interorganizational relationships found in different structured and unstructured social spaces in everyday life, which provide learning episodes.

Although the need for further studies on IOL and its governance remains, we understand that this chapter contributes to a better understanding and development of IOL, in addition to encouraging more theoretical and empirical researches in different interorganizational contexts. Aware of the need for more advanced and critical analysis on the topic, we corroborate with Ref. 15, which point out the future of IOL research depends on international academic collaboration and interdisciplinary perspectives and contributions. It is worth highlighting the importance of governance in different types of interorganizational relations. It facilitates the achievement of results and experiences in the interaction between different agents, including the IOL process.

Finally, we emphasize that we are contributing to the advancement of IOL research, facilitating its understanding through the six constitutive elements presented. Although the need for further studies remains, we expect that the debate presented here will contribute to a better understanding and development of IOL, in addition to encouraging further theoretical and empirical research in different interorganizational settings.

References

1. C. Inkpen and E.W.K. Tsang. Learning and strategic alliances. *The Academy of Management Annals*, **1**(1), 479–511 (2007).
2. T. Dacin, D. Reid and P.S. Ring. Alliances and joint ventures: the role of partner selection from an embeddedness perspective. In *Inter-organizational Relations*, S. Cropper, M. Ebers, C. Huxham and P.S. Ring (eds.), Oxford, UK: Oxford University Press (2008), pp. 90–117.
3. S. Cropper, M. Ebers, C. Huxham and P.S. Ring, *Handbook de relações interorganizacionais da Oxford*. Porto Alegre: Bookman (2014).
4. M.M. Crossan, H.W. Lane and R.E. White. An organizational learning framework: From intuition to institution. *Academy of Management Review*, **24**(3), 522–537 (1999).
5. M.M. Crossan, C.C. Mauer and R.E. White. Reflections on the 2009 AMR decade award: Do we have a theory of organizational learning? *Academy of Management Review*, **36**(3), 446–460 (2011).
6. R. Larsson, L. Bengtsson, K. Henriksson and J. Sparks. Barriers to interorganizational learning: Developing collective knowledge across corporate boundaries. In *Advances in Management Cognition and Organizational Information Processing*, Vol 6, C. Stubbart (ed.). JAI Press Inc (1999), pp. 115–147.
7. M. Easterby-Smith and M.A. Lyles. *The Blackwell Handbook of Organizational Learning and Knowledge Management*. Oxford: Blackwell Publishing (2003).
8. L. Knight and A. Pye. Network learning: An empirically derived model of learning by groups of organizations. *Human Relations*, **58**(3), 369–392 (2005).

9. Y. Engeström and H. Kerosuo. From workplace learning to inter-organizational learning and back: The contribution of activity theory. *Journal of Workplace Learning*, **19**(6), 336–342 (2007).

10. B. Nooteboom. Learning and innovation in inter-organizational relationships. In *The Oxford Handbook of Inter-organizational Relations*, S. Cropper, M. Ebers, C. Huxham and P.S. Ring (eds.) Oxford: Oxford University Press (2008), pp. 307–634.

11. J. Gibb, A. Sune and S. Albers. Network learning: Episodes of interorganizational learning towards a collective performance goal. *European Management Journal*, **35**(1), 15–25 (2017).

12. A. Rajala. Examining the effects of interorganizational learning on performance: A meta-analysis. *Journal of Business & Industrial Marketing*, **33**(4), 574–584 (2018).

13. R. Mozzato and C.C. Bitencourt. Understanding interorganizational learning based on social spaces and learning episodes. *Brazilian Administration Review*, **11**(3), 284–301 (2014).

14. A.R. Mozzato and C.C. Bitencourt, The process of interorganisational learning in the context of spatial agglomeration. *International Journal of Innovation and Learning*, **24**(2), 176–199 (2018).

15. J. Anand, L.B. Kringelum, C.O. Madsen and L. Selivanovskikh. Interorganizational learning: A bibliometric review and research agenda. *The Learning Organization* (2020) https://doi.org/10.1108/TLO-02-2020-0023.

16. M.M. Crossan, H.W. Lane, R.E. White and L. Djurfeldt. Organizational learning: Dimensions for a theory. *International Journal of Organizational Analysis*, **3**(4), 337–360 (1995).

17. L. Knight. Network learning: Exploring learning by interorganizational networks. *Human Relations*, **55**(4),427–454 (2002).

18. H. Bapuji and M. Crossan. From questions to answers: Reviewing organizational learning research. *Management Learning*, **35**(4), 397–417 (2004).

19. M. Holmqvist. Experiential learning processes of exploitation and exploration within and between organizations: An empirical study of product development. *Organization Science*, **15**(1), 70–81 (2004).

20. F. Mariotti. Exploring interorganizational learning: A review of the literature and future directions. *Knowledge and Process Management*, **19**(4), 215–221 (2012).

21. J. Verschoore, A. Balestrin and R. Teixeira. Network management and associated firms' outcomes: Multilevel analysis in the southern Brazilian context. *The Journal of Management and Governance*, **21**, 211–232 (2017).

22. K.G. Provan and P. Kenis. Modes of network governance: Structure, management, and effectiveness. *Journal of Public Administration Research and Theory*, **18**(2), 229–252 (2008).

23. C. Storey, A. Kocabasoglu-Hillmer, S. Roden and K. Ruyter. Governing embedded partner networks: Certification and partner communities in the IT sector. *International Journal of Operations and Production Management*, **38**(9), 1709–1734 (2018).

24. H. Berends and E. Antanacopolou. Time and organizational learning: A review and agenda for future research. *International Journal of Management Reviews*, **16**(4), 437– 453 (2016).

25. G. Corradi, S. Gherardi and L. Verzelloni. Through the practice lens: Where is the bandwagon of practice-based studies heading? *Management Learning*, **41**(3), 265–283 (2010).

26. S. Gherardi. *Organizational Knowledge: The Texture of Workplace Learning*. Malden, MA; Oxford, UK; Victoria, Australia: Blackwell Publishing (2006).

27. S. Gherardi. To start practice theorizing anew: The contribution of the concepts of agencement and formativeness. *Organization*, **22**(1), 1–19 (2015).

28. S. Gherardi and P.C.N. Souto. What do people do when they work? The contribution of practice-based studies to the understanding of working and organizing. In *Anais of the National Meeting of the National Association of Graduate Studies and Research in Administration*, Rio de Janeiro, Brazil (2013).

29. J.C. Jarillo. *Strategic Networks: Creating the Borderless Organization*. Oxford: Butterworth-Heinemann (1993).

30. T.M. Jorde and D.J. Teece. *Competition and Cooperation: Striking the Right Balance, Business & Public Policy*. Springer (1989).

31. B.J. Nalebuff and A.M. Brandenburger. *Co-opetição*. Rio de Janeiro: Rocco (1996).

32. J. Child. Learning through strategic alliances. In *Handbook of Organizational Learning & Knowledge*, M. Dierkes *et al.* (eds.), New York: Oxford University Press (2001), pp. 657–679.

33. R. Larsson, L. Bengtsson, K. Henriksson and J. Sparks. The interorganizational learning dilemma: Collective knowledge development in strategic alliances, *Organization Science*, **9**(3), 285–305 (1998).

34. A. Balestrin, L.M. Vargas and P. Fayard. Knowledge creation in small-firm network. *Journal of Knowledge Management,* **12**, 94–106 (2008).

35. H.R. Greve. Inter-organizational learning and heterogeneous social structure. *Organization Studies*, **26**(7), 1025–1047 (2005).

36. M. Easterby-Smith. Disciplines of organizational learning: Contributions and critiques, *Human Relations,* **50**(9), 1085–1113 (1997).
37. C.C. Bitencourt. Gestão contemporânea de pessoas: novas práticas, conceitos tradicionais. Porto Alegre: Bookman (2010).
38. B.-A., Lundvall, *National Innovation Systems: Towards a Theory of Innovation and Interactive Learning.* London: Pinter (1992).
39. S. Gherardi, D. Nicolini and F. Odella. Toward a social understanding of how people learn in organizations. *Management Learning,* **9**(3), 273–297 (1998).
40. A. Styhre, P-E. Josephson and I. Knauseder. Organization Learning in Non-writing Communities: The Case of Construction Workers. *Management Learning,* **37**(1), 83–100 (2006).
41. J. Sandberg and H. Tsoukas. Grasping the logic of practice: Theorizing through practical rationality. *Academy of Management Review,* **36**(2), 338–360 (2011).
42. S. Gherardi. Practice? It's a matter of taste! *Management Learning,* **40**(5), 535–550 (2009).
43. S. Gherardi. Practice-based theorizing on learning and knowing in organizations: An introduction. *Organization,* **7**(2), 211–223 (2000).
44. S. Gherardi. Situated knowledge and situated action: What do practice-based studies promise? In *New Approaches in Management and Organization,* D. Barry and H. Hansen (eds.). London: Sage (2008).
45. S. Gherardi. Knowing and learning in practice-based studies: An introduction. *The Learning Organization,* **16**(5), 352–359 (2009).
46. D. Nicolini, S. Gherardi and D. Yanow. *Knowing in Organizations: A Practice-Based Approach.* Armonk: M. E. Sharpe (2003).
47. D. Nicolini. Articulating practice through the interview to the double. *Management Learning,* **40**(2), 195–212 (2009).
48. S. Gherardi. Introduction: The critical power of the practice lens. *Management Learning,* **40**(2), 115–128 (2009).
49. P. MacDonald and M. Crossan. Learning to innovate: The process of learning between diverse organizations. *International Conference on Organizational Learning, Knowledge and Capabilities — OLKC 2010, Anais,* Northeastern University, Boston, Massachusetts, USA.
50. R. Janowiscz-Panjaitan and N.G. Noorderhavenarillo. Trust, calculation, and inter organizational learning of tacit knowledge: An organizational roles perspective. *Organization Studies,* **30**(10), 1021–1044 (2009).

51. E. Wenger. *Communities of Practice: Learning, Meaning, and Identity.* Cambridge: Cambridge University Press (1998).

52. W. Powell. Learning from collaboration: Knowledge and networks in the biotechnology and pharmaceutical industries. *California Management Review*, **40**(3), 228–240 (1998).

53. A. Contu and H. Willmott. Re-embedding situatedness: The importance of power relations in learning theory. *Organization Science*, **14**(3), 283–296 (2003).

54. M. Thompson. Structural and epistemic parameters in communities of practice. *Organization Science*, **16**(2), 151–164 (2005).

55. R.Van Wijk, J.J.P. Jansen and M.A. Lyles. Inter- and intra-organizational knowledge transfer: A meta-analytic review and assessment of its antecedents and consequences. *Journal of Management Studies*, **45**(4), 830–853 (2008).

56. D. Wegner, K. Faccin and P.C. Dolci. Opening the black box of small-firm networks: Governance mechanisms and their impact on social capital. *International Journal of Entrepreneurship and Small Business*, **35**(4), 559–578 (2018).

57. D. Wegner, E.K. Teireira and J.R. Verschoore. Modes of network governance: What advances have been made so far? *BASE-Revista de Administração e Contabilidade da Unisinos*, **16**(1), 2–26 (2019).

Part III

Innovation

11

Ideas Management: From a Management Perspective

Elina Mikelsone*, Aivars Spilbergs, Tatjana Volkova and Elita Lielā

Departments of Finance and Management,
BA School of Business and Finance,
Kr.Valdemara Street 161, LV-1013, Riga, Latvia

*elina.mikelsone@ba.lv

Many research studies have explored different idea management system (IMS) types and their applications in more than 400 enterprises. However, the question remains — how do these systems materialize in organizations and how do we manage them better to deliver product innovations, goal setting and achieving, and decision-making? This chapter aims to clarify IM perspectives from a managerial perspective and to elaborate the theoretical guidelines on choosing and applying the most appropriate IM approach to improve management performance. The methods employed include literature review (data collection: systematically data collection from scientific data bases; data analysis: content analysis); survey of $n > 500$ enterprises with web-based idea management systems (IMS) experience (data collection: survey;

data analysis: statistics); and case studies (data collection: web-based IMS creator secondary data; data analysis: content analysis). Research results highlight how the application of different IMS influences IM results in delivering product innovations.

11.1. Introduction

One of the management tools applicable in setting goals, improvement of decision-making, and delivering innovations, among other activities, is the idea management systems (IMS), for which research is topical. Thereby the research on IMS is both practical and theoretical. First, the use of IMS has already become a part of the innovation culture in organizations worldwide. IMS is used by many well-known organizations in various sectors such as Etsy, Panasonic, Sony, Electrolux, and Volvo. Second, there are research gaps in the literature about IMS as there are only a few studies on the use of IMS in organizations and even less about how to conceptualize and examine the impact of IMS on expected results. Third, there are no research studies on how different IMS application types impact idea management (IM) results. The relevance of this gap was confirmed in an additional study.[1] Therefore, this chapter aims to clarify IM perspectives from a managerial perspective and provide theoretical guidelines on how to choose and apply the most appropriate IM approach for setting and achieving goals and improving decision-making to deliver product innovations.

The main hypothesis blocks are the following:

- The impact of different types of IMS differs on the goals setting:
  - Active IMS application has helped to set the goals more than passive.
  - Internal IMS application has helped to set the goals more than external.
  - Mixed IMS application has helped to set the goals more than active.
- The impact of different types of IMS differs on the achievement of goals:
  - Active IMS application has helped to achieve goals more than passive.

- Internal IMS application has helped to achieve goals more than external.
- Mixed IMS application has helped to achieve goals more than active.
- The impact of different types of IMS differs on improvement of decision-making:
  - Active IMS application has improved decision-making more than passive.
  - Internal IMS application has improved decision-making more than external.
  - Mixed IMS application has improved decision-making more than active.
- The impact of different types of IMS differs on growth of new products:
  - Active IMS application has resulted in growth in the number of new products more than passive.
  - Internal IMS application has resulted in growth in the number of new products more than external.
  - Mixed IMS application has resulted in growth in the number of new products more than active.

Methods applied to test hypothesis and reach the aim are: literature review (data collection: systematically data collection from scientific data bases; data analysis: content analysis); survey of $n > 500$ enterprises with web-based IMS experience (data collection: survey; data analysis: statistics); and case studies (data collection: web-based IMS creator secondary data; data analysis: content analysis).

The theoretical foundation of this work is composed of a theory of adaptive structuring (AST). The ideas of Poole and DeSanctis, based on the theoretical frame of AST, have been used, starting with the article "Capturing the Complexity in Advanced Technology Use: Adaptive Structuration Theory."[2] The Leading Sources of AST are *MIS Quarterly*, *Organization Science*, and *Information Systems Research*. The work also uses the Diffusion/Adaptation Theory of Innovation — both from the point of view of introduction of the IMS and from the point of view of benefits; the Theory of Open Innovation and Closed Innovation — from the perspective of the sources involved in the IMS; the Resource-Based Theory, with IMS and stakeholders as a resource; design thinking, with IM as one of its sections; the Structuration Theory, which states the need to use the most relevant type of IMS; the Business Theory, emphasizing IMS as part of the business; the Theory of Situational Learning, focusing on the experience of IMS; and the Network Theory, which reflects the provision of IMS with ideas.

The novelty of the study could be summarized as follows:

(1) A framework for examining the impact of IMS use on results and benefits is created;
(2) IM and IMS concepts are distinguishable terms;
(3) A list of the benefits of the IMS, broken down by four benefits and a case-by-case analysis protocol for the use of IMS, which can be used in other studies are established; and
(4) The classification of the ways of using IMS and the impact on results is presented.

In summary, the empirical study has a practical meaning:

(1) The conclusions of the study can be used by companies that use web-based IMS and want to improve the results of ideas management and increase results. A theoretical and empirically based concept of IMS, highlighting the main similarities and differences between different IMS, can help in choosing the appropriate IMS. Classifications help to understand some classification criteria that could be used in practice when choosing IMS, while research highlights the benefits/uses of IMS.
(2) Empirically looking at the experience of various organizations with IMS, which can stimulate the use of IMS in a similar way, and the study provides an insight into a wide range of benefits from the use of IMS, which can stimulate new companies to start using IMS, while encouraging the existing ones to list the benefits of IMS use in more detail. The results of the study will help companies understand the results that can be achieved using different types of IMS.
(3) The results of the study can be used by IMS developers to recommend the most appropriate use of IMS for their customers based on the desired results of IMS and the benefits of their use.

11.2. Theoretical Aspects of IMS and Research Results

11.2.1. *Idea management and IMS*

The study concluded that IM was described in the context of innovation management,[3–9] IT literature and management literature,[10] human resources management,[3] knowledge-based management,[11] management psychology aspects,[12] etc.

In the IMS study, it is essential to look at what IM is, since IM literature gives more insight into the concept of IMS by revealing social[13] and structural IM elements.[14,15] The IM literature has mainly studied commercially available or privately developed IMS, their use, and potential improvements,[16,17] but there are researchers studying the development of new IMS.[18,19] For IM and IMS research trends based on structures and systems, see Table 11.1. On IM and IMS research trends' focus on diverse topics, see Table 11.2.

Table 11.1. IM and IMS research trends based on structures and systems.

Approach	Focuses
Systems	*Social capital, creativity, cognition etc.*
For example, Green, Bean and Snavely (1983); Nilsson, Elg and Bergman (2002); Van Dijk and Van Den Ende (2002); Flynn *et al.* (2003); Boeddrich (2004); Pundt and Schyns (2005); Vandenbosch, Saatcioglu and Fay (2006); Coughlan and Johnson (2008); Bjork and Magnusson (2009); Barczak, Griffin and Khan (2009); Tung, Yuan and Tsai (2009)	Creation of new IMS, classification, model
	Evaluation of IMS effectiveness influencing factors. Good practices
	IMS application and participant analysis
Structures	*Structure, design, features, process etc.*
For example, Fritz (2002); Wood (2003); Summa (2004); Voigt and Brem (2006); Yu, Chen and Shen (2006); Bakker, Boersma and Oreel (2006); Brem and Voigt (2007, 2009); Gamlin, Yourd and Paric (2007); Zejnilovic, Oliveria and Veloso (2012); Bothos, Apostolou and Mentzas (2012)	IMS tests
	Creation of new IMS, classification, model
	Evaluation of IMS
	IM effectiveness influencing factors
	Correlations
	Factor analysis

Source: See Refs. 3, 4, 6, 7, 10, 18, and 20–35.

Table 11.2.   IM and IMS research trends.

Approach	Focuses
Internal IM	IMS tests
For example, Iversen *et al.* (2009); Bansemir *et al.* (2009); Glassmann (2009); Klein *et al.* (2010); Bettoni *et al.* (2010); Selart and Johansen (2011); Shani *et al.* (2011); Moss *et al.* (2011); Deichmann (2012); Zejnilovic *et al.* (2012); Aagaard (2012, 2013); Poveda *et al.* (2012); Bassiti and Ajhoun (2013)	Creation of new IMS, classification, model Evaluation of IMS IM effectiveness influencing factors Correlations Good practices IMS application and participant analysis
Mixed IM	Correlations
For example, Fritz (2002); Nilsson *et al.* (2002); Voigt *et al.* (2006); Brem *et al.* (2007); Enkel *et al.* (2009); Brem *et al.* (2009); Sandstrom and Bjork (2010); Westerski and Iglesias (2012); Baez and Convertino (2012); Sandriev and Pratchenko (2014)	Good practices Literature review Interviews Creation of new IMS, classification, model IM effectiveness influencing factors
External IM	Creation of new IMS
For example, Bothos *et al.* (2008); Tung *et al.* (2009); Westerski *et al.* (2011); Bothos *et al.* (2012)	Correlation Good practices Crowdsourcing

Source: References 5, 7–9, 11, 13, 15, 18, 20, 27, 28, 32, 33, 35–49.

The chapter focuses on commercially available web-based IMS, their use, and impact on results. A study of commercially available IMS has been selected as a narrowing point in order to better identify the sample of the study. Table 11.3 presents the comparison between IM and IMS.

There are active, passive, internal, external, and mixed web-based IMS that are used by organisations as a management tool to manage ideas by several idea generation and evaluation processes systematically.

On the basis of potentially involved IM sources, IMS may be classified as internal IMS, external IMS, and mixed IMS. The internal IMS provides an opportunity for the IM to involve employees or specific departments in generating ideas for potential innovations. External IMS with mainly public platforms provide an opportunity to attract external

Table 11.3.   IM and IMS definitions.

IM — A process of idea generation, evaluation, and continuation

---

IMS — A tool, tool kit, or a complex system which provides systematic, manageable process of:

Idea generation (preparation, capture/ gathering of ideas, retention, enhancement)	Idea evaluation (screening, selection, retention)	Continuation of IM (concept development, distribution of ideas, support during implementation with repeated IM and rewarding, retention)

Additional characteristics: **these systems provide parallelism, anonymity, and transparency and are applicable for different kinds of idea generation and evaluation aims.**

---

sources of IM, such as society, customers, etc. The mixed IMS provides an opportunity to involve internal and external sources of IM, e.g. external sources of IM create ideas but internally assess them or vice versa. The mixed IMS offers extensive facilities for managing IM sources and ensuring that both internal and external IM can be used at any time.

Based on the focus of IMS, it can be classified as active and passive. This classification reveals that there is an IMS that passively gathers ideas that are not concentrated for a specific purpose, while the active IMS provides functions to gather ideas for specific purposes and includes options for evaluating ideas. For more details on IMS classifications, see Table 11.4.

11.2.2. *IM results*

In a rapidly changing environment, organizations need to find solutions faster than ever and IMS is one of such tools. From the authors' point of view, the application of open and mixed web-based IMS based on open innovations approach lead to delivering effective solutions, ensuring that stakeholders become co-creators of these solutions.

This classification follows the theoretical assumptions of open innovations.[50–55] Based on the focus of IMS, it can be classified as active and passive. This classification reveals that there is an IMS that passively

Table 11.4.   IMS classifications.

Classifications

Classification criteria: Based on the application focus

Passive IMS		Active IMS	
Functions	*Type of focus*	*Functions*	*Type of focus*
Focus on idea generation	Unfocused process	Focus on all IM dimensions	Focused process

Classification criteria: Based on the involved IM source

Internal IMS		External IMS		Mixed IMS	
Description	*Main IM source*	*Description*	*Main IM source*	*Description*	*Main IM source*
IMS that allows to involve only internal IM sources	Employees	IMS that allows to involve only external IM sources	Crowds, experts, clients, etc.	IMS that allows to involve internal and external IM sources	Employees, clients, experts, crowds, etc.

gathers ideas that are not concentrated for a specific purpose, while the active IMS provides functions to gather ideas for specific purposes and includes options for evaluating ideas. Table 11.4 provides an overview of IMS classifications. Open innovation can be defined as "a distributed innovation process based on purposely managed knowledge flows across organizational boundaries, using pecuniary and non-pecuniary mechanisms in line with the organization's business model."[56]

The open and mixed web-based IMS could be used during the ideation stage of any innovative activity of organization, e.g. for goals setting and its implementation, decision-making, ensuring product innovations, etc., as it fosters flow of ideas across and beyond organizational boundaries.

Goal setting is one of the most important steps in the management process. According to Mullins,[56] the goals are the foundational blocks upon which organizations and programs are built, and good goals are therefore essential management tools that must be employed by all results-oriented organisations.

The authors agree with Osohon[57] that goal setting is fundamental to organizational management, yet not every manager knows how to do it well.

One of the important goals of business development is to ensure business competitiveness by delivering product innovations. The Oracle White Paper in business and industrial contexts emphatically asserts that, "the organization that makes it a priority to develop quality, effective goals will succeed in its performance management, [and] in its business in general."[58] The authors would like to add that the same logic applies not only to quality development but also in prioritizing the delivery of innovations, etc.

According to Bratton *et al.*,[59] achieving goals is a basic expectation of every human activity. As was pointed out by Osahon,[57] the organizations or individuals working with no goals lack vital direction for their effort or destination for their journey. They exist functionally with no formal purpose.

The achievement of goals is the result of a management process and is impacted by many internal and external factors. Guo *et al.* state that the reasons for the inconsistent results of the formulation–performance relationship has not been discovered yet.[60] One of the enabling factors among many others impacting achievement of goals, from the author's point of view, is application of IMS during the implementation of goals, which lead to better management performance results.

IMS could be helpful in improving decision-making both for setting and implementing goals, as well for delivering product innovations. According to Alhawamdeh and Alsmairat,[61] the use of decision support systems help decision-makers in providing the required information on time, which helps to raise the effectiveness of the strategic decision, thereby having a direct impact on performance of the organization.

The usage of IMS for the ideation stage of innovative activities becomes a critical source for delivering product innovations. The authors agree with Reguia[62] that the continuance and the persistence of any company depends on its capacities to maintain its market place and face competition, which spreads rapidly and aggressively with the globalization and the expansion of the new technologies; while the product reflects the company's image, its entire success depends also on the product success through realizing (compliance) consumers' desires and needs and developing new products.

11.3. Research Methodology

Research background: The authors have explored that there are different IMS application types that could be used both locally and globally for goal setting and implementation, decision-making, and delivering product innovations, among others.

The research aim is to clarify IM perspectives from a managerial perspective and to elaborate the theoretical guidelines on choosing and applying the most appropriate IM approach to improve management performance.

Hypothesis testing approach is based on theoretical guidelines.[63] For hypothesis testing, the authors will use the proportion (Pi) of respondents who believe that the application of particular type of IMS helped to achieve the goals:

$$P_i = \frac{k_i}{n_i} \tag{1}$$

where k_i is the number of respondents who believe that the application of a particular type of IMS helped to achieve the goal and n_i is the number of respondents applying the particular type of IMS.

Null and alternative hypotheses are defined as follows:

$$H_0 : P_i - P_j \leq 0 \text{ and } H_A : P_i - P_j > 0 \tag{2}$$

As samples are simple random and independent, and $k > 80$ and $(n - k) > 30$, the difference of two proportions follows an approximate normal distribution and test statistic is calculated as follows:

$$z = \frac{P_i - P_j}{\sqrt{P_c * (1 - P_c) * \left(\frac{1}{n_i} + \frac{1}{n_j}\right)}} \tag{3}$$

where the pooled proportion (P_c) is calculated as follows:

$$P_c = \frac{k_i + k_j}{n_i + n_{Mj}} \tag{4}$$

Decision rule is to reject H_0 in favour of H_A, if z-statistic (z_{stat}) is larger than z-critical (z_α) values (1.645) for ($\alpha = 0.05$):

$$z_{stat} > z_\alpha \tag{5}$$

11.4. Findings of Hypothesis

11.4.1. *Application of different IMS types and goal setting*

The results of the survey, which show the extent to which different types of IMS helped to set the goals, are summarized in Figure 11.1.

Calculated proportions of respondents who believe that applications of a particular IMS type helped to set goals, pooled proportions, as well as z-statistics and corresponding p-values are summarized in Table 11.5.

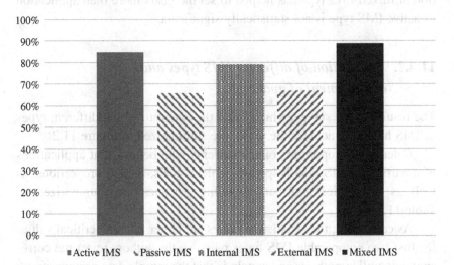

■ Active IMS ❖ Passive IMS ▨ Internal IMS ⁄ External IMS ■ Mixed IMS

Figure 11.1. Proportion of respondents who believe that application of particular IMS type helped to set the goals.

Table 11.5. Statistics for hypothesis testing about goal setting.

IMS Type	P_i	IMS Type	P_j	P_c	z_{stat}	p-value
Active	0.8454	Passive	0.8541	0.7876	5.3159	<0.001
Internal	0.7899	External	0.6699	0.7342	2.8549	0.002
Mixed	0.8867	Active	0.8454	0.8609	1.5094	0.066

As calculated, the z-statistics values are larger than the critical values for first two comparable IMS types pairs, therefore, the authors would reject the corresponding null hypothesis and conclude that the sample data provide strong evidence to support alternative hypothesis. Conclusions that the application of active IMS helped to set the goals more than the application of passive IMS and the application of internal IMS helped to set the goals more than the application of external IMS are also supported by low p-value (<0.0022).

As calculated, the z-statistic value is not larger than the critical values for the third comparable IMS types pairs, therefore, the authors cannot reject the corresponding null hypothesis and conclude that the sample data do not provide enough evidence to support alternative hypothesis — the difference in the proportions of respondents who believe that the application of mixed IMS type has helped to set the goals more than application of active IMS type is not statistically significant.

11.4.2. *Application of different IMS types and achievement of goals*

The results of the survey, which show the extent to which different types of IMS helped to achieve the goals, are summarized in Figure 11.2.

Calculated proportions of respondents who believe that applications of a particular IMS type helped to achieve goals, pooled proportions, as well as z-statistics and corresponding p-values are summarized in Table 11.6.

As calculated, the z-statistics values are larger than the critical values for first two comparable IMS types pairs, so the authors reject the corresponding null hypothesis and conclude that the sample data provide strong evidence to support the alternative hypothesis. Conclusions that the application of active IMS helped to achieve the goals more than the application of passive IMS and the application of internal IMS helped to achieve the goals more than the application of external IMS are also supported by a low p-value (<0.0025).

As calculated, the z-statistic value is not larger than the critical values for the third comparable IMS types pairs, so the authors cannot reject the corresponding null hypothesis and conclude that the sample data do not

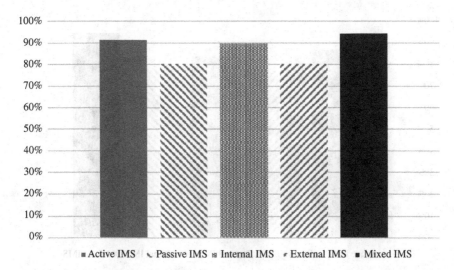

Figure 11.2. Proportion of respondents who believe that application of particular IMS type helped to achieve the goals.

Table 11.6. Statistics for hypothesis testing about achievement of goals.

IMS Type	P_i	IMS Type	P_j	P_c	z_{stat}	p-value
Active	0.9138	Passive	0.8000	0.8795	3.9724	<0.001
Internal	0.8954	External	0.8000	0.8514	2.8170	0.002
Mixed	0.9419	Active	0.9138	0.9243	1.3488	0.089

provide enough evidence to support alternative hypothesis — the difference in the proportions of respondents who believe that application of mixed IMS type has helped to achieve goals more than application of active IMS type is not statistically significant.

11.4.3. *Application of different IMS types and decision-making improvement*

The results of the survey, which show the extent to which different types of IMS has improved decision-making, are summarized in Figure 11.3.

Calculated proportions of respondents who believe that applications of particular IMS type has improved decision-making, pooled

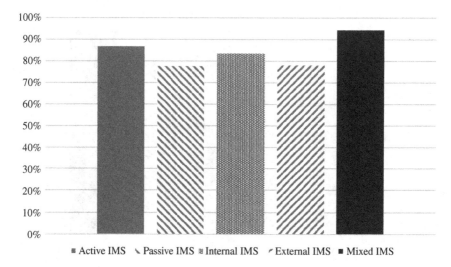

■ Active IMS ＼ Passive IMS ▦ Internal IMS ⟋ External IMS ■ Mixed IMS

Figure 11.3. Proportion of respondents who believe that application of particular IMS type has improved decision-making.

Table 11.7. Statistics for hypothesis testing about decision-making improvement.

IMS Type	P_i	IMS Type	P_j	P_c	z_{stat}	*p*-value
Active	0.8674	Passive	0.7742	0.8393	2.8931	0.002
Internal	0.8326	External	0.7816	0.8090	1.3669	0.086
Mixed	0.9419	Active	0.8674	0.8953	3.0872	0.001

proportions, as well as z-statistics and corresponding p-values are summarized in Table 11.7.

As calculated, the z-statistics values are larger than the critical values for the first and third comparable IMS types pairs, so the authors reject the corresponding null hypothesis and conclude that sample data provide strong evidence to support alternative hypothesis. Conclusions that the application of active IMS has improved decision-making more than the application of passive IMS and the application of mixed IMS has improved decision-making more than the application of active IMS are supported also by a low p-value (<0.002).

As calculated, the z-statistic value is not larger than the critical values for the second comparable IMS types pairs, so the authors cannot reject the corresponding null hypothesis and conclude that the sample data do not provide enough evidence to support alternative hypothesis — the difference in the proportions of respondents who believe that the application of the internal IMS type has improved decision-making more than the application of the IMS type is not statistically significant.

11.4.4. *Application of different IMS types and growth in the number of new products*

The results of the survey, which show the extent to which different types of IMS has resulted in growth of new products, are summarized in Figure 11.4.

Calculated proportions of respondents who believe that the application of a particular IMS type has resulted in the growth of the number of new products, pooled proportions, as well as z-statistics and corresponding p-values are summarized in Table 11.8.

As calculated, the z-statistics values are larger than the critical values for the first two comparable IMS types pairs, so the authors reject the corresponding null hypothesis and conclude that the sample data provide

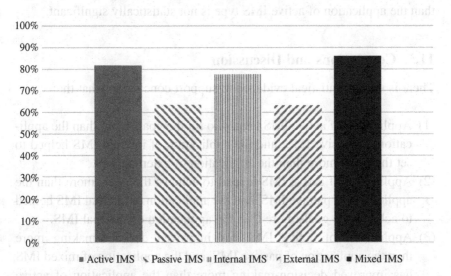

Figure 11.4. Proportion of respondents who believe that application of particular IMS type has resulted in growth of the number of new products.

Table 11.8.   Statistics for hypothesis testing about decision-making improvement.

IMS Type	P_i	IMS Type	P_j	P_c	z_{stat}	p-value
Active	0.8163	Passive	0.6344	0.7614	4.8618	<0.001
Internal	0.7741	External	0.6311	0.7079	3.3074	<0.001
Mixed	0.8605	Active	0.8163	0.8328	1.5038	0.066

strong evidence to support the alternative hypothesis. Conclusions that the application of active IMS has resulted in the growth of the number of new products more than the application of passive IMS and the application of internal IMS has resulted in the growth of the number of new products more than the application of external IMS are supported also by a low p-value (<0.001).

As calculated, the z-statistics value is not larger than the critical values for the third comparable IMS types pairs, so the authors cannot reject the corresponding null hypothesis and conclude that the sample data do not provide enough evidence to support alternative hypothesis — the difference in the proportions of respondents who believe that the application of mixed IMS type has resulted in the growth of the number of new products more than the application of active IMS type is not statistically significant.

11.5. Conclusions and Discussion

There is strong statistical evidence to support conclusions that the:

(1) Application of active IMS helped to set the goals more than the application of passive IMS, and the application of internal IMS helped to set the goals more than the application of external IMS.
(2) Application of active IMS helped to achieve the goals more than the application of passive IMS, and the application of internal IMS helped to achieve the goals more than the application of external IMS.
(3) Application of active IMS has improved decision-making more than the application of passive IMS, and the application of mixed IMS has improved decision-making more than the application of active IMS.

(4) Application of active IMS helped to achieve the goals more than the application of passive IMS, and the application of internal IMS helped to achieve the goals more than the application of external IMS.

(5) Application of active IMS helped to ensure growth of new products more than the application of passive IMS; the application of internal IMS helped to achieve the goals more than the application of external IMS; and the application of mixed IMS has ensured the growth of new products more than the application of active IMS.

The results of the study prove that different results can be achieved using different types of IMS. Therefore, the IMS developers must recommend the most appropriate type of IMS for their customers based on the desired results of IMS and the benefits of their use. The usage of IMS can be applied also for other management activities, and it is essential to continue research on the use of IMS in organizations to conceptualize and examine the impact of IMS on expected results.

Acknowledgment

This work has been supported by the European Regional Development Fund within the Activity 1.1.1.2 "Postdoctoral Research Aid" of the Specific Aid Objective 1.1.1 "To increase the research and innovative capacity of scientific institutions of Latvia and the ability to attract external financing, investing in human resources and infrastructure" of the Operational Programme "Growth and Employment" (N - 1.1.1.2/VIAA/4/20/670).

References

1. E. Mikelsone and E. Lielā. Idea management and organizational effectiveness: Research gap. *Journal of Business Management*, **12**(1), 4–24 (2016).
2. M.S. Poole and G. DeSanctis. Understanding the use of group decision support systems: the theory of adaptive structuration. In *Organizations and Communication Technology*, C.W. Steinfied and J. Fulk (eds.), Newbury Park: Sage (1990), pp. 173–193.

3. S.G. Green, S.A. Bean and B.K. Snavely. Idea management in R&D as a human information processing analog. *Human Systems Management*, **4**(2), 98–112 (1983).

4. M. Flynn, L. Dooley, D. Sullivan and K. Cormican. Idea management for organizational innovation. *International Journal of Innovation Management*, **7**(4), 1–26 (2003).

5. E. Bothos, D. Apostolou and G. Mentzas. A collaborative information aggregation system for idea management. In *Conference on Internet and Web Applications and Services, Proceedings of the International Conference in Athens*, Athens: IEEE, pp. 289–296 (2008).

6. J. Bjork and M. Magnusson. Where do good innovation ideas come from? Exploring the influence of network connectivity on innovation idea quality. *Journal of Product Innovation Management*, **26**(1), 662–670 (2009).

7. K.I. Voigt and A. Brem. Integrated idea management in emerging technology ventures. In *IEEE International Conference on Management of Innovation and Technology, Proceedings of the International Conference in Singapore, China*, Singapore: IEEE (2006), pp. 211–215.

8. H. Iversen, K. Kristensen, C.S. Liland, T. Berman, N. Enger and T. Losnedahl. *Idea Management: A Life-cycle Perspective on Innovation* (2009). Available at: http://www.ict-21.ch/com-ict/IMG/pdf/39_IdeaManagement_Kjetil_Kristensen_FINAL.pdf (Accessed 21 April 2018).

9. C. Sandstrom and J. Bjork. Idea management systems for a changing innovation landscape. *International Journal of Product Development*, **11**(3/4), 310–324 (2010).

10. F.Z. Yu, J. Chen and H.H. Shen. Idea management model for NPD fuzzy front end: Empirical analysis based on all-key-elements innovation in TIM. *Chinese Journal of Management*, **3**(5), 573–579 (2006).

11. B. Bansemir and A.K. Neyer. From idea management systems to interactive innovation management systems: Designing for interaction and knowledge exchange. *Wirtschaftinformatik Proceedings*, **1**(1), 860–870 (2009).

12. A. Pundt and B. Schyns. Fuhrung im Ideenmanagement — Der Zusammenhang zwischen transformationaler Fuhrung und dem individuellen Engagement im Ideenmanagement. *Zeitschrift fur Personalpsychologie*, **4**(2), 55–65 (2005).

13. M. Selart and S.T. Johansen. Understanding the role of value-focused thinking in idea management. *Creativity and Innovation Management*, **20**(3), 196–206 (2011).

14. D. Deichmann. *Idea Management: Perspectives from Leadership, Learning, and Network Theory*. Dissertation, ERIM, Netherland (2012).

15. A. Westerski. *Semantic Technologies in Idea Management Systems: A Model for Interoperability, Linking and Filtering.* Dissertation, Universidad Politecnica de Madrid, Madrid (2013).

16. A. Westerski, T. Dalamagas and C.A. Iglesias. Classifying and comparing community innovation in Idea Management Systems. *Decision Support Systems,* **54**(1), 1316–1326 (2013).

17. M. Bertetta. *The Role of Idea Management Systems for Innovation in Large Organizations: 3 Essays.* Dissertation, School of Business and Social Sciences, Aarhus University (2015).

18. E. Bothos, D. Apostoulou and G. Mentzas. Collective intelligence with web-based information aggregation markets: The role of market facilitation in idea management. *Experts Systems with Applications,* **39**(1), 1333–1345 (2012).

19. M. Lowe and J.E. Heller. PLM reference model for integrated idea and innovation management. Product lifecycle management for a global market. *IFIP Advances in Information and Communication Technology,* **442**(1), 257–266 (2014).

20. L. Nilsson, M. Elg and B. Bergman. Managing ideas for the development of new products. *International Journal of Technology Management,* **24**(5/6), 498–513 (2002).

21. C. Van Dijk and J. Van Den Ende. Suggestion systems: Transferring employee creativity into practicable ideas. *R&D Management,* **32**(5), 387–395 (2002).

22. H.J. Boeddrich. Ideas in the workplace: A new approach towards organizing the fuzzy front end of the innovation process. *Creativity and Innovation Management,* **13**(4), 274–285 (2004).

23. A. Pundt and B. Schyns. Fuhrung im Ideenmanagement — Der Zusammenhang zwischen transformationaler Fuhrung und dem individuellen Engagement im Ideenmanagement. *Zeitschrift fur Personalpsychologie,* **4**(2), 55–65 (2005).

24. B. Vandenbosch, A. Saatcioglu and S. Fay. Idea management: A systematic view. *Journal of Management Studies,* **43**(2), 259–288 (2006).

25. T. Coughlan and P. Johnson. Idea management in creative lives. *In Conference on Human Factors in Computing Systems, Proceedings of the International Conference,* NY: ACM (2008), pp. 3081–3086.

26. G. Barczak, A. Griffin and B.K. Kahn. PERSPECTIVE: Trends and drivers of success in NPD practices: Results of the 2003 PDMA Best Practices study. *Journal of Product Innovation Management,* **26**(1), 3–23 (2009).

27. W.F. Tung, S.T. Yuan and J.R. Tsai. A custom collaboration service system for idea management of mobile phone design. *Human Factors and Ergonomics in Manufacturing,* **19**(5), 494–509 (2009).

28. M. Fritz. Idea management enabler. *EContent,* **25**(8), 50 (2002).

29. A. Wood. Managing employees' ideas: From where do ideas come? *Journal for Quality & Participation,* **26**(2), 22–26 (2003).

30. A. Summa. Software tools to support innovation process. Focus on idea management. Working Paper No. 29, 15 June, Innovation Management Institute, Helsinki University of Technology (2004).

31. H. Bakker, K. Boersma and S. Oreel. Creativity (ideas) management in industrial R&D organizations: A crea-political process model and an empirical illustration of Corus RD&T. *Creativity and Innovation Management,* **15**(3), 296–309 (2006).

32. A. Brem and K.I. Voigt. Innovation management in emerging technology ventures — The concept of an integrated idea management. *Journal of Technology, Policy and Management,* **7**(3), 304–321 (2007).

33. A. Brem and K.I. Voigt. Integration of market pull and technology push in the corporate front end and innovation management — Insights from the German software industry. *Technovation,* **29**(1), 351–367 (2009).

34. J.N. Gamlin, R. Yourd and V. Patric. Unlock creativity with "active" idea management. *Research Technology Management,* **50**(1), 13–16 (2007).

35. L. Zejnilovic, P. Oliveira and F. Veloso. Employees as user innovators: An empirical investigation of an Idea Management System. *SSRN Electronic Journal* (2012). Available at SSRN: https://ssrn.com/abstract=2083422 (Accessed 25 November 2016).

36. B.S. Glassmann. *Improving idea generation and idea management in order to better manage the fuzzy front end of innovation.* Dissertation, Prude University, Lafayette (2009).

37. D. Klein and U. Lechner. Ideenmanagement im Rahmen von organisatorischem Wandel. *In MKWI 2010–IKT-gestutzte Unternehmens kommunikation proceedings,* Gottingen: Universitatsverlag Gottingen (2010), pp. 1831–1842.

38. M. Bettoni, W. Bernhard, C. Eggs and G. Schiller. Idea management by role based networked learning. *In 11th European Conference on Knowledge Management, Proceedings of the International Conference.* London: Academic Publishing Limited, (2010), pp. 107–116.

39. N. Shani and P. Divyapriya. A role of innovative idea management in HRM. *International Journal of Management,* **2**(1), 69–78 (2011).

40. B. Moss, D. Beimborn, H.T. Wagner and T. Weitzel. The role of innovation governance and knowledge management for innovation success. *In the 44th*

Annual Hawaii International Conference on System Science proceedings, Kohla: IEEE (2011), pp. 1–10.

41. A. Aagaard. Idea management in support of pharmaceutical front end of innovation. *International Journal of Technology, Policy and Management,* **12**(4), 373–386 (2012).

42. A. Aagaard. A theoretical model of supporting open source front end innovation through idea management, *International Journal of Business Innovation and Research,* **7**(4), 446–465 (2013).

43. G. Poveda, A. Westerski and C.A. Iglesias. Application of semantic search in idea management systems. In *Conference for Internet Technology Secured Transactions, Proceedings of the International Conference in London,* UK, London: IEEE (2012), pp. 230–236.

44. L. Bassiti and R. Ajhoun. Toward an innovation management framework: A life-cycle model with an idea management focus. *International Journal of Innovation, Management and Technology,* **4**(6), 551–559 (2013).

45. E. Enkel, O. Grassmann and H. Chesbrough. Open R&D and open innovation: Exploring the phenomenon. *R&D Management,* **39**(4), 311–316 (2009).

46. A. Westerski and A. Iglesias. Mining sentiments in idea management systems as a tool for rating ideas. *Paper presented at the International Conference on the Design of Cooperative Systems (COOP2012) of the Large-Scale Idea Management and Deliberation Workshop,* Marseille, France, 30 May–1 June (2012). Available at: http://www.gi2mo.org/files/papers/coop2012/opinions_coop2012_paper.pdf (Accessed 21 April 2018).

47. M. Baez and G. Convertino. Innovation cockpit: A dashboard for facilitators in idea management. *In ACM 2012 Conference Proceedings of the International Conference in Seattle,* Washington, USA, NY: ACM (2012), pp. 47–48.

48. A.R. Sandriev and O.V. Pratchenko. Idea management in the system of innovative management. *Mediterranean Journal of Social Sciences,* **5**(12), 155–158 (2014).

49. A. Westerski and C.A. Iglesias. Exploiting structured linked data in enterprise knowledge management systems: An idea management case study. *In Enterprise Distributed Object Computing Conference Workshops, Proceedings of the 15ᵗʰ IEEE International in Finland,* Helsinki: IEE, (2011), pp. 395–403.

50. H. Chesbrough. *Open Innovation: The New Imperative for Creating and Profiting from Technology.* Boston, MA: Harvard Business School Press (2003).

51. H. Chesbrough. *Open Business Models: How to Thrive in the New Innovation Landscape.* Boston, MA: Harvard Business School Press (2006).
52. L. Dahlander and D.M. Gann. How open is innovation? *Research Policy*, **39**(6), 699– 709 (2010).
53. O. Gassmann, E. Enkel and H. Chesbrough. The future of open innovation. *R&D Management*, **40**(3), 213–221 (2010).
54. J. West. and M. Bogers. Leveraging external sources of innovation: A review of research on open innovation. *Journal of Product Innovation Management*, **31**(4), 814–831 (2014).
55. H. Chesbrough and M. Bogers. Clarifying an emerging paradigm for understanding innovation. In *New Frontiers in Open Innovation*, H. Chesbrough, W. Vanhaverbeke, and J. West (eds.). Oxford: Oxford University Press (2014), pp. 3–28.
56. L.J. Mullins. *Management and Organisational Behaviour.* 5th ed. London: Financial Times, Prentice (1999).
57. O. Osahon. General concepts of goals and goal-setting in healthcare: A narrative review. *Journal of Management & Organization*, **24**, 1–18 (2018).
58. Oracle. Goal setting: A fresh perspective. White Paper. USA: ORACLE Taleo Cloud Service (2012).
59. J. Bratton, M. Callinan, C. Forshaw and P. Sawchuk. *Work and Organizational Behaviour.* Houndsmills, Basingstoke: Palgrave Macmillan (2007).
60. J. Guo, B. Zhou, H. Zhang, C. Hu and M. Song. Does strategic planning help firms translate slack resources into better performance? *Journal of Management & Organization*, **24**, 1–13 (2018).
61. M.H. Alhawamdeh and A.K.M. Alsmairat. Strategic decision making and organization performance: A literature review. *International Review of Management and Marketing*, *Econjournals*, **9**(4), 95–99 (2019).
62. R. Cherroun. Product innovation and the competitive advantage. *European Scientific Journal*, **1**, 147 (2014).
63. D. Moore, G. McCabe, L. Alwan and B. Craig. *The Practice of Statistics for Business and Economics.* 4th ed. New York: W.H. Freeman & Co (2016).

Maturity Model for Ideas Management

Aline de Brittos Valdati*,‡, *João Artur de Souza**,
Maria Isabel Sanchez Segura† *and Cynthya Garcia de Jesus*†

**Graduate Program in Knowledge Management and Engineering,
Federal University of Santa Catarina,
R. Delfino Conti, s/n — Trindade, Florianópolis — SC
88040–900, Brazil*

†*Computer Science and Engineering Department,
University Carlos III of Madrid, Madrid, Spain*

‡*alinevaldati@gmail.com*

The search for ideas, both internal and external, is increasing as innovation is treated as a strategic asset by organizations. Knowing how an organization manages ideas to innovate can be a crucial point at the beginning of the innovation process that will define its success or failure. To assess the management of ideas in organizations, this chapter proposes a maturity model for managing ideas. The model was developed based on an extensive literature review and field interviews with experts in the field of innovation. The maturity model has four levels (reaction, initiation, expansion, and maturation) and six dimensions (environment, preparation, generation, selection, and monitoring). It is expected that, when applied to organizations, they gain insights to improve the way they manage ideas for innovation. In addition, the model is a mechanism for both innovation management and knowledge governance when strategically aligned.

12.1. Introduction

Holding innovation contests that allow access to a diverse set of external knowledge is one of the practices performed by organizations in the search for new ideas.[1] Discussions about these initiatives and as mechanisms and tools that support them grow exponentially in the literature, such as the studies on crowdsourcing, ideation, collaborative idea generation, and idea storming.[2,3]

Even so, Brunswicker and Chesbrough[1] identified that companies make limited use of these actions to develop solutions. The reason is that sometimes they are insufficient as an independent practice because the external knowledge received is incomplete.

In addition to incomplete knowledge, when generating or systematically collecting ideas, the volume of ideas received increases exponentially. Gama[4] states that collaborative ideation is widely recognized as a practice of innovation, however, he concludes that capturing more ideas may not lead to better results. If the flow of new ideas is not organized and optimized, the benefits of gaining knowledge may not be realized by the organization.

In this context, Martini *et al.*[5] understand that the role of idea management is to serve as a catalyst mechanism that seeks to promote the integration of external and internal knowledge, to provide a network of collaboration and co-creation.[5]

However, for this to happen, when starting the systematic collection of ideas (external and internal), it is necessary to focus on the organizational structure and its ability to support this type of initiative.[1,4]

Analyzing the organizational structure to understand how an organization is dealing with innovation is a practice already established and used strategically to identify strengths and weaknesses.[6] These practices can be performed through a series of evaluation and audit mechanisms, which include the maturity models.[7,8]

These models understand that organizational capacities are developed through a series of desired or logical stages, from an initial to a more mature state.[9] They seek to determine how complete the organizational processes are, in relation to the literature, at a given time, which allow the organizational growth towards the desired level.[10] Therefore, they provide guidelines that can serve as a reference for both systemic implementation and improvements,[11] including assisting the organization's strategic decisions.

However, these models place little emphasis on the early stages of innovation, especially ideas, and disregard some important transformations in how innovation is being pursued by organizations — e.g. the search for external ideas and their integration with internal ideas and knowledge.

Therefore, we identified in the literature some important characteristics for the organization to be able to manage ideas in the initial stages of innovation. These in turn served as a basis for structuring the maturity model, namely:

(1) The understanding that ideas go through a flow and/or process from its generation to the beginning of development, which needs to be managed and optimized[12–14];
(2) The fact that this flow and/or process has opening points promoted by the concepts of open innovation, regarding the input and output of ideas and knowledge[5];
(3) The view that idea management initiatives should occur in an iterative manner[15]; and
(4) The understanding that idea management will be more effective in an organizational context supported by Knowledge Management (KM) through its technological and non-technological practices, techniques, and tools.[5,15,16]

Combined, these views complement the way ideas are treated and evaluated in the early stages of innovation, being the basis for us to present the proposition of the maturity model for the management of ideas and the implications, both at a managerial and strategic level, related to innovation management and knowledge governance.[17]

To define the main views that we will address in our model, Section 12.1 will discuss what we mean by ideas, as well as the main existing ideas management models and how they deal with the views mentioned above. In the same way, in Section 12.2 we identify the main maturity models related to innovation and how they deal with ideas.

In Section 12.3, we describe how the maturity model was developed. We use an extensive literature review and the opinions of 10 experts in innovation. In Section 12.4, we describe our proposal for a maturity model for idea management (MIM). It was created to meet the needs that, in the future, will represent a challenge for knowledge-based companies aware of the importance of working collaboratively and treating the management of ideas and knowledge strategically. Finally, Section 12.5 describes and summarizes our contributions to date and for future research. For this, we share practical and theoretical implications of the model, related to both innovation management and knowledge governance.

12.2. Idea Management

Idea management involves the interaction between explicit processes and systems and daily work practices,[18] being a process that involves stages of preparation, generation of ideas, improvement, evaluation, implementation, and development,[12] in which different players, both internal and external, exchange knowledge.[19]

The ideas and the action to manage them are incorporated in the initial innovation processes (front end), and this in turn influences the rest of the innovation process.[20]

To manage ideas, we need to understand them — for this, we define them from two points of view:

(1) **Business:** where one understands that an idea is an initial conception of a product (or service) and is related to an opportunity, problem, need, or trend[20-22]; and
(2) **Knowledge:** where one understands that an idea is composed of elements of knowledge, resulting from a knowledge-intensive process

in which there is a recombination of existing elements and other ideas.[14,23]

12.2.1. *Approaches for idea management*

Regarding the idea management models, based on an extensive integrative literature review, 20 approaches were found, from systems to frameworks that aim to manage ideas for innovation. From these approaches, the phases and structuring elements of the process and how they dealt with the factors of openness, knowledge, and iteration were analyzed, thus presenting a synthesis of the literature panorama on the management of ideas.

All 20 approaches describe stages for managing ideas: of which 16 specify players and functions and 18 present or foresee the use of practices, methods, and tools as support, both technological and non-technological. Therefore, the management triad — **processes**, **people**, and **technology** — are present in a general way in the approaches.

Regarding the **processes**, we observed the existence of stages, which, depending on the approach, differed in number and degree of details. We found phases such as preparation, generation, collection, filtering, categorization, enrichment, evaluation, selection, prioritization, and monitoring. These phases can be adapted and rearranged according to the context and served as the basis for the model proposal.

The players (**people**) are responsible for adding value to the process with their skills, competences, and knowledge and can assume different roles depending on the proposed approach. For example: the Idea Manager, responsible for running the idea program,[24–26] and the Ideator, responsible for providing the ideas that can be provided by employees, consumers, suppliers, and the community in general.[23,24, 26–28] Specialists have domain knowledge and they can be internal or external to the organization.[24] Finally, decision-makers are responsible for making decisions during the process, and they can be high-level managers, specialists, or the external community.[23,24,26]

Technology refers to the tools and techniques that the organization must have to support the processes of managing ideas. Therefore, each stage may require specific tools. For example, brainstorming, problem analysis, concept map analysis, focus groups with the client, and mapping of competing products are common for generating ideas.[29] Another example is the adoption of Idea Management Systems, which allows people (internal or external) to exchange information and knowledge[28] and, for this reason, they are supporters of various phases, from collection to selection of ideas.[12]

The literature on idea management presents consolidated concepts and elements that characterize it. However, when we analyze how organizations manage their ideas for innovation, other elements become important. As an example, for the management of ideas to act as an integrating element of knowledge and to have its flow optimized, the analysis of other elements is necessary, along with having KM as a guide through its practices, in addition to technical methods and tools.

KM is an integrated approach to the identification, creation, storage, sharing, and application of knowledge.[30] It is considered a supporter of the idea management, since it facilitates the knowledge necessary for the phases to be available. Examples of KM practices applicable to idea management include storytelling; communities of practice; collaborative physical spaces for new ideas[30]; and expertise finders, who connect people who need specific knowledge to people who have the knowledge.[30] It can also include advanced computational tools such as data mining to discover patterns, knowledge discovery in databases, and big data analytics. In addition, there are the techniques for storing ideas and knowledge, such as databases, blogs, business intelligence, and concept maps.[31]

Another element to be considered when evaluating the management of ideas in organizations is the **openness** factor. Although 10 approaches mentioning openness were found, they only focus on the search for external knowledge to generate ideas.[12,14,29] The **iteration** in the other phases is little explored, and an example is the use of collaborative tools to enrich and evaluate ideas.[16,28] Furthermore, it is not discussed in what contexts the opening would be appropriate.

Finally, the **evaluation** methods themselves are not clearly described, although some authors, such as Voigt and Brem[27] and Brem and Voigt,[13] argue about their need; Gerlach and Brem[12] present metrics to monitor and evaluate the management of ideas; and Glasman[14] focuses on control variables during the process. However, none of these works proposes a method to evaluate the management of ideas by looking at the organizational structure and comparing it with existing good practices and critical success factors.

Faced with the scenario presented, there is a way to be explored on how to evaluate the management of ideas in organizations, in addition to the triad processes, people, and technology, include KM and openness through interaction with partners.

12.3. Maturity Models for Innovation and Idea Management

Maturity models are conceptual models based on the idea that organizational capacities develop through a series of desired or logical stages, from an initial state to a more mature state.[9]

The maturity models originated in the area of software engineering and quality. However, they have crossed disciplinary boundaries, and today there are models in the most diverse areas of knowledge, including in the area of innovation. According to Frishammar,[6] these innovation maturity models are part of a class of models that aim to evaluate innovation in organizations in order to understand it and with better results.

To understand how the innovation maturity models have contemplated idea management, an integrative literature review was carried out, in which we identified two approaches that mention elements related to the ideas.

The first approach refers to models that include the management of ideas as a dimension to be analyzed.[7,32,33] These models focus on the generation of ideas, internal ideas, creativity, and institutionalization of the process of generating ideas.

The second approach includes the new maturity models, which are focused on open innovation, and emerged with the purpose of using ideas from external sources for innovation. However, we do not find in these approaches activities that explore in detail the process of managing ideas.

Thus, there is an opportunity for complementarity in these two approaches, both the need to institutionalize an idea management process (not just generation) and the need to look outside the organization to receive and capture external ideas.

12.3.1. *Structural principles of maturity models*

From the analysis of the models above, it was possible to identify the structural principles for a maturity model, such as:[34,35]

- **Levels** represent the transition states of maturity.
- **Dimensions or domains** group similar **attributes** in an area of importance to the subject and intent of the model.
- **Attributes** represent the main content of the model. They are based on observable practices, standards, or other specialized knowledge and can be expressed as characteristics, indicators, practices, or processes.
- **Assessment methods** facilitate assessment using the model as a basis. They can be formal or informal, led by specialists or self-applicable.
- **Improvement roadmaps** are used as benchmarking or to guide improvement efforts. They can prescribe methods to identify a scope of improvement, how to implement the improvement, and how to verify that it has occurred.

Following these principles and the fact that idea management needs to improve the evaluation methods, in Section 12.4, we propose our maturity model for idea management.

12.4. Development of the Proposed Model

For the development of the Maturity Model, we used De Bruin *et al.*[10] guidelines, which are divided into six stages: (1) Scope; (2) Design; (3) Filling in the model; (4) Testing the model; (5) Implementation; and (6) Maintenance. The testing, implementation, and maintenance stages are not the objectives of this work.

Stage 1: Define the model scope
It aims to determine the scope of application. It is important to define what distinguishes the model being created from the others. A literature review can be carried out to answer this question.[10]

The definition of the scope was based on the literature reviews on idea management (Section 12.2) and maturity models (Section 12.3). The literature review also made it possible to check whether any tool model had already been proposed for the problem in question. Therefore, it was found that there is no existing tool for this specific problem, but tools exist that permeate the problem, such as the innovation management maturity models that allude to idea management, and the models for idea management. Both bring subsidies for the development of our maturity model.

Stage 2: Define the model design

It refers to the definition of the model type and contributions to the organization.[10] The model is of the prescriptive type, directed at the performance of the business and indicates the way to reach the next levels of maturity when establishing a roadmap for improvements. The design was established in dimensions, levels, and attributes, with the latter detailing the first two.

Stage 3: Fill in the model

After defining the scope and design, the content must be decided. For that, it is necessary to identify what the maturity model will measure and how it will be done. The goal is to achieve domain components and subcomponents that are mutually exclusive and collectively exhaustive.[10]

In this case, the content to be evaluated is the management of ideas in organizations. It will be performed by comparing the critical success factors that classify the organization in levels.

The identification of domain components can be achieved through an extensive literature review and, later, interviews are used to conceptually validate and increase the list of critical success factors.[10]

In this way, an **extensive literature review** was carried out on idea management and maturity models. From this literature, the dimensions and levels of the model were defined, as well as an initial list of attributes (critical success factors) for each dimension.

Afterward, a **focus group** was held with six academic experts in order to validate the construct and the content validity in order to seek the convergence of opinions about the model and its elements.

In addition, the opinions of 10 specialists and managers working in the innovation area were considered. The **interviews** took place between November 2019 and March 2020 in three phases. In the first phase, there was the initial contact to present the research and for the interviewee to introduce himself. In the second phase, the interviewee performed the analysis of the maturity model. In the third phase, the interview was conducted following the script of the semi-structured interview. The interviews lasted about 1.4 hours each. All interviews were transcribed, resulting in approximately 100 pages in a text document. They were all analyzed using the thematic analysis technique.[a]

12.5. Proposal of a Maturity Model for Idea Management

In this section, we will present the maturity model of a Maturity Model for Idea Management (MIM).

12.5.1. *Overview: Objective, scope, and use of the model*

Objective: To represent the organizational capacities related to the management of ideas through a set of characteristics and attributes in order to provide a roadmap for continuous improvements.

    Scope: The scope of the proposed model is based on the understanding of four main visions:

(1) The process (or flow) through which ideas go from their generation to the beginning of development needs to be optimized and managed.
(2) The fact that this process has opening points promoted by collaboration with partners and the involvement of external actors.
(3) The understanding that KM makes the process of managing ideas more effective, through its technological and non-technological practices, techniques, and tools.
(4) The vision of agility, which concerns ideas management initiatives to flow in a process in a quick and iterative way.

---

[a]It is a method for identifying, analyzing, and reporting patterns (themes) within data. It organizes and describes the data set in rich detail and interprets various aspects of the research theme.

Use of the model: The model will be useful for managers of organizations that aim to identify the activities related to ideas and knowledge for innovation, aiming at improvements in management. It will also serve managers who are in place or plan to implement some initiative related to the management of ideas. In this way, it will be used to provide a roadmap for continuous improvement, as well as an implementation guide.

12.5.2. *Conceptual model*

The levels and dimensions that will be presented next are part of the conceptual model (Figure 12.1).

The **levels** represent the four transition states of the Maturity Model for Idea Management.

Level 1 — Reaction: The organization does not know what it is to manage ideas or the innovation process and is focused on its production processes.

Level 2 — Beginning: The organization begins to recognize that it needs to manage its ideas and knowledge for innovation or has already initiated some informal isolated action.

Level 3 — Introduction and **expansion:** The management of ideas and knowledge is being implemented and developed, as some activities and initiatives that characterize a structured flow are in progress.

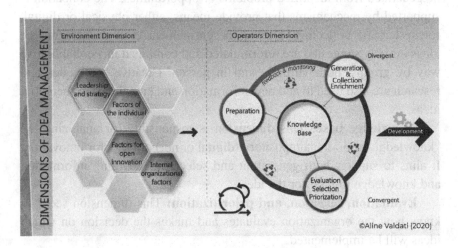

Figure 12.1. Dimensions of maturity model for idea management.

Level 4 — Refinement and maturation: The implementation of the management of ideas and knowledge is continuously evaluated for constant improvement and is integrated with the organizational culture.

The **dimensions** group similar attributes. In the Maturity Model for Idea Management, we identify two macro-dimensions: environment and operators.

Dimension I — Environment: It is understood that in this environment, leadership is committed and strategically aligned in order to promote new ideas, and individuals should be empowered and engaged to collaborate and create, immersed in a culture of tolerance to error and encouragement to learning and creativity.

Dimension II — Operators: They are the elements that operationalize the model; they are iterative with feedback elements and occur in a not necessarily sequential way: preparation; generation, collection, and enrichment; knowledge base; evaluation, selection, and prioritization; feedback and monitoring.

Preparation: The preparation dimension is responsible for analyzing how the organization defines the program guidelines as well as preparing the environment and the people involved.

Generation, collection, and enrichment: This dimension is responsible for analyzing the generation, collection, and enrichment of ideas. The generation is strongly supported by creative techniques, and ideas can be generated from identified problems or opportunities. The collection is supported by mechanisms that provide means, either physical or digital, for systematic collecting. During the enrichment or improvement, the ideas initially suggested are reformulated and combined in a collaborative way by groups, both virtually and in person. Creative techniques and research are also used to add new information and knowledge to the initial ideas.

Knowledge base: This dimension is responsible for analyzing the "knowledge base," i.e. a repository (digital or not) of ideas for innovation. It aims to support both generation and selection, providing information and knowledge to monitor the ideas.

Evaluation, selection, and prioritization: This dimension seeks to know how the organization evaluates and makes the decision on which ideas will be implemented.

Feedback and monitoring: This dimension analyzes how the organization monitors initiatives and ideas as well as how it recognizes those people involved in initiatives related to ideas for innovation.

Attributes were identified to define each dimension. The attributes represent factors that are critical to the successful management of idea initiatives. They were identified from the literature, and an initial list with 60 criteria success factors was formed. Subsequently, this list was presented to the experts and the 10 best scored criteria are presented in Table 12.1.

These success factors were used to characterize the dimensions and, in the future, can be used in the development of an evaluation method to check how organizations are in relation to the identified criteria and best practices for the management of ideas.

Table 12.1. Success factors for dimension of idea management.

Dimension	Success factors
Environment	• Strategic alignment; • Mindset, culture for innovation; • Top management involvement.
Preparation	• Structuring and planning the initiative; • Communication of the initiative; • Responsible for the initiative.
Generation, collection, and enrichment	• Collaboration; • Access to necessary knowledge; • Creativity.
Knowledge base	• Easy access to previously documented information and ideas.
Evaluation, selection, and prioritization	• Transparency: team that will select the ideas; • Structuring (criteria, weights); • Preventing the "kill disruptive ideas."
Feedback and monitoring	• Constructive feedback; • Recognition for those involved with the initiative (not just the "winners"); • Monitoring by means of metrics; • Relationship with organizational results; • Continuous learning through sharing success stories and recording lessons learned.

12.5.3. *Characterization levels*

When relating levels and dimensions, we define in more detail the characteristics of organizations for each level, which are presented by four basic questions: "Where are we?" i.e. at what level the organization is; "What are our characteristics?" which means knowing what the characteristics of the organization are by checking at what dimensions and level it is; "How far do we go in business?" to try to identify the business potential of the organization based on the level at it is, and, finally, "What do we have to do?" which is related to a possible roadmap for improvement.

Table 12.2 describes the characterization levels of our model based on these questions.

With the characterization of the levels, the conceptual maturity model makes it possible to characterize the organization for the management of ideas based on the four visions: process, KM, openness, and interaction (collaboration). In addition to providing insights for improvement.

12.6. Conclusion

This chapter presents a maturity model for managing ideas, which in addition to the triad of people, processes, and technology, advances the look at KM as an integrator of knowledge, both internal and external. Therefore, it is an unprecedented vision on how to evaluate the management of ideas in organizations, capable of meeting the needs that represent a challenge for knowledge-based companies, aware of the importance of working collaboratively, and treating KM and innovation in a strategic way.

The model is formed by four levels in which the abilities related to the management of ideas evolve from a reactive level, pass through a level of beginning and next expand until reaching the level of refinement and maturation.

Regarding the dimensions, we define an environment that deals with cultural leadership for innovation and one concerning operator that deals with preparation, generation, collection and enrichment, evaluation, selection and prioritization, and feedback and monitoring.

The proposed model, therefore, contributes to the scientific theory of innovation management, as it sets up a mechanism to assist in the

Table 12.2. Characterization levels.

	Characterization Levels	
	Level 1 — Reaction	Level 2 — Beginning
Where are we?	The organization does not know what the management of ideas or the innovation process is and is focused on its production processes.	The organization begins to recognize that it needs to manage its ideas and knowledge for innovation or has already initiated some informal isolated action.
What are our characteristics?	Focus on its production processes; it does not provoke but reacts to market stimuli.	Activities related to ideas are not formalized in the organization; ideas are collected and generated informally. The internal collaboration and fortuitous external collaboration is done through proximity or imposition. KM is not used in this process, so knowledge is completely informal and is not incorporated into ideas. There is no dedicated team and the leadership is not engaged. There is no policy of recognition and encouragement of creativity and tolerance for error. The results of the process are not measured or evaluated.
How far do we go in terms of business?	The chances of radical improvement are limited.	The chances of continually emerging innovative ideas are sporadic and individual capabilities are limited. There are obstacles to improvement and to achieving specific efficiency improvements. There is a process of improving essential activities and eliminating activities and functions that do not add value.

(Continued)

Table 12.2.   *(Continued)*

	Characterization Levels	
	Level 1 — Reaction	**Level 2 — Beginning**
What can we do?	Make management and employees aware of the importance of managing ideas and knowledge for innovation.	Map essential processes related to ideas and knowledge for innovation; Select processes to be worked on; Improve essential processes, including the input of some technological, non-technological, and practical ideas management tools; Redistribute resources and assign roles to people who will be disseminators; Define matrix of functions; Conduct pilot processes.
	Level 3 — Introduction and Expansion	**Level 4 — Refinement and Maturation**
Where are we?	The management of ideas and knowledge is being implemented and developed, as there are some activities and initiatives that characterize a flow.	The implementation of idea management is continuously evaluated for continuous improvement and is integrated with the organizational culture.
What are our characteristics?	Activities and elements of idea management are identified and with a level of structuring. Ideas are no longer generated, enriched, and selected informally. Collaboration (internal and external) still requires effort by the organization, as it is not part of the organizational culture or strategy. Some KM practices, methods, and tools are used, however, in isolation. The leadership and teams are already formed and are beginning to	The process is integrated with the organization's culture and processes. Actors' roles are defined. It is viewed strategically and supported by leadership and top management. It has the contribution of KM so that knowledge is easily accessible to employees, and its tools, methods, and practices are being used, i.e. there is a way that makes it possible to absorb and integrate knowledge and ideas. Collaboration and creativity, acceptance of error, and encouragement to learning are strongly stimulated and are part of the organizational culture. In addition, the focus

see value in optimizing the flow of ideas in the organization. Every idea management initiative needs mutual efforts and extra incentives to make it happen. There is no monitoring and control.

for new ideas, opportunities, and external collaboration is targeted. There is engagement and motivation for participation.

How far do we go in terms of business?

It is realized that ideas are already a source of new business and products. There is management of some isolated activities related to ideas and knowledge, and integration with auxiliary processes. The incorporation into the organizational culture starts.

High-quality ideas are implemented and developed in the form of new products or processes in the organization. There is integrated management of the ideas and KM processes with the essential processes of the organization. Creating and developing new ideas is in the organizational culture.

What can we do?

Adopt a structural model that includes the main defined functions. Integrate the ideas management practices, techniques, and tools already used with those of KM in order to start optimizing the flow of ideas. Implement and/or expand the idea management initiatives in the organization and with partners. Start monitoring initiatives and the flow of ideas and knowledge.

Monitor initiatives and the flow of ideas and knowledge. Monitor the organization's business definition; Continuously align/and adjust management initiatives across the organization.

improvement of innovation processes. In addition, it contributes to knowledge governance since it can be understood as being directly related to innovation, creativity, and problem solving. Therefore, it can also be considered a knowledge governance mechanism itself, when strategically aligned to the KM.

In a practical way, the model can be applied to organizations, as confirmed by the experts interviewed, to provide diagnosis on how organizations manage ideas in order to innovate.

As future work, we intend to continue developing the model with the construction of an instrument, possibly in the form of a questionnaire. Thus, it will be possible to carry out a more complete test in some selected organizations and, consequently, confirm the usefulness of the model in assessing their level of maturity in idea management.

References

1. S. Brunswicker and H. Chesbrough. The adoption of open innovation in large firms: Practices, measures, and risks a survey of large firms examines how firms approach open innovation strategically and manage knowledge flows at the project level. *Research-Technology Management*, **61**(3), 35–45 (2018).
2. A. Afuah and C.L. Tucci. Crowdsourcing as a solution to distant search. *Academy of Management Review*, **37**(3), 355–375 (2012).
3. K.J. Boudreau, and K.R. Lakhani. Using the crowd as an innovation partner. *Harvard Business Review*, **91**(4), 60–90 (2013).
4. F. Gama. Managing collaborative ideation: The role of formal and informal appropriability mechanisms. *International Entrepreneurship and Management Journal*, Springer, **15**(1), 97–118 (2019).
5. A. Martini, P. Neirotti and F.P. Appio. Knowledge searching, integrating and performing: always a tuned trio for innovation? *Long Range Planning*, **50**(2), 200–220 (2017).
6. J. Frishammar *et al.* Opportunities and challenges in the new innovation landscape: Implications for innovation auditing and innovation management. *European Management Journal*, **37**(2), 151–164 (2019).
7. P. Gupta. Leading innovation change-The Kotter way. *International Journal of Innovation Science*, **3**(3), 141–150 (2011).
8. E. Enkel, J. Bell and H. Hogenkamp. Open innovation maturity framework. *International Journal of Innovation Management*, **15**(6), 1161–1189 (2011).

9. P. Gottschalk and H. Solli-Sæther. Maturity model for IT outsourcing relationships. *Industrial Management & Data Systems*, **106**(2), 200–212 (2006).

10. T. De Bruin *et al.* Understanding the main phases of developing a maturity assessment model. *Australasian Conference on Information Systems (ACIS)* (2005), pp. 8–15.

11. R. Wendler. The maturity of maturity model research: A systematic mapping study. *Information and Software Technology*, **54**(12), 1317–1339 (2012).

12. S. Gerlach and A. Brem. Idea management revisited: A review of the literature and guide for implementation. *International Journal of Innovation Studies*, **1**(2), 144–161 (2017).

13. A. Brem and K. Voigt. Integration of market pull and technology push in the corporate front end and innovation management—Insights from the German software industry. *Technovation*, **29**(5) 351–367 (2009).

14. B.S. Glassman. Improving idea generation and idea management in order to better manage the fuzzy front end of innovation. Thesis, Purdue University (2009).

15. A. Hesmer and K-D. Thoben. Framework and IT-based toolset to support the early stages of collaborative innovation. In *2009 IEEE International Technology Management Conference (ICE)*, IEEE, (2009), pp. 1–14.

16. A. Gabriel, B.P. Chavez and M. Davy. Methodology to design ontologies from organizational models: Application to creativity workshops. *Artificial Intelligence for Engineering Design, Analysis and Manufacturing: AI EDAM*, **33**(2), 148–159 (2019).

17. A.L. Gerritsen, L. Alwin, M. Stuiver and C.J. Termeer. Knowledge governance: An exploration of principles, impact, and barriers. *Science and Public Policy*, **40**(5), 604–615 (2013).

18. A.V. Jensen. A literature review of idea management. In *DS 71: Proceedings of NordDesign 2012, the 9th NordDesign Conference*, Aarlborg University, Denmark (2012), pp. 22–24.

19. A. Westerski, C.A. Iglesias and T. Nagle. The road from community ideas to organisational innovation: A life cycle survey of idea management systems **7**(4), 493–506 (2011).

20. P. Koen, A. Bertels, M.J. Heidi and E.J. Kleinschmidt. Managing the front end of innovation—Part II: Results from a three-year study. *Research-Technology Management*, **57**(3), 25–35 (2014).

21. P. Koen *et al.* Fuzzy front end: Effective methods, tools and techniques. In *The PDMA Toolbook for new product development* P. Bellive, A. Griffin and S. Sommermeyer (eds.), New York: John Wiley & Sons, **1**(1), 81–91 (2002).

22. M. Stevanović and D. Marjanović. The continuous "fuzzy front-end" as a part of the innovation process. In *International Conference on Engineering Design, ICED11* Copenhagen, Denmark, **1**(1), 383–392 (2011).
23. M. Z. Murah, Z. Abdullah, R. Hassan, M. A. Bakar, I. Mohamed and H. M. Amin. A conceptual design of an idea management system. *International Education Studies*, **6**(6), 178–184, 2013.
24. E. Bothos, D. Apostolou and G. Mentzas, Collective intelligence for idea management with Internet-based information aggregation markets. *Internet Research*, **19**(1), 26–41 (2009).
25. C. Sandstrom *et al.* Idea management systems for a changing innovation landscape. *International Journal of Product Development*, **11**(3–4), 310–324 (2010).
26. A. Perez, F. Larrinaga and E. Curry. The role of linked data and semantic-technologies for sustainability idea management. In *International Conference on Software Engineering and Formal Methods*, Springer, Cham. (2013) pp. 306–312.
27. K. Voigt and A. Brem. Integrated idea management in emerging technology ventures. In *2006 IEEE International Conference on Management of Innovation and Technology. IEEE* (2006), pp. 211–215.
28. M. Alessi, A. Camilo, V. Chetta, E. Giangreco, M. Soufivand and D. Storelli. Applying Idea Management System (IMS) approach to design and implement a collaborative environment in public service related open innovation processes. *Complex Systems Informatics and Modeling Quarterly*, **5**, 26–38 (2015).
29. A. Aagaard. A theoretical model of supporting open source front end innovation through idea management. *International Journal of Business Innovation and Research*, **7**(4), 446–465 (2013).
30. Asian Productivity Organization (APO). *Knowledge Management Facilitators' Guide*. Japan. First edition (2010).
31. Asian Productivity Organization (APO). *Knowledge Management Facilitators' Guide*. Japan. Revised edition (2020).
32. A.T. Ueno. Modelo de avaliação da maturidade do processo de inovação como estratégia competitiva empresarial. Tese (Doutorado) — Curso de Engenharia e Gestão do Conhecimento, Centro Tecnológico, Universidade Federal de Santa Catarina, Florianópolis (2016).
33. A. Achi, C. Salinesi and G. Viscusi. Information systems for innovation: A comparative analysis of maturity models' characteristics. In *International Conference on Advanced Information Systems Engineering*. Springer, Cham. (2016), pp. 78–90.

34. S. Brunswicker, F. Sabine and F. Ehrenmann. Managing open innovation in SMEs: A good practice example of a German software firm. *International Journal of Industrial Engineering and Management*, **4**(1), 33–41 (2013).

35. M. Carcary. Design science research: The case of the IT capability maturity framework (IT CMF). *Electronic Journal of Business Research Methods*, **9**(2), 109 (2011).

Networked Innovation Laboratory Model for Public Sector

Willian Rochadel*, Aline de Brittos Valdati,
João Artur de Souza and Gertrudes Aparecida Dandolini

Graduate Program in Knowledge Management and Engineering,
Federal University of Santa Catarina,
R. Delfino Conti, s/n, Trindade, Florianópolis — SC
88040–900, Brazil

*willian.rochadel@ufsc.br

The aggregation of users' knowledge in public and private sector organizations involves a complex structuring of governance and its mechanisms to transform ideas into innovation. However, the individual, organizational, and environmental antecedents to innovation are capabilities that allow organizations to address the limitations to innovation capacity. This research arose due to the demand for an agency linked to public administration in Santa Catarina, Brazil, and the need for integration of the public agency that owns units with geographically dispersed teams. Thus, the concept of an innovation laboratory is an alternative to create spaces conducive to development, research, and innovation. This chapter presents a networked model for innovation laboratories in the public sector based on collective knowledge. From the literature review, we identified innovation practices in the public sector. As a result, we present the model that integrates four principles for the structuring of laboratories: (1) aggregation, (2) digital laboratory, (3) prototyping test, and (4) research groups. Thus, the model structure is a network space for knowledge integration and collaboration expansion. According to multilevel governance's current demands, this research collaborates with the organization of innovation laboratories for the public sector.

13.1. Introduction

Laboratories serve to experiment and transform ideas into knowledge. The potential of this knowledge depends on the application to deliver innovation, as "innovations derive from knowledge-based activities that involve the practical application of existing or newly developed information and knowledge" (Ref. 1, p. 46). In perspective on the outcome of this knowledge, innovation "is the multi-stage process whereby organizations transform ideas into new/improved products, service or processes, in order to advance, compete and differentiate themselves successfully in their marketplace" (Ref. 2, p. 1334).

In turn, innovation management models consider the openness through internal and external partners, thereby differentiating the ecosystem. The open innovation's dynamic promotes the permeability of knowledge at organizational boundaries driven by a relational system that considers the organization and its external partners, something contrary to the closed model.[3]

As an evolution of this concept, open innovation covers research academy, companies, and the development of public policies.[4] In this perspective, as these organizations seek to advance their innovation processes, their platforms, architectures, and systems progressively combine internal and external ideas to generate value.

Therefore, because it involves the public, private, and academic relationships, the mechanisms require a multilevel structure of Knowledge Governance. In this discussion, "the implementation of governance, capable of generating cooperation and guiding coordinated actions [...] for the collective good, in addition to the business, [...] as a new approach to intellectual property management from research and development" (Ref. 5, p. 30).

When considering the perspective of Knowledge Governance, the opening of a laboratory in the innovation ecosystem benefits both the public and private sectors, emphasizing citizen participation.[6] It promotes the relationship of knowledge between users and organizations in both sectors to capture new ideas for public services and collaboration in problem solving.[6]

From this interaction between public agencies and society, a laboratory space offers models, strategies, and tools that foster the process that generates innovation[7] and an area where one can test new business solutions with low-cost prototypes before they are implemented.[8] Therefore, it is useful to acquire a holistic view of the challenges to be faced and allow planning of solutions from different perspectives.[7]

Therefore, government innovation laboratories are like "islands of experimentation."[9] In a counterpoint of operational routines in public sector activities,[10] laboratories are conducive to the experimentation of new solutions, policies, and governance tools in the public sector.[11,12]

In this chapter, we propose a networked innovation laboratory model for the public sector. The literature review section addresses innovation in the public sector and laboratories. Section 13.3 describes the model with its practical principles and tools for governance focused on open participation at different network levels.

13.2. Literature Review

This section addresses the fundamental concepts and state of the art on innovation in the public sector and innovation laboratory.

13.2.1. *Innovation in the public sector*

Innovation in the public sector comprises developing and implementing a new idea to create or improve public value[a] within an ecosystem.[13]

---

[a]Public value are "products and results generated, preserved or delivered by the activities of an organization that represent effective and useful responses to the needs or demands of

Research on innovation capacity in the public sector points to the difficulties of the organizational structure and risks. According to the review by Timeus and Gascó,[14] research on the subject explored the factors that contribute to increase or prevent it in one of three levels of analysis: (1) the individual; (2) the organization; or (3) the environment.[15]

The individual level considers the risks that innovation requires typically. These risks are because professionals, every time, are reluctant to innovate. After all, risk-taking behavior is often discouraged in the public sector.[14,16,17] Even hierarchically, managers and other leaders focus only on operational and financial tasks, without time and resources to manage innovation processes.[18] However, the capacity for innovation in public services is optimized when a work culture supports professionals' confidence in their decisions and when they feel that management will not punish them for taking risks.[19]

The organizational level represents barriers to innovation capacity that include claims about the administrative work culture and the structure of public organizations.[14] Even public organizations' environments have rigid hierarchies and political divisions that inhibit cooperation between sectors and multilevel networks. Thus, it reinforces the "silo mentality," traditional roles, and inhibit employees' ability to generate innovative ideas.[20]

Therefore, research defines that the organizational structure needs support for innovation capacity. Recently, initiatives on open government have allowed new spaces for discussions and experimentation. These are the innovation labs that resemble startup incubators, but the focus is on public policies.[21]

13.2.2. *Innovation laboratories*

The combination of professionals and groups establishes inter-organizational networks capable of experimenting and innovating. Thus, innovation laboratories have become the preferred organizational tool to

---

the public interest and modify aspects of society as a whole or of certain specific groups recognized as legitimate recipients of public goods and services..." Decree No. 9,203 of November 22, 2017.

introduce innovation. The laboratories' organizational structure and commitment allow circumventing traditional public administration characteristics, often seen as barriers to innovation.[22]

Innovation labs operate in a separate but adjacent space from the rest of the organization. In this way, they can improve internal administrative efficiency and drive cultural change.[14] It is allowed in laboratories to experiment with new methods and monitor specialized knowledge because they are far from traditional organizational structures' problems and constraints. Thus, laboratories are perceived by governments as a way to introduce the capacity for innovation without interrupting the conventional bureaucratic structure.[21]

In Brazil, legislative proposal 7843/2017[b] provides for the obligation of public entities to "establish Innovation Laboratories, spaces open to the participation and collaboration of society for the development of innovative ideas, tools and methods for public management, the provision of public services and the empowerment of the citizen for the exercise of control over public administration."

The legislative proposal 7843/2017 also details the guidelines for Innovation Laboratories in:

I — an interinstitutional collaboration with society; II — promotion and experimentation of open and free technologies; III — use of agile software development and prototyping practices; IV — focus on society and the citizen; V — fostering social participation and public transparency; VI — encouraging Innovation; VII — support for entrepreneurship; VIII — strategic use of information in order to support decision-making and improve public management; IX — encouraging the participation of employees, interns and employees in their activities; and X — dissemination of knowledge in the field of public administration...

This project discusses the efficiency and effectiveness of the Brazilian public sector. The issue also originated the new fiscal regime of 2017 by the Constitutional amendment of the Ceiling of Public Expenditures No. 95 of December 2016.[c] Furthermore, the increase in costs in the actions

---

[b]https://www.camara.leg.br/propostas-legislativas/2141142.
[c]http://www.planalto.gov.br/ccivil_03/constituicao/emendas/emc/emc95.htm.

due to COVID-19 and social vulnerability[d] relates to discussions on how to create spaces for innovation in the public sector in cooperation with private initiative and open participation.

13.3. Model Proposal

This research arose from the demand for an agency linked to the public administration of the state of Santa Catarina, Brazil. The model required integrating the public agency with local teams, regional structures, and centralized management in the capital, Florianópolis.

The proposed model involved a literature review aimed to find the best practices in the public sector's innovation to structure a networked laboratory model.

Thus, the Networked Innovation Laboratory model presents four principles: (1) aggregation, (2) digital laboratory, (3) prototyping test, and (4) research groups. These principles are linked to a cyclical and backed process for laboratory dynamics (see Figure 13.1).

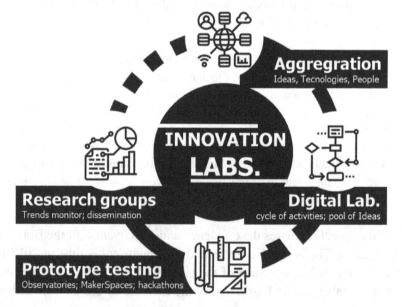

Figure 13.1. Networked innovation laboratories model for public sector.

[d]https://www.sbmt.org.br/portal/arboviroses-covid-19-e-vulnerabilidade-social/?lang=en.

Each principle consists of a combination of elements that they will detail in the following sections.

13.3.1. *Aggregation*

The first principle of the model is "aggregation." This principle combines and organizes the knowledge to co-create projects that will be supported by the other steps. The principle arose by observing successful practices in local teams of the public agency.

At this stage, the elements combine ideas, technologies, and people. These elements make up the knowledge base, a fundamental system for connecting skills and knowledge that will accompany the idea until its development. For this, the aggregation principle has as elements: internal and external partners; mapping of competencies and best practices; and defining open participation (see Figure 13.2).

The following topics describe in more detail the "aggregation" principle and the design of elements in levels to compose the model.

13.3.1.1. *Competencies and best practices mapping*

The mapping competencies and internal best practices are the initial and permanent activity of the model. In addition to identifying, mapping

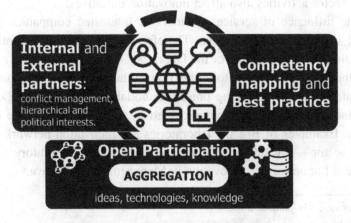

Figure 13.2. The aggregation principle.

constitutes an essential knowledge management activity for sharing knowledge with other public agencies.

As a later step, processes, activities and best practices need to be adapted to disseminate knowledge in each public agency that expresses interest. Therefore, Knowledge Base[23] assists in the choice of partners for training and monitoring of utilization strategies.

13.3.1.2. *Internal and external partners*

At the first level are the institutional partners directly linked to the public agency. Although geographically distributed, they make up an essential source of information and collaboration. Because this internal partner network is more robust than external partners, localized initiatives can result in rapid innovation when adapted and put into practice. As well, problems in common further motivate the search for solutions together.

However, conflicts of hierarchical and political interests can make this network risky.[20] Divergent interests impede cooperation between sectors and network development. In this way, it is vital to manage these conflicts to avoid or mitigate them.

At a second level, the model aggregates the hierarchy of the other partners. In each institution, the identification of the relationship network is undertaken by their skills and strategic people. Thus, external partners, companies, and other public agencies with direct and indirect links in public sector activities also affect innovation initiatives.

The influence of service providers or interested companies has an impact on innovation processes. Therefore, aggregation is essential for expanding the possibilities for the laboratory.

Other innovation laboratories also can collaborate as external partners. Laboratories with converging objectives collaborate to exchange knowledge and structure the services provided by the laboratory at the public agency. Examples of Brazil's laboratories are Innovation network in the public sector — InovaGov[e]; Management Innovation Laboratory — Lab. Ges[f]; and Laboratory of Innovation in Management — GNova.[g]

---

[e] http://inova.gov.br/junte-se-a-nos.
[f] https://labges.es.gov.br/quem-somos.
[g] http://gnova.enap.gov.br/sobre/quem-somos.

13.3.1.3. *Open participation*

Open participation discusses different ways of aggregating external knowledge.[24] Just as managers recommend projects based on their departments' needs, other users' ideas appear in campaigns made by the laboratory.[8] In this process of participation, decision-making is collaborative. It should involve all stakeholders necessary for a project's success, such as managers, other employees, laboratory members, company partners, and especially end-users. This constant interaction is fundamental, not only when deciding which project to develop but also throughout each process.[8]

In this context, open innovation approaches that have favored platforms and communities' emergence online optimize exploration of external knowledge.[25] In this sense, online participation campaigns gain space and voice to discuss problems, ideas, and developments in innovation environments, by society.[25] Therefore, understanding how to take advantage of crowd wisdom in the innovation process is strategic.[26]

In the Network Model, online and local actions promote society's participation in discussion, development, evaluation, and application. Thus, new sources and participatory user involvement enriches organizational knowledge.

13.3.2. *Digital laboratory*

The term "innovation laboratory" is a broad term in the public sector. The laboratories have different structures for experimenting and developing social and public solutions.[7]

A laboratory does not necessarily represent a permanent physical environment. The laboratories' units are permanent or temporary, physical or virtualized, composed of employees or inter-organizational teams, financed with the organization's resources or external funds.[7]

For the structure of a Network Model, the combination of physical and virtualized configurations is more coherent because the complexity of the aggregation of internal and external partners geographically dispersed would inhibit knowledge aggregation. Thus, a virtual environment can establish the initial meeting for the laboratory's operation and combination of knowledge.

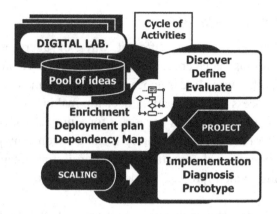

Figure 13.3.   The Digital Lab principle.

Figure 13.3 represents the functions of a digital laboratory. The principle of the Digital Laboratory operation begins with storage of the pool of ideas and the cycles of activities, with deliveries defined and accompanied by mentors. The progress is shared for discussion and enrichment by the community. The following topics explain how these functions work.

13.3.2.1. *Pool of ideas*

The pool of ideas serves as a Bank of Ideas with digital interaction for open participation. This system is the link with the previous principle, i.e. aggregation. In this interaction, idea management groups help collect feedback and monitor activities by promoting local experiences and sharing campaigns and initiatives.

Periodic events bring the different involved around a specific problem and serve as a "coffee of ideas," consisting of a discussion with small groups to create, enrich, and evaluate ideas.[27]

These conversations between each public agency's administrative staff also collect other specific ideas, needs, opportunities, or problems. At this point, the group prioritizes which ideas of the system are useful for the organizational context and which will go on to the cycle of activities.

13.3.2.2. *Cycle of activities*

The Digital Laboratory starts the cycle of activities. This cycle presents stages with deliveries and interactions for sharing, discussion, and enrichment of ideas. For this, we defined three phases: (1) Digital Lab; (2) Project; (3) Scaling.

As a basis for defining the cycle of activities, we identified the PSI Labs[28] and iLab[29] models. The PSI Labs model presents the "policy cycle," which classifies activities according to the following types (Ref. 28, p. 262):

(1) Identifying problems and informing the policy agenda (e.g. through research and/or data generation, analysis, or dissemination).
(2) Generating proposals and identifying potential solutions (e.g. through ideation, crowdsourcing, researching options).
(3) Testing solutions (e.g. prototyping, piloting).
(4) Decision-making (e.g. choosing solution/course of action, determining/producing policy).
(5) Implementing policy instrument(s) and/or scaling solutions.
(6) Monitoring and evaluating.

The iLab model defines the Project journey in six stages (Ref. 29, p. 295):

(1) Scoping: Scope the project topic with the department and sign a memorandum of understanding.
(2) Discover: Gathering user insights through interviews, focus groups, and/or observation.
(3) Define: Defining the challenge through a two-day workshop with stakeholders.
(4) Develop: Jointly create ideas with a broad user group, refine the concepts with a different user group, and test low fidelity prototypes with users.
(5) Deliver: Submit a business case to implement an integrated solution, upscale, and implement.
(6) Evaluate: Evaluate the process, outputs, and outcomes.

With regard to activities by Digital lab, we propose the formation of groups with virtual and local meetings. At first, the proposal is to "discover": problems, opportunities, or ideas. A perceived problem may be the stimulus for groups to present ideas. Otherwise, a local initiative or identified technology may be the opportunity for adaptation and application in different contexts.

From to "discover", the next step is to "define". That step is to describe and publish in the virtual environment. A moment to explain the group discussions that other users of the network will "evaluate." This assessment does not imply selection, but community participation in prioritization and interest. Combining this information in the digital environment will form the pool of ideas, a system for sharing, extracting data, and forming inter-organizational groups.

The "enrichment" activity consists of analyzing the organizational context and the knowledge structured in the previous activities.[30] In this activity, groups with common interests or proposals use this information to enrich the proposal.

The "deployment plan" consists of structuring the information in a formal project. For this, enrichment with different actors improves the project by identifying the scope, approach, execution, legal issues, costs, problems, or necessary improvements.

The "dependency map" activity comprises the complement of the project about responsibilities. Thus, it seeks professionals, companies, technologies, and talents to develop the project and the product.

The last activity devises the action plan to scale the project. Therefore, it formalizes how to carry out the implementation, diagnosis, and prototype of the project. The implementation involves putting a plan into action, hence the beginning of practical application in small initiatives. In parallel, the diagnostic activity performs the organizational analysis to put the project into practice and identify what attitudes are necessary to scale. Finally, a prototype is generated for verification in the production environment, resulting in further review steps or the initiative's expansion.

13.3.3. *Prototype testing*

The prototype testing tangibles the ideas and innovative capabilities of laboratories. The goal is to experiment and present a quick return for registration in the knowledge management system, thereby formalizing and improving what will become an innovation.[1]

The innovation laboratories advocate the creation of knowledge management systems.[14] In Barcelona,[14] this strategy has encouraged innovation laboratories to implement specific systems and processes to absorb, organize, and use new knowledge. Thus, the system manages the knowledge generated by the initiatives and makes a continuous flow of improvements.

Figure 13.4 illustrates the prototype testing principle and highlights the different strategies and phases of prototypes. As strategies, we identify the hackathons, makerspace, and incubators in the literature to create and promote practical initiatives.

The observatory operates in all phases with assistance to projects in three main stages. Because of the agency's distributed characteristics, we divided the phases into local communities, regional groups, and collective presentations. The prototype follow-up activities are described in the following sections.

13.3.3.1. *Innovation observatory*

The project phases are local communities, regional groups, and collective presentations. According to the cycle of activities, small groups are involved in formalization and sharing in local communities.

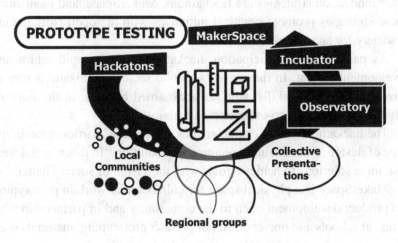

Figure 13.4. The prototype testing principle.

After contributing to the pool of ideas, the observatory brings together different teams to form regional groups. Thus, the innovation observatory acts in all phases with assistance to projects to create groups, mentoring, and support in searching for resources.

The project then needs an incubation moment with mentoring by researchers, invited professionals, and public agencies' managers in an observatory. For this, presentation events at the Innovation Observatory help to search for resources in public notices or organizations that promote innovation. In this context of group formation, the need for specialists arises. The specialists will assist in the development of projects with mentoring and innovation strategies.

In the case of laboratories in Barcelona,[14] the innovation strategy guided the laboratories' operations and helped systematize the innovation process, which, according to the interviewees, included risk management.[14]

Among the categories for analysis in the risk management of these projects are: (1) operational risks; (2) the agency's image/reputation risks; (3) legal risks (compliance); (4) financial/budgetary risks; (5) risks to integrity; (6) risks of information and communication technology; (7) environmental risks; (8) strategic risks; and (9) people management risks.

13.3.3.2. *Hackathons, MakerSpace, and incubator*

Other innovation strategies are Hackathons, MakerSpace, and incubators. These strategies promote practical initiatives with the open participation of society for specific solutions.

As part of open participation, hackathons have a rapid return and development format. In these events, public sector organizations turn to citizens with unique skills, who are nicknamed hackers, in the hope of solving a problem, or co-executing an activity.[6]

The hackathon's main characteristics are citizens' participation in the stage of design, creation, and execution of a solution.[6] In this way, hackers customize solutions to achieve goals with the vision of society better.

MakerSpace is a physical space for collaborative work in prototyping and product development open to the community and in partnership with technical schools and universities. For product prototyping, materials such as prototyping boards, sensors, single-board computer (Raspberry, Arduino), tools, and 3D printers are available. These spaces also serve for the hackathons and events that seek the development of solutions.[1]

Furthermore, business incubators are an area to relate startups with solutions for the public sector. They provide working conditions and an ecosystem for startups to develop their first products with potential for the sector.

13.3.4. *Research groups*

The principle of research groups covers the end and the beginning of the model. This model is employed because research groups, in this context, are integrated into the laboratory and serve as monitoring agents, provide knowledge and ideas, and disseminate results.

A research group has the responsibility to develop research, science outreach, and education to discover technical-scientific responses to the public institution's strategic challenges. Its principle is to act in a network (multidisciplinary, interdisciplinary, or transdisciplinary) collaboratively and search for continuous learning with other entities and other research groups to strengthen knowledge areas, as shown in Figure 13.5.

This principle's conception is related to the concept of a research group of the Brazilian National Council for Scientific and Technological Development (CNPq). CNPq describes a research group as "a group of researchers, students and technical support personnel organized around

Figure 13.5. The integration principle.

the execution of lines of research according to a hierarchical rule based on experience and technical-scientific competence."[31]

Therefore, groups come together with scientific researchers and technical-practical staff, community, and various participants in search of solutions and joint discoveries around research lines, aiming to discover innovative solutions that add public value.

13.3.4.1. *Trend monitor*

When monitoring trends, the research group directs the realization of the projects. It has the desired composition, a general coordinator, and leaders of thematic research groups, responsible for publications, dissemination, and evaluation of the group and the secretary-general.

The group assists in developing research that can be individual, collective, and thematic. Also, in each thematic group, a team of collaborators, researchers, and students continues the search for new research and opportunities. Thus, ordinary alignment meetings maintain the interaction between members and the consistency of research.

13.3.4.2. *Dissemination of results*

Another point is the technical-scientific responses. This function is the academic dissemination and communication of the results to society. The availability of knowledge repositories, technical-scientific journals, and events promotion is vital to maintain the laboratory cycle and participants' collaboration.

This disclosure is in line with the principles provided for by legislative proposal 7843/2017, which states that "[the results] developed in the Innovation Laboratories will be of free and public use and domain shared through non-restrictive free licenses."

13.4. Conclusion

The creation of open spaces allows the public sector to experiment with ideas without interrupting the traditional structure.[7] From this approach, a Networked Innovation Laboratory for the public sector becomes an environment conducive to participation and collaboration in developing ideas and identifying problems and opportunities. This conception differs by analyzing the knowledge of the extended network of internal and external partners, such as service providers and society.

For the structuring of a laboratory, integrating this knowledge and stimulating initiatives outside the hierarchical structures characterized the network model's proposal formed by four principles: (1) **aggregation**, (2) **digital laboratory**, (3) **prototyping test**, and (4) **research groups**.

The aggregation starts with open participation and structured knowledge flows. The involvement of different actors contributes collectively to generate and enrich the knowledge. When structuring this knowledge, the laboratory recognizes the capacity for innovation in the organizational structure itself.

The next principle is the creation of a digital laboratory to structure the cycle of activities. Thus, the cycle of activities is the enrichment and improvement of knowledge to elaborate projects.

Then, the prototyping test principle systematizes knowledge for the effective application and expansion of projects. Currently, local communities, regional groups, and collective presentations involve teams to get a product or service concept.

Finally, there are the research groups that set up the model in a cycle. These groups are responsible for developing knowledge and disseminating the laboratory results academically and technically, presenting the value of innovations to society. Likewise, they monitors trends that will encourage the continuation of innovation cycles, researching and identifying strategic challenges for the organization.

Thus, the results perceived from the perspective of governance collaborate in the structuring of new laboratories. In particular, as it presents an open space for aggregating knowledge and expanding collaboration, the model acts as a mechanism for knowledge governance.

The relationship occurs since the establishment of innovation laboratory benefits both the public and private sectors, emphasizing citizen participation. It promotes the knowledge relationship between users and organizations from both sectors to capture new ideas for public services and collaboration in solving problems. In this way, it is consistent with one of governance's purposes, which is to generate cooperation for the collective good.[5]

In future work, the model's development will focus attention on the phases of: (1) Implementation; (2) Follow-up; (3) Diagnostics; and (4) Results. Such a discussion is fundamental to define the laboratory's mission and its value to the institution and society and its relationship with the Corporate University Model in Network,[32–34] by the practical experiences of structuring research and innovation in the public sector.

Acknowledgments

This study was financed in part by the Coordenação de Aperfeiçoamento de Pessoal de Nível Superior — Brasil (CAPES) — Finance Code 001.

References

1. OECD/Eurostat. *Oslo Manual 2018: Guidelines for Collecting, Reporting and Using Data on Innovation.* 4th ed. Luxembourg: OECD Publishing (2019).
2. A. Baregheh, J. Rowley and S. Sambrook. Towards a multidisciplinary definition of innovation. *Management Decision,* **47**(8), 1323 (2009).
3. H.W. Chesbrough. *Open Innovation: The New Imperative for Creating and Profiting from Technology.* Cambridge, MA: Harvard Business School Press (2003).
4. M. Bogers, H. Chesbrough and C. Coins. Open innovation: Research, practices, and policies. *California Management Review,* **60**, 5 (2018).
5. P. de Sá Freire, G.A. Dandolini, J.A. de Souza, T. Caetano Silva and R. Moreira Couto. Governance of Knowledge (GovC): The state of the art over the term. *Biblios,* **69**, 21 (2017).
6. G. de Ferreira and J. S. Farias. The Motivation to Participate in Citizen-Sourcing and Hackathons in the Public Sector. *Brazilian Administration Review,* **15**, 3 (2018).
7. C. Galhardo. Laboratory of innovation in the public sector: A study on the MobiLab Da Cidade de São Paulo. Universidade Nove de Julho (2019).
8. MJV Technology & Innovation. Laboratório de Inovação, (2019). https://conteudo.mjv.com.br/ebook/laboratorio-de-inovacao
9. D. Schuurman and P. Tõnurist. Innovation in the public sector: Exploring the characteristics and potential of living labs and innovation labs. *Technology Innovation Management Review,* **7**, 7 (2017).

10. H. Vibeke Carstensen, C. Bason and D. Christian Bason. Powering collaborative policy innovation: Can innovation labs help? *Sociology: The Innovation Journal*, **17**(1), 25 (2012).

11. A. Yazdizadeh and A. Tavasoli. Living labs as a tool for open innovation: A systematic review. *International Journal of Humanities and Cultural Studies*, **3**, 15 (2016).

12. M. Gascó. Living labs: Implementing open innovation in the public sector. *Government Information Quarterly*, **34**(1), 90 (2017).

13. J. Chen, R.M. Walker and M. Sawhney. Public service innovation: A typology. *Public Management Review*, **22**(11), 1674 (2020).

14. K. Timeus and M. Gascó. Increasing innovation capacity in city governments: Do innovation labs make a difference? *Journal of Urban Affairs*, **40**(7), 992 (2018).

15. H. Gieske, A. Van Buuren and V. Bekkers. Conceptualizing public innovative capacity: A framework for assessment. *The Innovation Journal: Public Sector Innovation Journal*, **21**(1), 25 (22016).

16. D. Albury. Fostering Innovation in public services. *Public Money Management*, **25**(1), 51–56, (2005).

17. L. Brown and S.P. Osborne. Risk and innovation. *Public Management Review*, **15**(2), 186 (2013).

18. A. Agger and E. Sørensen. Designing collaborative policy innovation: lessons from a Danish municipality. In *Public Innovation Through Collaboration and Design*, C. Ansell and J. Torfing (eds.), 1st ed. London: Routledge, pp. 206–226 (2014).

19. L.M. Ricard, E.H. Klijn, J.M. Lewis and T. Ysa. Assessing public leadership styles for innovation: A comparison of Copenhagen, Rotterdam and Barcelona. *Public Management Review*, **19**(2), 134 (2017).

20. E. Sørensen and J. Torfing. Collaborative innovation in the public sector. *Innovation Journal*, **17**(1), 1 (2012).

21. R. Karo and E. Kattel. Innovation bureaucracy: Does the organisation of government matter when promoting innovation? *Papers in Innovation Studies* No 2015/38, 25 (2015).

22. P. Tõnurist, R. Kattel and V. Lember. Innovation labs in the public sector: What they are and what they do? *Public Management Review*, **19**(10), 1455 (2017).

23. R. Young. *Knowledge Management Tools and Techniques Manual*. Tokyo: Asian Productivity Organization (2020).

24. W. Rochadel. *Identification of Criteria for Evaluation of Ideas: A Method Using Folksonomy*. Brazil: Federal University of Santa Catarina (2016).

25. C. Riedl, I. Blohm, J.M. Leimeister and H. Krcmar. Rating Scales for Collective Intelligence in Innovation Communities: Why Quick and Easy Decision Making Does Not Get it Right. Proceedings of Thirty First International Conference on Information Systems, (2010). https://papers.ssrn.com/sol3/papers.cfm?abstract_id=1714524

26. J. Prpić, P.P. Shukla, J.H. Kietzmann and I.P. McCarthy. How to work a crowd: Developing crowd capital through crowdsourcing. *Business Horizons*, **58**(1), 77 (2015).

27. A. D. B. Valdati, J. A. De Souza and G. A. Dandolini. *Systemic representation of idea management: A proposed framework*. Brazil: Federal University of Santa Catarina (2019).

28. M. McGann, E. Blomkamp and J.M. Lewis: The rise of public sector innovation labs: Experiments in design thinking for policy. *Scientific Policy*, **51**(3), 249 (2018).

29. A. Whicher and T. Crick. Co-design, evaluation and the Northern Ireland Innovation Lab. *Public Money and Management*, **39**(4), 290 (2019).

30. W. Rochadel, A. de B. Valdati, J.A. de Souza and G.A. Dandolini. Idea Maturity Model. In *16th International Conference on Information Systems Technology and Management CONTECSI 2019* (São Paulo, 2019).

31. CNPq. Brazilian National Council for Science, Technology and Development (n.d.).

32. P. de Sá Freire, G. Dandolini, J.A. de Souza and S.M. da Silva. Process of implementation of the Corporate University in Network (UCR). *Revista Espacios*, **37**(23) (2016).

33. G.A. Dandolini, P. de Sá Freire and J.A. de Souza. Implementation process of Corporate University in Network (CUN). *International Journal of Innovation Education Research*, **5**(12), 101 (2017).

34. S. Maria da Silva, G.A. Dandolini, P. de Sá Freire, J. Artur de Souza, W. Rochadel and A. De Brittos Valdati. Purpose of the use of technologies in the contemporary models of Corporate University. *International Journal of Innovation Education Research*, **6**(8), 55 (2018).

Cross-Sector Partnerships in Social Innovation Initiatives: A Multiple Case Study in Portugal

Michele Andréia Borges, Márcia Aparecida Prim* and João Artur de Souza

Graduate Program in Knowledge Management and Engineering,
Federal University of Santa Catarina,
R. Delfino Conti, s/n, Trindade, Florianópolis — SC
88040–900, Brazil

*marciaaprim@gmail.com

Social innovation has evolved as an important mechanism to respond to global social challenges and the social demands of territories. A relevant feature of its process is the collaboration between multiple actors, through the formation of cross-sector partnerships, which include, in its definition, the involvement of various sectors of the economy, beyond the community and the individual himself. The underlying complexity of the relationships formed demands a systemic look at the dynamics of these partnerships, as well as participatory governance. Through a multiple case study approach on social innovation initiatives in Portugal, this chapter aims to understand how partnership relations for social innovation are established. The results allowed identifying the essential elements to the partnerships and thus present guidelines to support the development of cross-sector partnerships for social innovation initiatives. Although the empirical scenario is in Portugal, the guidelines are supported by theories and scientific results at a global level, and are flexible and adaptable in order to obtain adherence to other cultural, political, social and economic contexts.

14.1. Introduction

Social innovation has proved to be a viable alternative to solve local social demands, combat major global challenges, and incite systemic changes (i.e. changes in fundamental attitudes and values, strategies and policies, and organizational structures and processes), from the perspective of sustainability in its triple dimension (social, environmental, and economic), involving the government, companies, the third sector, and, above all, civil society.[1–3]

As its name suggests, social innovation is a social process of value creation and, therefore, this process cannot be closed. It must provide the actors' interaction and collaboration so that more effective and sustainable social transformations occur.[4–6] However, although recent studies suggest that the formation of collaborative partnerships has significant potential in the success of social impacts, some obstacles need to be overcome.[7]

Collaboration requires efforts to be established in the daily lives of people and organizations, since it involves trust, commitment and alignment of values and beliefs between the parties involved.[5,8] The synergy between socio-economic sectors is complex and generates not only benefits but also costs.[9]

The lack of concrete objectives with the partnerships is a challenge presented to the evaluation of the efficiency and effectiveness of partnerships in social initiatives.[7] Governance is another factor that is sensitive to social innovations.[1–11] Hubert[1] explains that there is a lack of coordination between the various actors involved in social innovation. This lack of coordination has implications, such as overlapping roles and social activities and subcritical or political interventions that may be inconsistent or that overlap on each other.

That said, it is understood that coordinating the social innovation process with partners is complex. In this sense, the objective of this chapter is to understand the dynamics of partnerships through a study on multiple cases and, based on that, to propose a set of guidelines to support the development of cross-sector partnerships in social innovation initiatives. The multiple case study was carried out with 20 social innovation initiatives in Portugal, through document analysis and semi-structured interviews. The initiative includes actions and solutions that can be a product, service, process, or methodology, linked to the most diverse areas of social intervention (health, education, environment, etc.).[12]

The guidelines were created with a focus on four categories: (1) partnership planning, (2) mapping and ways to make them official, (3) evaluations focused on results, and (4) governance. These guidelines are permeated by attributes arising from the social capital of partnerships, such as values, beliefs, collaboration, trust, commitment, and transparency, among others. In this sense, governance is a vital element in partnerships.[13]

Social initiatives are part of a historical context, whether to solve basic survival needs or economic or social needs.[14] The discussions, both in the academic and economic and political fields, take place daily and this debate leads us to think in a more inclusive and collaborative way and with the purpose of creating social value.[4–11] A widely known definition in the literature is the one by researchers Murray *et al.*[15] For these authors, social innovation can be new ideas that meet social needs and create new social relationships. In this sense, they are good for society and increase their capacity for action.

However, social innovation has been defined in other ways by other researchers, with no consensus in the literature and being perceived with various meanings.[2] While the discussion remains about a universally accepted concept, the importance of social innovation as an important mechanism for responding to global social challenges and the social demands of territories is not questioned.

Some essential factors that explain the importance of social innovation in society are sustainable growth; job security; increased competitive capacity; the growing number of non-profit organizations developing economic activities to support their social mission; the emergence of a variety of markets and projects; and non-market-based business strategies, aimed at solving social problems and growth opportunities for innovation and experimentation derived from the current global recession environment.[5–16]

More than isolated initiatives, social innovation is a social process of value creation and thus partnerships and collaborative actions between multiple actors are key elements for its dissemination, effectiveness, and sustainability.[8] Social innovation can be understood as a process or as a result.[15–17] Until 2010 it was oriented, in most cases, to its result and developed a social value produced from paternalistic environments.[18] In the sense of processes, for social innovations to be effective, they need to be intentional, organized, systematized, and coordinated. The understanding of social innovation oriented to the process takes into account the steps developed, from its creation to its implementation.

14.1.1. *Social innovation process*

The innovation process is recognized, in general, by three major phases[16]: the first directed to the treatment of opportunities and the generation of ideas; the second to development, which involves the concept of creating a prototype, and lastly, the moment of implementation, diffusion, and commercialization.[15]

In the specific context of social innovation, Mulgan[9] was one of the first researchers to analyze and describe its process. She concluded that social innovation processes go through six stages, not necessarily sequential, and that feedback loops can occur between them. The stages identified by Mulgan[9] were:

(1) *Prompts*: Refer to the diagnosis of social needs and challenges, considering the symptoms and causes of the problem. At this stage, the involvement of partners is vital for the correct identification of society's demands.
(2) *Proposals*: Refer to the generation of ideas. This entire stage must be carried out cooperatively, with a view to propose creative and innovative solutions to deal with the diagnosed needs and challenges.

(3) *Prototypes:* Refer to the development and prototyping of the generated idea. At this stage, the ideas are tested in practice.

(4) *Sustainability:* That is when the idea becomes an everyday practice. At this stage, it is especially important to create strategies and business models that support the financial sustainability of the social initiative in the long term.

(5) *Scaling:* Refers to the scaling and diffusion of the idea, i.e. the phase that uses a series of strategies to disseminate innovation in different contexts and with different partners.

(6) *Systemic change:* Is the stage that involves the interaction of multiple transformative and long-term elements such as diverse actors and partners, new business models, laws and regulations, and new paradigms in the way of thinking and acting. Changes considered systemic usually involve new structures composed, in many cases, of several minor innovations.[15,16]

Cunha and Benneworth[17] present the social innovation process in six phases, being:

(1) *Generation of ideas:* Proposing solutions to the social problem encountered, usually with a variety of actors involved;

(2) *Protected space:* A place to experiment and to put this plan into action;

(3) *Demonstration:* Application of the new solution in order to assess whether the idea is viable and works effectively;

(4) *Expansion:* It is the decision to expand, if the scale solution is possible;

(5) *Establish a pilot support team:* In order to develop and improve the innovative solution, maintaining the protected space;

(6) *Codification:* It will involve several individuals to contribute to increasing the scale of the solution, new contexts, places, or circumstances.

Patias *et al.*[18] present a more robust model of social innovation, elaborated from previous models. In this model, social innovation can emerge at any time, through a presented social problem. It stems from moments of crisis or other adversities in a given scenario or time. The coalition stage demands a collective effort so that the projects and proposals are a time to raise ideas and develop prototypes, to achieve the objectives set. The deployment and maintenance phases are for project execution. This phase can start through a pilot project. They are extremely important, because at that moment, errors and correction needs can be identified, as well as the sustainability of the project and measurement. In the scale and replicability phase, the potential of social innovation to achieve its objectives, whether local, regional, or global, is verified. It is in moments of change and transformation that social innovation is consolidated. The supposedly final phase is the analysis of the impact of social innovation.

The social innovation process will vary considerably depending on the initial problem and the actors and partners involved, especially if the innovation in question is developed by third sector organizations, the business sector, or the State. Therefore, understanding the interrelationships between the stages of the social innovation process and how they develop through the particularities of partnerships, entities that promote innovation and the particularities of innovation itself, are still a challenge in the field of social innovations.

14.1.2. *Cross-sector partnerships*

When talking about cross-sector partnerships, it is expected to involve formal organizations from the third sector, business sector, and public sector, but the scope of this type of partnership goes beyond these formal organizations and involves people and informal groups.

According to Nelson and Zadek, cross-sector partnerships are defined as "people and organizations from the public, private, business, and civil sectors that engage in mutually beneficial, innovative relationships to respond to social goals assumed by all, combining their resources and skills" (Ref. 9, p. 14).

Corroborating, van Tulder et al.[7] state that cross-sector partnerships are, therefore, expected to deliver improved and innovative solutions to economic, social, and environmental problems through the combination of the capacities and resources of organizational actors in different sectors. However, the effectiveness of partnerships depends on multiple factors.

Thus, the triumph of cross-sector partnerships depends on an entire dynamic process that is permeated by characteristics belonging to the dimensions of the context, purpose, participants/actors, organization, and evaluation, and the alchemy between these dimensions is composed of elements such as trust, collaboration, commitment, integrity, values, transparency.[19]

14.1.3. *Governance*

The notion of governance of cross-sector partnerships concerns the balance of roles, responsibilities and capacity of different levels of government (local, regional, national, and global) and the involvement of different actors or sectors of society (public, private, non-profit organizations and citizens.[20]

In this context, a new look should be given to governance to meet the challenges of social innovation, which differs from traditional models, and it should seek to answer the questions: how companies can conciliate the creation of economic and social value? How can governments create an enabling environment that balances regulatory frameworks with voluntary approaches and market incentives to better meet citizen needs?[19]

To face these challenges, Nelson and Zadek[19] suggest a new form of governance that considers: (1) active citizen participation, adopting innovative strategies to mobilize more citizens at both the political and practical levels; (2) more coordinated and efficient approaches within and among existing government institutions; (3) greater dialogue between governments and profit and non-profit sector organizations; and (4) greater transparency and accountability on the part of government and business in terms of priorities, investments, and results.

In a more operational discourse on the governance of cross-sector partnerships, Roth *et al.*[21] propose a governance model that has as its theoretical core the seminal work by Beagles et al.[22] and the works by Oxley[23] and Albers.[24] This model defines governance as:

> The governance consists of the definition of rules, criteria for decision making, responsibilities, and limits on the autonomy and action of participants. It is created by the organizations involved and at the same time it affects

them, because it implies the definition of rules that they themselves must follow. The role of governance is not to manage, but to delimit management (Ref. 21, p. 112).

In this way, Roth *et al.*[21] operationalize their model based on structural dimensions (form of organizations and established regulation) and instrumental dimensions (related to management, organization, regulation, and control instruments).

14.2. Methodology

This is a qualitative research. The strategy chosen was the case study that aims to answer *how* and *why* a certain phenomenon occurs. In addition, it was decided to carry out a multiple case study in order to obtain a greater robustness of the unit under analysis, which is the cross-sector partnerships, within the context of social innovations.

14.2.1. *Multiple case study*

The cases were selected based on the criterion sampling strategy. According to Gray (Ref. 13, p. 149), in the criterion sampling, the sample is selected based on the main focus of the study, from which all the chosen cases must meet this criterion. Thus, the criteria established were: (1) initiatives considered as social innovation and (2) social innovation initiatives that contain a network of partners.

The social innovation initiatives in Portugal were identified in the aforementioned Map of Innovation and Social Entrepreneurship and the Oporto Center for Social Innovation. In all, 20 social innovation initiatives agreed to participate in the research. The initiatives belong to 11 areas of social intervention, according to the MIES classification:[25] environment, preservation, and recycling; community development, agriculture, and food industry; active aging and/or support to the vulnerable elderly and/or combating isolation; support to disabled people for development of skills; ludic and/or cultural and/or sports initiative; poverty reduction (one initiative); youth development (one initiative); employability and/or entrepreneurship (one initiative); health (one initiative); and inclusive tourism (one initiative).[26]

The Northern Region initiatives that are part of this study have a social impact at the local, national, Portuguese-speaking countries, and international (other countries) levels. The Central Region initiatives have social impact at local, regional, and national levels. The initiatives belonging to the Alentejo Region have a social impact only at local level.

The beneficiaries of the initiatives converge with their areas of intervention, thus, the cases studied present different types of beneficiaries (elderly, young people in vulnerable situations, individuals in poverty, individuals with disabilities, schools, communities, etc.). The proposed solutions are aimed at the development of methodologies or techniques to solve a social or environmental demand, and are integrated actions that involve the provision of services to the community, creation of products with social and environmental impact, and training and awareness-raising actions for the community.

14.2.2. *Data collection and data analysis*

The data collection was carried out entirely in Portugal, from October 2015 to September 2016, and was based on three data sources: documents semi-structured interviews, and questionnaire.

The interviews aimed to focus the collection of data on the participants' own experience with regard to concrete and symbolic aspects regarding the research problem. The interviews were of the semi-structured type, i.e. with open questions, adherent to the objective of the research, that guide the interviewer along the narrative of the interviewee. Twenty managers participated in this stage, one per initiative of social innovation studied.

The main theoretical pillar of the questionnaire was the Framework for Evaluating Partnership Network for Social Change, from Canada's *Centre for Social* Innovation,[27] and the EQUAL Development Partnership Guide.[20] The adherence to the questionnaire was partial: of the 20 interviewees, 13 answered the questionnaire. The analytical strategy used to analyze the data set was through the triangulation of multiple data sources, which allow convergence and fusion of the various sources used[28] and generate richer and more reliable findings and results. To triangulate the data, Bardin's Thematic-Categorical Content Analysis[25] methodology was used. The organization of the content analysis occurred from the execution of the pre-analysis, exploration of the material, and treatment of the results.[25]

14.3. Results: Presentation of the Guidelines

The descriptive analysis of the ecosystem, processes, and results of cross-sector partnerships in social innovation initiatives in Portugal allowed us to infer that the dynamics of partnerships is determined mainly by the social objectives of each initiative and the specific objectives with the partners. In addition to this factor, the way social innovation processes are implemented, some analytical components (planning, development, and evaluation) and governance also stand out as relevant macro-processes for partnerships.

The proposed guidelines were designed through the relationship between three metaphorical macro-components: axis, helix, and grid. Figure 14.1 shows the relationship between the macro-components that are part of the proposed guidelines to support the development of cross-sector partnerships for social innovation initiatives.

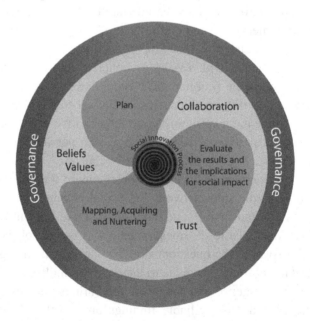

Figure 14.1.   Macro-components of cross-sector partnerships.

The **axis** is the process of social innovation, ranging from the recognition of a social demand to systemic changes. It is along this process that cross-sector partnerships will be established.

The **helices** represent analytical components where cross-sector partnerships will be made tangible. First helix: planning stage; second helix: development stage (mapping, acquiring, and nurturing partnerships); and third helix: the partnership evaluation stage.

Governance is the grid that "protects" the axis and the helices, i.e. it establishes the strategies, rules, and limits of the partner network management. It is noteworthy that the dynamics of cross-sector partnerships is permeated by attributes arising from the social capital of the partnerships, such as values, beliefs, collaboration, trust, commitment, and transparency, among others.

14.3.1. *Axis — Social innovation process*

Although its definition is not unanimous in academia, the concept of social innovation is recognized by a body of characteristics that are predominant or essential to it. Among these characteristics, we highlight the dimension of originality and novelty for a given context; the improvement in the quality of life of the beneficiaries; its endurance in time and respect for the environment; and solutions to the real problems of people, among others.

Recognizing these characteristics and observing them throughout the social innovation process is a form of bargaining in the acquisition of partners and is also a strategy to maintain and nurture partnerships over time. In this sense, the guidelines for the macro-component (axis) are defined: (1) identify the level of compliance with the characteristics of social innovation in your initiative, in order to enhance partnerships; and (2) monitor the characteristics of social innovation throughout its process.

14.3.2. *Partnership planning helix*

The partnership planning phase is one of the most important phases, as it defines what is intended with the partners (objectives) and what strategies will be adopted to achieve success with the partnership and the implications on social impacts. Thus, it is relevant that, in the planning phase, the social and operational objectives with the partnerships, the types of partners required for the initiative, the verification and adequacy to the level of formality of the initiative, and the participation in structures supporting social innovation are taken into consideration. The guidelines for the macro-component helix — the planning helix — are:

(1) Reflect on how the partner or network of partners can meet the social objectives of the initiative.
(2) Identify the types of resources (tangible or intangible) that are available and/or will be requested from each partner.
(3) Define whether the partner will complement resources (tangible or intangible) throughout the initiative or will only provide resources on time.
(4) Establish, jointly, the roles and functions that the partner will play in the initiative.
(5) Question whether the initiative requires the collaboration of companies, the third sector, the government, beneficiaries, academies, or a specialized center.
(6) Question whether the initiative requires the collaboration of different types of partners, whether companies, third sector, government, beneficiaries, universities, or specialized centers.
(7) Check the need and feasibility of institutionalizing the project through the creation of a non-profit company or institution, or if there is an existing institution.
(8) Check the need to adapt the regulations of the institution promoting the social innovation initiative in order to meet the requirements and standards of partner institutions.

Regarding the social objectives, these are related to the intervention or social purpose of the initiative. In addition, the roles and functions that the partner will develop in the initiative must be jointly established. It is important to say that the objectives should be established a priori, but they should also be sufficiently flexible to changes and the emergence of new objectives.

Regarding the formality of the initiative, two major scenarios were identified: social innovation initiatives that are conceived by social entrepreneurs or informal groups of individuals and initiatives that emerge within an institution (companies, non-governmental organizations, universities, etc.). Finally, in the planning phase, the involvement of the initiative with support structures for social innovation (centers, institutes, government programs) must be taken into account. These structures, in addition to supporting the project at the core of each social innovation phase, foster a network of relationships with other entities that may become partners in the project in question.

14.3.3. *Partnership development helix*

Developing partnerships involves mapping, acquiring, and nurturing these partnerships over time. The empirical analysis demonstrated that social innovation initiatives must use a series of strategies to map, acquire, and nurture partnerships, from making the aggregate knowledge clear to establishing negotiation techniques, relationships, and communication, among others. Table 14.1 points out these strategies and guidelines.

Within this macro-component of partnership development, there is a need to make clear that the "doors" of the promoting initiative are always open to partners, so that moments of informal relationship with the representatives of the partnerships, as well as work in co-creation may arise. Using technologies to encourage participation (social networks, synchronous communication technologies, taking photos of certain occasions) is also relevant, as they increase the visibility of the partnerships.

14.3.4. *Partnership evaluation helix*

An evaluation of the results of the proposed solution was observed in the social innovation initiatives, however, this evaluation has not been a central focus. The evaluation of partnerships allows to reinforce some measures, change others, adopt new measures, establish changes in the governance of the network, establish new objectives, adopt strategies to foster commitment, trust, and collaborative participation of partners,

Table 14.1. Strategies and guidelines for the macro-component partnership development helix.

Strategies	Guidelines
Aggregated knowledge	(1) Demonstrate the innovative character of the initiative and the scientific and/or practical rigor of the proposed solution.
	(2) Explain the proposed solution knowledge in the form of a methodology, as it demonstrates the capacity of the managers of the initiative to structure, systematize, and organize knowledge, so that it can be shared and replicated.
	(3) Present the partial or full results of the proposed solution, in order to generate credibility and trust in the initiative.
Negotiation	(4) Present the tangible and/or intangible benefits of forming the partnership; the so-called win-win partnerships.
	(5) Emphasize participation in the fulfillment of the partner organization's own social mission, especially in the case of third sector and public sector organizations.
	(6) Show that they can work in a complementary way, whether related to tangible or intangible resources.
	(7) Show to potential partners, especially beneficiaries, the potential of the initiative to improve people's living conditions and/or the environment.
	(8) Demonstrate that partnerships help to reduce social costs.
	(9) Demonstrate that partnerships lead to the mutual improvement of the organization's practices.
	(10) Demonstrate that there is an economic return due to the positive visibility or the reach of a new market niche.
	(11) Demonstrate that the partnership can ensure resources.
	(12) Offer the proposed solution to the potential partner. For example, if the initiative's solution is to train individuals for a given area, then enable the partners to take advantage of that training, so that they can integrate into the initiative and strengthen the feeling of belonging.
Relationship source	(13) Identify government programs and policies.
	(14) Identify collaboration networks, learning networks, or thematic networks in which the initiative can be inserted.
	(15) Identify influential people who are aligned with the initiative's proposal.
	(16) Participate in events, forums, and meetings focused on the social intervention theme.
	(17) Use personal networks to form partnerships.

Table 14.1. (*Continued*)

Strategies	Guidelines
Communication	(18) Invest in the communication of the initiative on the web and social networks.
	(19) Use didactic and dynamic means to present the initiative to partners.
	(20) Present the beneficiaries and other partners' reports.
	(21) Publicize awards and recognition titles.
	(22) Use inclusive local and friendly language.
	(23) Visit the organizations and the group of beneficiary actors to present the initiative.
	(24) Constantly share and disseminate information and experiences in order to nurture the established partnerships.
	(25) Publicize their support and formally thank partner organizations.
	(26) Hold commemorative events to strengthen the connection.
	(27) Use the personal contact network as a means of publicizing and disseminating the initiative.

innovate in processes, establish new projects together and make changes in the proposed solution itself.

(1) Evaluate the processes and results of the partnership, both for the common purpose and for the individual agendas of each partner.
(2) Evaluate the efficiency of partnerships at the input level and the implementation and execution of activities, through a cost-benefit analysis and of partnerships in terms of management and the interaction of partners in the network.
(3) Evaluate the effectiveness of partnerships in terms of performance related to the social objective of the partnership, through a comparative analysis of partner organizations that have the same social objective.
(4) Use holistic measuring instruments.

It is important to emphasize the possible need to obtain human resources for the management and evaluation of partnerships, which can be both collaborators already established in the project or in the promoting entity, as well as the inclusion of other people or competent entities in the management and evaluation of cross-sector partnerships.

14.3.5. *Governance — Grid*

The governance of the network of partners is one of the sensitive topics for cross-sector partnerships. In the proposal presented, governance is the "protective grid" of the dynamics of cross-sector partnerships throughout the process of social innovation, since it allows delimiting the partnerships, in a notion characterized by flexibility and adequacy of practices to meet the needs of collective strategies[24] and by the balance of roles, responsibilities, and capacities of the different levels of local, national, regional, and global government and the different actors or sectors of society — public, private, and civil society organizations and individuals.[22] The guidelines for the macro-component governance are presented below:

(1) Encourage a non-centralized governance in a single institution and increase the coordination, in order to ensure the coherence of actions.

(2) Reflect on whether the network partners, or some of them, will have autonomy to manage and coordinate the activities of the initiative.

(3) Allocate human resources dedicated to managing the partnerships.

(4) Foster the involvement of partners in the project's decisions and directions that directly or indirectly affect the partnership.

(5) Enable a board of directors or advisory group to support the decisions of the initiative.

(6) Establish formal protocols with partners, in order to make transparent the commitments between the parties, the gains from the partnership, legal caveats, among other critical issues in the development of the partnership.

(7) Encourage informality of relationships in the partnership continuum. Maintain assiduous and transparent communication in the critical phases of the project to which the partners are linked.

(8) Promote occasional meetings, in person or virtual, in order to keep the partnership relationship active.

(9) Frequently disseminate the results of the activities developed with the partners, the social results of the project, and general information that can strengthen the partnership relationship.

In the matter of the formality of each network partner, the initiative must assess the need for this formalization. In the initiatives studied in this survey, the formality has generally proved relevant for establishing the commitments, costs, and benefits of the partnership; but, on the other hand, the initiatives have shown that the relationship between partners, in the exchange of information, communication, and decision-making, is based on an informal understanding, and that this establishes a trust and an affective commitment that feeds the effectiveness of the established commitments and generates a virtuous circle of trust.

Communication, in terms of frequency, is variable; as Mulgan[9] informs, it is innocent to think that the communication among actors in a collaborative union will be carried out all the time. The empirical results of this research showed that communication depends on the phases of the project and is carried out when necessary. However, when it comes to communication in terms of dissemination of results, accountability, and processes and novelties of the initiative, these should be disseminated frequently, as it provides transparency and credibility, fosters trust among partners, helps to positively disseminate the initiative, brings partners closer together, makes them more active in the initiative, and helps in the acquisition of more partners, should this evolution in the network dimension be necessary.

Changes in the governance structure are a topic that should not be denied. Therefore, the governance model must be planned and redesigned according to the direction of the partnerships, always thinking about the social mission of the initiative. Finally, one must question intermittently which governance structure is desirable to the network of partners throughout the process of social innovation.

14.4. Conclusions

The social innovations studied showed their innovative potential in solutions that, in some cases, the object itself was not apparently innovative, but the way in which the proposed solution was conducted proved to be innovative. This form boils down mainly to intentionality and professionalism, which go beyond passion and empathy for social causes.

This professionalism was materialized by the careful development of methodologies that support social actions, many of them with a scientific basis, supported by collaborative partnerships with universities and research centers. The descriptive analysis of the ecosystem, processes, and results of the cross-sector partnerships in social innovation initiatives allowed to infer that the dynamics of the partnerships is determined, mainly, by the social objectives of the initiative and by the specific objectives with the partners.

Thus, each initiative has its own particularity in terms of the involvement of the actors that are partners in the initiative. However, the description of the dynamics of partnerships indicates that the complementarity of tangible and intangible resources between the parties involved is a critical factor for the success of the initiative, which generates benefits for both parties, such as, for example, the fulfillment of the social mission, both for the promoter and for public and third sector entities, avoiding overlapping roles.

In view of this professional proposal, the need for partnerships became evident. Partnerships help, above all, to sustain and disseminate the proposed solution. The cases studied showed that this support is linked, mainly, to a perspective of complementing tangible and intangible resources, where collaboration between the parties helps to avoid overlapping roles of organizations for society, generate know-how beyond what was initially planned, to increase the possibility of changes in current legislation and to involve the beneficiaries beyond a passive participation.

Describing the dynamics of cross-sector partnerships allowed us to understand that the social innovation initiative is aligned with a wide range of actors, a mix of partners from different sectors and sectors of activity, individuals, and communities. This diversity is positive and is in line with the perspective of complementing resources and lasting partnerships. Diversity helps to reach different audiences and alert them to social issues from different points of view.

In addition, the cases studied helped to demystify that in social projects it is doubtful to negotiate benefits for both parties, especially when it involves organizations in the business sector. Through the analysis of the data it was observed that the benefits for both parties fosters the involvement of the actors, where, when they are inserted in a context of collaborative partnerships, learning is gained, and certain prejudices are broken.

The dynamics of partnerships is regulated by governance, although it can be seen that in most initiatives there is no formally institutionalized governance model in the network. However, governance elements such as the centrality of management, the formalization of commitments, the deliberation of partners' autonomy, and communication mechanisms, among others, are present throughout the partnership relationship and directly or indirectly interfere in its success.

In addition, the descriptive analysis of the dynamics brought us evidence that the involvement of partners in the phases of the social innovation process was more accentuated in the phases of development and prototyping, sustainability, and dissemination, although both the literature and the description of the empirical reality show the importance of the beneficiaries' participation (whether active or passive), in the diagnosis phase of the problem.

Acknowledgments

This study was financed in part by the Coordenação de Aperfeiçoamento de Pessoal de Nível Superior — Brasil (CAPES) — Finance Code 001.

References

1. A. Hubert. *Empowering People, Driving Change: Social Innovation in the European Union.* Luxemburg: Publications Office of the European Union (2011).
2. M. Edwards-Schachter and M. Wallace. Shaken, but not stirred: Sixty years of defining social innovation. *Technological Forecasting and Social Change*, **119**, 64–79 (2017).
3. T. Nyseth and A. Hamdouch. The transformative power of social innovation in urban planning and local development. *Urban Planning*, **4**(1), 1–6 (2019).
4. K. Soma, S.W.K. van den Burg, T. Selnes and C.M. van der Heide. Assessing social innovation across offshore sectors in the Dutch North Sea. *Journal of Ocean and Coastal Management*, **167**, 42–51 (2019).

5. M.J. Sanzo, L.I. Alvarez, M. Rey and N. Garcia. Business–nonprofit partnerships: A new form of collaboration in a corporate responsibility and social innovation context. *Service Business*, 1–26 (2015).

6. J.W. Selsky and B. Parker. Platforms for cross-sector social partnerships: Prospective sensemaking devices for social benefit. *Journal of Business Ethics*, **94**(1), 21–37 (2011).

7. R. van Tulder, M.M. Seitanidi, A. Crane and S. Brammer. Enhancing the impact of cross-sector partnerships. *Journal of Business Ethics*, **135**(1), 1–17 (2016).

8. J.L. Klein, J.M. Fontan, D. Harrisson and B. Lévesque. The Quebec system of social innovation: A focused analysis on the local development field. *Finisterra*, **47**(94), 9–28 (2012).

9. G. Mulgan. The process of social innovation. Innovations — Technology, governance. *Globalization,* **1**(2), 145–162 (2006).

10. A. Etxezarreta, G. Cano and S. Merino. Las cooperativas de viviendas de cesión de uso: experiencias emergentes en España. CIRIEC-España, *Revista de Economía Pública, Social y Cooperativa*, **92**, 61–86 (2018).

11. P.P.C. Gentil, L.O. Guimarães, D.C. Pereira, A.M. Diniz and I.B. Ckagnazarof. Governança territorial e inovação social nos processos de desenvolvimento regional em territórios de mineração: um modelo teórico em construção. *Cad. Escola Brasileira de Administração Pública e de Empresas — EBAPE. BR* **17**, 509–522 (2019).

12. M.A. Borges. Dinâmica das Parcerias Intersetoriais em Iniciativas de Inovação Social: da descrição à proposição de diretrizes. 278 f. Tese (Doutorado em Engenharia e Gestão do Conhecimento) — Universidade Federal de Santa Catarina (UFSC), Florianópolis, Brasil (2017).

13. D.E. Gray. *Pesquisa no mundo real*. Porto Alegre: Penso (2012).

14. G. Cajaiba-Santana. Social innovation: Moving the field forward. A conceptual framework. *Technological Forecasting and Social Change*, **82**, 42–51 (2014).

15. R. Murray, J. Caulier-Grice and G. Mulgan. The open book of social innovation. London: The Young Foundation. National Endowment for Science, Technology and the Art-NESTA (2010).

16. A.A. Santos Delgado. Framework para caracterizar la innovación social sobre sus procesos. Tese (Doutorado em Engenharia e Gestão do Conhecimento) — Florianópolis: Universidade Federal de Santa Catarina, (2016).

17. J. Cunha and P. Benneworth. Universities' contributions to social innovation: Towards a theoretical framework. University of Twente, School of Management and Governance — IGS (2013), pp. 1–31.

18. T.Z. Patias, C.M. Gomes, J.M. Oliveira, D. Bobsin and B.B. Liszbinski. Modelos de Análise da Inovação Social: O Que Temos Até Agora? *Revista Brasileira de Gestão e Inovação*, **4**(2) 125–147 (2017).

19. J. Nelson and S. Zadek. Partnership alchemy: New social partnerships in Europe. Copenhagen: The Copenhagen Centre (2002).

20. Comissão Europeia. *Guia para as parcerias de desenvolvimento EQUAL*. Lisbon: European Commission (2004).

21. A.L. Roth, D. Wegner, J.A.V. Antunes Júnior and A.D. Padula. Diferenças e inter-relações dos conceitos de governança e gestão de redes horizontais de empresas: contribuições para o campo de estudos. *Revista de Administração*, **47**(1), 112–123 (2012).

22. J.E. Beagles, L. Mercken and L. Scott. Awareness of evidence-based practices by organizations in a publicly funded smoking cessation network. *Journal of Public Administration Research and Theory*, **23**(1), 133–153 (2012).

23. J.E. Oxley. Appropriability hazards and governance in strategic alliances: A transaction cost approach. *Journal of Law Economics an Organization*, **13**(2), 387–409 (1997).

24. S. Albers. *The Design of Alliance Governance Systems* Köln: Kölner Wissenschaftsverlag (2005).

25. L. Bardin. *Análise de Conteúdo*. São Paulo, Brazil: Edições 70 (2011).

26. IES and IPAV. *Mapa de inovação e empreendedorismo social — 1a fase*. Lisbon: Social Business School (2015).

27. E. Malinsky and C. Lubelsky. *Network Evaluation: Cultivating Healthy Networks for Social Change*. Toronto: Centre for Social Innovation and Canada Millennium Scholarship Foundation (2010).

28. R.K. Yin. *Estudo de caso: planejamento e métodos*. 4th ed. Porto Alegre: Brookman (2010).

https://doi.org/10.1142/9789811224119_0015

Highlighting the Paths of Social Innovation

Daniela de Oliveira Massad*, Rosane Malvestiti, Ricardo Pereira
and Gertrudes Aparecida Dandolini

Graduate Program in Knowledge Management and Engineering,
Federal University of Santa Catarina,
R. Delfino Conti, s/n, Trindade, Florianópolis — SC
88040–900, Brazil

*danimassad@gmail.com

This chapter specifically addresses the topic of social innovation, with the aim of showing the direction that its research is heading. This was done by following the methodological guidelines of an integrative literature review. After a detailed analysis of the selected articles, a contextualization of the area was made. A remarkable point is the disagreement regarding the concept of social innovation that generates fragmentation and stagnation in the evolution of this research area. Next, we tried to make a prognosis on social innovation research, raising questions about health problems, sustainability, economy, urban and rural spaces, arts, and culture, and identifying some trends that could occur, mainly, post-pandemic, in face of social problems to be solved. A list of items for future research and a framework are proposed as a result of the analyses. The need for research to investigate the pillars of social innovation (such as entrepreneurship, sustainability, and education), governance for social innovation, partnership formation processes, the process of social innovation, the use of technologies, and the dynamics of social innovation ecosystems, among others, is highlighted. It is expected that this study will be useful to assist in guiding social innovation initiatives, considering its potential to transform society.

15.1. Introduction

This chapter was written between May and October 2020. Such information should be irrelevant for a scientific publication that, in principle, is made of texts elaborated not to expire. However, humanity is experiencing a sui generis situation in which the only certainty at this moment is that of rapid change.

This context reminds of the need to rethink concepts and revisit theories, so that new paths can be traveled with security, provided with the necessary knowledge to drive this new world that is being presented to us every day. Furthermore, it is expected that society will be able to learn from the diverse problems and adversities that the coronavirus pandemic and the world economic crisis are bringing.

Sustainable development with its various dimensions (social, economic, environmental, and cultural) is increasingly necessary in this pandemic world with environmental problems and social and economic inequalities. Changes are being demanded both by organized groups in favor of sustainability, and by large financial market organizations and investors, which, more recently, have begun to demand environmentally sustainable, socially responsible, and governance practices by the organizations, through Environmental, Social, and Corporate Governance (ESG) indicators.

In this sense, companies are expected to be driven by changes and innovation, to propose new paradigms of products, processes, and services for the world to come. Technology is positioned as a great ally in this process. However, innovation and technology are not enough to solve existing social problems. For this reason, many authors have proposed a form of innovation capable of meeting social needs, and yet provoking a transformation in society: social innovation.

Social innovation has been studied by several research fields such as: management and economics sciences, arts and creativity, local development, psychology, and social entrepreneurship[1] and has been consolidated as a relevant theme in the discussion on the solution of social problems, which can often be complex, and require systemic action.[2]

Despite being a growing focus of studies in the last decade, the academy has not yet reached consensus on its definition. However, its characteristic of presenting answers to unresolved social questions through the collaboration of various actors and the participation of society is considered a fundamental factor.[3-5] The striking aspect of social innovation is to request the participation of representatives of society and organizations, both in the public and private sectors, as well as the need to analyze the governance relations of social problems, a field of research that is still little explored, mainly in a micro-perspective, at the level of analysis of social innovation governance, and with a lack of indicators for its measurement.[6]

The present work, instigated by these profound transformations of society that more than ever will need the support of science in order to overcome the crisis that affects it, aims to provide an overview of the last five years of research on social innovation, seeking evidences to suggest a list of topics for research on this field.

Thus, in order to fulfill the proposed objective, a study is presented that consolidates the work on social innovation through an integrative review. This type of research has the advantages of reducing bias, possessing the possibility of being replicable, resolving the controversy between conflicting results, and providing a reliable basis for decision-making, providing the construction of a panorama on the subject, in addition to providing subsidies for future works that seek to improve the available concepts.[7-10]

The methodological path consisted of three stages:

(1) Review planning, identification of the research problem, and elaboration of the protocol that guided the study.
(2) Bibliographic survey in the Scopus and Web of Science databases using the expression ("Social innovation" AND "literature review"

OR "integrative review" OR "systematic review"), filtered by title, abstracts, and keywords, with time delimitation from 2015 to 2020, searching articles and reviews published in English, Spanish, and Portuguese. The data extraction was carried out on May 23, 2020, returning 121 publications. After screening the works, with the elimination of duplicates and those that did not fit the research proposal, 62 publications were selected, 35 of which were excluded after the initial reading, for not presenting information adhering to the scope of the work. Eleven articles from the Scientific Electronic Library Online (SciELO) database were also included, making up the final portfolio with 37 articles, which served as a theoretical basis for this study.

(3) This chapter is structured in two main parts: contextualization and prognosis. The first presents the construct and portrays the evolution of research on social innovation. The second seeks evidence of trends in the theme, in addition to proposing a list of research subjects on social innovation. This work is concluded with a summary of the results found and the theoretical and practical implications of studies on social innovation.

15.2. Social Innovation: Contextualization

Social innovation (SI) has a relatively recent and uncertain history[11] and has been discussed with more intensity for some decades and recognized for its complexity.[2,12]

The construct emerged as an analytical concept prior to technological innovation, in early academic studies of areas such as sociology, management, and community psychology, and in recent decades it has advanced through other areas such as creativity and environmental and political studies, among others, also as a normative concept, i.e. it is inherently "good" and stimulated by governments and public policies.[13]

It is, therefore, an area of research that benefits from inter- and multidisciplinary approaches, involving different disciplines from diverse academic communities.[14] The investigation of SI by considerably diverse and heterogeneous fields of scientific knowledge contributed to the expansion of research on the theme.[1]

Over the past 20 years, research on SI has increased significantly,[12] conducted mainly to solve increasingly complex socio-economic and environmental problems, and by its characteristic of presenting answers to these questions through collaboration between public and private organizations and the involvement of society.[3-6,14]

Apparently, studies on the subject presented a rebirth in social psychology in the early 2000s; however, in the last decade, there has been an increase in research developed by scholars of management and entrepreneurship, more precisely of social entrepreneurship, although there is not such a prominent community in the area.[14]

Social innovation can benefit from advances in technological innovation research; however, it requires a new paradigm[11,14] that is deeper, creative, and guided by IS processes,[15] with a differentiated approach that takes into account its complexity and contextual dimensions.[11] In this sense, the systemic view contributes significantly to the analysis of SI, as it considers its multidimensional and complex aspect.[2]

Despite all the research on the concept of social innovation, this field of study still needs a theoretical systematization, due to its diffusion and terminological dissent, with room for new contributions both in theory and in practice.[11]

With the lack of a common definition, the authors strive to search for conceptual delimitation, and, mainly, to identify factors that represent the distinguishing characteristics of SI[1,5] and key elements of dimensions of social innovation[3].

García-Flores and Martos (Ref. 5, p. 262) propose that social innovation refers to "practices or initiatives carried out by the community that, based on the products, services or models they generate, or through the process designed to achieve their objectives, they reach solutions that give a better response, in an alternative and creative way, to social problems or needs." They analyze characteristics pointed out by agents involved in social innovation processes and identify 29 key factors of social innovation, distributed into five pillars: social and cultural elements; political and institutional support; knowledge and facilitating mechanisms; spatial components; and entities and mechanisms that determine the corporate and social productive structure.[5]

In turn Hernández-Ascanio et al.[3] classify the definitions of social innovation into five dimensions: (1) social innovation manager, (2) main objective of social innovation, (3) capacity for social transformation, (4) process cycle, (5) and disciplinary implication or predominant dimension.

The IS relationship with sustainable development is based on the alignment of its characteristics,[16] as the SI constitutes positive responses to social problems[17] and ways of materializing collective actions to promote the social change or transformation necessary to achieve development sustainable,[4] in all its dimensions and not only in the environmental aspect.[18]

It is perceived that the transforming power of IS has been increasingly recognized and researched,[12] establishing its understanding as a process of social transformation capable of empowering individuals and making communities the protagonists of their stories.[19]

Finally, IS promotes social inclusion, quality of life and well-being of human beings, change in social relationships, and engagement and mobilization, improving the society's capacity to act,[12] filling the institutional voids,[20,21] and providing an alternative to the neoliberal system.[22] Van der Have and Rubalcaba[14] corroborate this thought by stating that IS encompasses two common components: (1) a change in social relations, systems, or structures and (2) the satisfying of a shared human need or the solution of a socially relevant problem.

15.3. Research Trends and Proposals for Future Studies on SI

From the relationship between the different contexts, levels of analysis, sub-themes that relate the SI with other areas of knowledge, and the different organizational processes in which the SI can be analyzed, possible topics for future studies emerge.

The articles studied suggest some approaches for future studies on SI, such as social movement theory,[23,24] which arise from the failure of governments[21] and inefficiency of traditional business models in meeting social demands;[24] transformational change theory,[12,24] which seeks to understand how SI relates to the context[24] and creates change and transforms existing systems;[12] power relations and the perspective of multiple SI actors;[24] institutional theory,[24] which understands SI as an eminently collective phenomenon, product of interaction and application of knowledge and resources;[13,23,24] and structuration theory,[24] in which SI, as a transformative force, results from the interrelationship between agents, institutional structures, and social systems.[24,25]

The dynamics of social innovation and its transformative capacity are increasingly becoming the focus of discussion in the academia.[12] The transformative power will depend on the promotion and dimensioning of practices by local initiatives, replicating them and translating them also into public policies, regulations, or new markets.[26]

Thus, starting from a local development strategy, Monteiro[27] proposes a model of IS that articulates two fundamental axes — (1) an instrumental axis, which contemplates sectorial innovations added to local governance practices and the valuation of externalities and (2) a political axis that incorporates the activation of learning communities linked to the principle of social mission and transformative vision.

In the current era, in which local development is increasingly based on knowledge, social innovation presents itself as a way of providing answers to social questions and promoting local development, from a perspective based on knowledge and value creation.[28]

Saldivar *et al.*[29] identify an ecosystem conducive to the use of new technologies, where more and more cities and civil society organizations have organized experiments in participatory and direct democracy, with the support of technology. However, according to the authors, the academy still needs to advance on this issue and make use of technologies to assist in the development of innovative platforms that can promote collaboration and the strengthening of society.

The diversity of approaches, objectives, and methodologies applied to the study of social innovation and sustainability leads to the need for more research on these themes,[17] requiring an inter- and multi-disciplinary approach[14] with different perspectives, studying different sectors and bringing academics and other professionals closer to society's issues. Following this logic, Bayuo *et al.*[30] propose to train students as social entrepreneurs, connecting universities with communities, and co-producing knowledge. In this way, the efforts to promote sustainability stimulate the university community, contributing to the construction of greener and more sustainable communities.[31]

However, few studies address the institutional and structural changes in incentives that influence universities to integrate SI in their teaching, research, and the so-called third mission activities.[30] Arteaga *et al.*[32] state that there is a need to develop educational approaches that contribute to higher levels of complexity of the student's thinking and promote student skills acquisition as active citizens and entrepreneurs.

Research on social innovation, also motivated to solve society's problems, faces the problem of a lack of incentives, as it is not the type of research that is patentable or rewarded academically, receiving support mainly from the private sector.[30] As examples, it is worth highlighting the development of technologies for the use of renewable natural resources[31] and assistive use of technology.[33]

Social innovation has always been engaged in solving the social problems of the underprivileged and in an urban and organizational environment, but it is expanding into agribusiness. As an example, the study by Patias *et al.*[34] explored the local productive arrangements of family agro-industries from the point of view of social innovation, highlighting that the formation of the arrangements has a decisive impact on the economic and social development of the region in which it is inserted, being considered a SI, with emphasis on governance as a central construct and its culture of coalition with public, private, and third sector actors in the search for solutions to social needs, allowing greater autonomy and agility in decision-making. This characteristic of governance in the arrangements is an element of social innovation that until now has been presented as superficial.

Considering the various incidents related to food safety that caused panic and undermined the confidence of the population, Wu *et al.*[35] observed the benefits of the change from governance to social co-governance encompassing society, therefore, as something more effective, flexible, inclusive, and economic, emphasizing open dimensions for the development and helping to manage food safety risks, which is a social innovation for this sector.

Following this logic, the study by Satalkina and Shpak[36] on the development of the social macro-environment in SI activities within organizations pointed out that the macro-environment is distinct and cannot be controlled, but can be a strategic indicator for SI actions and, thus, gain a role in the economic development.

Civil society actors and their social and environmental concerns and initiatives have the capacity to boost sustainability in cities.[26] Thus, social innovations in urban spaces are directly linked to sustainable development, as they tend to incorporate important spatial dimensions.[37] For the purpose of analysis, Ardill and Oliveira[37] subdivided them into three categories: (1) spatial planning and community development; (2) governance; and (3) co-production and service projects. The findings observed in the three groups indicated that end-user collaboration for local urban development is central to the process of change.

Profitable social innovations may become a trend: an example is the case of the complex Portuguese Association MIRO of sports activities (soccer and athletics) in Penacova, which, according to Vieira *et al.*,[38] has an impact on the development and promotion of social innovations with revenues of one million euros per year. Its goal, in addition to social innovations, has great emphasis on solving local social problems. The Association receives various contributions and donations, with state and municipal subsidies being the two main sources of funding.[38]

The concept of social innovation ecosystem (SIE) emerges as a network of different actors (government, civil society, and companies), based on interconnected dynamics, of a complex nature, on several scales.[25] Thus, SI could be evaluated in terms of networks (public and private), activities (learning, reproduction, and collaboration), and roles (diffusing new technologies, use, and economize) and considered a supplement for the national innovation system.[39]

The collaborative action of multiple actors and the protagonism of society in the construction of social innovation initiatives, together with the transformative role of social innovation, will be increasingly necessary to deal with the complexity of social problems and challenges of the current century, requiring a systemic and comprehensive vision to orchestrate the elements involved.[2]

In this sense, observing several interrelated categories that clarify the process of forming partnerships (partners, means of identification, motivation of partners and criteria to form the partnership, facilitators, and difficulties of the formation process), it is possible to say that intersectoral partnerships will be of great value in social innovation initiatives.[40] This understanding is necessary, as it seems difficult to negotiate benefits among stakeholders in social projects, and so a social responsibility approach focused on legal obligations toward society shifts to an empowerment approach, in which everyone is co-responsible for a better society,[40]

Some problems are treated primarily by SI, such as accessibility difficulty,[41] the secondary or assistive use of technology by people with disabilities,[36] and the precarious conditions of urban life under the view of SI.[42] Karadima and Bofylatos,[42] seeking an intersection between SI and policy formulation, concluded that those most in need are more open to alternative forms of life, more creative, co-creative, and socially mature, which facilitates the re-engagement of these people located in the periphery and their inclusion in decision-making processes.

In the context of open social innovation, the entrepreneurship and collaborative economy are relevant,[43,44] and it is at the level of local governance and civil society that social value is created in this field.[43] Open innovation strategies seem to be a good pathway for the continual growth of social enterprises.[44]

In this same approach of the collaborative action of SI, Sauer and Hiete[45] studied how multi-stakeholder initiatives in the mining industry can contribute to social innovation both as a governance approach, in which stakeholders cooperate with each other, and in changing practices for social benefit by implementing responsible mining, going beyond the limits of authority-based governance.

In terms of governance, there is still much to be developed in the field of social innovation. Howaldt *et al.*[46] found that much of the social innovation initiatives they researched were inserted in a framework of policy programs, but in initiatives related to poverty reduction and sustainable development, the role of the umbrella organization is more relevant.

Regarding the COVID-19 pandemic, it is worth mentioning that the concerns addressed by Patias *et al.*[34] and Ardill and Oliveira[37] suggest an inverted movement, a return to the rural space, especially after the pandemic.

The occurrence of several publications on social innovation focusing on meeting social needs related to the health of the population,[41,47] whose vulnerabilities have been increased and exposed even more with the COVID-19 pandemic, is justified.

Although it does not have a single definition and definite function,[47] social innovation in health requires special attention to transform society, not only in countries experiencing a poverty scenario but also in developed countries where failures in their healthcare systems were observed, being strongly impacted by the pandemic.

The aspects of the social entrepreneurship, their relationship with SI[48,49] and the action of the social entrepreneur to the social change,[3] combining practices and knowledge with a social mission, as well as developing partnerships[48] need a theoretical clarification. The political ideology can influence social entrepreneurs and without this perspective, it is difficult to address the complexity of social entrepreneurship.[49]

There is a growth in SI as a hybrid collaborative innovation between the third sector, the public sector, and/or business actors, in which the division between profit and guidelines for non-profit organizations in the sectors of the informal and social economy are increasingly more out of focus, due to the commercialization of the third sector and the advancement of multisectoral collaboration; innovation in the business sector, focused on social actions, needs, and the social market; and the dissemination of corporate social responsibility and corporate practices of SI.[13]

An under-researched topic, although useful, is the issue of how SI can be used to complement technical changes. More detailed theoretical and empirical work on the complementarities between SI and technological changes can benefit studies on innovation. Another relevant, but unanswered, research question is whether the sources of creativity for social innovation differ from those for technological innovation.[12]

The following are some suggestions for future research identified in the articles studied.

- Definition of social innovation processes and identifying challenges and related mechanisms.[3,22,23,28]
- Analysis of the best use of opportunities offered by technology and big data to improve the performance and quality of SI processes; how situated or shared technologies can contribute to civic collaboration patterns interactions; secondary use of technologies.[28,29,33]
- Higher education involving SI projects.[30]
- Researches on innovative approaches, strategies, and models to optimize the performance of social innovation processes.[28]

- Diffusion and dissemination of innovative mechanisms and processes (such as the creation of a value chain) in the social economy within the scope of discussions on open social innovation.[43]
- Research on the dynamics of open social innovation involving social companies and collaborative economies in the world.[44]
- Studies on social innovation initiatives in health, for the production of knowledge in the area and development of the concept.[35,38,47]
- Sustainability, with development of technologies for the use of renewable resources.[31]
- More detailed and specialized studies on the links between social innovation and knowledge-based perspectives of local development and value creation.[29]
- Analysis of cultural and institutional factors of society's capacity for social innovation.[17]
- Comparative analysis of the dynamics of SIEs in different places, cities, and countries.[25]
- Descriptive studies and model proposals that address the relationship between non-profit or Third Sector organizations and SI.[15,20]
- Elaboration or improvement of existing strategic models for local social innovation, from an analytical perspective and from the practices they can generate.[27]
- Investigation on different governance approaches (based on authority or multiple stakeholder initiatives) for each type of social problem, assessing effectiveness and contingency factors.[45]
- Investigation on the influence of different institutional systems (political, financial, educational, labor, and cultural) on social innovation projects; and the main differences between social innovation processes in emerging and developing markets and in developed countries.[21]
- Analyses of: the interaction between different actors in social innovation projects, to fill institutional gaps in a multidimensional context; the differences in the results of institutional gaps overcome by social innovation projects in different contexts; the main governance strategies for multiple actors, and if they can be different in different contexts.[21]
- Researches that develop a concept of social innovation that addresses different sectors, types of partners, policy fields, and transversal

themes, with an emphasis on empowerment and user involvement as necessary drivers for social innovations.[46,49]

- Studies that better investigate the relationship between collaborative processes of social innovation and their urban spatial outcomes, articulated as the co-production of places of social innovation, as well as replicating and diffusing local initiatives to other localities.[26,37]
- Researches that explores the fundamental aspects that define social entrepreneurship, considering the different schools of thought, and analyze their relationship with SI.[20,48]
- Understanding the process of forming partnerships (partners, means of identification, motivation of partners, and criteria for forming the partnership, facilitators and difficulties of the training process) for SI.[40]
- Deeper and mainly empirical researches on the relationship between SI and social transformation, investigating the role of social actors, whether transformations are desirable or not, and success factors such as scale, durability, and impact.[12]

15.4. Interconnection Structure

This study ends with the proposal of a framework (Figure 15.1) that makes correlations with the proposals for future studies presented in the previous section and the whole theory studied. As can be seen in the figure, SI is considered the main construct and connects to three major areas: (1) education, (2) sustainability, and (3) entrepreneurship, considered as motor bases. Each motor base has its own activator that, together with the others, generates drivers or questions for studies that need to be developed. The outermost circle shows the possible results of SI.

Therefore, education has, as its own activator, the multi- and interdisciplinary knowledge that starts from joining the attempts of creating knowledge oriented to social innovation. Sustainability has common good as its activator, guided by social innovation. Entrepreneurship has as its own activator the social change necessary to solve social problems.

Common drivers for the areas include a specific concept, governance, partnership formation process, best use of technology, and the dynamics of SI ecosystems.

The results of SI processes can be health, social justice, economic balance, environmental preservation, empowerment, and culture and arts.

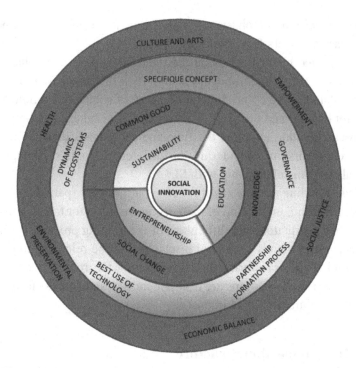

Figure 15.1.   Framework of future studies on SI, prepared by the authors.

Thus, the relationship becomes dynamic and involves all areas facilitating both its application and its understanding.

It is important to emphasize that the elements that compose this framework need more research to explore the relationships between them and their effects on social innovation, as well as the results (social transformation) of social innovation (empowerment, quality of life, etc.). Governance, in particular the governance of the network of actors, is highlighted as an element of extreme relevance to the SI, given the diversity of stakeholders that an SI initiative involves.

15.5. Final Considerations

This study intended to make a contextualization of the field of social innovation, based on an integrative review of other reviews. A detail observed was the dissent regarding the characterization of social innovation. This is explained by the inter- and multi-disciplinary approaches of the field, which encompass researches related to psychology, management, engineering, sociology, regional development, creativity, urbanism, and co-production, among other themes.

In the prognosis, first an overview of research on social innovation was analyzed in order to identify which areas have aroused the interest of researchers in the development of new knowledge, reconciling the current rapid changes with the needs to be met.

Issues of health, improvement in agrarian life with the exodus from the cities to the countryside, and remote working are highlighted themes.

The concern with teaching social innovation, especially in higher education, which in turn favors social transformation, is also a prominent issue.

Entrepreneurship and the role of the social entrepreneur also proved to be a prominent area in the studies on SI.

Then, guidelines for further research are indicated, suggesting several contexts where the research on social innovation may proceed, such as the process of forming partnerships to promote the common good, governance of networks developed by the various stakeholders, understanding the ecosystem social innovation, the use of technology, and the diffusion of mechanisms for open innovation, among others. Finally, a framework was elaborated that presents in a condensed form the authors' suggestions for future studies and that can assist in directing the social innovation research and identifying trends.

In general, it is possible to affirm that social innovations are explicitly planned to adapt to a context in which meeting social needs is necessary, as a way to improve people's well-being and quality of life, in addition to taking into account the environment and business.

Acknowledgments

This study was financed in part by the Coordenação de Aperfeiçoamento de Pessoal de Nível Superior — Brasil (CAPES) — Finance Code 001.

References

1. A.S.V. Pacheco, M.J. Santos and K.V. Silva. Social innovation: What do we know and do not know about it. *International Journal of Innovation and Learning*, **24**(3), 301–326 (2018).

2. D. de O. Massad, P.C. Lapolli, F.K. Feliciano, L. Nascimento and E.M. Lapolli. Contribuições da teoria geral de sistemas para a mudança sistêmica da inovação social. In *A Produção do Conhecimento nas Ciências Sociais Aplicadas 4*, W.D. Guilherme (ed.), Ponta Grossa: Atena Editora, pp. 131–144 (2018).

3. J. Hernández-Ascanio, P. Tirado-Valencia and A. Ariza-Montes. El concepto de innovación social: ámbitos, definiciones y alcances teóricos, *España, Revista de Economía Pública, Social y Cooperativa*, **88**, 165–199 (2016).

4. S.E.N. Correia, V.M. de Oliveira, M.J. da S. Feitosa and C.R.P. Gomez. Inovação Social para o Desenvolvimento Sustentável: um caminho possível. *Administração Pública e Gestão Social*, **10**(3), 199–212 (2018).

5. V. García-Flores and L.P. Martos. Social innovation: Key factors for its development in the territories. *Revista de Economía Pública, Social y Cooperativa*, (97), 245–278 (2019).

6. A. Unceta, J. Castro-Spila and J.G. Fronti. The three governances in social innovation. *Innovation: The European Journal of Social Science Research*, **30**, 406–420 (2017).

7. C. Forza. Survey research in operations management: A process-based perspective. *International Journal of Operations & Production Management*, **22**(2), 152–194 (2002).

8. J.P.T. Higgis and S. Green (eds.) *Cochrane Handbook for Systematic Reviews of Interventions*. The Cochrane Collaboration, March version 5.1.0 (2011). Available at: www.handbook.cochrane.org.

9. R.J. Torraco, Writing integrative literature reviews: Guidelines and examples. *Human Resource Development Review*, **4**(3), 356–367 (2005).

10. R. Whittemore and K. Knafl. The integrative review: Updated methodology. *Journal of Advanced Nursing*, **52**(5), 546–553 (2005).

11. G. Cajaiba-Santana. Social innovation: moving the field forward: a conceptual framework. *Technological Forecasting and Social Change*, **82**, 42–51 (2014).

12. J. Dias and M. Partidário. Mind the ap: The potential transformative capacity of social innovation. *Sustainability*, **11**(16), 1–17 (2019).

13. M. Edwards-Schachter and M. Wallace. 'Shaken, but not stirred': Sixty years of defining social innovation. *Technological Forecasting and Social Change*, **119**(March), 64–79 (2017).

14. R. Van der Have and L. Rubalcaba. Social innovation research: An emerging area of innovation studies? *Research Policy*, **45**(9), 1923–1935 (2016).

15. J. Hernández-Ascanio and M. Rich-Ruiz. Characterization of third sector organizations from the perspective of social innovation. A case study approach. *Innovation*, **30**(75), 71–86 (2020).

16. R. Malvestiti, Y.D.S. Figueiredo and D. Esteves. Desenvolvimento susten-tável e sua relação com inovação social e negócios sociais, In *Inovação social, negócios sociais e desenvolvimento sustentável*, G.A. Dandolini, J.A. Souza, R. Pereira and R. Malvestiti (eds.), Nova Xavantina, MT: Pantanal (2020), pp. 42–56.

17. F. Periac, A. David and Q. Roberson. Clarifying the interplay between social innovation and sustainable development: A conceptual framework rooted in paradox management. *European Management Review*, **15**(1), 19–35 (2018).

18. R. Pereira, D.O. Massad, F.L. do Canto and G.A. Dandolini. The interrela-tionship between sustainable development and social innovation: A bibliometric study. In *Proceedings of IDEAS, Smart Innovation, Systems and Technologies*, L. Pereira, J. Carvalho, P. Krus, M. Klofsten and V. De Negri (eds.), Springer (2020), Cham, pp. 480–489.

19. M.A. Prim, D.O. Massad and G.A. Dandolini, Inovação social: da essência ao seu poder de transformar, In *Inovação social, negócios sociais e desen-volvimento sustentável*, G.A. Dandolini, J.A. Souza, R. Pereira and R. Malvestiti (eds.), Nova Xavantina, MT: Pantanal (2020), pp. 13–28.

20. F. Adro and C.I. Fernandes. Social innovation: A systematic literature review and future agenda research. *International Review on Public and Nonprofit Marketing*. **17**(1), 23–40 (2020).

21. M.R. Agostini, L.M. Vieira and M.B. Bossle. Social innovation as a process to overcome institutional voids: A multidimensional overview. *Revista de Administração Mackenzie*, **17**(6), 72–101 (2016).

22. M. Gregoire. Exploring various approaches of social innovation: A franco-phone literature review and a proposal of innovation typology. *Revista de Administração Mackenzie*, **17**(6), 45–71 (2016).

23. A.A. Silva and J. Almeida, Palcos de inovação social: atores em movimento(s). Sociologia: *Revista da Faculdade de Letras da Universidade do Porto*, **30**, 35–54 (2015).

24. M. Agostini, L. Vieira, R. Tondolo and V. Tondolo. An overview on social innovation research: Guiding future studies. *Brazilian Business Review*, **14**(4), 385–402 (2017).

25. C. Andion, G.D. Alperstedt and J.F. Graeff. Ecossistema de inovação social, sustentabilidade e experimentação democrática: um estudo em Florianópolis, *Revista de Administração Pública*, **54**(1), 181–200 (2020).

26. M. Wolfram and N. Frantzeskaki. Cities and systemic change for sustain-ability: Prevailing epistemologies and an emerging research agenda. *Sustainability* (Switzerland). MDPI AG 8, (2016).

27. A. Monteiro. What is social innovation? Conceptual malleability and practical implications. *Dados*. **62**(3), 1–34 (2019).
28. V. Ndou and G. Schiuma. The role of social innovation for a knowledge-based local development: insights from the literature review. *International Journal of Knowledge-Based Development*, **11**(1), 6–25 (2020).
29. J. Saldivar, C. Parra, M. Alcaraz, R. Arteta and L. Cernuzzi. Civic technology for social innovation: A systematic literature review. *Computer Supported Cooperative Work*, **27**(3–6), 1215–1253 (2018).
30. B.B. Bayuo, C. Chaminade and B. Göransson. Unpacking the role of universities in the emergence, development and impact of social innovations — A systematic review of the literature, *Technological Forecasting and Social Change*, **155** (June), 1–11 (2020).
31. C.A.L. Quiroz, M.P.L. Calle and A.D.Q. Derfrey. La universidad verde: percepciones de la comunidad universitaria en el proceso de transformación hacia la sostenibilidad. *Revista Virtual Universidad Católica del Norte*, May(57), 157–174 (2019).
32. I.H. Arteaga, C. Pérez Muñoz and S.R. Castañeda. University students' educational interests and perspectives on Social and Solidarity Economy, *CIRIEC-España Revista de Economía Pública, Social y Cooperativa*, **Diciembre** (94), 91–121 (2018).
33. I.M.F. Oomens and C. Scholten. Inclusion in social innovation through the primary and secondary use of technology: A conceptual framework. *International Review of Applied Economics*, **34**(5), 672–686 (2020).
34. T.Z. Patias, D. Bobsin, C.M. Gomes, B.B. Liszbinski and L.I. Damke. Family agro-industry clusters from the social innovation perspective, *Revista de Administração Mackenzie*. **17**(6), 191–215 (2016).
35. L. Wu, P. Liu, Y. Lv, X. Chen and F.S. Tsai. Social co-governance for food safety risks. *Sustainability*, **10**(11), 1–14 (2018).
36. L. Satalkina and N. Shpak. Evaluation of the influence of the macro-environment on the social innovation activity of enterprises. *Organizacija*, **51**(1), 36–48 (2018).
37. N. Ardill and F.L. Oliveira. Social innovation in urban spaces. *International Journal of Urban Sustainable Development*, **10**(3), 207–221 (2018).
38. N.D.S. Vieira, A.C.Q. Barbosa, C. Parente and D.P.T. Lopes. Contribution to social innovation theory and practice: Lessons from a Portuguese Association. *Administração Pública e Gestão Social*, **10**(1), 12–21 (2018).
39. H. Fulgencio and H. Le Fever. What is the social innovation system? A state-of-the-art review. *International Journal of Business Innovation and Research*, **10**(2/3), 434–452 (2016).

40. M.A. Borges, G.A. Dandolini and A.L. Soares. O processo de formação de parcerias intersetoriais em iniciativas de inovação social em Portugal. *Análise Social*, **1**(234), 118–143 (2020).
41. C.B. Sampedro-Palacios and J. Pérez-Villa. A Inovação Social como ferramenta na transformação de uma sociedade inclusiva, *Prospectiva* [online], **28**(Jul/Dec), 93–119 (2019).
42. D. Karadima and S. Bofylatos. Co-living as a means to re-engagement. A literature review. *Design Journal*, **22**, 751–762 (2019).
43. C.H. Shin. A conceptual approach to the relationships between the social economy, social welfare, and social innovation. *Journal of Science Technology & Policy Management*, **7**(2), 154–172 (2016).
44. J.J. Yun, K.B. Park, C.J. Im, C.H. Shin and X. Zhao. Dynamics of Social Enterprises—Shift from Social Innovation to Open Innovation, *Scientific & Technological Society*, **22**(3), 425–439 (2017).
45. P.C. Sauer and M. Hiete. Multi-stakeholder initiatives as social innovation for governance and practice: A review of responsible mining initiatives. *Sustainability*, **12**(1), (2020).
46. J. Howaldt, D. Domanski and C. Kaletka. Social innovation: Towards a new innovation paradigm. *Revista de Administração Mackenzie*, **17**(6), 20–44 (2016).
47. D.M. Castro-Arroyave and L.F. Duque-Paz. Documentary research on social innovation in health in Latin America, Infectious Diseases of Poverty. *BioMed Central Ltd.*, **9**, 1–8 (2020).
48. J. Macke, J.A.R. Sarate, J. Domeneghini and K.A. Silva. Where do we go from now? Research framework for social entrepreneurship. *Journal of Cleaner Production*, **183**, 677–685 (2018).
49. H. Jarrodi, J. Byrne and S. Bureau. A political ideology lens on social entrepreneurship motivations. *Entrepreneurship and Regional Development*, **31**(7–8), 583–604 (2019).

Part IV

University Innovation

16

University Governance for Innovation: How to Nurture Creativity Through a Successful Academic Entrepreneurship Process

Valério Vincenzo De Luca* and Alessandro Margherita†‡

**Department of Economic and Entrepreneurship Sciences,
Catholic University 'Our Lady of Good Counsel',
Rr. Dritan Hoxha, Tirana, Albania*

*†Department of Engineering for Innovation, University of Salento,
Campus Ecotekne, Via Monteroni sn, 73100 Lecce, Italy*

‡alessandro.margherita@unisalento.it

Higher education institutions are today significantly impacted by a number of social and technological transformations. A different archetype of university is emerging, which requires a new governance model able to drive the creation of new socio-economic value into a complex and challenging scenario. This chapter is focused on understanding how universities can valorize the creativity and innovation potential of territories and communities through a governance model supporting academic entrepreneurship. The interest is on analyzing the organizational conditions under which universities can have a central role in stimulating economic growth through industrial research, technology commercialization, entrepreneurial development, and new venture creation. A review on university governance and academic entrepreneurship literature is used to discuss the pillars of the entrepreneurial transformation of higher education institutions and universities. We then present seven successful cases of academic entrepreneurship in Albania and Italy to provide examples of entrepreneurship-oriented governance in two different political, institutional, economic, and cultural contexts. Finally, we derive some conclusions, also based on the comparison of the two scenarios, and identify a recommendation framework in terms of: (1) innovation triggers; (2) key stakeholders; (3) processes and enabling policies; and (4) performance reporting approaches.

16.1. Developing a "New" Concept of University

Several disruptive technological factors are driving unprecedented transformations in most organizations, industries, and societies. Along with the emergence of new wicked societal challenges and sustainability issues (e.g. Sustainable Development Goals defined by the United Nations), and trends like global mobility and lifelong learning, this is generating new requirements and opportunities to build innovative research and higher education systems. In particular, the ability to engage many stakeholders and integrate multiple areas of human knowledge into a strong problem-solving and value-creation approach is crucial for policy-makers and professionals in the contemporary university scenario.

How will universities look like in the near future? Which management frameworks are needed to guide the transformation of current higher education institutions into exponential and high-impact learning systems? Successful innovative experiences such as the Singularity University, and consolidated leading examples like the Massachusetts Institute of Technology and the Stanford University, demonstrate the increasing attention toward a new model of university, which is able to integrate disciplines and address the disruption factors ("singularities") in the society to create a new generation of business and social leaders. The emerging university archetype is increasingly *global* and *networked* (able to connect many stakeholders worldwide) and *digital* (leverages the potential offered by digital technologies), but also *ecological* (focused on the environment), *responsible* (sustainable and ethic), and *holistic* (integrative, pluralistic).

Universities are key actors able to create virtuous synergies for knowledge creation and dissemination, and a new model of leadership is needed to take advantage of the entrepreneurial potential lying within territories and societies. Universities have the potential to drive sustainable development of regions but they require a number of facilitation factors such as a diverse institutional set-up, a committed leadership, as well as alliances with bridging organizations.[1] In the contemporary scenario, it is crucial the implementation of a knowledge governance approach as an interdisciplinary view that goes through the fields of knowledge management, organizational studies, strategy, and human resources management.[2]

The governance of universities needs to facilitate academic entrepreneurship as a strategy and a process and to develop a culture of innovation and sustainability in the current transformation era. The call for a new responsibility in business, environmental, and social terms is a multiperspective challenge, and a purposeful, conceptual model and best practices are thus needed to drive policy-makers and university managers.

In such a scenario, the main research curiosity of this chapter is related to understanding how university governance can trigger academic entrepreneurship through technology-oriented research, entrepreneurial development, and venture creation. After an introductory discussion on university governance and academic entrepreneurship (Sections 16.2 and 16.3), we present seven successful cases of academic entrepreneurship in Italy (Section 16.4) and Albania (Section 16.5). Finally, we derive some conclusions and a recommendation framework useful for policy-makers and higher education managers (Section 16.6).

16.2. University Governance: Toward an "Exponential" Model

A combination of structural, cultural, and environmental factors has generated transformations and reform processes in public universities in the last 20 years. University governance reforms, when talking of public universities, are a reflection of the broader *new public management* reforms that are focusing on increasing efficiency in public organizations. Through reforms, universities change their formal relations with other national authorities and policy-makers in terms of autonomy in financial, management, and decision-making matters. On the other hand, reforms also generate more requirements in terms of reporting, scrutiny, and control systems, financial incentive systems, and pressure to get resources.

However, besides efficiency and control, the reform of university governance should be addressed to enhance the value-creation potential of higher education institutions. Like business entities, universities need to find a dynamic to adapt to the demands of the knowledge-based economy,[3] which create a growing pressure on universities and implicitly generate major changes in their organizational model. The university is an engine for generating intellectual capital and creating value in the local community and society. Academic governance needs thus to be directed to improve the relationship among intellectual capital creation, entrepreneurship development, and local economic progress through the development of an entrepreneurial ecosystem with start-ups and research spin-offs.[4]

The strategic and operational logic of a university has a deep impact on the values and activities of stakeholders and ultimately shapes the broader innovation and entrepreneurial activities. A new organizational logic, termed the "academic enterprise" emerges and adds new to the more established academy, bureaucratic, and market logics. The academic enterprise is inherently entrepreneurial, and its reliance on faculty and student entrepreneurship is a tool for broad-scale social and economic transformation.[5] Literature has addressed the representation, modelling, and analysis of contextual influences on academic entrepreneurship and the impact of institutional variables and initiatives in promoting academic entrepreneurship.[6] Reference 7 has analyzed the implementation of Good University Governance (GUG) and Intellectual Capital.

Leveraging the discussion in the corporate and business management field, a set of individual and organizational factors can drive the success of an entrepreneurial orientation and the deriving activities in the university context. Whereas at individual level, the presence of technical innovators (e.g. PhD students, researchers), innovation champions (e.g. management professors), and knowledge brokers (e.g. institutional leaders) is relevant, team collaboration, senior management support, and dedicated facilities and projects are crucial organizational dimensions to sustain academic entrepreneurship.

There is an opportunity to create "exponential" universities able to leverage collective intelligence, open innovation, and digital technologies to address wicked societal challenges and drive fast-growth dynamics in the institutions and the society. Universities need a model of governance and a conducive "mindset" typical of an exponential organization,[8] thus including a tough commitment to growth, a strong stakeholder orientation, a holistic view of the university and the society, and a consolidated risk-taking and experimentation approach.

16.3. The Affirmation of the Entrepreneurial University

The Bayh–Dole Act in 1980 represented a disruption in the conception of the university as an ivory tower and generated a rapid escalation in commercial knowledge transfers from US universities to firms through mechanisms such as licensing agreements, research joint ventures, and university-based start-ups. Today, universities not only provide human resources and knowledge but also strongly contribute to the socio-economic development. The successful achievement of this mission is connected to a close collaboration with government and industry,[9] even if the commercialization of university research faces many challenges in adapting a context optimized for exploration to the task of exploitation.[10]

The shift in the nature of academic research is supported by historical factors like the decrease and stringency in research funding, with a simultaneous increase in the costs of research, which motivates policy-makers to ask for tangible benefits.[11] Policies aimed at promoting entrepreneurship and commercial knowledge transfer have been welcomed by universities as a way to build relationships with external stakeholders and enhance regional growth, and as a potential source of revenue.[12]

In a new paradigm where the commercialization and application of knowledge is the needed condition for innovation[13] and sustainable socio-economic development,[14] universities have started developing a new organizational setting able to promote entrepreneurship in the academic context inside and outside the university. The process of introducing such configuration includes three stages. First is "activation," to spark an interest in entrepreneurship within students through activities like boot-camps and hackathons. Second is "education," i.e. formal programs to provide the foundation of entrepreneurship, like bachelor and PhD programs. Third is "incubation," to accelerate the development of start-ups and support their access to the market.

Reference 15 proposed a conceptual model for developing the entrepreneurial university, including formal factors such as entrepreneurial governance and support measures, informal factors like entrepreneurial attitudes and reward systems, resources such as human and physical capital, and capabilities like prestige, networks and alliances. Building on such comprehensive view, five dimensions of analysis can be identified as facilitators of academic entrepreneurial performance.

First, "context" or environment is fundamental for innovation, entrepreneurship, and entrepreneurial behavior.[16] Best examples of universities, mainly top ranked, as key nodes in regional innovation systems come from the most competitive regions in the world in terms of economic growth, workforce qualifications, and number of international firms in new or high-technology sectors.[17] Reference 11 found that proximity and regular contacts between actors are the best ways to develop research programs matching industrial needs, which is why clusters and industrial parks are fundamental.

Second, "human and social capital" is crucial for knowledge transfer and the activation of entrepreneurial activities. Actors include not only scientists and engineers patenting ideas but also academicians consulting or participating in the board of private companies. Network capital, in the form of investments in strategic relations to gain access to knowledge, mediates the relationship between entrepreneurship and innovation-based regional growth.[18]

Third, "infrastructure" refers to innovation and entrepreneurship centers within (or connected to) the university such as incubators, accelerators, hubs, and other spaces where entrepreneurs, professionals, and students can join, collaborate, organize activities, share knowledge, and develop innovative ideas. Incubators and technology transfer offices are support mechanisms in the process of creation of university spin-offs enabling the flow of resources, fostering mutual trust, awarding credibility to the new firms, and building legitimacy in transactions.[19]

Fourth, "entrepreneurial activities" include business courses and training; coaching and mentoring events with academics, professionals, alumni, and start-up founders; seminars and conferences; award and recognition programs; research projects; inspirational talks; events for scouting ideas (e.g. hackathons); patenting and licensing; and services for students, entrepreneurs, start-ups, and small and medium enterprises (SMEs) (e.g. support for crowdfunding campaigns[20]).

Finally, "outputs" refer to tangible or intangible measurable results of the entrepreneurial university. Some of them are a natural and direct consequence of the "entrepreneurial activities," such as patents, licenses, joint research contracts, and spin-off companies, whereas others reflect their influence in areas like partnerships and collaborations, network reinforcement, number of enrolled students, branding, and private funding.

These five dimensions strongly characterize the entrepreneurial approach and governance of a modern university. The challenge for an entrepreneurial university is to produce and share new knowledge with an application in the "real world" and to educate people to develop concrete solutions to relevant problems. In line with a sustainable view of the university,[21–23] academic entrepreneurship is also aimed to generate sustainable innovation for the society and provide answers to the complex demands of our society.

16.4. Academic Entrepreneurship and Successful Governance in Italy

16.4.1. *Introduction*

From the early 1990s, the Italian Ministry granted greater autonomy to academic institutions, allowing them to manage their budgets, design teaching programs, and introduce statutes and regulations for managing organizational and scientific activities. Universities therefore created internal mechanisms to support academic entrepreneurship, namely the exploitation of university-owned IP and the creation of academic spin-offs and the consultancy activities of academics. The majority of Italian STEM universities put policies meant to efficiently regulate these activities.

A crucial change for technology transfer and the creation of an academic entrepreneurship model in Italy was a national law regulating the effective commercialization of research results through academic start-ups. The law (legislative decree n. 297/1999) specifically fostered the creation of research spin-offs, by introducing the possibility for public researchers to be formally involved in the creation of a spin-off or in other technology transfer projects between a university/PRO and a firm, while keeping their position and wage. In 2004, the PNICube association (including today about 50 universities and academic incubators) was established to enhance technology transfer and to stimulate the creation of innovative university-based companies.

Academic spin-offs are a successful channel in transferring knowledge generated by the university and fostering economic growth. Coherently, a wide range of policies has been implemented in Italy to encourage their formation to spur innovation and local economic development. Of course, the nature and characteristics, including the economic and market sustainability, of academic entrepreneurship initiatives are strongly influenced by the motivation of creation. At this regard, based on a sample of 613 Italian academic spin-offs established over the period 2006–2012, a study found that necessity-oriented academic spin-offs are associated with higher survival profiles, while opportunity-oriented spin-offs exhibit higher post-entry growth rates.[24]

16.4.2. *Illustrative cases*

In the Italian scenario, there are different experiences of successful entrepreneurship development within an academic context. Three interesting cases of academic entrepreneurship and governance are the Polytechnic of Milan, with the PoliHub incubator; the Luiss Business School, with the initiative Luiss Enlabs; and the University of Naples Federico II (in partnership with Città della Scienza) with the project Campania NewSteel.

PoliHub ranks in the "World Top 5" of university incubators, according to the 2019/2020 UBI Global World Rankings of Business Incubators and Accelerators. PoliHub is a Start-up District & Incubator of the

Polytechnic of Milan. It is engaged to transform innovative ideas into entrepreneurial projects in fields which span from hi-tech to design, from gaming to social networks, from mechanics to informatics security, from medical devices to energy. PoliHub addresses innovators, developers, makers, designers, and managers to put to the test their capabilities and ideas. It also addresses entrepreneurs wanting to grow their business and looking for synergies with new high-potential ideas, products, and services. A selection committee evaluates ideas, helping to identify the weak points and to strengthen the winning features. PoliHub offers access to the large network of the Polytechnic of Milan, the Foundation, and the consortia (MIP, Cefriel, and PoliDesign). The Incubator selects talented people, leverages their strengths, and identifies weaknesses to create competitive teams. The Hub also offers administrative, legal, communication, and press services; ICT consulting and operational support; assistance in scouting funds with venture capital and business angels; and direct contact with Polytechnic professors and researchers, managers, entrepreneurs, and experts.

Luiss Enlabs is the business accelerator of LVenture Group, born from a joint venture with the Luiss University. With a success rate of 80% in terms of investments collected by the start-ups that have concluded the program and an internationally established methodology, the accelerator aims to transform the most promising early stage digital start-ups into the success companies of the future. The *Global Finance Magazine* has included Luiss EnLabs in the ranking of the 25 World's Best Financial Innovation Labs 2019. In its program, the selected start-ups can access to a funding up to 160,000 euros from LVenture Group, which is among the most important European venture capital companies. The incubation program includes a period of five months within an ecosystem of talents, university researchers, and professors, investors, and corporations. The incubator also leverages a network of expert advisors able to coach on aspects such as product development, business model innovation, communication and marketing strategy, legal assistance, and fundraising.

The Campania NewSteel is a certified incubator promoted by the City of Science and the University of Naples Federico II. It represents an important reality in south Italy. The incubator hybridizes the established experience of the City of Science in supporting the creation of more than

150 companies with the research infrastructures, innovation excellence, and new talent creation specialization of the University Federico II. It offers a large spectrum of services, such as tutoring and mentoring, consulting on Industry 4.0 and fast prototyping, intellectual property protection, financial consulting, and testing, The Campania NewSteel represents one of the most important initiatives in Italy to support the development of innovative start-ups and spin-offs.

Other relevant Italian universities hosting active incubators and successful academic entrepreneurship initiatives include Polytechnic of Turin, Scuola Superiore Sant'Anna of Pisa, Ca'Foscari University of Venice, Bocconi University, University of Basilicata, University of Ferrara, University of Padova, University of Palermo, University of Rome Tor Vergata, and University of Udine.

16.5. Albanian Universities Toward Entrepreneurship

16.5.1. *Introduction*

Albania completely changed its social and economic paradigm less than 30 years ago with the end of communism, and today the county is still in an embryonic stage in terms of entrepreneurial development (the country is positioned 83 out of 137 in the Global Entrepreneurship Index). The start-up sector is quite underdeveloped, with most activities at pre-ideation and ideation phases.

The Ministry of Innovation and Public Administration dissolved in 2017 and its responsibilities are today distributed in different departments, with no joint strategy. A legal framework for start-ups is currently being developed, but the overall support by the government is limited and cooperation with support organizations is weak. In addition, the banking and financing system is unfavorable for start-ups because they focus on the local market, and its size is not attractive for investors looking forward to the growth perspectives. The only help to the underfinanced start-up sector is represented by grants, but amounts are too small to create an impact. Despite these challenges, other contexts (e.g. Switzerland or Israel) showed evidences that is possible to take advantage of reduced dimensions and a closer and collaborative stakeholders' network with recurring interactions.

In Albania, entrepreneurship is seen as a necessity rather than an opportunity. In fact, 'the high unemployment rate pushes many young people looking for self-employment. This is a significant pool of talent the start-up ecosystem can build on and motivate to become entrepreneurs, even though investments in the ecosystem remain insufficient. While Innovation Nest is seeking to set up Albania's first Network, and South East Ventures has committed to invest, no start-ups have been funded yet. Alternative sources of financing, such as crowdfunding and peer-to-peer lending, miss the legal basis. In addition, there are social and cultural aspects unfavorable to entrepreneurship, like corruption, low trust, in particular to the government[25] and unfair competition from the informal economy.[26]

Despite the generic difficulties throughout the country, there is a big difference between Tirana and the other regions, with a strong migration flow from smaller cities and rural areas to the capital. Only NGOs tried to support entrepreneurs outside Tirana, and most universities lack the capacity to implement start-up programs and depend on international funds (e.g. Instrument for Pre-Accession Assistance [IPA] and Erasmus Plus). Nevertheless, some initiatives are challenging the status quo. For example, the mayor of Korçe has the ambitious goal of strengthening the ICT sector to retain talent and offer remote employment opportunities, and the municipality is offering fiscal incentives for tourism, handicraft, and ICT sectors. In addition, the mayor of Elbasan is cooperating with the university of the city to create an "Innovation Centre."

University–industry collaboration is limited by the lack of funds and trust, and higher educational institutions miss the outreach to the industry that could create demand for start-up products and services. Furthermore, the private sector is mostly characterized by small enterprises reducing the capacity of the industry to absorb and introduce innovations. In addition, government policies are frequently taken from different European legislations without a real local adaptation.

In the university, entrepreneurial activity is prevented by little practical experience, lack of role models and success cases, and a low motivation to pursue entrepreneurship as a career choice. Moreover, only a few private universities, mainly located in Tirana, have the resources to introduce extra-curricular activities and motivate staff, while public universities are facing with reducing number of enrolled students, resulting in lower budgets. Therefore, innovation and entrepreneurship are not on the agenda of many universities, and the few incubation programs are not continuous and staff capacity is somehow inadequate.

Despite the contextual and institutional conditions not being specifically favorable for academic entrepreneurship in Albania, a number of strengths, such as the very young population speaking many languages, a high number of university graduates, and a growing IT services sector, are driving the emergence of a number of extremely interesting university initiatives. Such experiences demonstrate the emergence of a new approach to university governance able to create new value for the Albanian society.

16.5.2. *Case studies*

We used unstructured interviews to gather relevant information on five Albanian universities, i.e. Polis University, Metropolitan Tirana University and Professional College of Tirana (more consolidated in terms of entrepreneurship), Our Lady of Good Counsel, and Luarasi University (with more recent initiatives).

Regarding entrepreneurial activities, Polis University is one of the top Higher Education Institution (HEI) in Albania. The Vice Rector Elona Karafili and the Innovation Factory Coordinator Valerio Perna explained that the concept of entrepreneurship was introduced with the creation of the university (the founder is an entrepreneur and one of the most important businessmen of Albania). Since the beginning, a course of entrepreneurship and other classes on pitching and financing have been taught, and, later, a professional MBA has been introduced in partnership with a French business school. The entrepreneurial dimension was not limited to the educational area but relies on the human capital as many academics are closely connected with private businesses. One of the main objectives of the University is to fill the systemic gap with industry and create connections between students and professionals. In addition, the alumni network is a great resource and is involved in post-diploma training, mentoring, and role model inspirational sessions. The most important entrepreneurial project is the development of the Incubator and the

FabLab, which represent a novelty in Albania. In Polis, there is not a dedicated structure for entrepreneurship, but the university staff invests time in the entrepreneurial activities and each department has a person in charge to deal with industry relationship. Key points in the Polis operating model are the leadership of Vice Rector for the entrepreneurial activity and a lean decision-making process, even more important in the start-up context.

The Metropolitan University was founded in 2010 and, in 2014, it created the Metroresearch Center, an NGO composed of two entities: Metropolitan Incubator and Metropolitan Geospatial Center. As explained by its Director Pleurat Rexhepi, the Incubator aims at encouraging students and young professionals (not only from MTU), in identifying and implementing new ideas in information technology and other fields of expertise. It offers incubation and acceleration services for start-up businesses in ICT and other domains. The concept of entrepreneurship is intricately linked with the university since its foundation and is well emphasized in the university vision. This is reflected also in the programs and courses offered and in the engagement of the staff. MTU has dedicated people for innovation and entrepreneurship: academic staff from faculty (35), Innovation Centre staff (10), Business Incubator staff (7), and Research Centre staff (20). One of the main strengths of the university is its structured governance with a strong leadership.

The Professional College of Tirana (KPT) shows some similarities with Polis. As stated by the administrator Diana Biba, the idea to teach students "not only a profession but how to be entrepreneurs" was introduced since the very beginning, as the founding partners are entrepreneurs themselves. KPT started two new courses in "Basics of entrepreneurship" and "E-commerce." In addition, the study program "Office Administration" was added to the academic portfolio of the Professional College of Tirana for the academic year 2018–2019, and it aims to prepare young professionals and entrepreneurs for the new job market. There is not a formal group, but responsibilities are shared between lecturers in charge of the course "Basis of Entrepreneurship," mentors of KPT HUB, the Head of the Department, and the Students Information Office. Three persons are mostly involved, besides the students participating in the KPT HUB.

The Catholic University "Our Lady of Good Counsel" is a private university offering joint programs with Italian faculties, and a significant part of the staff is from Italy. The first related entrepreneurship initiative has been introduced in 2019 with the formation of an informal group appointed by the Rector for the creation of an academic incubator. Relying on the international nature of the university, agreements with international stakeholders for joint programs, internships, and service provision to entrepreneurs have been established, and a call for projects with focus on medical sciences has been launched. On the other hand, entrepreneurship is not formally present in the educational area, but, in some cases, academics provide entrepreneurial related knowledge in their course.

In "Luarasi" University, the human capital is the major resource for entrepreneurship as many of academics are closely connected with the industry or work for private businesses. In fact, the interviewee Afrim Osmani is a professor in Management and Innovation but also a former entrepreneur. The entrepreneurial approach in 'Luarasi' University dates back to 2018 with a convention between academics believing in the importance of the practical application of knowledge for real life and market challenges. Hence, entrepreneurial subjects have been introduced and open lectures with entrepreneurs have been organized. Key factors are the will of academics to spread entrepreneurial culture and the strong involvement of the Vice Rector in the entrepreneurial activities, together with the participation of heads of departments in the informal group. The university is planning to develop an incubator in the near future.

16.6. Discussion and Conclusions

Ensuring effective university governance and leadership is more important than ever, given the contemporary transformations of higher education institutions and their functions and role in the society. The ability to address wicked societal challenges through a new, open, and collective intelligence approach, and the valorization of potential offered by digital technologies to create a new entrepreneurship ecosystem, require a new governance model.[27–29] Universities are asked to create new intellectual capital for the progress of societies[30] and to valorize creativity as a foundation of academic entrepreneurship.[31]

We studied seven illustrative cases from Albania and Italy as examples of entrepreneurial development and university governance for innovation in both developing and more mature and consolidated scenarios. The analyzed cases showed that the entrepreneurial activities depend mainly on the initiative of academics, and that human and social capital is a critical success factor when government policies and formal structures and practices are missing or underdeveloped.

Some relevant considerations emerged from the analyses of cases. The discussion can be structured along four areas to provide a recommendation framework for university managers and policy-makers: (1) key triggers of innovation for university governance; (2) key stakeholders involved and engagement of the same; (3) institutional and industrial processes and enabling policies; and (4) performance measurements and reporting approaches. Table 16.1 reports a number of main considerations and recommendation for the governance of universities.

Table 16.1. A recommendation framework for university governance.

Dimensions	Recommendation for Governance
(1) Key triggers of innovation or transformation	(i) Increase awareness on exponential trends in society and technology; (ii) Promote an entrepreneurial culture and mindset fostering initiatives; (iii) Support commercialization and application of knowledge through collaboration with industry.
(2) Stakeholders and their engagement	(i) Stimulate recurring interactions and proximity; (ii) Ensure separation and transparence of tasks and responsibilities; (iii) Arrange dedicated structures for networking, collaboration, and contamination.
(3) Processes and enabling policies	(i) Provide incentives for human capital (academic staff and students) involvement; (ii) Include entrepreneurial theory and practice in educational programs offered; (iii) Ensure specific services to support patenting and innovation.
(4) Performance and reporting system	(i) Take into account sustainability into an integrated performance evaluation approach; (ii) Establish indicators for intangible results, like human and social capital enrichment; (iii) Relativize results to the context and the starting point.

University governance should realize the potential offered by exponential technologies into an increasingly complex business environment where opportunities evolve in networked ecosystems. This requires approaches based on collaborative interactions where the university management adopts a holistic view of the organization and its role in society. Universities can become "accelerators of excellence" or "Excelerators" if they manage to adopt the right mindset and vision and the proper organizational configuration.

Updating the initial idea that the entrepreneurial university is "a global phenomenon with an isomorphic developmental path, despite different starting points and modes of expression,"[32] our study means that the shift toward the new model is an entrepreneurial experience itself. Whereas success examples and standard practices and guidelines are available worldwide, inputs and stimuli are mostly local, and universities should thus strive for adaptation to the context and the available resources. They should build creative solutions into an integrated formal and informal (legal and cultural) framework and pursue the achievement of an entrepreneurial model able to contribute to innovation and development.

The creative application of knowledge is the new aim, and it is extensively embedded in human capital development. As a consequence, the governance model needs to bet on flexibility, motivation, and incentives based on performance, and foster collaboration with entities holding complementary assets or strategies. This will allow the university to rise up as a stakeholders' facilitator, trust generator, and knowledge manager in our fast-changing society.

Acknowledgments

We are grateful to the colleagues providing their knowledge and expertise for the analysis of the Albanian cases. In particular, the Vice Rector Elona Karafili and the Innovation Factory Coordinator Valerio Perna (Polis University); the Head of Rectorate's Cabinet and Research Project's Director Besa Mançka and the Metropolitan Incubator Director Pleurat Rexhepi (Metropolitan Tirana University); the Administrator Diana Biba (Professional College of Tirana); and the Professor of Management and Innovation Afrim Osmani ("Luarasi" University).

References

1. S. Sedlacek. The role of universities in fostering sustainable development at the regional level. *Journal of Cleaner Production*, **48**, 74–84 (2013).
2. P.D.S. Freire, G.A. Dandolini, J.A.D. Souza, T.C. Silva and R.M. Couto. Knowledge Governance (GovC): The State of the Art about the Term: Brapci 2.0. *Biblios*; *Journal of Librarianship and Information Science*, **69**, 21–40 (2017).
3. P.K. Wong, Y.P. Ho and A. Singh. Towards an "entrepreneurial university" model to support knowledge-based economic development: the case of the National University of Singapore. *World Development*, **35**(6), 941–958 (2007).
4. M. Lupan and R. Bejinaru. Perspectives of university governance for the development of entrepreneurship. *The USV Annals of Economics and Public Administration*, **19**(29), 74–81 (2019).
5. M.M. Crow, K. Whitman and D.M. Anderson. Rethinking academic entrepreneurship: university governance and the emergence of the academic enterprise. *Public Administration Review*, **80**(3), 511–515 (2020).
6. B.B. Fischer, G.H.S.M. de Moraes and P.R. Schaeffer. Universities' institutional settings and academic entrepreneurship: Notes from a developing country. *Technological Forecasting and Social Change*, **147**, 243–252 (2019).
7. N. Hidayah, A. Badawi and L. Nugroho. Implementation of good university governance and intellectual capital in university context. *International Journal of Commerce and Finance*, **5**(2), 1–7 (2019).
8. S. Ismail, *Exponential Organizations: Why New Organizations are Ten Times Better, Faster, and Cheaper than Yours (and What to Do About it)*. New York, NY: Diversion Books, Singularity University Book (2014).
9. J. Dzisah and H. Etzkowitz. Triple helix circulation: the heart of innovation and development. *International Journal of Technology Management & Sustainable Development*, **7**(2), 101–115 (2008).
10. A.J. Nelson. From the ivory tower to the start-up garage: Organizational context and commercialization processes. *Research Policy*, **43**(7), 1144–1156 (2014).
11. C. Hussler, F. Picard and M.F. Tang. Taking the ivory from the tower to coat the economic world: Regional strategies to make science useful. *Technovation*, **30**(9–10), 508–518 (2010).
12. L.M. Branscomb, F. Kodama and R. Florida. *Industrializing Knowledge: University-Industry Linkages in Japan and the United States*. Cambridge, MA: MIT Press (1999).

13. P. Braunerhjelm, Z.J. Acs, D.B. Audretsch and B. Carlsson. The missing link: knowledge diffusion and entrepreneurship in endogenous growth. *Small Business Economics*, **34**(2), 105–125 (2010).

14. M. Wagner, S. Schaltegger, E.G. Hansen and K. Fichter. University-linked programmes for sustainable entrepreneurship and regional development: How and with what impact? *Small Business Economics,* **56**, 1141–1158 (2021).

15. M. Guerrero and D. Urbano. The development of an entrepreneurial university. *Journal of Technology Transfer*, **37**(1), 43–74 (2012).

16. R. Grimaldi, M. Kenney, D.S. Siegel and M. Wright. 30 years after Bayh–Dole: Reassessing academic entrepreneurship. *Research Policy*, **40**(8), 1045–1057 (2011).

17. E. Garnsey and P. Heffernan. High-technology clustering through spin-out and attraction: The Cambridge case. *Regional Studies*, **39**(8), 1127–1144 (2005).

18. R. Huggins and P. Thompson. Entrepreneurship, innovation and regional growth: A network theory. *Small Business Economics*, **45**, 103–128 (2015).

19. M.T. Hansen, H.W. Chesbrough, N. Nohria and D.N. Sull. Networked incubators. *Harvard Business Review*, **78**(5), 74–84 (2000).

20. V.V. De Luca, A. Margherita and G. Passiante. Crowdfunding: A systemic framework of benefits. *International Journal of Entrepreneurial Behavior & Research*, **25**(6), 1321–1339 (2019).

21. P. Ghisellini, C. Cialani and S. Ulgiati. A review on circular economy: The expected transition to a balanced interplay of environmental and economic systems. *Journal of Cleaner Production*, **114**, 11–32 (2016).

22. L. Velazquez, N. Munguia, A. Platt and J. Taddei. Sustainable university: What can be the matter? *Journal of Cleaner Production*, **14**(9–11), 810–819 (2006).

23. S. Schaltegger and M. Wagner. Sustainable entrepreneurship and sustainability innovation: categories and interactions. *Business Strategy and the Environment*, **20**(4), 222–237 (2011).

24. A. Civera, M. Meoli and S. Vismara. Engagement of academics in university technology transfer: Opportunity and necessity academic entrepreneurship. *European Economic Review*, **123**, 103376 (2020).

25. C.C. Williams and B. Kosta. Evaluating institutional theories of informal sector entrepreneurship: Some lessons from Albania. *Journal of Developmental Entrepreneurship*, **24**(2), 1950009 (2019).

26. A. Bitzenis and E. Nito. Obstacles to entrepreneurship in a transition business environment: the case of Albania. *Journal of Small Business and Enterprise Development*, **12**(4), 564–578 (2005).

27. G. Elia and A. Margherita. Can we solve wicked problems? A conceptual framework and a collective intelligence system to support problem analysis and solution design for complex social issues. *Technological Forecasting & Social Change*, **133**, 279–286 (2018).

28. G. Elia and A. Margherita. Digital entrepreneurship ecosystem: How digital technologies and collective intelligence are reshaping the entrepreneurial process. *Technological Forecasting & Social Change*, **150**, 119791 (2020).

29. G. Rizzatti and P. de Sa Freire. Learning governance (GovLearn): The state of the art on the terms. *Espacios Magazine*, **41**(3), 16 (2020).

30. G. Secundo, A. Margherita, G. Elia and G. Passiante. Intangible assets in higher education: mission, performance or both? *Journal of Intellectual Capital*, **11**(2), 140–157 (2010).

31. B. Kalar. The role of creativity in the context of academic entrepreneurship. Creativity *and Innovation Management*, **29**(2), 254–267 (2020).

32. H. Etzkowitz, A. Webster, C. Gebhardt and B.R.C. Terra. The future of the university and the university of the future: Evolution of ivory tower to entrepreneurial paradigm. *Research Policy*, **29**(2), 313–330 (2000).

17

Knowledge Ecosystems, Universities, and Innovation in Small and Medium-Sized Enterprises: Establishing a Knowledge Infrastructure Governance Theoretical Framework and Conditions for Success

Joyline Makani[*,§]*, Angelo Dossou-Yovo*[†,¶] *and*
Michelle McPherson[‡,**]

[*]Faculty of Management
Dalhousie University, Halifax, Nova Scotia, Canada B3H 4R
[†]Department of International Studies,
York University, Toronto, Ontario, Canada

319

‡*Dalhousie University,*
Halifax, Nova Scotia, Canada

§*Joyline.Makani@dal.ca*

¶*angelody@Glendon.Yorku.ca*

****michelle@scienceatlantic.ca*

Scholars underscore the advantages of knowledge ecosystems, where local universities play a central role in advancing innovation within the system. Nonetheless, to date, no research has elucidated what knowledge ecosystems factors drive innovation success in small and medium enterprises (SMEs). Further, the elements modelling effective SME and university relationships and knowledge infrastructure governance are still a blur. Utilizing the meta-synthesis approach, this study provides a thematic review of existing evidence relating to knowledge ecosystems, university-firm collaboration, and innovation success in SMEs. An SME innovation and knowledge infrastructure governance framework, including 16 factors classified under 3 actor layers (SME [knowledge & learning processes], embedded university, and integrated knowledge community), was obtained. The framework, coupled with activity examples, will allow universities, SMEs, policy-makers, and scholars to obtain a clearer understanding of how to leverage university–firm collaborations to create successful knowledge communities fostering innovation success in SMEs. Further research could explore and provide criteria and measures to assess the impact and direction of the relationships and governance factors outlined in the framework.

17.1. Introduction

Knowledge is considered an indispensable asset for small businesses today, and a strong knowledge infrastructure governance is viewed as fundamental to their innovative processes. Universities, as generators of knowledge and providers of continuous learning opportunities, are reckoned as organizations that perform a key role in innovation processes. As such, researchers have called attention to the advantages of geographic co-location hotspots of universities with existing innovation processes.[1]

They highlight that characteristics of these co-locations offer core advantages of continuous flow of knowledge between and among enterprises. Scholars refer to the hotspots as knowledge ecosystems where local universities play a central role in advancing innovation within the system.[1,2] Surprisingly, to date, no research has elucidated what knowledge ecosystems factors drive innovation success in small and medium enterprises (SMEs). Further, the elements modelling effective SME and university relationships are still a blur. Specific to SME innovation collaboration activities, scholars are calling into question networks governance and modes of engagement among actors. Specifically, they are asking what and how contextual factors within university–SME collaboration relationships contribute to success in innovation.

To date, the complete literature on knowledge ecosystems, universities, and innovation, as it pertains to steps of the innovation processes, has not been reviewed in a single study. As a result, a summary of the current evidence regarding university–firm collaboration and factors of success in innovation in relation to SMEs does not exist. To that effect, this study contributes to the SMEs, innovation, and knowledge management literature by thematically reviewing and synthesizing the literature on university–firm collaboration and the contextual factors within knowledge ecosystems that drive SME innovation success. Our goal is to propose a new framework, depicting the dynamic and complex nature of actors, vehicles of collaboration, and the contextual factors within a knowledge infrastructure contributing to innovation success.

The rest of the chapter is organized as follows. In Section 17.2, we present the background, theories, and questions underscoring our study. In Section 17.3, we provide the theoretical foundations. This is followed by description of the methodology used in this study in Section 17.4. We then discuss our study results and present a comprehensive multi-dimensional framework in Section 17.5. In Section 17.6, we provide a discussion of our study contributions, implications, limitations, and future directions.

17.2. Background

The current economy is recognised as the knowledge economy, in which, as Ref. 3 explained, the real and controlling resource and the absolutely decisive "factor of production" is knowledge. Scholars consider knowledge as a fundamental factor shaping the outcome of the innovation process in firms today.[4] The underlying premise is that innovation is essentially "about knowledge — creating new possibilities through combining new knowledge sets."[5] Innovation in SMEs has been researched through a variety of approaches over many years.[6] These studies employ variable definitions of SMEs, which can cause problems in synthesizing their findings. In this study, we define an SME as a "business establishment with 1–499 paid employees."[7] In addition, innovation researchers use a variety of labels to define innovation depending on whether the focus is on the organization or the geographic location and the environment of the organization. Our focus is on firm-level innovation while recognizing that innovation is an interactive process that can lead to a diversity of possible outcomes. Thus, we adopt the Ref. 8's broad definition of innovation. This definition underscores firm-level innovation as underpinned by the capacity of a firm to explore new knowledge and exploit it "to introduce new products and services ahead of competitors, to anticipate consumer needs or even to create them. (...) to decide to change its market geographically, virtually, or creatively. (...) to change how goods and services are produced and delivered to reduce cost, improve efficiency, and increase convenience for customers. (...) [And] to convert creativity, market and customer knowledge, and technology into marketable innovations."[9] In short, it recognizes the knowledge-driven approach as a necessary process in building effective capabilities for innovation success in firms today.

In the literature the importance of inter-organizational relationships as an extension of firms' internal knowledge bases is underscored.[10] The benefits of the extent and breath of external knowledge linkages to firm innovation have been well documented.[11,12] A firm's exposure to dissimilar, complementary bodies of knowledge is recognized as actuating new ideas and creativity,[13] and together with managing internal knowledge flows, strong linkages to and knowledge flows from various external partners, particularly in uncertain environments, are identified as leading to improved innovation outcomes.[14] Scholars also point to serendipitous or chance encounters within the knowledge ecosystem as having a key role to play in innovation as they expose individuals to new sources of data, information, and knowledge that can be combined with their own current stock and lead to new discoveries and the creation of new knowledge.[15] Prior literature has also highlighted universities as key external links and core sources of knowledge contributing to innovation success in firms and explored firm characteristics that influence its ability to utilize new knowledge which is transferred from universities. However, researchers have criticized the narrow view taken by prior studies that tend to focus on "the commercialization of research results and on mechanism of technology transfer such as science parks and incubators, liaison offices, or intellectual property."[16] They point to the predominance of research as exploring flow of knowledge between universities and firms from a university-centric perspective, focusing primarily on the role of the university as the knowledge producer and placing emphasis on the process of knowledge transfer or commercialization of university research through patenting, licensing, and university spin-offs.

Collaboration with other organizations is noted as contributing to the increase in the innovation performance of SMEs "as they encounter liabilities of 'smallness.'"[17] But much of the work in the area of university–firm collaboration and knowledge transfer has focused on large firms. SMEs possess greater innovative capacities than large firms in terms of innovations per employee[18]; are likely to be more innovation-oriented[19]; "appear to be able to utilize their university-based associations to leverage their internal R&D to a greater degree than large firms,"[20] and, driven by a lack of resources, are more eager to build efficient and durable relationships with their ecosystem to create innovation.[21] The need for further research that examines knowledge exchange and knowledge exploitation, and the complementarities across innovative processes in SMEs is thus stressed.

17.3. Theoretical Foundations and Research Questions

Inspired by the opportunity to assess what business and innovation scholars have learned thus far, we embarked on a journey to thematically review the prevailing SME literature relating to knowledge ecosystems, university–firm collaboration, and innovation. Our aim was to build upon scholarship and practice in this area by synthesizing the representative literature, identifying themes and patterns, and creating a conceptual framework.[22] This framework depicts new perspectives on the dynamic and complex nature of actors, spaces, vehicles, and contextual factors of collaboration within ecosystems contributing to SME innovation success. A number of theories were used to provide a focus for the research and to provide boundaries to its scope.[23] Below, we unpack the particular theories and hypothesize the impact they may have on the innovation processes of SMEs.

17.3.1. *Knowledge ecosystems, Ba, and absorptive capacity*

Scholars and business managers today are recognizing the value of employing the ecosystem metaphor for understanding the governance of knowledge infrastructure defined by complex network of business relationships within and across industries and communities. In this study, we adopt the knowledge ecosystem lens to investigate knowledge infrastructure and collaborative practices in relation to their benefits to the SME innovation process. We define knowledge infrastructure as the set of "systems and institutions that enable the creation and sharing of ideas and the reliable transfer of information from person to person and group to group."[24] The systems approach has been used in previous studies to study innovation. In the innovation literature, researchers have examined the systemic dimension of innovation at many different levels (e.g. the actors considering spatial or geographic limits,[25] sectoral limits,[26] and technological limits.[27] Our approach to investigate the SME innovation process is different as we rely on the knowledge ecosystem concept, a concept emerging from the information systems literature. Our aim is to understand how knowledge processes in general, and in SMEs specifically, shape firm-level innovation processes at the critical stages such as the generation and development of new ideas, leading to a new technological concept, the research and development (R&D), and the commercialization of newly developed products.[28] Following Ref. 29, we categorize knowledge processes as including the following types of focuses: knowledge creation (the development of new knowledge, and innovation), intra-organizational knowledge sharing (the movement of existing knowledge between different organizational actors, both within and between departments and hierarchical levels), and knowledge acquisition (the successful acquisition, storage and documentation of external knowledge).

Significantly, in examining the role of knowledge in shaping innovation dynamics in SMEs we reckon that "at its core, innovation is a path-dependent, cumulative activity that involves multiple actors."[30] It is defined by each actor actively pursuing opportunities to expand their knowledge base so as to be able to implement a new or significantly improved product, process, and service menu. We thus, understand knowledge ecosystems as complex networks of actors "where local universities and public research organizations play a central role in advancing technological innovation within the system."[2]

Importantly, in this study we view knowledge ecosystems as complex systems defined by both the structures of, and relationships between, interacting actors. The core focus of knowledge ecosystems is the creation of new knowledge through joint research work, collaboration, or the development of knowledge base.[31] We consider the main outcome of a knowledge ecosystem as new knowledge and recognize that this outcome is shaped by the networks of actor nodes where the knowledge is created and retained. The relationships between the actors play a central role and underscores the flow, exploration, and exploitation of data, information and knowledge. Pertinent to our research is the view that innovation is an "integrating mechanism between the exploration of new knowledge and its exploitation for value co-creation."[31] Actors within the ecosystem work together "in iterative processes of trial and error to bring about the successful commercial exploitation of a new idea."[32] Innovation often requires novelty of sources, i.e. exposure to dissimilar, complementary bodies of knowledge gives birth to new ideas and creativity. As Ref. 13 observed, "knowledge creation depends on a capacity to coordinate the exchange of complementary pieces of knowledge owned by a variety of actors within and between organizations." Thus, from a governance perspective, a crucial feature that defines success is the presence of what Ref. 1 described as an anchor tenant, i.e. "a scaffolding that, either intentionally or unexpectedly, assists subsequent connections," and an actor "who neither directly competes with nor dictates to the other organizations that inhabit the community." Therefore, we can expect that universities, as actors present in the knowledge ecosystem, are more likely to be anchor tenants.

Ba (shared space or context)[33] represents a core element of the ecosystem context that facilitates knowledge creation and innovation processes.

Ba refers to the shared physical and virtual spaces where people can communicate, interact, and collaborate as well as "shared mental space in terms of common assumptions, values, practices, and knowledge that people can develop and share".[34] As Ref 33 argued an appropriate *ba* is necessary to support and facilitate each type of knowledge conversion (socialization, externalization, combination, internalization processes), thereby underscoring the fact that key considerations should be placed on the type of *ba* required to support different knowledge creation and innovation processes. If the ecosystem context in which people are participating in knowledge creation and innovation activities is inappropriate, it is likely to inhibit people's efforts to communicate, interact, and collaborate. However, not much empirical literature is available on the topic of *ba*, or the relationship between different types of *ba*, knowledge processes, and innovation processes.[34] Therefore, we can expect universities to provide and cultivate the appropriate *ba*, which enables the transfer, exchange, and exploitation of knowledge for value co-creation.

At the firm level, we recognize the relevance of the concept of absorptive capacity[35] to this study. Following Ref. 34, we define absorptive capacity as a firm's "ability to understand, absorb, and use external knowledge." We contend that a firm's ability to successfully innovate depends on its ability to identify, assimilate, transform, and apply external knowledge.[35] Thus, we posit that in order to be receptive to knowledge networks, SMEs need to build their absorptive capacity capabilities, i.e. harness the ability to utilize effectively external sources of knowledge. Therefore, we can expect enhanced absorptive capacity in SMEs collaborating within knowledge ecosystems defined by universities acting as anchor tenants as well as providing and cultivating the appropriate *ba*.

17.3.2. *The Canadian setting*

Contextualizing the findings of this study within Canada has several major advantages. First, considerable attention has been paid to the role of universities in business innovation as Canadian stakeholder communities' focus on mapping out strategies to strengthen university-firm collaboration and boost business innovation.[36] The insights from this literature allow us to delve into whether and how university–firm collaboration-driven knowledge processes shape firm-level innovation processes. Second, internationally, Canada is recognized for both its quantity and quality of scientific research.[37] However, "Canada's existing research strengths have not translated into sufficient applied research, technology, or innovation outcomes."[38] This perhaps suggests issues and problems in the way Canada's knowledge ecosystems are designed and function, i.e. the way in which new knowledge is created and disseminated and how businesses incorporate that knowledge into both existing and new products. Third, policy-makers in Canada are investing more time and money on regional knowledge ecosystems that foster innovation as evidenced by the government's recent investments in "Innovation Superclusters," emphasizing the development of ecosystems that are characterized by flows of knowledge.[38] This places a stronger emphasis on SMEs as partners in the ecosystem as it focusses on "creating the right partnerships for developing new innovation ecosystems that bridge the gaps from science, to commercialization."[38] However, to date, there is still limited understanding of how within these ecosystems innovation in Canadian SMEs is motivated.

17.3.3. *Research questions*

More formally, the following questions summed our study:

(1) What factors defining knowledge infrastructure governance (institutions, actors, *ba*, actor interaction, and interdependencies) offer information that can contribute to our understanding of value co-creation and capture and innovation success in SMEs?

(2) To what extent does the presence of universities in a knowledge ecosystem provide the "anchor tenant" needed to enhance the capacity to coordinate the exchange of complementary pieces of knowledge owned by a variety of actors within and between organizations which results in new knowledge creation and success in innovation in SMEs?

(3) How does the presence of universities in a knowledge ecosystem enhance the provision and cultivation of the appropriate *ba* enabling the transfer, exchange, and exploitation of knowledge for value co-creation and success in SME innovation?

(4) To what extent does a knowledge ecosystem, defined by strong university–SME collaborations, enhances the absorptive capacity capabilities of an SME which results in more high-impact innovation processes and outcomes? and

(5) How does the presence of universities in a knowledge ecosystem enhance value co-creation and capture and innovation success in SMEs in Canada?

17.4. Research Methodology

On the basis of scattered knowledge concerning effective knowledge ecosystems, universities, and innovation, specifically in SMEs, our study adopted an evaluative approach.[22] Evaluative studies are associated with inductive designs and they enable richer theoretical contributions "where emphasis is placed on understanding not only 'how effective' something is but also 'why.'"[22] We thematically reviewed the literature using a comprehensive strategy to locate existing literature, evaluate contributions, analyze and synthesize findings, and present the evidence.[22] In collecting the data, we followed a two-step strategy. First, we focused on networks of collaboration together with the key contextual factors within knowledge ecosystems that positively influence innovation in general, and specifically SME innovation processes. We did so, not only to align with our theoretical argument on knowledge ecosystems and innovation processes at the firm level but also to gain access to reliable and measurable written evidence of innovation success in SMEs. Second, we focused on the factors underlying successful knowledge ecosystems in Canada. We employed the meta-synthesis approach,[39] a method of inquiry that does not entail a secondary data analysis of the primary data from the selected studies nor an integrated review of literature on a given topic but instead entails an analysis of the findings of these studies.[40] Although more prevalent in the medical and health-related disciplines, evidence exists which details the use of meta-synthesis research designs in several disciplines, including business and management.[39] The purpose of meta-synthesis is theory development, high-level summarization, and generalization to provide more access to the findings for practical applications.[41] The meta-synthesis method served our goal of developing a comprehensive framework well. Reference 41's seven-step meta-synthesis methodology was adapted for this study. We categorize the seven-step meta-synthesis methodology steps into four major steps: (1) searching and selecting studies; (2) classifying and rating the selected articles; (3) synthesizing findings; and (4) presenting the synthesis results. Below we provide a discussion of the four steps.

17.4.1. *Searching and selecting articles*

An extensive systematic search was conducted to identify evidence relevant to our research. First, one member of the research team ran several variations of search terms such as: (*"knowledge ecosystem" OR "knowledge hub" OR "knowledge cluster" OR "collaborative R&D"*) *AND* (*"small and medium sized enterprise*" OR SME* OR "small business*"*) *AND universit* AND* (*innovation OR commercialization*) in 10 of the most popular and most recognized databases of record for academic research, (e.g. ABI Inform, Business Source Complete, Scopus, and Web of Science). Second, we searched within selected major journals in management and innovation. Articles published in such journals shape the perception of the extent of the topic areas and policies and the direction of future research. In a third method, we searched 58 repositories assembled by the Canadian Association of Research Libraries.[a] Reference lists of the retrieved articles were also reviewed to identify additional articles. In summary, we are confident that our search to locate relevant evidence for the study was exhaustive.

Our inclusion criteria included scholarly/academic research papers, theses, dissertations, or grey literature with findings relevant to our research. The inclusion of a breadth of evidence minimizes bias against non-published research literature. The exclusion criteria included no condition of interest; not outcomes of interest (new or significantly improved product, or process, implementation); and not written in English or French. In order to maximize the number of potentially qualified documents, specific cut-off dates were not applied. Our aim was to prioritize papers that appeared to be relevant, rather than particular study types or

[a]https://www.carl-abrc.ca/advancing-research/institutional-repositories/repos-in-canada/.

research that met specific methodological processes.[42] The retrieved articles were initially assessed for inclusion by reviewing their titles using keywords. Filtering results by keywords is considered a useful and efficient approach of zeroing in on the most relevant articles, in particular when searches yield a high number of results[43] — in our case, over 800 (n = 858). All three researchers screened each paper for inclusion independently. Any disagreements were discussed, but emphasis was placed on not rejecting any disputed papers. Uncertainties or conflicts were resolved by consensus. This reduced the sample to 314. Most (~85%) studies in the sample were published in the last 20 years. We conducted a bibliometric analysis utilizing a data classification form developed by the research team to assist in systematically identifying characteristics of each article. For empirical articles, to aid in the appraisal of study quality, our research team developed a 15 point-scale quality rating matrix. Two team members independently applied the quality rating matrix to a subset of identified empirical studies (n = 10). The two members then discussed their quality rating approaches and any discrepancies between their ratings. An "overall" percentage of agreement was calculated; the resulting value (0.88) was well above the minimal threshold (0.70), as suggested by Ref. 44. One member of the research team then rated the remainder of the selected studies. We agreed to include only those empirical articles that had an overall score higher than 10/15 (n = 79). Non-Empirical literature (e.g. reports) were also reviewed and included in the analysis (n = 24).

17.4.2. *Synthesizing findings*

We used NVivo 12 Plus software program to store, organize, and analyze the data. To code the data, we employed a combination of an inductive and a more deductive approach. The inductive approach was conducted through an open coding of the data. We created an initial synthetic coding scheme derived from the literature, building upon Ref. 45. The process was kept as descriptive as possible in line with the guidelines for inductive research.[46] Categories were refined as they were applied to the data, a process that enabled our "theoretical driven scheme to grow and to adapt in response to the exigencies of the data."[45] Cohen's Kappa was used to calculate interrater reliability, resulting in a score of 0.84. Then, we moved to deduction analysis, i.e. we grouped open codes into more abstract bundles based on axial coding, a process employed to find relationships between categories and subcategories.[47] The output of this step was 16 higher-order themes which were identified as contributing to our understanding of value co-creation and capture and innovation success in Canadian SMEs. We then explored and integrated the relationship of the higher-order themes into a conceptual framework, summarizing how the data fit together and fit with existing theory.

17.5. Results and Discussion

By completing the steps of the meta-synthesis method, an SME innovation and knowledge infrastructure governance framework was developed (see Figure 17.1). It includes 16 factors, which were classified under three actor layers (SME, university, and the knowledge community). At its center is the SME as the focus of success in innovation; encircling the SME is the embedded university, underscoring its significant role as the anchor tenant driving the success; and encircling both SME and embedded university is the integrated knowledge community. Since the focus of the framework is on highlighting knowledge infrastructure governance

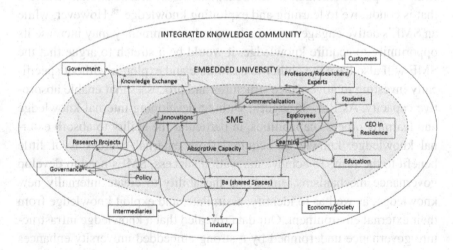

Figure 17.1.   SME innovation and knowledge infrastructure governance framework.

factors contributing to successful collaborations and innovation in SMEs, arrows indicating relationships between attributes or between attributes and outcomes within the same circle of factors have been omitted for simplicity's sake. Below we describe the three actor layers while exploring the answers to our research questions and discussing the extent to which the presence of the university in the ecosystem explains SMEs' successful innovation outcomes. We also assess whether these outcomes are primarily an aggregation of both the structures of, and relationships between, interacting actors.

At firm level, the importance of knowledge and learning to innovation success are undisputed by scholars. Governance factors contributing to innovation success in SMEs are defined by a knowledge infrastructure that nurtures new and expansive patterns of thinking and supports continuous actor learning. An analysis of our data revealed an SME's level of collaboration within an integrated knowledge community as an important mechanism through which employees continually learn and engage "in successful exploration — recognizing and integrating new knowledge external to one's domains of expertise."[15] Notably, our data revealed the importance of community collaboration as not limited only to R&D as vital to the SME innovation process, but also much innovation activity is revealed to rely on "highly skilled workers, on interactions with other firms and public research institutions, and on an organisational structure that is conducive to learning and exploiting knowledge."[8] However, while an SME's active engagement in a knowledge community may increase its opportunity to acquire knowledge, it would be a stretch to argue that the SME will also have the ability to assimilate and exploit it without specifically investing in governance structures and processes that enable absorptive capacity. As Ref. 35 argues, without developing internal knowledge and learning process capabilities, in particular the ability to absorb external knowledge, knowledge acquired from external sources is of little benefit to the firm. To achieve innovation success, SMEs need to develop governance mechanisms, enhancing the ability to create internally new knowledge, as well as to identify, assimilate, and exploit knowledge from their external environment. Our data revealed that a knowledge infrastructure governance underpinned by a strong embedded university enhances the absorptive capacity capabilities of an SME, which results in more high-impact innovation processes and outcomes.[10] Notably, the data revealed a recursive relationship between SME learning and absorptive capacity.[48] Continuous learning in a particular area enhances the SME's knowledge base in that area, which further increases its absorptive capacity and, thus, facilitates more learning in that domain.[49] In line with Ref. 35, we therefore, argue that an SME's willingness to invest in creating absorptive capacity is influenced by the incentives for learning that it perceives in its environment, in particular through proximity and engagement with an integrated knowledge community anchored by an embedded university as discussed below.

The essence of building strong, integrated knowledge clusters is underscored in the literature as a possible way of effecting innovation and commercialization success in SMEs. SMEs are presented as having limited resources and are described as suffering from the "liability of smallness,"[50] which hinders their ability to permeate the innovation market. As well, "compared to larger businesses, SMEs have fewer resources to manage globalization challenges, which include navigating the export ecosystem, learning different operating rules, targeting customers, validating products and attracting financing."[51] Nonetheless, the data reveals that in order to enhance their innovation and commercialization success, SMEs need to collaborate with different external partners and institutions[52] and that the breadth and depth of such external linkages coupled with proximity (space, time, or relationship) significantly improves their ability to innovate and commercialize successfully.[53] Notably, the flows of knowledge, learning, and innovation in SMEs are presented as strongly influenced by geographical distance.[54] Physical and mostly relational proximity are revealed as "extremely important in order to develop interorganisational relations that can lead to innovation."[55] For example, at the most crucial stage of commercialization, SMEs are shown to look to external sources within their proximity as vehicles of access to knowledge on marketing and sales channels.[53] In other words, close-knit networking and alliances, specifically strong integrated clusters enhancing collaboration between firms, and with universities, are revealed to offer SMEs highly effective vehicles for leveraging scarce public resources and aligning policy strategies across the different jurisdictional scales — e.g. federal, provincial, and municipal.

However, from a knowledge ecosystems perspective, we feel that the term community describes the collaborative activities and behaviors (which can be described as community-friendly and supportive) occurring in the knowledge ecosystem spaces better than the term cluster. In fact, defining the clusters as integrated knowledge communities considers the full spectrum of actors, institutions, and resources necessary to ensure effective knowledge exchange among community members in order to maximize the innovation and commercialization potential of the SME. Regardless of the model adopted to facilitate knowledge flows to and from SMEs, the underlying premise in our framework is that proximity or geographic location matters. We also emphasize the importance of *ba*. A good example of an integrated knowledge community is the MaRS Discovery District, located adjacent to the University of Toronto and major downtown teaching and research hospitals. MaRS supports knowledge flows and technology transfer across a broad range of sectors. Among its unique services, the MaRS Incubator provides space for academics, researchers, entrepreneurs, mentors, and investors across the innovation spectrum with the opportunity to meet, share ideas, and collaborate.[36] The MaRS' embedded executive program places executives with technology ventures in Ontario to support these firms in achieving growth milestones.[51] We believe unique, governed integrated programs such as these motivate actors within the knowledge community to participate in shared problem solving and/or to make complementary investments. Pursuant to the embedded program frame of thinking, we therefore introduce the notion of embedded university as the core pillar of a successful integrated knowledge community fostering SME innovation success, as discussed below.

In Canada, with regard to exchange and creation of knowledge, SMEs are reported as being disadvantaged over the large firms.[55] For instance, Ref. 55 observed SMEs within the aeronautics sector as very much dependent on the larger firms and often marked by competition, leading to their hesitancy to cooperate and to exchange information with other businesses. On the other hand, it is evident that a university presence within a knowledge community is crucial to the construction of a strong community that fosters knowledge exchange among all the actors within the community, leading to successes in innovation and commercialization. Due to the person-embodied nature of knowledge exchange, universities are considered core community tenants, and their proximity or embeddedness in the knowledge community is critical.[36] Thus, in our framework, we underscore the role of the university, as the actor intermediary instrumental to the reduction of SMEs' dependence on the larger firms, by facilitating business interactions with other actors. The embedded university is the much-needed anchor tenant, i.e. "a scaffolding that, either intentionally or unexpectedly, assists subsequent connections" and an actor "who neither directly competes with nor dictates to the other organizations that inhabit the community."[1]

The framework highlights the importance of multidirectional knowledge exchange, thus going "beyond traditional, unidirectional 'knowledge transfer' from academia to industry."[56] The data reveals the continuous exchange of knowledge between SMEs and university researchers as helpful in framing the problems that are solved in the university labs and ultimately lead to the development of innovative solutions that align with the SME's needs. It is evident also that an embedded university actively builds a network of university–firm–industry–customer relationships, enabling effective knowledge exchange. Customer participation in a knowledge community may significantly increase the odds of successfully translating innovation capabilities into new service offerings.[57] Also highlighted is the value of university professors and students, active within integrated communities, as boundary spanners, facilitating connections between SMEs and various networks they are in. See Refs. 58 and 36 for more details. Thus, the framework establishes a community-centric governance view in which the focus of an embedded university is not on "one-way outbound"[55] transfer of knowledge, but on the creation of an alliance of diverse stakeholders who may not naturally have a common platform for interaction.

We refer to the GreenCentre Canada at Queen's University as exemplifying the crucial role played by a university embedded in a community. Anchored by Queen's University, the GreenCentre Canada, which was established by PARTEQ Innovations and the technology transfer office of Queen's University in 2009, with funding from the Governments of Ontario and Canada, is self-described as "an all-in-one commercialization 'ecosystem' that includes everything from technical and market assessment, scale-up and testing to intellectual property protection, business management and financial resources."[36] The knowledge infrastructure governance in this case exemplifies an SME-centered and university-anchored knowledge community built to address SMEs' "liability of smallness,"[50] as illustrated by the following testimonial from a small start-up company:

> We came to GreenCentre with a formula for our adhesive technology that worked well in the lab but did not have a clear path (...) for scale up production. GreenCentre tested our material on large-scale equipment, leveraging their industry network, and developed a procedure and recommendations for a manufacturing process. [59]

In addition, our framework, in line with Ref. 60, presents a more expansive view of university contributions to innovation and commercialization success in SMEs. We do not limit universities "to a simple factor of production" but instead recognize them as a multifaceted "creative force in the economy."[60] We present the embedded university as providing key resources contributing to the enhancement of the SME's capabilities to utilize research partnerships, boundary-spanning personnel, and other organizational policies to increase their absorptive capacity.[48] In Canada, many scholars have documented universities, such as University of British Columbia in the West Coast, University of Toronto, York University, and McGill University in Central Canada, and Dalhousie University in the Atlantic Region, as playing an integral role in providing SMEs, not only with new knowledge to drive the development of innovative ideas but also a supply of highly-qualified graduates, which facilitate the development of local expertise and a well-informed and connected customer base.[36] Universities, on top of providing critical inputs for SMEs' innovative activities, such as training and consultancy, also attract brilliant students, providing a localized market for highly skilled labor, which in turn may help enhance the SMEs' absorptive capacity capabilities for external knowledge as well as the "capabilities of appropriating the results of their own research efforts."[61] For example, singled out in the literature as being of great value to SMEs are the co-op and internship programs offered in Canadian universities. Recently the Government of Canada endorsed the benefits of such programs by investing CA$498,099 to enable 48 industrial engineering co-op students at Dalhousie University to work with 16–20 SMEs based in Nova Scotia.[62] As the Honourable Navdeep Bains, Minister of Innovation, Science and Economic Development and Minister responsible for ACOA aptly stated:

> The Government of Canada knows that innovation in the workplace is essential to create economic growth. Co-op students and interns can make important contributions to help SMEs ... to build on their global competitiveness.[62]

The data also revealed that an embedded university provides the appropriate variety of *ba* enabling the transfer, exchange, and exploitation of knowledge for value co-creation and SME innovation success. That is, *ba* for: networking (e.g. conferences and workshops designed to assist SMEs in connecting to other community actors), knowledge exchange (e.g. participation in seminars, programs and courses), services (e.g. the provision of an incubator, CEO in Residence), and support (e.g. the promotion of innovation and commercialization, publicity and recognition, workforce development).[36] These different types of *ba* enable SMEs to gain access to knowledge and contacts by facilitating a wide use of knowledge, increasing value of complementary assets and the likelihood of reciprocal behavior among community actors. What differentiates university *ba* from ordinary human interaction is "the concept of knowledge creation."[33] *Ba* provides a platform for advancing individual and/or collective knowledge creation. In essence, a university *ba* is "both an incubator of knowledge as well as a container of knowledge."[33] It is from such knowledge infrastructure that a transcendental perspective integrates all information needed for innovation and commercialization. For instance, the education *ba* at universities is revered as providing an opportunity for students at all levels (undergraduate and graduate), faculty, postdoctoral researchers, and CEOs in residence to engage in effective knowledge creation activities at both the theoretical and practical level.[56]

17.6. Conclusions

Our main contribution in this study is the presentation of a comprehensive SME Innovation and knowledge infrastructure governance framework. Our framework, coupled with in-depth descriptions and activity examples, allow universities, SMEs, policy-makers, and scholars to obtain a clearer understanding of how to leverage university–firm collaborations to create successful knowledge infrastructure, fostering innovation and commercialization success in SMEs. At the heart of our framework lies a novel appreciation of university–SME collaboration as a core mechanism to improve a SME's knowledge base, learning, and innovative process conditions.

Importantly, our study advances important governance elements modelling knowledge infrastructure, SMEs, and university relationships in the Canadian context. Canada is described as "a nation of small firms."[38] Thus, while the literature points to large firms in Canada as more likely to collaborate with universities, it is paramount from the data and discussion above that policy-makers focus more on building governance structures of strong, integrated knowledge communities, anchored by embedded universities. As Ref. 63 argued, Canadian policy-makers need to focus on encouraging collaboration between smaller firms and universities because small firms are found to be more innovative per dollar of R&D. We believe an integrated knowledge community, as presented in our framework, is also essential in advancing the Government of Canada's plan "to create an "IP Marketplace," which will become a centralized portal for all innovating businesses, small, medium and large, to create a searchable list of all intellectual property held by government and academia, to aid in licencing and commercialization.[38] Our study contributes to the existing knowledge on knowledge infrastructure and SME innovation and may help to formulate governance policies that foster the creation of successful innovation communities on the Canadian landscape. Further, our study makes several contributions related to knowledge ecosystems and business innovation. First, we expand current notions of university–industry collaboration beyond processes of knowledge transfer or commercialization of academic research to also include its benefits to firm-level innovation processes, a topic that is gaining in currency. Second, we enhance the literature on business innovation by bringing deeper understanding on innovation in SMEs. Importantly, our study results are also relevant for managers in SMEs since they provide explanation on how collaboration with knowledge community actors can be beneficial to SMEs for innovation and the commercialization of SMEs new products. For instance, managers may initiate collaborations with universities and recognize and actively manage their *ba,* absorptive capacity capabilities, and organizational impediments, so as to improve the translation of knowledge and thereby broaden their organization's innovative focus and success.

Our study has its recognized limitations. First, because our framework is conceptually intricate, it might have brought to light some previously neglected factors and relationships while failing to capture others. We are hopeful that this comprehensive framework will provide a vehicle to help integrate the wealth of research on knowledge infrastructure governance, universities, and innovation in SMEs in order to advance both research and practice. Future research is needed in which the connections among actors, roles, processes, and capabilities are empirically investigated and addressed more explicitly. We also encourage scholars to compare the influence of different facets and conceptualization of *ba* on SME innovation. Also, considering that the boom of ecosystem started about five to six years ago and the implementation of this perspective is observed mostly in entrepreneurship studies and is very limited in innovation studies, future research is therefore needed that incorporate more empirical publications in innovation studies adopting a knowledge ecosystem perspective, thus enabling the application of a more robust meta-synthesis approach. Second, data for our review were gathered from a few selected databases, albeit 10 of the most recognized academic databases of record. The selected databases might have omitted some relevant research. Third, the exclusion process employed may have also omitted some relevant research. However, we believe that our inclusion of the documents retrieved from Canadian Institutional repositories, together with the rigorous procedure of our thematic review, have reduced the probability that the omitted research would have contained information that would critically alter our analysis and conclusions.

References

1. J. Padgett and W.W. Powell. *The Emergence of Organizations and Markets.* Princeton: Princeton University Press (2012).
2. B. Clarysse, M. Wright, J. Bruneel and A. Mahajan. Creating value in ecosystems: Crossing the chasm between knowledge and business ecosystems. *Research Policy,* **43**(7), 1164–1176 (2014).
3. P. Drucker. *Post-capitalist Society.* 1st ed. New York: HarperBusiness (1993).

4. A. Richtnér, P. Åhlström and K. Goffin. "Squeezing R&D": A study of organizational slack and knowledge creation in NPD, using the SECI model. *Journal of Product Innovation Management*, **31**(6), 1268–1290. (2014).

5. J. Tidd, J. Bessant and K. Pavitt. *Managing Innovation: Integrating Technological, Market and Organizational Change.* Chichester: Wiley (2005).

6. J. Kitching and D. Smallbone. Literature review for the SME Capability to Manage Regulation project. (2010). Available from https://eprints.kingston. ac.uk/id/eprint/12064/1/Kitching-J-12064.pdf

7. Government of Canada. Key Small Business Statistics (2019). Available at: https://www.ic.gc.ca/eic/site/061.nsf/eng/h_03090.html#point2–1 [cited Dec 12, 2020].

8. OECD/Eurostat. *Oslo Manual: Guidelines for Collecting and Interpreting Innovation* Data, 3rd edn. Paris: OECD Publishing (2005).

9. K. Lynch and M.A. Sheikh. Innovation dividend = stronger productivity growth. *Policy Options*, **32**(8), 22 (2011)

10. U. Lichtenthaler. Open innovation: Past research, current debates, and future directions. *Academy of Management Perspectives*, **25**(1), 75–93 (2011).

11. A. Leiponen, and C.E. Helfat, Innovation objectives, knowledge sources, and the benefits of breadth. *Strategic Management Journal*, **31**, 224–236 (2010).

12. J.H. Love, S. Roper, and P. Vahter. Learning from openness: The dynamics of breadth in external innovation linkages. *Strategic Management Journal*, **35**(11), 1703 (2014).

13. R. Boschma. Proximity and innovation: A critical assessment. *Regional Studies*, **39**(1), 61–74 (2005).

14. T. Felin and T.R. Zenger. Closed or open innovation? Problem solving and the governance choice. *Research Policy*, **43**(5), 914–925 (2014).

15. F. Nagle, and F. Teodoridis. Jack of all trades and master of knowledge: The role of diversification in new distant knowledge integration. *Strategic Management Journal*, **41**(1), 1–19 (2020).

16. M. Guerrero, D. Urbano, A. Fayolle, M. Klossten and S. Mian. Entrepreneurial universities: Emerging models in the new social and economic landscape. *Small Business Economics*, **47**(3), 551–563 (2016).

17. A.J.J. Pullen, P. Weerd-Nederhof, A. Groen and O. Fisscher. Open innovation in practice: Goal complementarity and closed NPD networks to explain differences in innovation performance for SMEs in the medical devices sector. *Journal of Product Innovation Management*, **29**(6), 917–934 (2012).

18. Z.J. Acs and D.B. Audretsch. Innovation in large and small firms: An empirical analysis. *American Economic Review*, **78**(4), 678–690 (1988).

19. V. Scuotto, D.G. Manlio, S. Bresciani and D. Meissner. Knowledge-driven preferences in informal inbound open innovation modes. An explorative view on small to medium enterprises. *Journal of Knowledge Management,* **21**(3), 640–655 (2017).

20. A.N. Link and J. Rees. Firm size, university-based research, and the returns to R&D. *Small Business Economics,* **2**, 25–31 (1990).

21. A. Mina, E. Bascavusoglu-Moreau and A. Hughes. Open service innovation and the firm's search for external knowledge, *Research Policy,* **43**(5), 853–866 (2014).

22. M. Saunders, P. Lewis and A. Thornhill. *Research Methods for Business Students,* 8ᵗʰ ed. New York: Pearson (2019).

23. C. Teddlie and A. Tashakkori. *Sage Handbook of Mixed Methods in Social & Behavioral Research.* 2ⁿᵈ ed. Thousand Oaks, CA: SAGE Publications (2010).

24. J. Riel and L. Roger. *In the Know: A Call for the Redesign of Our Knowledge Infrastructure.* Rotman School of Management, Toronto: University of Toronto Press (2015).

25. B. Lundvall. *National Systems of Innovation: Toward a Theory of Innovation and Interactive Learning.* London: Anthem Press (2010).

26. F. Malerba. Sectoral systems of innovation: A framework for linking innovation to the knowledge base, structure and dynamics of sectors. *Economics of Innovation and New Technology,* **14**(1–2), 63–82 (2005).

27. B. Carlsson and R. Stankiewicz. On the nature, function and composition of technology systems. In *Technological Systems and Economic Performance: The Case of Factory Automation* (1995), pp. 21–56.

28. A. Dossou-Yovo. Capacité d'innovation des petites et moyennes entreprises et contribution des organisations intermédiaires dans l'industrie des logiciels d'application multimédia à montréal (2011). PhD thèse [cited Dec 12, 2020] Available from: https://archipel.uqam.ca/3900/1/D2113.pdf

29. T. Andreeva and A. Kianto. Knowledge processes, knowledge-intensity and innovation: A moderated mediation analysis. *Journal of Knowledge Management,* **15**(6), 1016–1034 (2011).

30. O. Alexy, G. George and A. Salter. Cui Bono? The selective revealing of knowledge and its implications for innovative activity. *Academy of Management Review,* **38**(2), 270–291 (2013).

31. K. Valkokari. Business, innovation, and knowledge ecosystems: How they differ and how to survive and thrive within them. *Technology Innovation Management Review,* **5**(8) (2015).

32. K. Laursen and A. Salter. Open for innovation: The role of openness in explaining innovation performance among UK manufacturing firms. *Strategic Management Journal,* **27**, 131–150 (2006).

33. I. Nonaka and H. Takeuchi. *The Wise Company: How Companies Create Continuous Innovation.* New York, NY: Oxford University Press (2019).
34. D. Hislop, R. Bosua and R. Helms. *Knowledge Management in Organizations: A Critical Introduction.* 4th ed. Oxford: Oxford University Press (2018).
35. W.M. Cohen and D.A. Levinthal. Absorptive capacity: A new perspective on learning and innovation. *Administrative Science Quarterly,* **35**, 128–152 (1990).
36. A. Bramwell, N. Hepburn, and D.A. Wolfe. Growing innovation ecosystems: University-industry knowledge transfer and regional economic development in Canada. University of Toronto. Final Report, 62 (2012).
37. Government of Canada. *Positioning Canada to Lead: An Inclusive Innovation Agenda* (2016). [Internet] [Cited 2020 Dec 12] Available from https://www.ic.gc.ca/eic/site/062.nsf/eng/h_00009.html.
38. Innovation, Science and Economic Development Canada *Building a Nation of Innovators* (2019). [Internet] [Cited 2020 Dec 12] Available from https://www.ic.gc.ca/eic/site/062.nsf/eng/h_00105.html.
39. M. Van Rijmenam, T. Erekhinskaya, J. Schweitzer and M. Williams. Avoid being the Turkey: How big data analytics changes the game of strategy in times of ambiguity and uncertainty. *Long Range Planning,* **52**(5), 1–21 (2019).
40. S. Yahyapour, M. Shamizanjani and M. Mosakhani. A conceptual breakdown structure for knowledge management benefits using meta-synthesis method. *Journal of Knowledge Management,* **19**(6), 1295–1309 (2015).
41. M. Sandelowski, S. Docherty and C. Emden. Qualitative metasynthesis: Issues and techniques. *Research in Nursing & Health,* **20**(4), 365–371 (1997).
42. J. Makani, M. Durier-Copp, D. Kiceniuk and A. Blandford. Strengthening deeper learning through virtual teams in e-learning: A synthesis of determinants and best practices. *International Journal of E-Learning & Distance Education,* **31**(2), 1–16 (2016).
43. S. Fainshmidt, A. Pezeshkan, M. Lance Frazier, A. Nair and E. Markowski. Dynamic capabilities and organizational performance: A meta-analytic evaluation and extension. *Journal of Management Studies,* **53**(8), 1348–1380 (2016).
44. J. Cohen. A coefficient of agreement for nominal scales. *Educational and Psychological Measurement,* **20**, 37–46 (1960).
45. M.S. Poole, A.H. Van de Ven, K. Dooley and M.E. Holmes. *Organizational Change and Innovation Processes: Theory and Methods for Research.* Oxford: Oxford University Press (2000).

46. A. Hargadon and R.I. Sutton. Technology brokering and innovation in a product development firm. *Administrative Science Quarterly*, **42**(4), 716–749 (1997).

47. A. Strauss and J. Corbin. *Basics of Qualitative Research*. Thousand Oaks, CA: Sage. (1998).

48. P.J. Lane, B.R. Koka and S. Pathak. The reification of absorptive capacity: A critical review and rejuvenation of the construct. *Academy of Management Review*, **31**(4), 833–863 (2006).

49. E. Autio, H.J. Sapienza and J.G. Almeida. Effects of age at entry, knowledge intensity, and imitability on international growth. *Academy of Management Journal*, **43**(5), 909–924 (2000).

50. G. Santoro, A. Ferraris, E. Giacosa and G. Giovando. How SMEs engage in open innovation: A survey. *Journal of the Knowledge Economy*, **9**(2), 561–574 (2018).

51. MaRS Discovery District *MaRS* (2019). [Internet] [Cited 2020 Dec 12] Accessed from https://www.marsdd.com/.

52. S. Brunswicker and W. Vanhaverbeke, Open innovation in small and medium-sized enterprises (SMEs): External knowledge sourcing strategies and internal organizational facilitators. *Journal of Small Business Management*, **53**(4), 1241–1263 (2015).

53. S. Lee, G. Park, B. Yoon and J. Park. Open innovation in SMEs—An intermediated network model. *Research Policy*, **39**(2), 290–300 (2010).

54. M.R. Della Peruta, M. Del Giudice, R. Lombardi and P. Soto-Acosta. Open innovation, product development, and inter-company relationships within regional knowledge clusters. *Journal of the Knowledge Economy*, **9**(2), 680–693 (2018).

55. B. Hassen, J.L. Klein and D.G. Tremblay. Interorganizational relations, proximity, and innovation: The case of the aeronautics sector in Montreal. *Canadian Journal of Urban Research*, **21**(1), 52–78 (2012).

56. E.B. Acworth University–industry engagement: The formation of the Knowledge Integration Community (KIC) model at the Cambridge-MIT Institute. *Research Policy*, **37**(8), 1241–1254 (2008).

57. L.V. Ngo and A. O'cass. Innovation and business success: The mediating role of customer participation. *Journal of Business Research*, **66**(8), 1134–1142 (2013).

58. S. Yusuf. Intermediating knowledge exchange between universities and businesses. *Research Policy*, **37**(8), 1167–1174 (2008).

59. GreenCentre. *Testimonials* (2020). [Internet] [Cited 2020 Dec 12] Accessed from https://www.greencentrecanada.com/working-with-us/testimonials/

60. M.P. Feldman, and D.F. Kogler. The contribution of public entities to innovation and technological change. In *Handbook of Technology and Innovation Management*, S. Shane (ed.), Chichester (West Sussex, England): Wiley (2008), pp. 431–459.

61. S. Breschi and F. Lissoni. Knowledge spillovers and local innovation systems: A critical survey. *Industrial and Corporate Change*, **10**(4), 975–1005 (2001).

62. Dalhousie University, Science, Information Technology, Engineering Co-operative Education Office News. Local businesses benefit from Dalhousie University's top Industrial Engineering undergrads (2018). Available from https://www.dal.ca/faculty/site/news_events/news/2018/09/18/local_ businesses_benefit_from_dalhousie_university___s_top_industrial_ engineering_undergrads.html

63. I. Currie. Government policies to encourage university-business research collaboration in Canada: Lessons from the US, the UK and Australia. *Centre for the Study of Living Standards Research Reports* (No. 2011–02) (2011).

The Corporate Education System and the Governance of Knowledge and Organizational Learning: A Method for Assessing the Maturity of the System

Marta Silva Neves, Patrícia de Sá Freire and
Talita Caetano Silva*

*Engineering and Knowledge Management,
Federal University of Santa Catarina, Brazil*

*marta_neves242@gmail.com

Nowadays, the more learning we bring into organizational environments, the more prepared organizations become to instantiate multilevel governance, which is characterized by the development of a dynamic balance between autonomy, insertion, and regulation of multiple actors.

This is possible with the management of cognitive and behavioral processes that contemplate the shared vision of the network involved, generating collective and continuous development. Such processes are characteristic of learning governance, and constitute the agenda of the Corporate Education System (CES). In this study, we highlight the CES as a strategic tool for multilevel and learning governance. A mature learning organization necessarily creates sustainable development mechanisms. Thus, a CES maturity diagnostic method was proposed in order to establish strategies for the governance of organizational learning and the development of the system itself. For accessibility reasons, a public financial organization located in the South of Brazil was chosen. In the case study with a qualitative approach, significant gains were identified in the application of the proposed method, emphasizing the importance of accurate mapping of the learning network involved and active performance of the participants identified in validation, decision-making, content, and evaluation processes, among others. It is suggested to apply the method in other contexts so that it can be refined with continuous improvements.

18.1. Introduction

Multilevel Governance is characterized by a dynamic balance between autonomy, insertion, and regulation between multiple players[1] and requires governance of organizational learning, i.e. the more the learning, the more one is prepared to instantiate governance at various organizational levels. Within this context, learning governance encompasses cognitive and behavioral processes that contemplate the shared vision of the participants about the organization, creating and developing a collective organization, and mitigating knowledge management risks and costs.[2]

However, learning governance can also be considered a metaphor for individual learning, which runs through intuition, interpretation, integration, and institutionalization.[3] Thus, it is necessary that the individual learns so that the groups integrate this knowledge and, from this integrated group knowledge, organizational learning takes place, changing the organization's practices, processes, and technology.

These processes that start in the human mind and add value to the organization are the agenda of the actions of the CES; hence the importance of portraying the CES as one of the main tools for multilevel governance. Back in 1999, Ref. 3 showed the importance of the multilevel approach in the organizational learning process: even though its genesis is in the individual, its effectiveness is realized in the context of organizations.

The reflections hitherto highlighted — in addition to the impacts, developments, and maturity the CES drives within Brazilian organizations — are problematizations that drove the development of this research. In the timeline of the CES, it can be highlighted that, since 1920, actions for the development of people and organizations reverberate in the maintenance and improvement of essential competences.[4] It can be considered that the act of learning translates, in fact, into a high-power engine to optimize the operationalization of work, this being a key factor for the achievement of strategic objectives.

When dealing with the theme "Maturity," a construct that is also a target of this study, some important meanings were identified in widely disseminated dictionaries, such as "the moment of what is in the last stage of development; evolution [...]; State of people or things that have reached full development: behavioral, mental maturity..."[5] Bringing them to the organizational context, maturity models receive different domains, however, in relation to corporate education, their handling and understanding is still incipient.[6]

There are certainly several challenges inherent to the process of organizational maturity in CES, such as the lack of maturation in the organizational context, which can occur, e.g.: (1) due to the fact that it is centered on training individuals for the tasks; (2) due to the lack of alignment with the strategic planning guidelines, not extending the educational actions to the fixed or fluid players of the organizational network; or (3) due to difficulties in implementing indicators that enable the governance of organizational knowledge and learning, thus compromising the measurement of their impact on organizational results.[7]

The scientific literature on CES points to a more recent study on its stages. When refining the cut for the Brazilian scenario, it was identified that the Training, Development, and Education (TD&E) actions mostly focus their efforts on the third stage, i.e. corporate education.[8] The major challenge is in expanding the focus of the actions, which are mostly directed strictly to tasks. For this expansion to be achieved, the basis should be the understanding that knowledge management and organizational learning have become essential for the longevity of organizations, adding value to products and brands.

For example, in the study of Ref. 2, it was identified that learning governance is crucial to promote the processes of continuous improvement with respect to organizational learning, knowledge governance, and knowledge management. Still, in that study, the authors point out that, on the one hand, such factors combined foster the organizational performance; on the other hand, it is necessary to have mechanisms that govern learning with a focus on ensuring the knowledge evolution cycle. In this study, it is proposed that this challenge can be answered by maturity mechanisms of Corporate Education Systems (CESs).

Faced with this scenario, we sought to propose a **method for diagnosing the CES maturity in order to establish strategies for the governance of organizational learning and, specifically, the development of the system itself.** For reasons of accessibility, a public financial organization located in southern Brazil was selected. Using the case study methodology and qualitative approach, it was possible to identify that there is a multilevel understanding about the investigated phenomenon. As an application and analysis instrument, the Kraemer questionnaire, which is an instrument validated in public security organizations, was used.

18.2. Stages of the CES and its Developments in the Knowledge Society

The demands and changes manifested by contemporary society encourage education to have a solid performance in training for work, considering the technological complexity, globalization, reconfiguration of productive practices, and labor flexibility, among others.[9] Such changes have a direct impact on the individual level — on decisions and career paths and on the development of new essential competencies — and, at the organization level, on the sustainability of the business and strategy.

In this context, processes related to human development are called upon to be more aligned and actively collaborative with organizational strategies and businesses, management of knowledge and skills, talent retention, motivation for the collaborative work, and high performance, among other aspects.[10–15]

Academic universities introduce concepts and weave the relationships between them, creating an environment of curiosity.[16] This context is an opportunity for the organization to complement itself with CESs, as they encourage the contextualization of concepts as learning results from daily engagement in the problems and challenges of the organization's activities.[17]

In the evolutionary process, the Networked Corporate University (NCU) is a more contemporary model created and consolidated by Ref. 18. Six stages of corporate education are identified, which characterize the NCU Model, comprising Training Department, e-learning Platform, Corporate Education, Corporate University, Stakeholder University, and Networked Corporate University.

The first stage, Training Department, is characterized as training for the task, aimed at internal actors, with low interconnection between them and low education technology, without aligning learning with business strategies.

The second stage, e-learning Platform, is aimed at internal actors, with a focus on training for the task, through high use of educational technologies, expanding the interconnection, but without alignment between business and learning strategies.[19]

Corporate Education, the third stage, directs its TD&E actions to internal actors, with the use of education, interconnection, and training technologies for the task, with courses and programs aligned with organizational strategies. It is worth noting that this is the most common stage in the Brazilian scenario.[7]

The fourth stage, Corporate University, is aimed at internal and external actors in the production chain, with the learning focus expanded from training for the task to the development of management and strategic education in line with the organizational objectives. The use of educational technologies is part of this stage, providing interconnection between the actors, whether employees, customers, or suppliers, in educational experiences that contribute to implementing organizational strategies in human, economic, financial, technological, social, and environmental terms.[20]

The Stakeholder University stage, the fifth model, shows greater breadth in reaching the actors, which goes beyond the production chain and involves all those interested in the results of the organization. At this stage, partnerships with academic universities, learning based on relationships and interactions through collaboration, generating social capital, and the strategic alignment of the organization with stakeholders all are present, resulting in individual and collective learning. In addition to these characteristics, the use of educational technologies and the focus of learning on the task, management, and strategy are also present.

The sixth stage, identified as the NCU Model, focuses on educational actions that go beyond human (individual learning) and structural (shared knowledge) to relational capital, as development depends on the relationships between individuals, groups, and organizations. This model proposes using Knowledge Management practices, techniques, and tools, which act as collaborative and sharing mechanisms, cooperation and connectivity between the organization, employees, universities, science and technology institutes, suppliers, consumers, and participants in the productive and social arrangements, generating value for all stakeholders.[18] The NCU Model perceives each individual as a potential "recipient" of knowledge, which drives the creation and development of human capital at its most diverse levels (individual, group, organization). Thus, essential knowledge is identified and strategically integrated into the organization through intelligent environments and learning application. At this stage, the eminence of actions aimed at accelerating the learning curve and transferring learning to work practice is clear.[7] The maturity of the stages represented in the NCU Model aims to serve the organization in its development and ecosystem.

The stages of the CES provide organizational capabilities to meet the challenges inherent to the Knowledge Society.

18.3. Organizational Maturity

Biology introduced the concept of maturity from the development of living beings, considering its unfolding into pre-defined stages. This concept was integrated into organizational studies as organizations began to be analyzed from a closed to an open system.[21] Close to that time, Ref. 22

talks about the life cycles of organizations and their growth phases, considering periods of evolution and revolution, and influencing authors in the conception of maturity models.

These stages are based on structural patterns in view of the context and challenges they face, enabling the identification and adaptation of actions according to the needs of each stage.[23]

In addition to the maturity models from the perspective of life cycles, other models were developed with a focus on potential performance. Ref. 24 points out that, in the life cycle view, the final stage must be reached, while in the model focused on potential performance, the stages are options for the organization's progress, advancing or not to the following stages. Most of the available models have as a reference the potential performance[24] as well as the perspective adopted by the tool and study adopted in this research. These models favor evaluating the competence, capacity, or level of qualification of the characteristics of a stage, using established criteria as a reference.[25]

Although they differ in some factors, they are all characterized by the number of stages of maturity, name of each stage, and their respective identification summaries, in addition to the method for specifying the level at which the organization is located.[26]

As for the format of the models, Ref. 25 highlights that they can be descriptive, prescriptive, or comparative. The descriptive describes the level of mastery in a stage, without indicating performance. The prescriptive emphasizes the level of mastery and the performance. The comparative format develops analogies that favor benchmarking in organizations.

The Capability Maturity Model (CMM), developed by the Software Engineering Institute, presents five levels of maturity with respective characteristics — initial, managed, definite, predictable, and optimizing — providing essential elements to managers, as well as actions and strategies for improvement.[27] Other models were derived from the CMM, including the Capability Maturity Model Integration (CMMI), in which Ref. 24 identifies better software development practices, combining concepts of software, systems engineering, and product development

In this sense, the maturity models derived from CMM favor identifying a product development process, but not equally corresponding to define the organization's development.[23] Reference 24 states that many methods were created without a recognizable model. In this sense, Ref. 25 highlights that there is little documentation about models that are theoretically solid, rigorously tested, and widely accepted. So, this latter author presents a framework for developing maturity models composed of five stages: scope, design, filling, testing, implementation, and maintenance.

The models present different perspectives, designs, methodologies, and implementations. When identifying criticisms of the models and the theorizing of authors, Ref. 6 developed a maturity model based on the framework of Ref. 25. Thus, the Kraemer instrument proposes the identification of maturity levels, stages, and visions of a CES, making it possible to analyze and classify the reality.

It is a self-application instrument, without interference from a consultant or researcher, composed of 26 statements related to each stage described: training department, e-learning, corporate education, corporate university, stakeholders' university, and corporate network university; and the corresponding visions of the CES.[a]

It is important to emphasize that, in order to be considered mature, the CES needs to be leveraged as a strategic tool for the governance of knowledge and organizational learning and, therefore, we seek to **propose a method for the diagnosis of maturity of the CES** from the use of the Kraemer questionnaire to identify the stage of maturity and the actions necessary for its evolution in a financial organization.

18.4. Methodological Procedures

The case study consists of a research strategy that allows understanding the dynamics of a phenomenon from its particularities. Reference 28 mentions that the resource must be used when a phenomenon cannot be hermetically isolated from its real existence. This study — considered a case study — was carried out between December 2018 and March 2019. In order to comply with the requirements of the method, some important steps for the concreteness of the research were defined by the authors of this chapter.

---

[a]http://btd.egc.ufsc.br/?p=2563.

18.4.1. *Identification of gaps based on the scientific research*

To begin understanding the maturity assessment mechanisms of the institution's CES, the stages of evolution were identified based on articles and theses related to the themes "Corporate Education Maturity," "Corporate Education Systems," and related topics, where it was possible to realize the relationship with the visions that generate the implementation and operation, as well as the necessary steps to be worked on to improve the maturity level of the stages. These interlaces were presented in Section 18.2.1 of this chapter.

18.4.2. *The field — Selection of the institution*

The selected financial institution is 92 years old, is located in southern Brazil, and has a structure of 53 administrative units and 518 branches located in 5 Brazilian states. The work of its 10,107 employees is divided into the bank administrative units and the branches. In addition to these employees, there are 1,512 high school and university interns, and 454 young apprentices.[b] There are also 4,132 outsourced workers, covering surveillance, cleaning, IT, general services, call center, and transportation services.

The institution started its activities in 1928 with only 30 employees and an internal organization distributed into two portfolios: economic and mortgage. In 1958, the bank had 1,635 professionals. The education and training of these professionals was based on the work environment itself. In 1966, the corporate education process was formalized, creating a sector aimed at training professionals, in line with the organizational strategy. Then the professional duties began to be aligned with the business operations and organizational strategy, creating important milestones.

Faced with the maturing of this trajectory, in 2014, the institution decided to upgrade the concept of training management to the concept of Corporate University, with the objective of further guiding the quality of the teaching–learning process. These aspects, according to the research,

---

[b]Brazil's *Young Apprentice Program* offers job opportunities for young people aged 14–18 years.

contributed to strengthening the qualification of the institution's professionals to work in the market, as well as with partners and the community in general. In terms of organizational structure, the Corporate University is made up of 35 direct employees: 26 are employees, 7 are interns, and 2 are young apprentices. Regarding instructors and tutors, there are approximately 600 employees from administrative units and the network of branches.

The trajectory of the organization's Corporate Education corresponds to the trends in corporate education identified in the scientific literature already presented in this study, which were characterized by going through the training and education of employees for the development of operations; expanding to align with the organizational strategy; and starting to develop operational, tactical, and strategic capacities, skills, and attitudes, from the internal public to those involved in the value chain, stages highlighted by Ref. 18. It was understood that this field presents fertile ground for the development of the research.

18.4.3. *Procedures*

Phase I was developed between December 2018 and January 2019, with 10 employees from the organization's Corporate University as participants. This first application of the questionnaire aimed to collect the perception about the maturity stage of corporate education by those who have functions focused on the education processes in the organization.

Phase II took place between February and March 2019, covering 100 employees of the institution, corresponding to approximately 1% of the institution's total staff. This broader application of the questionnaire aimed to collect the impressions of people working in different functions and organizational areas at the Corporate University.

The invitation to participate in Phases I and II was made by telephone contact with each participant. After the invitations were sent, the Free Informed Consent Form was employed and the questionnaire was sent via e-mail.

The data collected from both Phases were recorded in an Excel® spreadsheet, subsequently easing categorizations, filtering by categories, and analyses.

18.4.4. *Research subjects — Selection of participants*

The research subjects involved in Phase I were: five instructors, four coordinators, and one manager. In Phase 2, 30 instructors, 2 tutors, 2 mentors, and 1 collaborator participated in theses boards, with 2 collaborators for personal testimonials, 1 Libras (Brazilian Sign Language) Interpreter, and 62 participants in educational activities.

As can be seen, in Phase I, 10 employees with direct and indirect relation with the Corporate University were involved, corresponding to instructors, coordinators, and managers. Of the 10 employees, 9 work at the institution's headquarters and 1 at a unit located in the Greater Porto Alegre; all involved in administrative operations, with 5 acting as leaders and 5 as led. Still at this phase, the profile of the participants is characterized by being 50% women; 10% with up to 5 years of experience at the Corporate University; 60% with up to 10 years in the organization; and 30% up to 35 years of age.

In Phase II, of the 116 participants invited to participate in the research, 100 people responded to the Kraemer questionnaire in full, presenting the following profile: 51 men and 49 women; 61 from Porto Alegre and its Metropolitan Region, 34 from other regions of the state of Rio Grande do Sul, and 5 from the state of Santa Catarina; two predominant ranges of time with the company: from 6–10 years and from 11–20 years; proportionality of leaders and led being 50/50; 37 professionals involved with commercial operations and 63 with administrative operations; and with 38 developing educational activities in conjunction with the Corporate University. More data will be shown in the Results section.

18.4.5. *Tools*

To carry out the organizational diagnosis, in both phases, the Kramer questionnaire was used, which describes the stages of the CES. As already said, from the stages described, 25 statements are derived, which are marked according to the Likert scale from 1 to 5, 1 being the lowest and 5 the highest level of adherence in the organization.

The concentration of responses allows tagging the stages with the following degrees: not started, started, in progress, readiness, and maturity.

In the data collection of Phase I, there was an initial presentation of the questionnaire to the participants, aiming at the relationship between the theoretical study and the direct applicability regarding the progressive tasks, including the initial diagnosis of the CES. Of the 10 participants, this introduction took place in person for 8 people and by telephone for 2 other people. For the data collection of Phase II, a mapping of possible participants was carried out, considering geographic locations, functions, time of organization, and involvement with educational processes, among others.

18.4.6. *Data analysis*

To analyze the maturity stages determined, it was necessary to go through three steps: the **pre-analysis**, in which the data from the answered questionnaires were organized, systematizing the statements marked in an Excel® spreadsheet. For this, a general reading of the collected material was performed, considering the levels of the stages and visions of CES maturity. The **exploration of the material** occurred based on counting and classification rules, determining the stages and the comparison of perceptions between Phases I and II. The **treatment of the results** obtained and the interpretation were carried out with the condensation and the highlighting of the information for analysis, allowing interpretations, inferences, and reflective and critical analysis.

18.5. Presentation of Results

It was initially noticed that there was gender equality in both phases: Phase I, 5 women, 5 men; Phase II: 49 women and 51 men.

Regarding the geographic distribution, there was greater variability of regions in Phase II, notwithstanding the purpose of the questionnaire to reach the largest possible number of people.

The people's time in the organization was predominantly longer than 10 years in both phases.

Another important fact is that, in Phase I, more participants were led (95%) than leading (5%); in Phase II, the relationship was equitable between the leaders (50%) and the led (50%).

In Phase II, workers were identified from the commercial (37%) and administrative (63%) areas, while in Phase I, 100% of the participants were from the administrative area.

As for involvement with the Corporate University, several functions were directly or indirectly involved in both phases. In Phase I, there were five instructors, four coordinators, and one manager. In Phase II, there were 30 instructors, 2 tutors, 2 mentors, 1 collaborator in thesis boards, 1 Libras interpreter, 2 collaborators for personal testimonials, and 60 trainees.

As for the number of records, in Phase I, the instrument was evaluated by 10 participants, and 250 responses were recorded and represented by the initials of the respondents' names. The total of 250 responses were distributed into each stage according to the corresponding statements. Thus, 70 responses were for Training Department (TD); 20 for e-Learning (EL); 30 for Corporate Education (CE); 50 for Corporate University (CU); 50 for Stakeholder University (SU); and 30 for Networked Corporate University (NCU).

Through the concentration of responses, the identification of the highest score obtained by each stage showed its corresponding maturity level, being TD — Readiness (28 points out of a total of 70); EL — Maturity (19 points out of a total of 20); CE — Maturity (12 points out of a total of 30); CU — Readiness (18 points out of a total of 50); SU — Readiness (24 points out of a total of 50); and NCU — In progress (11 points out of a total of 30), as shown in Figure 18.1.

In Phase II of the diagnosis, in which 100 participants answered the questionnaire, 2,500 responses were recorded in an Excel® spreadsheet, using an alphabetic code for the list of participants, without identifying them. The 2,500 responses were distributed at each stage according to

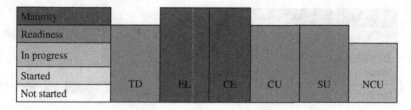

Figure 18.1. Maturity levels — Phase I.

corresponding statements. Thus, there were 700 responses for Training Department (TD); 200 for e-Learning (EL); 300 for Corporate Education (CE); 500 for Corporate University (CU); 500 for Stakeholder University (SU); and 300 for Networked Corporate University (NCU).

The tabulation of the data revealed the concentration of points obtained by each stage, expressing the corresponding maturity level, being TD — Maturity (232 points out of a total of 700); EL — Maturity (178 points out of a total of 200); CE — Readiness (99 points out of a total of 300); CU — Readiness (153 points out of a total of 500); SU — Readiness (152 points out of a total of 500); and NCU — Readiness (92 points out of a total of 300), as shown in Figure 18.2.

In order to develop the analysis, it is important to emphasize that Phase I of the diagnosis was characterized by professionals directly linked to the Corporate University or with frequent activities with it, while Phase II counted on participants who are users of the Corporate University services and also those who develop educational actions with less proximity to the CE than those of Phase I. To facilitate the description and analysis of the diagnosis process, the expressions group I and group II will also be adopted for the participants of Phase I and Phase II, respectively.

Regarding the Training Department Stage, a more critical analysis of the respondents in Phase I is perceived in relation to that manifested by the participants in Phase II, both by the score and by the registered comments recorded. Among the points identified for strengthening are: reinforce the survey of training needs; evaluate the effects of training on work behavior; and assess the impact of training on the organization's performance.

The perception of the two groups of participants regarding the E-Learning Stage was similar and led the Distance Learning offered to be

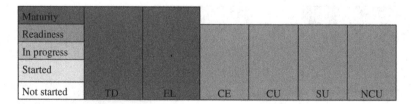

Figure 18.2.   Maturity levels — Phase II.

considered as at the Maturity level. Among the points for improvement is the expansion of access to external stakeholders.

As for the Corporate Education Stage, while the members of Phase I think that the Maturity level of this stage was reached, highlighting the importance of strengthening the competence-based management, those in Phase II consider that it is at the Readiness level, due to the need to reinforce the provision of educational actions for managerial development.

The level of Readiness was maintained for the Corporate University Stage for both groups of participants. There is a similar understanding as for increasing the orientation of courses by learning paths and developing courses for external audiences.

The Stakeholder University Stage also obtained a similar perception by the participants of Phase I and Phase II, indicating the level of Readiness in the maturity scale. There is the same understanding about learning networks and identifying the possibility of strengthening them, including external relations. To achieve it, it is clear that it is necessary to encourage the use of interactive technologies to promote sharing and collaboration between people.

For the members of group I, the Networked Corporate University Stage was understood to be In Progress, considering their analysis of the previous stages, and the need to expand the offer of courses that develop dynamic capabilities for innovation. On the other hand, the participants of group II perceive it at the level of Readiness, although they also express that the CES has the potential to be more dynamic, including stakeholders

Finally, it is worth noting that the participants in Phase I who work directly at the Corporate University have knowledge about the limitations of planning, execution, and evaluation of the educational areas. However, it can be seen from the results that the CES users' perception is more condescending with distance education actions and networking.

18.6. Proposal of the Method of Application of the Kraemer Model for the Diagnosis of CES Maturity

From the study and the experience of self-application of the instrument to representatives of the network involved in the Corporate University of the analyzed organization, the willingness to engage in dialogue and understand the CES under an evolutionary perspective in order to reach a level of Networked Corporate University, as well as to advance in the maturity of this system, was perceived.

In this research, important steps and aspects for the involvement and collaboration of the participants were identified, characterizing the design as a **method** of diagnosis of maturity of the CES in order to establish strategies for the governance of organizational learning and, specifically, the development of the system itself, systematized as follows:

The **first step** consisted of a survey on data from the institution to be studied, critical knowledge, and key people related to the Corporate University. This step was carried out by synchronous digital means and face-to-face interviews with leaders and managers related to corporate education. Thus, it was possible to define the sample based on organizational complexity, the content of knowledge essential to the business, and the relationship of the diverse actors with the education and development processes.

The identification of participants from the interviews can also be enhanced using the Snowball non-probabilistic sampling technique, i.e. the selected individuals invite new participants of their network, strengthening the engagement with the study as they demonstrate understanding its purpose.

The **second step** consisted of data collection, which occurred through a previous presentation of the purpose of the study, in person or online, individually or in groups. To this end, it was sought to provide an understanding of the CES and the stages that comprise it; present the instrument and its filling, considering its self-applicability; and clarify how to fill out the Free and Informed Consent Form.

As a facilitator to the participants for the self-application of the instrument, the researcher needs to be aware of the importance of being available for the clarification of doubts and to record the contributions that the respondents may add to the collection process. In addition, it is important to continuously monitor the return of the questionnaire completed and Consent Form by the respondents.

The **third step** consisted in documenting the data collected so the socio-demographic information, such as age, gender, and location, was considered, in addition to the professional information, such as function, time in the organization, involvement in corporate education processes, etc. The identification of the profile of the participants favors the reliability of the sampling dimension, besides the categorization and subsequent filtering.

Still in the recording, there was the compilation of the statements related to the stages of maturity of the CES pointed by the participants, making it possible to observe the concentration of perceptions manifested: not started, started, in progress, readiness, and maturity.

The **fourth and last step** was the analysis of the data, beginning with a pre-analysis starting from counting and classification, and including the complementary notes. It is worth emphasizing the importance of data treatment through categorization and interpretation of the concentration of scores and perceptions regarding the maturity levels of the CES. The analysis was then performed, establishing relationships between worldview, stages, and maturity levels, favoring the identification of strategic objectives to be implemented to reach the CES' desired stage.

From the data analysis, the methodological path showed basic strategies that enabled to envision the reach of the NCU model. To implement the strategies identified by stage, they were analyzed and related to the proposed method, highlighting the necessary steps, the practices to be realized, and the challenges to be considered, which are analyzed under the perspective of worldview, stage, strategic goals for evolution, methodological steps, good practices, and implementation challenges.

18.7. Final Considerations

The study development based on the application of the Kraemer questionnaire demonstrated that the tool is suitable for application in the public banking sector, since it favored the approach of the organization with the evaluation of the maturity of its CES, facilitating the identification of the stage in which it is and the possible elements, good practices, steps related to the method, and challenges to be managed to obtain the evolution to the next stage.

As the next study, it is suggested that the steps followed here be applied in other contexts, in order to generalize the possibilities of using this method. It is also worth expanding the sample of respondents to the instrument and conducting a long-term monitoring of the action plans designed after the maturity diagnosis.

As pointed out, the challenges associated with CESs are countless, and the lack of maturation in the organizational context can increase the difficulties of implementing systems to assess the effective impact of educational actions on the business. It is important to emphasize that the CES will be mature when it becomes a strategic tool for the governance of organizational knowledge and learning.

The method presented is based on the Corporate University Model, which privileges the theoretical currents of learning governance and multilevel governance. This means, in a more objective form, and far from being reductionist, that a precise mapping of the learning network involved is required, as well as the active performance of the participants, in the processes of validation, decision-making, content, and evaluation, among others.

The study reveals gains in the deepening of the model presented here, both for the academy and for the practice in organizations, when considering the greater assertiveness in investments and efforts aimed at human and organizational development.

Therefore, this theme should become the agenda of scholars and professionals in the field.

References

1. G. Knopp. Governança social, território e desenvolvimento. *Perspectivasem Políticas Públicas*, **4**(8), 53–74 (2011).
2. G. Rizzati and P.S. Freire. Mecanismos da Governança da Aprendizagem Organizacional. *Proceedings Suceg*, **2**, p. 1049–1067 (2019).
3. M.M. Crossan, H.W. Lanee and R.E. White. An organizational learning framework: From intuition to institution. *Academy of Management Review*, **24**(3), 522–537 (1999).
4. L. Morin and S. Renaud. Participation in corporate university training: Its effect on individual job performance. *Canadian Journal of Administrative Sciences*, **21**(4), 295–306 (2004).
5. Dicio. Significado de Maturidade. Available at: https://www.dicio.com.br/maturidade/ (Accessed May 18, 2020).

6. R. Kraemer. Modelo de maturidade do sistema de educação corporativa. Dissertação (Mestrado), UFSC (2018).

7. T.C. Silva. Framework Ponte TAP: Gestão da curva de aprendizagem para a efetivação da transferência de aprendizagem para a prática do trabalho. Tese (Doutorado), UFSC (2019).

8. P.S. Freire, G.A. Dandolini, J.A. Souza and S.M. Silva. Processo de implantação da Universidade Corporativa em Rede (UCR). *Espacios*, **37**(23), 1–26, (2016).

9. A.C. Barros Jr. Sujeito e empresa capitalista contemporânea num impasse: entre o laço social neurótico e o perverso. Dissertação (Mestrado), São Paulo (2009).

10. G. Hamel and C.K. Prahalad, The core competence of the corporation. *Harvard Business Review*, **3**, 3–15 (1990).

11. A.T. Nicolai and J.M. Dautwiz. Fuzziness in action: What consequences has the linguistic ambiguity of the core competence concept for organizational usage? *British Journal of Management*, **21**(4), 874–888 (2010).

12. K.J. Meier and A. Hicklin. Employee turnover and organizational performance: Testing a hypothesis from classical public administration. *Journal of Public Administration Research and Theory*, **18**, 573–590 (2007).

13. K. Xie and F. Ke. The role of students' motivation in peer moderated asynchronous online discussions. *British Journal of Educational Technology*, **6**(42), 916–930 (2011).

14. A. Oliveira and L.Pombo. Estratégias de ensino mediadas pelas tecnologias no modelo Edu Lab. *Revista Indagatio Didactica*, **8**(1), 1–20 (2016).

15. D.I.D.P. Albuquerque, D.J.G. Perez, M.C.S. Del-Masso and E.T.M. Schlüznez. Elementos norteadores para orientação na Educação a Distância. *Inovação e Formação*, **1**(1), 129–143 (2015).

16. V. Szoboszlai, J. Velencei and Z. Baracskai. Post-experiential education: From knowledge to 'knowing'. *Acta Polytechnica Hungarica*, **11**(10), 235–247 (2014).

17. R. Paton, G. Peters, J. Storey and S. Taylor. Corporate universities as strategic learning initiatives. In *Handbook of Corporate University Development: Managing Strategic Learning Initiatives in Public and Private Domains*, by R. Paton, G. Peters, J. Storey and S. Taylor (eds.), London, UK: Gower Publishing, pp. 5–16 (2012).

18. P.S. Freire, G.A. Dandolini, J.A. Souza, A.C. Trierweiller, S.M. Silva, D. Sell, R.C.S. Pacheco, J.L. Todesco and A.V. Steil. Universidade Corporativa em Rede: Considerações Iniciais para um Novo Modelo de Educação Corporativa. *Espacios*, **37**(5), 1–20, (2016).

19. A. Margherita and G. Sencudo. The emergence of the stakeholder university. In *Open Business Innovation Leadership: The Emergence of the Stakeholder University*, A. Romano (ed.) London: Palgrave Macmillan (2009), pp. 170–206.
20. J.J. Phillips. *Corporate universities*. HRD Trends Worldwide, 73–97 (1999).
21. L.V. Bertalanffy. *Teoria Geral dos Sistemas*. Petrópolis: Vozes (1975).
22. L.E. Greiner. Evolution and revolution as organizations grow. *Harvard Business Review*, **50**, 37–46 (1972).
23. G. Escrivão and L.S. Silva. Knowledge management maturity: Critical reflections and identification of gaps. *13th European Conference on Knowledge Management*, Cartagena. ECKM (2012), pp. 1542–1552.
24. R. Wendler. The maturity of maturity model research: A systematic mapping study. *Information and Software Technology*, **54**(12), 1317–1339 (2012).
25. T. De Bruin, R. Freeze, U. Kaulkarni and M. Rosemann. Understanding the main phases of developing a maturity assessment model. *16th Australasian Conference on Information Systems*, ACIS 2005 Proceedings, Sydney, p. 1–12.
26. A.P. Nascimento, M.P.V. Oliveira, M.B. Ladeira and H. Zanquetto. Pontos de transição: a escalada rumo à maturidade de Sistemas de Gestão da Qualidade. *Gestão & Produção*, **23**(2), 250–266 (2016).
27. J. Feng. A knowledge management maturity model and application. *PICMET '06 — Technology Management for the Global Future*, Istanbul (2006), pp. 1251–1255.
28. R. Yin. *Case Study Research: Design and Methods*. London: Sage (1986).

Maturity Criteria of the Networked Corporate University Model to Support Knowledge and Organizational Learning Governance

Graziela Grando Bresolin*, Patricia de Sá Freire and Solange Maria da Silva

Graduate Program in Knowledge Management and Engineering, Federal University of Santa Catarina, Florianópolis, Santa Catarina, Brazil

**grazielabresolin@gmail.com*

The Corporate Education System is an important strategic tool for promoting the development of skills essential for the job market.

However, this chapter discusses the context of network learning, specifically the contemporary model of the corporate education system, named Networked Corporate University (NCU). This model develops a continuing education environment that manages and institutionalizes networked learning. It is composed of eight guidelines that determine the degree of alignment of the organization with the model. The aim of this research is to propose the criteria for the assessment of the maturity of the NCU model. To achieve this objective, the qualitative approach of exploratory and descriptive purposes was chosen through a narrative bibliographic review. The results describe eight criteria of the maturity of the NCU, comprising Governance, Reach, Stakeholder Recognition, Interconnection, Technology, Focus, Level, and Knowledge Management (KM) and Governance. For each criterion, specific indicators have been developed, measured from the lowest to the highest scales, for monitoring the adherence the organizations to the NCU guidelines. These criteria support the development of Knowledge Governance (KGov) and Organizational Learning Governance (LGov) aligned to the NCU model.

19.1. Introduction

The digital transformations allied to the context of the knowledge society require the employees to seek continuous learning and develop hard and soft skills in order to keep themselves always updated and flexible with organizational changes.[1–3] In addition, innovations and business interactions promote the extension of learning processes beyond the boundaries of organizations, facilitating initiatives involving a broad network of participants,[1] in order to achieve the organization's strategic objectives and adapt to the accelerated changes in the knowledge society.[2]

The development of a Corporate University to network with an open innovation approach through partnerships with academic universities, professional associations, suppliers, communities, and customers allows organizations to become learning network. Organizations that adopt this innovation approach by obtaining external expertise from their network represent opportunities for value creation. Consequently, it provides the opportunity to operationalize the corporate strategy, integrating internal and external competencies.[3]

In this context, the contemporary model of the corporate education system emerges, named Networked Corporate University (NCU).[2] This model was defined by Freire *et al.*[2] as an intelligent environment of continuing education, physical or virtual, that manages and institutionalizes a culture of networked learning. As a networked model, it promotes integration, collaboration, and co-creation between organizations, collaborators, academic universities, science and technology institutes, suppliers, consumers, and other participants in social productive arrangements for the development of human, social, and relational capital.

Therefore, the NCU can be configured as a strategic model that aims to support Knowledge Governance (KGov) and Organizational Learning Governance (LGov) as it aids in the advancement of the maturity of the organizational KM and the strategic area of people development, eliminating gaps of individual, collective, and institutional skills of the network.

The NCU model can contribute to the measurement of an organization's performance.[3] However, the appropriate evaluation for Corporate Universities that operate in networks integrate indicators and criteria that consider strategic objectives and interaction with the external environment.[4]

The NCU model needs appropriate measures that go beyond conventional indicators and criteria, as it needs to consider its learning network and the eight guidelines that underpin the model. To measure and identify the level of maturity the organization is at in relation to the guidelines proposed by the NCU model, it is necessary to create criteria, indicators, and scales.

According to the context presented, the aim of this research is to propose the criteria for the assessment of the maturity of the NCU model. To achieve this objective, the qualitative approach using exploratory and descriptive purposes was chosen. The guidelines that support the NCU model were described and characterized through a narrative bibliographic review of theoretical and empirical publications.

19.2. NCU Model

The NCU model is defined as an intelligent continuing education environment, physical or virtual, that manages and institutionalizes networked learning.[2] The model was developed based on the theories of Social Constructivism, Organizational Learning, and Andragogy. With application of the elements of the Neo-learning methodology, for the planning, execution, and multilevel evaluation of educational programs. The model is composed of eight guidelines that guide the programs of Training, Development, and Education (T,D&E) and subsidize the learning processes at individual, group, intraorganizational, interorganizational, and network levels.[5]

The NCU proposes to apply Neo-learning as a methodological support for teaching and learning, in order to attend the cultural and socio-emotional transformations imposed by the competencies of the new digital generation and to distribute responsibility and autonomy among the educational triad (student-teacher-education institution). The Neo-learning methodology, as a new motivating mechanism for the learning process of young adults, and its transfer into practice, establishes guidelines and strategies for the use of active, agile and co-production methodologies, through the application of andragogical, experiential and expansive principles, which are decisive for the promotion of a dialogical environment; role exchange between teachers and learners and; knowledge sharing for collaboration and co-production of the educational triad and the learning network stakeholders. Moreover, Neo-learning provides elements that facilitate multidimensional planning, effective execution, and multilevel evaluation of learning trails, which are crucial to the elimination of knowledge gaps essential to organizational development.

In the NCU model, learning is seen as a strategic organizational process, as it contemplates the integration of different business areas and organizations by adopting collaboration and networking as a new paradigm.[2,6] The learning strategy is aligned with the business strategy, and the creation of knowledge is based on relationships between the different stakeholders of the network. There is extensive use of new collaborative technologies and methods, techniques, and tools of KM to expand and develop of dynamic capabilities for innovation. Also, the NCU can be considered a strategic model to support KGov and LGov.[2,6]

For this, the NCU model predicates a creation of the network learning that involves all stakeholders, internal and external. For learning to happen at the multilevel, the knowledge created and shared must be managed in order to expand the reach of the target audience and the promotion of learning for all participants.[2]

19.2.1. *The guidelines of the NCU model*

The NCU model is composed of eight guidelines that structure the model and guide the programs of T,D&E, called KM, KGov and LGov, Reach, Stakeholder Recognition, Interconnection, Technology, Focus, and Level. Silva and Freire[5] observe that these guidelines are related to the decisions that will determine the organization's alignment with the NCU model.

19.2.1.1. *KM*

The KM guideline involves the identification of critical knowledge, focusing on the consonance between the strategy of operation, management, and network organization. This guideline covers network learning, organizational memory, and knowledge retention. Furthermore, the educational programs use methods, techniques, and tools of KM to instrumentalize the organizational memory and compose an observatory of knowledge and identification of knowledge gaps. In summary, the KM guideline deals with the use and combination of sources (human and non-human) and types of knowledge (tacit and explicit) for the creation of the intelligent environment of continuing education that seeks to institutionalize a culture of networked learning.[2,6-8]

For Chen *et al.*,[9] with the development of corporate universities, the scope and functions of knowledge managed is deepened to contemplate the connections outside the organization. As a result of the knowledge network, the model of NCU is not limited to knowledge transfer and knowledge creation and begins to support and promote innovations. The knowledge network is extended to departments in the organizations, employees, customers, communities, universities, and research institutions.

In addition, the NCU guides and influences the acquisition, sharing, and creation process of internal and external knowledge and achieve the effective integration of externally acquired knowledge with existing knowledge.[9] In this sense, KM provides methods, techniques, and tools for sharing information and knowledge, creating organizational structures that facilitate human and organizational development policies to support the creation of networks and partnerships for the development of network participants.[10] The knowledge created and shared during these relationships must be managed and supported by the governance of knowledge and learning.[7]

19.2.1.2. *KGov and LGov*

To promote stakeholder inclusion and involvement, governance is needed that is aligned with the learning network. Supporting the collaboration of stakeholders who are interested in the success of the organization and the impact of the results on the ecosystem of which they are a part requires a governance that is equally dynamic and responsive to the needs of the network to maintain mechanisms that are appropriate to the context and interests of its internal and external stakeholders, so that all participants achieve their strategic objectives.[11,12]

The NCU promotes a governance model that considers KM processes, stakeholder fluidity, and learning networking. Therefore, KGov and LGov promotes greater effectiveness in the flow of knowledge and in building the learning network.

From the perspective of Rizzatti,[13] KGov is part of a system that governs and recognizes the inter- and intra-organizational learning processes generated by the relationships of individuals, groups, and institutions that are part of the organizational ecosystem. For the author, LGov is considered a larger system than KGov, because it governs the knowledge, mechanisms, and processes that support learning, from the individual level to the level in networks.

The LGov framework proposed by Rizzatti[13] is composed of four mechanisms: KGov, KM, Organizational Learning Cycle, and Knowledge Cycle; four components: Shared Mental Model, Shared Vision and Common Purpose, Reliable Information and Dynamic, and Self-Organizing Capability; and two learning environments: BA and collaborative environment.

19.2.1.3. *Reach*

The reach guideline is related to the scalability, integration, and flexibility of intra- and inter-organizational learning networks. It corresponds to the identification of internal and external stakeholders of the productive chain of the organizational ecosystem. This guideline defines who will be the target audience of educational programs. For the NCU model, the audience corresponding to the internal stakeholders are employees and leaders and the external stakeholders, from suppliers and customers, to even business partners and communities influencing the organizational strategy.[7] This guideline including fixed partners, proposed by the Stakeholder University (SU)[14] model, but moves forward to accept fluid and dynamic partners, as in the case of the NCU model.[2]

From the strategic planning, the stakeholders considered indispensable to the achievement of organizational objectives become the target audience of educational programs. NCU suggests that the educational programs be offered to the maximum number of stakeholders, including internal and external.[12]

Castells[15] affirms that networks have their characteristic flexibility, scalability, and capacity. Flexibility is the ability of networks to reconfigure according to changing environments and maintain objectives by changing their components and finding new connections. Scalability is the ability to expand or decrease size. The capacity of networks is related to a wide range of configurations.

The stakeholders are classified by Koehler *et al.*[12] at four levels according to their reach: intraorganizational stakeholders, the value chain, the social network, and the organizational ecosystem. At the intraorganizational level, it is restricted to the organization's employees. The value chain level encompasses the direct participants that are part of the organization's value chain — for instance, suppliers, customers, and society. At the network level, it includes the entire learning network of the organization, including fixed or dynamic partners of the productive and social arrangements of the organizational ecosystem.

This last level is contemplated by the NCU model, because when considering society and networked learning, T,D&E programs should contemplate all stakeholders that can positively or negatively influence the achievement of the organization's strategic objectives.

19.2.1.4. *Stakeholder recognition*

The reach directive defines which stakeholders will be involved in the educational programs. For this, it is necessary to identify and recognize their needs and expectations during the design of programs aligned with strategic planning to promote the management of relational capital and learning networks.[16]

Marguerita and Secundo[14] conceptualize the stakeholders of an organization as the parties that have interests and that interact directly and indirectly to achieve the organizational strategy. Stakeholders are considered individuals or groups that contribute, voluntarily or not, to the achievement of organizational strategies. In other words, they are individuals or groups that affect and are affected by strategic decisions, while they are responsible for corporate results, whether positive or negative.

The NCU model recognizes everyone — i.e. individual, group, or other organization — as a part of the learning network. It also understands how information and knowledge are acquired, created, absorbed, applied, and shared among these participants, contributing to the improvement of the learning network. Thus, the educational programs try to cover the largest number of internal and external stakeholder in the organizational network, focusing on the development of relational, social, and human capital.[16]

Once the stakeholders that will be included in the learning networks have been identified, it is necessary to recognize the interrelationships between the nodes of this network. This understanding is indispensable to create a shared vision that will motivate them to participate and produce collaboratively.[15]

After identification and recognition, it is necessary to classify the stakeholders as primary or secondary and define their degree of interest and influence in the organization. Finally, it is necessary to analyze the degree of influence and interest of each one of stakeholder, so that the best decision can be made in the management of the learning network relationship.[16]

The NCU model subsidizes the memory of the network, as there is openness and fluidity for the input and output of stakeholders,[16] becoming an interface for the relationships between learning networks for the development of skills, behaviors, culture, and shared values.[1,17]

19.2.1.5. *Interconnection*

After defining the scope and identifying and recognizing the stakeholders to be considered by NCU, they should be involved in educational programs. The interconnection guideline is related to the promotion of integration, inclusion, and interactivity of different stakeholders for the sharing of knowledge and consolidation of environments for networked learning.[18]

For organizations to respond more quickly to changes in the external environment, it is necessary to implement increasingly sophisticated initiatives, tools, and techniques for learning and development of employees, supported by digital technologies.[19]

In this context, it is understood that learning networks are dependent on the interconnections of the actors of the corporate education system, which can be accomplished in multiple ways. Information and communication technologies become decisive for the effectiveness of the interconnection of the learning network. At NCU, the interconnections happen in a dynamic and constant way, in all senses, between all the different stakeholders involved.[18]

In the interconnection guideline occurs the use of collaborative technologies to create a connection environment that promotes learning without limitations of time and physical space, facilitating the monitoring of the performance of participants, in addition to expanding networked learning. This is done with the intention of fostering, managing, and implementing the learning network, involving the different actors of the ecosystem. Therefore, technology allows for plurality of actors and greater participation in the network, and this possibility of participation is integrated with data processing and the generation of knowledge that can affect various aspects of organizations, including the human relationship.[18]

19.2.1.6. *Technology*

The educational technology guideline, in turn, refers to the use of technologies focused on streamlining and optimizing networked learning, envisaging the creation and sharing of knowledge to innovation. This guideline subsidizes the choices regarding the technologies used in educational programs to optimize the process of learning in networks.[2,6,20]

For Silva and Freire,[21] the education technologies guideline is related to which digital or analog; synchronous or asynchronous; face-to-face, hybrid, or distance; and innovative or traditional technologies should be selected and used by the NCU educational programs to support and facilitate individual, group, and organizational learning.

Thus, the choice of educational technologies should be made in a way that helps to achieve the intended objectives, in order to energize and facilitate learning and promote interaction, connection, and collaboration of participants.[22]

Networked learning promotes the development of information and communication technologies to reach stakeholders. In this way, learning environments have been transformed into virtual learning environments with the objective of leveraging new opportunities, entering new world markets, and developing deeper relationships with customers and the ecosystem. The NCU model aims at integrating different business areas and organizations and adopts collaboration and networking as a new paradigm.[23]

19.2.1.7. *Focus*

The focus guideline offers educational programs aimed at the development of technical and soft skills of employees, aligned with organizational objectives, covering the tactical, operational, and strategic levels. This guideline is related to the strategic increase of corporate learning, which extends from training to task, to the broadest forms of professional development.[24]

In summary, this guideline for the NCU model is classified into three dimensions: strategic, tactical, and operational. The strategic dimension focuses on human development that aims to promote co-creation and co-production for the implementation of the strategy. The tactical dimension focuses on delivery and aims to align organizational goals with the development of individual competencies. The operational dimension focuses on the task, because it refers to improving the efficiency of the individual in the organization, in the accomplishment of their tasks.[24]

These three dimensions have their degree of importance for the development of individual competences of professionals, contributing to the organizational development.[24] The degree of adherence of the focus guideline is measured by observing how strategic there is in learning, which can be low, medium/low, high/medium, or high.[14]

In other words, this guideline determines the decision of what is the focus of each educational program, whether operational, tactical, or strategic. This decision, then, will define the percentage of operational, tactical, or strategic courses of each educational program that will be developed by NCU.

19.2.1.8. *Level*

The level guideline orients the development of educational programs regarding the level of involvement of internal and external stakeholders, which may include employee-oriented actions as well as learning processes aimed at the entire network of values of the organization. In other words, the level guideline refers to the educational programs offered that must be aligned with the organization's strategic planning.[25]

The taxonomy developed by Antonelli *et al.*[1] is called content coverage, and the three levels proposed are used for the NCU model. The generalist level is concerned with developing training to disseminate the organizational culture to as many employees as possible, making them multipliers of the culture of the organization in search of a shared vision and the achievement of strategic objectives. The managerial level develops management and leadership skills aligned with organizational strategies, aiming to strengthen the link between strategy and operation. The technical level focuses on developing specific technical and operational skills, seeking to train employees at the operational level of the organization to perform specific activities and tasks aligned with the strategic challenges of the organization.

The NCU[2,6] defining one level does not necessarily exclude the others. The transition between levels is not a requirement, but it is necessary to define the model to be implemented. Educational programs can be developed to instruct by repetition and practice (training), create knowledge (capacitation), or gradual development (formation). In the NCU model, the educational programs are offered in different levels of education, both in presential and online, with certification and properly aligned with the organization's strategic planning.

19.3. The Purpose of Maturity Criteria of the NCU Model

The NCU must thus constantly justify its contribution to the measurement of the organization's performance. However, at the same time, it is critical to identify and measure the impact of NCU model on the organization.[3] Cappiello and Pedrini,[4] in their research, found that stakeholder-based evaluation is appropriate for corporate universities operating in networks, as they integrate indicators and criteria that take into account strategic objectives and interaction with the external environment. Thus, the potential added value of the NCU needs appropriate measures that go beyond conventional indicators and criteria, as it needs to consider its learning network and the eight guidelines mentioned above.

In accordance with De Bruin *et al.*,[26] the maturity consists of the ability to measure and evaluate domain capabilities at a determined point in time. For this study, maturity criteria are classified as descriptive, as they report the current situation of a determinate domain, but do not provide information for its performance improvement or how to reach the highest levels, including the phases of scope, design, and populate.

The first phase in the development of a maturity model is the definition of application and utilization limits.[26] To contemplate the NCU model, the scope approaches the internal and external stakeholders of the organization's learning network that are influenced by and influence the organization.[16]

The second phase is to determine a design or architecture for the model that forms the basis for the future development and application.[26] The maturity of the NCU model is composed of eight criteria, indicators, and scale of 1 to 4 that the organizations can control and measure.

Third phase, called populate, comprises the decision about the content of the model, identification of what needs to be measured in the maturity evaluation, and how this can be measured.[26] For this stage, it was necessary to identify the criteria, for which the literature review was used to provide the necessary data and theoretical basis to elaborate the maturity criteria of the NCU model.

The maturity criteria of the NCU model are composed of eight criteria: Governance, Reach, Stakeholder recognition, Interconnection, Technology, Focus, Level, and KM and Governance. Each proposed criterion contains specific indicators. The indicators developed determine how the criteria will be analyzed. The scales contemplate four levels, low, medium/low, high/medium, or high, 1 being the lowest and 4 the highest. The highest level represents that the organization contemplates the NCU model.

19.3.1. *Governance*

The governance is the strategic direction, with a broader vision of internal and external stakeholders, understanding that each one influences management.[11] The governance criterion is the institutionalization of learning and KGov. The indicators are represented by the percentage of evolution of the institutionalization of KGov and LGov. It is used on a scale of: (1) Low institutionalization (25%); (2) Medium institutionalization (>25% up to 50%); (3) Regular institutionalization (>50% up to 80%); and (4) High institutionalization (>80%).

19.3.2. *Reach*

The guideline reach should include all stakeholders who can positively or negatively influence the achievement of the organization's strategic objectives, even if these can be dynamic and fluid.[12] From this perspective, an NCU needs to propose criteria for evaluating the T,D&E programs based on the ability to produce new knowledge and readiness for application in the practice of work and interact the learning network of the organization.

The criterion Reach is related to the Capillarity of the T,D&E programs, including the internal and external public that compose the ecosystem of action of the organization. The indicators represent the reach rate with the weighting of the composition rates and diversity of participants. The scales used are: (1) Low Reach (distribution rate <25%); (2) Medium Reach (distribution rate 25% up to 50%); (3) Regular Reach (distribution rate >50% up to 80%); (4) High Reach (distribution rate >80%).

19.3.3. *Stakeholders recognition*

The stakeholders recognition criterion uses the GUTAI tool is defined for Freire *et al.*[27] as a mechanism that facilitates multicriteria prioritization and is used to support decision-making by organizations. Multicriteria are suggested when the problem involves qualitative and quantitative characteristics, not always easy to measure and with possible adverse points. The logic of problem prioritization proposed by GUTAI helps to analyze situations in an objective and rational way.

In line with the NCU model, Freire *et al.*[28] suggest that the GUTAI tool be used as an analysis and classification method to select, prioritize, and propose investments in educational programs with a view to eliminate skills gaps and then proposed to address the:

(1) Gravity of the competence gap that it pretends to eliminate, being related to the strategic objectives of the organization.
(2) Urgency of eliminating this gap for the resolution of strategic problems of the organization.
(3) Tendency to aggravate the problem generated by the skills gap.
(4) Achievement of the educational programs — whether it reaches only one individual, one group, several groups, or the entire organization or learning network.
(5) Impact of educational programs for the achievement of strategic objectives, improvement of operational results and financial management of the T,D&E area to obtain the materials, production, and execution.

The stakeholder's recognition criterion is composed of the mapping of skills gaps and recognition of the expectations and learning needs of actors and stakeholders. The indicator is the index of use of the multicriteria model and GUTAI tool for mapping and prioritization of skills gaps. The scales are:

(1) The diagnosis is performed in a limited way and is based on the empirical observations and impressions of the areas when requested.
(2) An effective diagnosis model is applied, but there is no standard for comparability between requests and prioritization is a subjective process.

(3) An effective diagnosis and prioritization model is applied, but it is not aware of all the standards used.

(4) The multicriteria model and the GUTAI tool are applied to identify and prioritization of skills gaps, and the entire organization knows how to use the tool.

19.3.4. *Interconnection*

The interconnection in turn arises from the use of collaborative technologies to manage promotion, integration, inclusion, and interactivity of the learning network, involving the different participants of the ecosystem.[18] The interconnection criterion is the consolidation of learning networks for the development of human, relational, and social capital. The indicators present an index of Collaborative Representativeness of institutionalized learning networks. The scales are of: (1) low collaborative representativity (<25%); (2) medium collaborative representativity (25% up to 50% of objectives of the achieved networks); (3) regular collaborative representativity (>50% up to 80% of objectives of the achieved networks); (4) High collaborative representativity (>80% of objectives of the achieved networks).

19.3.5. *Technology*

The network learning recommends the development of information and communication technologies for integration, inclusion, and interactivity of the different stakeholders in order to dynamize and optimize the learning process in networks.[2,6,20,23] The technology criterion uses collaborative technologies to promote integration, inclusion, and interactivity of network participants. The indicator is represented by the percentage of institutionalization of information, communication, and knowledge systems. The scales start from:

(1) There are no information, communication, and knowledge systems institutionalized for use.

(2) There are information systems, but still weak communication and knowledge systems institutionalized for use.

(3) There are information and communication systems institutionalized, but there are no knowledge systems that offer collaborative technologies for integration, inclusion, and interactivity of the participants.

(4) There are information, communication, and knowledge systems institutionalized, providing collaborative technologies for integration, inclusion, and interactivity of the participants.

19.3.6. *Focus*

The focus criterion was elaborated in accordance with Margherita and Secondo,[14] who considered the focus as how strategic there is in learning, which can be low, medium/low, high/medium, or high. For the NCU model, the indicator of the focus criteria corresponds to the percentage of distribution of educational programs among operational, managerial, and strategic themes.[24] The scales are:

(1) The distribution of educational programs among the themes is realized by the direction.

(2) The distribution of educational programs among the themes is carried out by randomly meeting the demands of the organization areas.

(3) The intention of distribution of educational programs among the operational, managerial, and strategic themes is already perceived, but there is no strategy for this distribution.

(4) There is an increase in educational programs in some of the themes and the strategy applied to achieve strategic objectives of the institution is perceived.

19.3.7. *Level*

The level criterion represents the educational programs, and their knowledge trails are composed of modules distributed in the six levels: initial formation, teaching formation, continuing education courses, dissemination of knowledge, specialization, and graduate course. The indicator is the percentage of distribution of educational programs among the six levels of formation. The scales are represented by:

(1) The distribution of the educational programs among the six levels of formation is made by political force.
(2) The distribution of the educational programs among the six levels of formation is made randomly, attending to the demands of the areas of the organization.
(3) The intention of distribution of the educational programs among the six levels of formation is already perceived, but there is no strategy for this distribution.
(4) There is an increase of the educational programs in some of the six levels, and the strategy applied for the reach of strategic objectives of the organization is perceived.

19.3.8. *Governance and KM*

The last criterion, Governance and KM, is composed of mechanisms, components, and learning environments, formal, informal, and relational, generated by governance and KM for the optimization of NCU results.[13,29] The indicator is represented by the number of mechanisms, components, and learning environments of the organization. The scales are:

(1) There is no governance structure and there is no institutionalization of mechanisms, components, and learning environments.
(2) There is a governance structure, but without the institutionalization of mechanisms, components, and learning environments.
(3) There is a governance structure and there is the institutionalization of some mechanisms, components, and learning environments.
(4) There is a governance structure and there is the institutionalization of mechanisms, components, and institutionalized learning environments.

19.4. Conclusion

This research proposes the criteria for the assessment of the maturity of the NCU model. From the narrative literature review, it was possible to describe the guidelines and to propose eight criteria of the maturity of the

NCU, comprising Governance, Reach, Stakeholder Recognition, Interconnection, Technology, Focus, Level, and KM and Governance. For each criterion, specific indicators have been developed contemplating from the lowest to the highest scales for monitoring the adherence of the organizations to the NCU guidelines.

The guidelines presented in this study establish that T,D&E programs are aligned with the organizational strategy that aims at co-creating and co-producing value for the network of stakeholders. They provide an experiential, expansive, and collaborative learning environment, utilizing KM methods, techniques, and tools. Furthermore, it respects and supports the mechanisms, components, and environments of KGov and LGov, focusing on the development of human, relational, and social capital of the organization.

For future work, it is suggested to continue the stages of testing, implementation, and maintenance[26] of the criteria proposed in organizations, thus providing empirical research. Additionally, it is suggested to develop prescriptive maturity criteria, which allow the indication of how improvements can be made to contemplate the higher levels of maturity of the NCU model. In relation to the NCU model, the development of a multilevel evaluation model that considers the criteria proposed in this research is suggested.

Acknowledgments

This study was financed in part by the Coordination for the Improvement of Higher Education Personnel-Brazil (CAPES)-Finance Code 001.

References

1. G. Antonelli, G. Cappiello and G. Pedrini. The corporate university in the European utility industries. *Utilities Policy*, **25**, 33–41 (2013).
2. P.S. Freire, G.A. Dandolini, and J.A. Souza. Implementation process of Corporate University in Network (CUN). *International Journal for Innovation Education and Research*, **5**(12), 101–126 (2017).
3. L. Rhéaume and M. Gardoni. The challenges facing corporate universities in dealing with open innovation. *Journal of Workplace Learning*, **27**(4), 315–328 (2015).

4. G. Cappiello and G. Pedrini. The performance evaluation of corporate universities. *Tertiary Education and Management*, **23**, 304–317 (2017). https://doi.org/10.1080/13583883.2017.1329452

5. T.C. Silva and P.S. Freire. Universidade corporativa em rede: Diretrizes que devem ser gerenciadas para a implantação do modelo. *Revista Espacios*, **38**(10), 1–22 (2017).

6. P.S. Freire, G.A. Dandolini, J.A. Souza and S.M. Silva. Corporative University in Network: Initial considerations towards new model of corporate education. *International Journal of Development Research*, **7**(11), 17207–17216 (2017).

7. T.C. Silva and P.S. Freire (2017). Universidade corporativa em rede: diretrizes que devem ser gerenciadas para a implantação do modelo. *Espacios*, **38**(10), 1–22 (2017).

8. I. Nonaka and H. Takeuchi. *Gestão do conhecimento*. Bookman: Porto Alegre (2008).

9. Y. Chen, Y. Xu and Q. Zhai. The knowledge management functions of corporate university and their evolution: Case studies of two Chinese corporate universities. *Journal of Knowledge Management*, **23**(10), 2086–2112 (2019).

10. C. Prince and J. Stewart. Corporate universities — an analytical framework. *Journal of Management Development*, **21**(10), 794–811 (2002).

11. F. Kempner-Moreira and P.S. Freire. Redes de Aprendizagem e Capital Relacional: uma introdução aos valores distintivos da UCR. Universidade Corporativa em Rede: diretrizes iniciais do modelo. Curitiba, CRV (2019).

12. F.S. Koehler, P.S. Freire and F. Kempner-Moreira. *Alcance como diretriz para o modelo UCR*. Universidade Corporativa em Rede: diretrizes iniciais do modelo. Curitiba, CRV (2019).

13. G. Rizzatti. Framework de Governança da Aprendizagem Organizacional. Tese (Doutorado em Engenharia e Gestão do Conhecimento). Universidade Federal de Santa Catarina, Florianópolis, Brasil (2020).

14. A. Margherita and G. Secundo. The emergence of the stakeholder university. In *Open Business Innovation Leadership*, A. Romano (ed.), Palgrave Macmillan, London, 170–207 (2009).

15. M. Castells. *Communication Power.* New York: Oxford University (2004).

16. P.S. Freire and A.F. Loth. *Reconhecimento dos stakeholders como diretriz para o modelo UCR*. Universidade Corporativa em Rede: diretrizes iniciais do modelo. Curitiba, CRV (2019).

17. M. Allen. What is a next-generation corporate university?. In *The next generation of corporate universities*, M. Allen (ed.), John Wiley and Sons, San Francisco, 3–16 (2007).

18. F. Kempner-Moreira and P.S. Freire (2019). Interconexão como diretriz para o modelo UCR. Universidade Corporativa em Rede: Diretrizes iniciais do modelo. Curitiba, CRV (2019).

19. L. Ryan, C. Prince and P. Turner. The changing and developing role of the corporate university post-millennium. *Industry and Higher Education*, **29**(3), 167–174 (2015). doi: 10.5367/ihe.2015.0256

20. G. Izidorio, G.G. Bresolin, P.S. Freire and R.C.S. Pacheco. Tecnologia da educação como diretriz para o modelo UCR. Universidade Corporativa em Rede: Diretrizes iniciais do modelo. Curitiba, CRV (2019).

21. T.C. Silva and P.S. Freire. Diretrizes para implantação e gestão. Universidade Corporativa em Rede: diretrizes iniciais do modelo. Curitiba, CRV (2019).

22. W. Rochadel, A.B. Valdati, P.S. Freire, G.A. Dandolini and J.A. Souza. Tecnologias digitais para um novo modelo de educação corporativa: universidade corporativa em rede (UCR). In *Inovação em educação: perspectivas do uso das tecnologias interativas*, P.J. Fiuza and R.R. Lemos (eds.), Paco Editorial, Jundiaí (2017).

23. R. Kraemer. Modelo de maturidade do sistema de educação corporativa. Dissertação no Banco de Teses e Dissertações do EGC, do Programa de Pós-Graduação em Engenharia e Gestão do Conhecimento (2018).

24. R.W. Aires, C.A.R.L. Canto and P.S. Freire. *Foco como diretriz para o modelo UCR*. Universidade Corporativa em Rede: diretrizes iniciais do modelo. Curitiba, CRV, 227–234 (2019).

25. C.A.R.L. Canto, R.W. Aires and P.S. Freire. *Nível como diretriz para o modelo UCR*. Universidade Corporativa em Rede: diretrizes iniciais do modelo. Curitiba, CRV, 235–244 (2019).

26. T. De Bruin, R. Freeze, U. Kaulkarni and M. Rosemann. Understanding the main phases of developing a maturity assessment model. In *16th Australasian Conference on Information Systems,* ACIS (2005).

27. P.S. Freire, F. Kempner-Moreira and G. Izidorio. Gutai COVID-19: apoio à governança multinível da pandemia. Instituto Stela, Florianópolis (2020).

28. P.S. Freire, F. Santos and S.M. Silva. Cadeia de Valor Proposta pelo Modelo de Universidade Corporativa em Rede. *I Seminário Internacional de Universidade Corporativas e Escolas de Governo*. December, Florianópolis, Brasil (2017).

29. P.S. Freire, G.A. Dandolini, J.A. Souza, T.C. Silva and R.M. Couto. Knowledge governance (GovC): The state of the art about the term. *Biblios*, **69**, 21–40 (2017).

Index